Nationalist Passions

Sylvic Forsythe

402 - 393 - 8929 .

Nationalist Passions

STUART J. KAUFMAN

Cornell University Press

Ithaca and London

First published 2015 by Cornell University Press

First printing, Cornell Paperbacks, 2015

Printed in the United States of America

Library of Congress Cataloging-in-Publication Data

Kaufman, Stuart J., author.
    Nationalist passions / Stuart J. Kaufman.
        pages cm
    Includes bibliographical references and index.
    ISBN 978-0-8014-5345-8 (cloth : alk. paper)
    ISBN 978-1-5017-0056-9 (pbk. : alk. paper)
    1. Ethnic conflict—Political aspects—Case studies.   2. Ethnic relations—Political aspects—Case studies.   3. Conflict management—Political aspects—Case studies.
4 Multiculturalism—Political aspects—Case studies.
5. Nationalism—Case studies.   I. Title.

    HM1121.K38 2015
    305.8—dc23   2014045670

Cornell University Press strives to use environmentally responsible suppliers and materials to the fullest extent possible in the publishing of its books. Such materials include vegetable-based, low-VOC inks and acid-free papers that are recycled, totally chlorine-free, or partly composed of nonwood fibers. For further information, visit our website at www.cornellpress.cornell.edu.

Cloth printing   10 9 8 7 6 5 4 3 2 1

Paperback printing   10 9 8 7 6 5 4 3 2 1

Contents

237 ÷ 3
79 per day
(3 page summary)
+ 3 page

Acknowledgments

The first things any scholar needs to research and write a book are time and money; for these essential commodities I thank the University of Delaware, which provided so much of both. Funding for this project came from the university's Department of Political Science and International Relations, a General University Research grant, and a grant from the Center for International Studies. I also benefited from sabbatical leave and a course release generously granted by the university, which gave me additional time to research and write this book. An earlier version of chapter 2 was first published as "Symbols, Frames and Violence: Studying Ethnic War in the Philippines," *International Studies Quarterly* 55, no. 4 (December 2011), pp. 937–58. Some portions of chapters 3 and 4 also appeared previously in "Symbolic Politics or Rational Choice? Testing Theories of Extreme Ethnic Violence," *International Security* 30, no. 4 (Spring 2006), pp. 45–86.

In approaching this project, I have tried to be simultaneously ambitious in my goals and humble about my knowledge. In the latter quest I was aided by my keen realization of how little I knew about my cases before I began researching them. This book would not have been possible if not for the generous assistance of numerous genuine regional experts and residents of the areas I studied, for which I am deeply grateful. For the Philippines case, my colleague Alice Ba provided the essential first contacts that got me started. On the ground in Mindanao, Benny Bacani and Rufa Guiam provided invaluable assistance in helping me proceed. Assistance also came from Rommel Banlaoi, Hermann Kraft, Rudy Rodil, Sol Santos, and a number of local experts and participants who generously gave of their time to speak with me. Satoshi Machida, Wang Yu, and Dina Delias provided able help as research assistants for that case.

For help with my research in South Africa, my greatest thanks go to Hermann Giliomee, who went above and beyond the call of collegial duty in aiding me in this project and making possible whatever success I have achieved. I also thank the dozens of participants in South Africa's transition process who agreed to be interviewed, including F. W. de Klerk, Barend du Plessis, Mac Maharaj, and others whose names I have kept confidential. The Human Sciences Research Council generously shared some of its invaluable survey data, the F. W. de Klerk Foundation was highly cooperative, and Maxi Schoeman kindly provided a home away from home at the University of Pretoria. Other scholarly colleagues who provided great help in South Africa include Stephen Ellis, Neville Alexander, Denis Beckett, Anthony Butler, Fanie Cloete, Andre du Toit, Pierre du Toit, Deon Geldenhuys, Roland Henwood, Anthea Jeffery, Koos Malan, Bob Mattes, Lawrence Schlemmer, Annette Seegers, Thula Simpson, A. J. Venter, and David Welsh. Andre Dumon was invaluable as research assistant and translator. Jeff Pieres helped me with hard-to-find information, and Brendan O'Leary kindly read and provided detailed feedback on an early version, which he also arranged for me to present at a comparative politics symposium at the University of Pennsylvania. I thank those colleagues at Penn for their feedback as well.

My research in Tanzania got its initial boost from Gretchen Bauer and Aili Mari Tripp, who helped me enormously in getting started. Bruce Heilman was my invaluable first point of contact, and Jingu John Kiang'u was superbly helpful as my research assistant; Kelvin Mathayo kindly translated articles from the Swahili-language press for this project. Assistance also came from Theodora Bali, Paul Bjerk, Jessica Mushi, Allen Rugambwa, and the Tanzanian Studies Association.

. Back home, my wife Nita provided not only the love and support that kept me going but also the graphic design expertise that produced the maps, flowcharts, and elements of the cover art that grace this volume. My child, Sam, provided both useful feedback on the introduction and constant reminders about the other things that make life worth living. Ron Hassner and Marc Ross read the whole manuscript and provided detailed and immensely useful comments. Feedback on one or more chapters was also provided by Gretchen Bauer, Zoltan Buzas, Bob Denemark, Marie Desrosiers, Kara Ellerby, Phil Jones, Aaron Karnell, Chaim Kaufmann, Neophytos Loizides, Omar McDoom, Donald Rothchild, Stephen Saideman, and Crawford Young; Daniel Kinderman, David Wilson, and other members of the Department of Political Science and International Relations Faculty Research Seminar also provided useful comments. Sam Gaertner and other members of the Psychology Department's brownbag symposium on social psychology also provided valuable theoretical insights. Any errors that may be contained in this work are solely the responsibility of the author.

Nationalist Passions

Introduction

Ethnic Relations and Symbolic Politics

Ethnic conflict is a plague of our time, at least partly to blame for most contemporary warfare.[1] In 2012, the three most violent wars ongoing were largely ethnic in character: the civil war in Syria, pitting mostly Sunni Arab rebels against an Alawite-dominated government, and the wars in Pakistan and Afghanistan, in which Pashtun-dominated Taliban groups opposed governments dominated by Punjabis (in Pakistan) and Tajiks (in Afghanistan). Overall, thirty-two armed conflicts each killed at least twenty-five people in 2012, and the vast majority of these conflicts were ethnic, at least in part. Looked at differently, these "ethnic" conflicts were also nationalist ones, pitting different national identities against each other. For example, Europe saw a continuing insurgency by Chechen nationalists in southern Russia; Africa experienced fights between the Arab government in Sudan and various non-Arab ethnic rebels; and in Asia the Kachin minority was rebelling against Burmese majority rule in Myanmar, all among other examples.[2]

Yet if most wars are at least partly ethnic, it is also true that most ethnic relationships are peaceful. Indeed, most countries are multiethnic, and most of them manage relations between ethnic groups relatively quietly. The aim of this book is to explain how both of these facts can be true at the same time. How does ethnic peace work? How can it be maintained? Why do ethnic relations sometimes become contentious? And what causes some ethnic relationships to descend into all-out war or even genocide?

The contrast between Sudan and Tanzania illustrates the puzzle. These two East African siblings gained independence within five years of each other, Sudan in 1956 and Tanzania in 1961, and at birth they shared many qualities. Both were among the largest countries in Africa by both area and population and were among the poorest countries in the world. Both were also highly diverse, each including over one hundred different ethnic groups speaking a wide variety of languages, further divided between Christians and Muslims. Both were led at independence by leaders determined to

1

impose the most widely spoken language among each country's Muslims (Arabic in Sudan, Swahili in Tanzania) as the national language for all. According to World Bank analyses, this set of traits—large size, poverty, and linguistic and religious diversity—put both countries at serious risk of political instability or civil war.[3]

Yet despite these shared qualities, the two countries followed opposite paths from the beginning. Sudan suffered repeatedly from horrific ethnic violence, experiencing two civil wars between the Muslim north and the non-Muslim south: the first from 1962 to 1972 and the second, genocidal in scale, from 1983 to 2005. Just as that second war, estimated to have killed over two million people, was finally coming to an end, a third one started in the western region of Darfur, raising yet again the specter of a Sudanese genocide. South Sudan finally achieved independence in 2011, as a result of a peace deal with the Sudanese government, but within two years it too began experiencing internal ethnic violence.

Tanzania, in contrast, remained at peace, with hardly a hint of ethnic tensions on the Tanzanian mainland. While Sudanese politicians were rallying their supporters for war, Tanzanian politicians were seeking votes with promises to build roads, dig wells, and create jobs.

This book explains such contrasts: why some ethnically diverse countries, like Tanzania, feature constructive national politics focused on economic development and experience little ethnic tension while others, like Sudan, fall into the worst kind of ethnic wars. In trying to answer this question, I reach resolutely across the boundaries between social sciences for two reasons. First, there are no simple answers to questions like this. If I focused only on the issues of interest to economists or to sociologists, I would not get very far with my explanation. Second, while conceding the importance of psychological, cultural, sociological, and political *issues*, I also had to respect those disciplines' accumulated *evidence* by ensuring that my explanation would be consistent with the facts established by scholars in those disciplines.

Once we consider the range of what is known in different disciplines, it becomes even clearer that there is no simple answer—no silver bullet explanation of the causes of ethnic war and peace. Rather, ethnic war happens when many things go wrong, usually when the culture, psychology, sociology, and politics all work together to create a spiral of escalating violence. Ethnic peace, similarly, is stable only when most or all of those factors work together to maintain it. If some factors favor peace while others favor conflict, the result is often an in-between kind of contentious politics that is tumultuous but not very violent. The factors that matter most can be summarized as follows:

1. Cultural factors: Do the most prominent ethnic or national narratives promote hostility to other groups in the country, or acceptance of them?

And do these narratives encourage the resort to violence to settle political disputes? Sudan's national narrative asserted the superiority of Arabs and Muslims, promoting conflict with non-Arabs, and Arabs and non-Arabs alike have self-images as warrior peoples. Tanzania's national narrative, in contrast, asserted a common identity for all Tanzanians and promoted cooperation.

2. Social psychological factors: Are the groups in the country prejudiced against each other? In Sudan, Arabs cultivated vicious prejudices against non-Arab "Africans"; in Tanzania, ethnic biases were milder and were resolutely discouraged.

3. Threat perceptions: Do the groups see each other as threatening? Northern Sudanese felt that southerners threatened their values and identity, and southern Sudanese knew that northerners threatened their lives. Tanzanians, however, did not see each other as threatening, in part because of the lack of prejudice.

4. Public opinion: If people do feel hostility and fear, do these feelings translate into political support for mobilizing and taking action against the rival group? In Tanzania, with little hostility and fear, there is little support for policies aimed against other groups. In Sudan, however, there was a great deal of northern public support for the actions against southerners—such as the imposition of Islamic law—that sparked the civil war.

5. Leadership and organization: Do leaders frame political issues in ways that fan the flames of hostility or that calm them? And are these leaders backed by organizations that can mobilize large groups to act? In Tanzania, founding leader Julius Nyerere framed issues as common challenges for Tanzanians and used the organizations of the ruling party and the government to promote common action to address those challenges. In Sudan, President Jaafar al-Numayri, who signed a peace treaty with the south in 1972, later began framing issues to mobilize Islamist sentiments and used state institutions against southerners, leading southern leaders to create rebel organizations in response.

Considering all of these factors poses a problem: How can we put them together into a coherent explanation? I argue that the only way to do so is to jettison the usual assumption made by most political scientists and economists that political behavior is "rational" and instead to focus on the fact that people make decisions primarily on the basis of their biases, prejudices, values, and emotions. The theoretical approach I use to put these ideas together is symbolic politics theory.

Summing up these ideas, the symbolist theory of ethnic conflict in its simplest form is as follows. The basic principle of symbolic politics is that because people make decisions based primarily on their biases and emotions,

Symbolic Politics Theory

3

the way leaders gain support is by using symbols to appeal to those biases and emotions. Thus the path to ethnic war would start with bias and emotion—people who dislike and fear each other. Many such people nurse vicious prejudices, repeat nasty stereotypes about the other group, and so are quick to see the others as a threat. The more widespread such predispositions are, the more suitable the situation is for the emergence of rabble-rousing leaders who exploit fear and hatred to amass power and then organize people for conflict and war. Ethnic and nationalist conflicts, therefore, are not the results of uncertainty, misunderstanding, or poverty. They are usually triggered by naked grabs for power aimed at subordinating one group to another, with power-hungry leaders supported by deeply bigoted public opinion and with the organizational muscle to implement their plans. Peace is stable only when these factors point the other way: group narratives promote unity, prejudice is low, and people do not feel threatened, so leaders cannot succeed even if they try to stir up conflict.

This picture raises a question: Is it possible to have an ethnic or national movement that mobilizes millions but stays peaceful? Can you mobilize an ethnic or national group without playing on hate and fear? The obvious place to look for an example is with the founder of modern nonviolent mobilization, Mohandas Gandhi. The answer, it turns out, is mixed: Gandhi *did* mobilize millions in a mostly nonviolent struggle for Indian independence, but in the process he was forced to give up on trying to bridge the Muslim-Hindu divide, with terrible consequences in later years. This failure ultimately killed Gandhi himself, as he was assassinated in 1948 by Nathuram Godse, an extremist Hindu who felt Gandhi had betrayed the Hindu cause.

This book, therefore, starts with two questions: Why do ethnic wars sometimes occur, and (to paraphrase songwriter Dan Fogelberg) how do we make peace stay? To answer these questions, the book examines six different cases. It begins with three cases that did escalate to full-scale ethnic war, in the Philippines, Sudan, and Rwanda, examining whether conflicts occurring in such different places all followed the pattern expected by symbolic politics theory. The book next considers two cases of group contention that fell short of all-out war: Gandhi's efforts in India in the 1920s, and the African National Congress's campaign against apartheid in the 1990s. Finally, the book considers the happy puzzle of Tanzania's relative peace, examining not only how Nyerere built a political system that submerged ethnic tensions but also how it continued to operate with that effect after Nyerere's retirement and a transition to democracy. The idea is to examine places different enough to allow creation of a theory that applies virtually anywhere, at least in the developing world, and that can explain political processes as diverse as the maintenance of peace in Tanzania, Gandhi's limited control over his followers, and Sudanese president Numayri's shift from making peace in 1972 to provoking war in 1983.

What Is Ethnic (or Nationalist) Conflict?

One difficulty in answering these questions is in defining what exactly we are talking about. I use the catchall term *ethnic conflict*, but the "ethnic" divides in these cases are quite different. In Tanzania, ethnic groups are differentiated mostly by language. In India, the key issue was national independence from British colonial rule, though the "communal" divide between Muslim and Hindu Indians was also unavoidable. In Sudan and the Philippines, the key divide was between Christian ethnic groups and Muslim ones. In South Africa and Rwanda, the groups were defined locally as "racial," though neither South Africans nor Americans would see any racial difference in Rwanda. The question we need to address is whether these can all be lumped together as "ethnic."

I will argue in this book that all of these different kinds of identities work about the same way psychologically, and as a result they also work much the same way socially and politically. So it makes sense to lump them together, as many scholars do,[4] even though most do not. The literatures on ethnicity, nationalism, and race are mostly separate from each other, but one of my goals is to bring them together. I therefore typically refer to all of these kinds of conflicts as "ethnic."

For a formal definition, no one has yet improved on Max Weber's simple statement that an ethnic identity is defined by a "subjective belief" in "common descent . . . whether or not an objective blood relationship exists."[5] In other words, we might think of an ethnic group as an "imagined family."[6] Jews, for example, see themselves as descendants of the biblical Abraham and Isaac, Arabs trace their ancestry to Abraham and Ishmael, and Croats trace their origins to a medieval family led by five brothers.

This simple notion of an imagined family logically requires all of the other elements that typically go into definitions of ethnicity.[7] Most obviously, for an ethnic group to exist, there have to be a family name and narratives that assert the connection so its members believe they are family. They must also have some elements of culture in common, though which elements matter may vary: some families do not mind if members convert to a different religion or speak a different language with their spouses, but other families will ostracize members for such behavior. In the terms anthropologists use, this means that ethnic identity is ascriptive; most people are born into it. While people can change group identities, for example, through marriage, adoption, or religious conversion, most stay within the group they are born into.

Since the family relationship is imagined, ethnic identity is subjective. Ethnic diversity cannot be reliably measured worldwide by statistics on language use or religious affiliation, because those differences do not always matter to people. The only way to tell people's ethnic identity is to ask them: an individual's ethnic identity depends mostly on what he or she thinks it is

[handwritten margin note: Max Weber Definition]

and partly what others in society think it is. An ethnic *group* consists of the people who mutually accept each other as members. Sometimes there is a discrepancy: some German Jews in the 1930s, for example, wanted to be considered German, but they were rejected by the Nazi government and society. Discrepancies of this kind are one sort of ethnic conflict.

More generally, an ethnic conflict is a conflict between groups that are distinguished by ethnic identity. Of course, the groups in conflict are never entirely united. As Rogers Brubaker has pointed out, ethnic conflicts are largely between *organizations* that claim to be acting on behalf of their groups.[8] But there are always some moderates who try to stand aside. Also, as Stathis Kalyvas has pointed out, people often use the excuse of ethnic fighting to pursue other agendas.[9] Some take the opportunity to loot, and others are organized crime figures fighting more for "business opportunities" than for group ideals. Still others may focus on taking revenge against personal enemies, and some are just thugs and sadists.[10]

Even so, a conflict like the one in the Philippines is "ethnic" because recruitment is along ethnic lines on one or both sides. Virtually all members of Muslim rebel groups in the Philippines were Muslims, while those fighting for the government side were virtually all Christians. Also, these conflicts are ethnic because the political justification—and therefore the political support—are based on appeals to ethnic identity. In other words, not only are the conflicting sides defined by ethnic identity but the conflict is largely *about* competing ethnic identities, even if tangible goods like land, jobs, or political power are also at stake.

To repeat, however, ethnic conflict is usually peaceful. Violent ethnic conflicts, as in Rwanda or Darfur, tend to be the best known, but in most places where ethnic identity is important, conflict between ethnic groups takes place through normal routines of politics. Russia, for example, has about one hundred different ethnic groups—not just Russians but Tatars, Bashkirs, Ossetians, Chuvash, and many others—but except for Russians' relations with Chechens, their contacts are usually peaceful. It is important to keep this in mind: any kind of disagreement may be a conflict. The question of this book is why ethnic conflict is sometimes unimportant, sometimes contentious but nonviolent, and occasionally violent.

How to Build a Theory

Another premise of this book is that since it is asking a complicated question, we cannot expect that a simple answer will be satisfactory. Unfortunately, the tendency in academia is to attempt just that: to insist on too much parsimony, which usually translates into trying to explain very complicated problems with very simple theories.

To illustrate the issue, let us return to the puzzle of Jaafar al-Numayri and Sudan's second civil war. A few years after signing a peace treaty granting political autonomy to the non-Muslim south in 1972, the previously secular Numayri began cultivating an image of himself as a devout Muslim. He allied himself with the fundamentalist National Islamic Front, ultimately going as far as attempting to impose shari'a law on the mostly Christian and animist southerners. In response to these moves, military units dominated by southerners finally rebelled in 1983 and were joined by wave after wave of fellow southerners eager to join the fight. Despite desultory peace talks, the fighting continued to increase even as the toll of violence increased in the south and the popularity of the war decreased in the north.

Why did this civil war break out? The first answer—and the one most people miss—is that this is not really one question but several. Why did Numayri begin to cultivate the image of a devout Muslim and ultimately try to impose Islamic law on the south, violating the autonomy deal he had signed? Why did so many northerners support those moves and the war that followed? Why did Numayri and his successors continue the war even as the costs grew? Why were southern military officers so quick to lead a rebellion after they, too, had agreed to peace, and why did so many southern civilians seek them out to join in their fight? What we need to answer these questions is not a simple, one-size-fits-all theory but a general perspective that helps us understand the whole flow of events.

ONE-FACTOR THEORIES OF ETHNIC CONFLICT

Some scholars try to argue that the causes of ethnic conflict or civil war boil down to one factor. One theory, popular with some economists and political scientists, suggests that the answer to all of these questions is *because they can.* Implicitly starting from the assumption that everyone wants to maximize his or her own power and wealth, this approach takes it for granted that of course leaders like Numayri will exploit the weak for their own benefit if they can. What distinguishes peaceful countries from those with civil wars, in this view, is the *opportunity to rebel*: the southerners rebelled because they had the chance. The main cause of civil war, these theorists argue, is therefore weakness of government institutions, usually as a result of poverty in the country; motivation does not matter. If a country is poor, its government will be weak; if its territory is large and mountainous, then there will be inaccessible areas where rebels will be free to operate. In these circumstances, the logic goes, groups like Sudan's southerners are likely sooner or later to rebel for some reason or other.[11] These scholars' conclusion is "Feasibility rather than motivation is decisive for the risk of rebellion."[12]

The first half of this assertion is clearly correct: it is obvious that opportunity or "feasibility" is vital. Rebellions will be nipped in the bud if the government is very strong and capable. Studies have also found that ethnic civil wars are more likely when the potential rebels are concentrated in one region and that ethnic dissidents escalate their demands when they receive external support, as Sudanese southerners did from Ethiopia and elsewhere.[13] Opportunity structure—government weakness, concentration of ethnic minorities, external support for rebels, and so on—does tell us something about where civil war is likely to break out.

On the other hand, opportunity does not tell us everything; even opportunity theorists' studies show that other factors also matter. One finds, for example, that ethnic diversity, poverty, and a previous civil war all make a new civil war more likely.[14] All of these factors point more to motive than to opportunity. First, if ethnic diversity is important (even though their measure of it is flawed), this is probably because more ethnic diversity implies more ethnic grievances. Similarly, a previous civil war suggests leftover resentments that can flare up again. As for the effect of poverty, it is best understood in light of a separate finding: that more economic and political equality across groups makes civil war less likely.[15] In other words, the poverty that is most likely to provoke a civil war is *unequal* poverty, the kind that seems to be the result of ethnic discrimination. Even government weakness (as in Sudan) may be the result of ethnic conflict rather than the cause of it: the government may be weak because excluded ethnic groups do not support it. Ultimately, opportunity theorists' own analysis shows the limits of their approach: one of their prominent studies finds that opportunity factors explain little more than one-fourth of the variation between civil war and peace.[16] It seems clear that civil wars, including ethnic wars, are caused not only by opportunity but also by economic or political grievances—that is, motives.

A related approach, sometimes employed by opportunity theorists, tries to deal with the problem of motivation by arguing that leaders' policies that result in war are "rational," that is, logical efforts by the leaders to pursue their own interests. War, with all of its costs and destructiveness, is in this account the ironic result of the rational pursuit of self-interest because of two common dilemmas: commitment problems (essentially distrust) and information failures (mostly misperceptions of the other side's intentions).[17] I have shown elsewhere that this is often untrue: ethnic war leaders like Numayri are typically so obvious in their hostility that misperception is not much of a problem and questions of trust are irrelevant.[18] However, even to the extent that these problems do matter, pointing them out only raises another question: Why are problems of distrust and misperception overwhelming in some cases but manageable in others? Rational choice theorists have no systematic answer to this question.[19]

[margin note: Opportunity vs. Motive]

SINGLE-DISCIPLINE THEORIES

Alternative approaches recognize that complex social processes cannot be reduced to one single cause, but they typically limit themselves to a single perspective, usually that of one discipline in the social sciences. For example, a popular approach to explaining social turmoil of all kinds focuses not so much on *where* rebellions are likely to break out but rather on *how* and *when* they do. This approach, favored by sociologists, is known as the "mobilization" school, which asks, how and when do insurgent groups mobilize the resources they need to rebel? This approach focuses on three main issues: how would-be rebels perceive their opportunities, how they use social organizations to mobilize supporters, and how their leaders present or frame the issues involved. The main focus of attention is on the middle part—not just formal organizations, but also informal networks: friends, families, or business or other associates. A key role in this story is played by societal "brokers," people who can connect different social networks and get them to join a common movement.[20]

In explaining the Sudanese conflict, this approach would start with framing—Numayri's decision to play down his secular ideas and frame his leadership in Islamist terms. His power as head of state gave him both the opportunity and the organization he needed to implement these ideas, and his alliance with the Islamic Front broadened his base of support. Of course, Numayri's Islamist frame made it easy for rebellious southerners to frame their message in terms of self-defense against forced Islamization. Sudan's relatively weak army and huge territorial expanse gave the rebels their opportunity. The key rebel organization was built in part on the personal network of ex-rebels from the previous civil war and on personal ties among southern schoolchildren who flocked to the rebel standard.

The trouble with this approach is that, as its leading practitioners agree, it considers *why* a rebellion occurs to be essentially the same question as *how* it occurs.[21] To these scholars, the reason for the Sudanese conflict is simply that Numayri and the rebels saw their opportunities, framed their messages, and then used organizations to mobilize their people for war. What is missing from this story is again the "why" of motive: Why did Numayri move so decisively toward Islamism at the risk of the peace that he had built, why were the southern military officers so quick and determined in their rebellion, and why did the people, northerners and southerners alike, go along?

Many sociologically inclined theorists argue against even trying answer these questions of motive. For example, Charles Tilly, a founder of the mobilization school, explicitly rejected "the claim that individual and collective dispositions explain social processes," suggesting that psychology and culture are irrelevant. Instead he insisted on "interpersonal transactions as the basic stuff of social processes"—that is, only sociology matters.[22] Here again we have the insistence on a one-size-fits-all approach that simply cannot explain some key questions. For example, in Rwanda, why was the idea of genocide on the agenda at all, when it usually is not in ethnic and racial conflicts? In Sudan, why were Numayri's religious appeals popular with his people, and why were southerners so repelled by that message? The answer has to be, at least in part, psychological or "dispositional."

BUILDING COMPLEX THEORIES — *Interdisciplinary Levels*

When we apply these lessons to explaining ethnic politics, with all of its different facets, the logical conclusion is that we need to draw on many different theoretical approaches to make sense of it. We cannot get a satisfactory answer with a one-factor theory or even a single-discipline theory. The question, then, is how multiple theories can be brought together in a coherent way. Other sciences offer ideas for a path forward.

An example is the physics of why the sun (or any other star) shines and can do so for billions of years. The process is explained by a model that combines several different physical principles. The story begins with gravity, which compresses the stellar material. When gravitational pressure is strong enough to push atomic nuclei very close together, as happens in the stellar core, it brings into play the strong nuclear force, leading to nuclear fusion— the same process that powers hydrogen bombs. These fusion reactions in turn generate immense amounts of heat energy (according to Einstein's formula, $E = mc^2$), causing thermodynamic effects that push the material in the star to expand. Some of these effects are explained by Newton's laws governing kinetic energy; others by quantum mechanics.

The stability or instability of the star depends on the balance between the forces of gravity holding the star together and the thermodynamic forces (generated by the fusion reactions) that threaten to blow it apart. If fusion reactions suddenly increase in power, generating enough energy to overcome the force of gravity, the star explodes in a supernova. If gravity overcomes the thermodynamic forces, the star collapses, perhaps into a neutron star. If all of these forces remain in equilibrium—as they have in our sun for billions of years—the star can remain stable. Ultimately, however, any star begins running out of fuel, setting the stage for its demise in explosion, collapse, or some combination of both.[23]

The point of explaining this model from physics is to emphasize that it works only by considering the effects of several different physical forces that operate according to different principles. No physicist would argue that parsimony requires dropping any of these forces from the explanation. None would say, "I have demonstrated the importance of the gravitational force; therefore the strong force is irrelevant."[24] Without any of them, the equations would not work to account for what actually occurs.

Yet this is what social scientists like Tilly are doing when they make claims like "Interpersonal transactions [are] the basic stuff of social processes" while rejecting "the claim that individual and collective dispositions explain social processes." Their argument is that only "transactional" sociology matters; psychology and anthropology are irrelevant. While social science is, of course, different from physics in many ways, the differences only strengthen my argument because social processes are less deterministic—and in that sense, more complicated—than physical ones. Individual people can choose what they will do in ways that individual atoms cannot. This brings up a related complication: some of these processes, such as public support for a policy, happen at the level of individuals, while others, such as social mobilization, happen only on a societal scale. Therefore, we have to include theoretical insights from different disciplines (e.g., psychology for individual-level processes, sociology for societal mobilization) if our explanation is to make sense. The challenge is to find a way to show how these explanations relate to each other to generate a coherent theory.

The Symbolic Politics Synthesis

One strength of the mobilization approach proposed by Charles Tilly and his associates is that it includes the insights of the opportunity school. If we use a metaphor from criminology, we can say that he argues that social movements are explained by a combination of "means" (such as organization) and "opportunity." The problem with this approach is that motive is necessary, too. Anyone with a steak knife and a dinner partner has both means and opportunity to commit murder; the reason that steak houses are not slaughterhouses is that the diners lack motive. Similarly, the means and opportunity to launch a social movement exist all the time in any democracy rich in civil society organizations such as churches and labor unions. However, since they usually lack motive, these groups' members rarely flock to the streets in protest.

Like the model of stellar behavior explained in the preceding section, the theory proposed in this book includes a combination of several factors pushing and pulling in different directions to explain an outcome—in this case, how ethnic groups relate to each other. As in criminology, this theory includes motive as well as means and opportunity. The means of fighting, as noted by mobilization theory, boils down to two key factors: *leadership* (which involves how leaders frame the issues at stake) and *organization*. I add two key elements of motive, based on important findings in social psychology: *symbolic predispositions*, such as prejudice and ideology, and *threat perceptions*. Including both factors makes intuitive sense: people are most likely to support confrontation with a rival ethnic group if they dislike that group and see it as threatening. I include opportunity by counting it mostly as part of the perceived threat: people support the fight only if the idea of fighting seems less threatening than the idea of not fighting (and leaving

11

the adversary unopposed). Other aspects of opportunity work by facilitating organization.

To sum up, the symbolic politics theory presented here posits that the way relations between ethnic groups play out in any country depends on four main factors: *symbolic predispositions, perceived threat, leadership,* and *organization.* In bringing these ideas together, I am recasting the symbolic politics theory proposed decades ago by David Sears and Murray Edelman so that it includes both more recent findings in psychology and neuroscience and the insights of the mobilization approach. As discussed here, therefore, symbolic politics theory is about symbolic predispositions and threat perceptions, as in Sears's version, but it also includes leadership and organization and suggests psychological reasons for their importance.

In proposing this theory, I am arguing for a paradigm shift in political science and related fields away from the notion that human behavior should be seen as "rational."[25] I have several reasons for this. First, people rarely do the kind of value-maximizing cost-benefit analysis that rational choice theory assumes is the basis of their behavior: How often do any of us carefully list the pros and cons of any choice we face? Rather, people's decisions are more often intuitive "gut reactions" than rationally calculated acts, and are mostly governed by biases and emotions. Rational choice theorists would respond by saying that they do not assume that people actually make such calculations but only that they act "as if" they did. I argue, however, that it is better to base a theory on the way people actually decide instead of on an "as-if" assumption that is false.

Second, rational choice theorists assume that people base their decisions on a clear and consistent preference ordering—they assume, that is, that people know what they want and that those desires are stable. Again, however, this is false. Politics is largely about politicians responding to changes in popular mood—status anxieties, security fears, and so on—that lead to changes in priorities. It is also about politicians seeking, usually by manipulating popular emotions, to get people to change their preferences to support the politician's program. Assuming fixed preferences and rational decision making takes the politics out of political analysis and leaves rational choice theorists dismissing most of what politicians do as meaningless "cheap talk." It is not; that "cheap talk" is one of the main ways politicians seek and keep power.

The symbolic theory of politics is better than theories that assume rational behavior because it fixes these problems. Instead of assuming a single universal rationality, it is based on the recognition that different people react differently to similar circumstances based on their biases, prejudices, values, and ideology—their symbolic predispositions. It also considers how preferences shift with emotions. In explaining political conflict, the key emotions are fears—more precisely, feelings of threat either to physical security or to status, identity, or economic prospects. Additionally, symbolic politics theory ("symbolist theory" for short) explains how leadership works: usually not by appealing to logic or rational interests but by making emotional appeals to identity, ideology, or prejudice. Finally, it integrates consideration of organization into analysis of these other factors when it is too often kept separate.

Since the notion of symbolic predispositions is unfamiliar to most, let us turn now to examining what they are and why they matter.

SYMBOLIC PREDISPOSITIONS AND SYMBOLIC POLITICS

To define them more carefully, symbolic predispositions (SYPs for short) are durable inclinations people have to feel positively or negatively about an object.[26] When people are confronted with anything that symbolizes the liked or disliked object, they tend to feel the corresponding emotion. The symbol may be something very specific, such as a person's name or photo, or something more abstract, like a national flag. Racial prejudice has a broader effect, inducing negative emotions in response to anything associated with the disliked racial group.

To clarify, when I discuss symbolic predispositions, I do *not* mean either a symbol or an emotion; I mean a person's consistent inclination to *react* to a specific symbol with a particular emotion. For example, many Americans have strong SYPs about the U.S. president: some are deeply supportive of the incumbent; others are inclined to hate or despise him. However, few Americans spend their days filled with love for or rage against the president. The emotion emerges only when triggered by a symbol—anything that reminds people of the president. As a result, when told that the president supports a certain policy, these Americans react in polarized ways: opponents tend to get angry and denounce the president's view, while supporters typically feel sympathetic and back the president. The SYP is this inclination to feel either sympathy or hostility when one is reminded about the president.

Symbolic predispositions play a central role in this theory because they powerfully influence how people react to almost anything. First, SYPs help to determine what threats people perceive: if they are prejudiced against a group, they are more likely to see that group's actions as threatening in some way. Second, SYPs about ideology help determine how people respond to perceived threats: people with a hawkish ideology will tend to favor confrontation, while dovish types will favor accommodation. SYPs also influence how people will respond to organizations: they will support organizations that appeal to symbols they like and oppose organizations that appeal to symbols they dislike. Finally, SYPs influence how people respond to leadership: if people have positive feelings about a particular leader, they are more likely not only to follow that leader but also to support the ideas that leader proposes.

A well-known experiment illustrates how subtly and powerfully SYPs influence people's perceptions. In the study, participants were shown a photo of either a black person's or a white person's face—flashed on a screen for only 0.2 seconds—followed by a photo of either a handgun or a tool (such as a pair of pliers), also flashed for 0.2 seconds. Participants who had seen a black face were more likely to mistake the tool for a gun than were those who were shown the white face.[27] This bias was linked to negative stereotypes: the more familiar participants said they were with the stereotype of black men as dangerous, the more likely they were to misperceive the tool as a gun. The obvious implication, demonstrated in study after study, is that people with this symbolic predisposition are likely to see a group of black people as more threatening than a group of white people engaged in the same behavior.

The way SYPs work in politics is illustrated in a classic study of the 1978 California tax revolt by David Sears and Jack Citrin. What the authors found was that three symbolic predispositions—feelings about government, feelings toward blacks, and feelings about welfare—were key influences on people's views on the tax revolt, which aimed to cut California's property taxes.[28] Activists made interest-based arguments on both sides: supporters argued for the obvious benefits of tax cuts, while opponents pointed out that since property taxes were the primary funding source for the school system, cutting those taxes would reduce school budgets and impair school quality, producing less educated and less productive graduates.

The argument that people believed, however, depended mostly on their SYPs. People with a symbolic predisposition against "big government" tend to believe that government wastes money, so they rejected the school-funding argument, assuming—even if they had children in school—that cutting taxes would reduce government waste rather than school quality. People inclined to appreciate government, on the other hand, tended to see the benefits of generous school funding—even if they did not have children in public school. Furthermore, opposition to "big government" was closely tied to prejudice: people with negative feelings toward black people were particularly likely to be skeptical of government spending, suspicious that their tax revenues were being diverted for the benefit of undeserving racial minorities. The symbols of "big government," "welfare," and "taxes" were so strongly associated in these people's minds that they tended to overlook the fact that property taxes went primarily to schools and not at all to welfare. As a result, they supported the 1978 property tax cut.

In contrast to the role of SYPs—and counter to the assumptions of rational choice theory—tangible interests did not matter much in explaining people's views: being a homeowner (and therefore a payer of property taxes) was much less important than SYPs in explaining people's attitudes, and having children in school did not matter at all. These findings illustrate the general logic of symbolic politics theory. Some specific material interests like property tax bills matter, but others, like funding for one's child's education, may not matter at all. Instead, most of the time in politics, symbolic predispositions—ideology, values, prejudice, and so on—are what matter most. Thus we are back to the basic principle of symbolic politics, which I can now state more formally: because people make decisions based primarily on their symbolic predispositions, the way leaders gain support is by using symbols to manipulate those SYPs.

For explaining ethnic conflict, the key implication is that stronger prejudice should lead to more contentious ethnic politics. Thus in the California tax revolt example, moderate racial prejudice led to a sort of covert racial politics in which nonracial symbols were used to harness racist attitudes to help drive the tax cut movement. Some reports identified a similar kind of politics behind some Tea Party leaders in the 2010s.[29] In cases of stable ethnic peace, however, such prejudices are usually weak or absent. For example, when probed for their opinions, both Russians and Tatars in Tatarstan steadfastly refuse to endorse ethnic stereotypes about each other.[30] Cases of ethnic war, in contrast, feature blatant prejudice, sometimes to the point of dehumanization. Thus Christian Filipinos both feared and despised Muslims as primitive and bloodthirsty warriors who needed to be converted to Christianity, and Rwandan Hutu derided Tutsi as alien interlopers and "cockroaches" who needed to be exterminated.

PERCEPTIONS OF THREAT

Studies of prejudice tell us more about how SYPs influence what threats people perceive and how those threat perceptions shape their attitudes and behavior.[31] The kind of threat perception mentioned in the California example is "symbolic" threat, the belief that another group threatens one's own group's values. In other cases, the issue is a threat to status: thus some Christian conservatives in the United States allege a "war on Christmas" because they feel that the public use of neutral terms such as *holidays* instead of explicit references to Christmas threatens to displace Christianity from what they see as its rightful, dominant place in American culture. Perceptions of these kinds of "social threats," in turn, tend to lead people to support discrimination against the threatening out-group.

Studies in another branch of psychology, "terror management theory," have shown that physical threat—even a subtle reminder of the potential of death—has an even stronger effect.[32] Physical threat influences people to become more aggressive, nationalistic, intolerant, and indifferent to other groups' suffering and more supportive of nationalistic or ethnocentric leaders or speakers. The implication for ethnic conflict is obvious: if people feel physically threatened, they are much more likely to support aggressive actions that are likely to lead to violent clashes. Overwhelming threat, of course, may lead people to submit, not to fight, but less overwhelming levels of threat motivate people to fight in self-defense.

Another consideration is the source of threats: By whom do people feel threatened? This applies both to leaders and to followers. Leaders have to balance the potential threat posed by rival ethnic groups against other potential threats to their power—including, in many cases, potential threats from ethnic extremists in their own group. Which is scarier, confronting the ethnic rival or confronting one's own extremists? Ordinary potential rebels have to make a similar judgment if the government is unfriendly: Do they face a greater threat if they let the government's discrimination continue unchallenged or if they try to rise up to oppose it?

To summarize, feelings of threat are critically important because their presence or absence promotes different patterns of politics. If there are no internal ethnic threats, the symbolic predispositions that matter for politics tend to be personal or ideological ones: feelings about politicians, parties, and political platforms. Prejudice plays a role, but it does not dominate. Politics therefore tends to be primarily about distributing economic goods. When feelings of group threat are strong, on the other hand, ethnic politics is likely to become contentious (if the concern is social threats) or violent (if the fear is of physical threats).

LEADERSHIP AND FRAMING

While SYPs are important, it is obvious that prejudiced attitudes cannot lead to ethnic conflict without the leadership to direct those attitudes into social action. By *leadership* I refer primarily to leaders' rhetoric and the political strategy behind it; as mobilization theory also suggests, this rhetoric is best analyzed in terms of the way different issues are "framed" or presented. The most effective frames will, among other things, appeal to the symbolic predispositions of their audience. Leaders use these frames as part of a political strategy to gain and hold power, to get support for their desired policies, and often to mobilize supporters for concerted political action.

When a group challenges the political status quo, it often mobilizes by framing the issue as one of injustice.[33] That is, the group's leaders frame all of their grievances in terms of one master narrative arguing that they are being treated unjustly. In this book, Gandhi's mobilization of Indians against the British Empire is an example. All of Gandhi's particular arguments were focused around the notion that the existence of the British Empire was unjust and that the British should, in the terms of one of his last campaigns, "quit India." Framing issues in terms of injustice, if effective, can lead to mass mobilization that is contentious but not necessarily violent. Gandhi achieved just that, with the aim of redistributing political power from the British to the Indians.

When feelings of a physical threat to the group are present, it is tempting for a politician to frame other issues in terms of this ethnic threat—tempting, but dangerous. The temptation is to use the "terror management" effect to induce people to shift their views in support of the politician's "tough stand." Also, if the threatening group is the object of prejudice, then the prejudice and fear can reinforce each other: the prejudice makes the other group seem more threatening, while the threat seems to justify the prejudice and hardens it. Finally, it is easy to frame issues of material interest in ethnic terms: poor groups claim they are not getting their fair share of government resources, rich groups argue they are overtaxed to provide the others with undeserved benefits, and so on. The stronger the prejudice, the less truth there needs to be in these charges for them to be believed.

This strategy is dangerous, however, because it is often self-defeating. Promising to "protect" his group from a "threatening" rival group, a chauvinistic politician like Serbia's Slobodan Milošević may provoke a violent response from the other side that leads to less security for his people, not more. Promising to secure "deserved" economic benefits for his people, the chauvinist leader may get a destructive war that leaves most of them worse off. Promising himself that this course will propel his political career, the politician may find that it instead leads eventually to his own death (as in the case of Chechen leader Jokhar Dudaev) or fall from power (as in the case of Milošević). And if he sees the peril and attempts to dismount the tiger, seeking ethnic accommodation to head off conflict, he may still be devoured. This is what happened to Sri Lankan premier S. W. R. D. Bandaranaike in the early 1960s: he had come to power on a platform of "Sinhala [language] only," but after he shifted course and attempted a compromise with the Tamil minority, he was assassinated by an extremist fellow-Sinhalese.

ORGANIZATION

The last of the key factors influencing ethnic politics is organization. No matter how silver-tongued and charismatic, any leader needs to be backed by an organization if he or she is to accomplish large social or political goals. Even in routine politics, the ethnic leader must become either a politician backed by a party organization or at least an interest-group leader backed by an ethnic lobbying organization in order to have much effect. Creating a social movement or an ethnic militia requires even more organizational capability, involving the backing of the government, a political party, an ethnic social organization, or some other social network. Sustained contentious or violent politics does not happen without organization. Since this basic point is easy to understand, I do not expand on it here; details on the role of organization are presented in chapter 1.

PATTERNS OF ETHNIC POLITICS

The outcome I am trying to explain in this book is the amount or intensity of ethnic conflict and, relatedly, the way that conflict is managed. As mentioned earlier, we need to distinguish between not only cases of war and peace but also cases in the middle, where ethnic relations are contentious—often involving raucous social movements and sometimes some rioting—but do not result in civil war. The objective is to understand what politics is like in each type of case and why it is like that. If we consider the politics of ethnic peace, however, it becomes clear that it can take two completely different forms. One possibility is the repressive peace of a dictatorship: Brezhnev's Soviet Union, for example, experienced ethnic peace because the KGB eliminated all opportunity for rebellion. The other possibility is what we might call an inclusive peace, as in a working democracy where ethnic groups' concerns are addressed in routine politics without the need for violence or mass contention. In sum, to use social science terminology, there are four different possible values of the dependent variable: war, contentious politics, repressive peace, and inclusive peace.

According to symbolic politics logic, the most important factor explaining which outcome is reached is the kind of threat perceived by members of an ethnic group (particularly one that is out of power). Repressive peace results from perceptions of an overwhelming threat from the state that prevents any kind of ethnic mobilization. War results from a physical threat severe enough to motivate the group to mobilize in self-defense but not so overwhelming that resistance is hopeless. Contentious politics results from perceptions of social threats to a group's identity, status, or economic interests, which motivate the creation of a social movement by the ethnic group. Inclusive peace, finally, occurs when no significant threats are perceived, so ethnic group members feel no need to mobilize politically.

As it happens, studies of U.S. politics and foreign policy by Theodore Lowi and William Zimmerman have identified several different patterns of politics, three of which clarify what politics is like in three of these situations.[34] The first pattern is the politics of *distribution*, which occurs when political stakes are low and outcomes are "symmetrical," or fairly evenly distributed. An example is pork-barrel politics, in which each group receives a share of government spending. This is what inclusive ethnic peace looks like: ethnic groups perceive only minimal threats because their concerns are addressed through the routine processes of politics before they come to feel threatened.

In contrast, the politics of *redistribution* is what happens when the outcomes sought do not have symmetrical effects—some groups would gain and others would lose. An example is a policy of racial or ethnic preferences, such as U.S. affirmative action policies, which benefit racial minorities to the disadvantage of other groups. The higher stakes in these situations motivate the concerned groups to mobilize social movements to pursue their goals.

Table I.1 Patterns of (ethnic) politics

Main Threat Perceived	Pattern of Politics	Quality of Ethnic Relations
Overwhelming physical threat	Politics of submission	Repressive ethnic peace
Physical threat to ethnic group	Politics of protection	Ethnic violence or war
Social threat to ethnic group	Politics of redistribution	Contention among movements
Minimal threat	Politics of distribution	Inclusive ethnic peace

This is what contentious politics looks like: one group mobilizes in the belief that the status quo threatens its group interests, status, or identity, while the other countermobilizes because the first group's demands for redistribution threaten its interests, status, or identity.

The third pattern is the politics of *protection*, which occurs when people perceive a physical threat from another group and respond by mobilizing for violent group defense behind a leader who promises to protect them. This is the pattern that can result in ethnic war.

While there are some cases of repressive ethnic peace in U.S. politics—especially the Jim Crow South and the treatment of Native Americans in many cases—neither Lowi nor Zimmerman theorized what the resulting pattern would look like. To fill in this gap, I label it the politics of *submission*, which occurs when the threat from the state overwhelms any inclination to challenge it, so there is no open contention over ethnic issues. These four patterns are summarized in table I.1.

Considering the different kinds of nonviolent or low-violence situations is central to the purpose of this book. My goal is to show not only why ethnic war happens but also why and how ethnic peace happens and when an intermediate, contentious-but-not-too-violent pattern emerges. Just as we need to know how a healthy human body works to understand what goes wrong to cause a disease such as cancer, we have to understand how a healthy body politic works to head off ethnic conflict if we want to understand what goes wrong to drive the system into mass demonstrations or war.

WHY PATTERNS CHANGE: PROCESSES OF MOBILIZATION

To analyze in more detail how a political system can move from one pattern to another, we must keep in mind that different steps toward conflict happen at different times. As discussed earlier, the four main factors that explain these outcomes are prejudice and other SYPs, threat perception, leaders' framing, and organization. When mobilization occurs, these factors typically work in a sequence of four steps, with each step involving a different subset of these four factors. The overall process is illustrated in figure I.1.

The first step, which happens over the long term, is the evolution of *prejudice* and other symbolic predispositions, which depend in part on the image

19

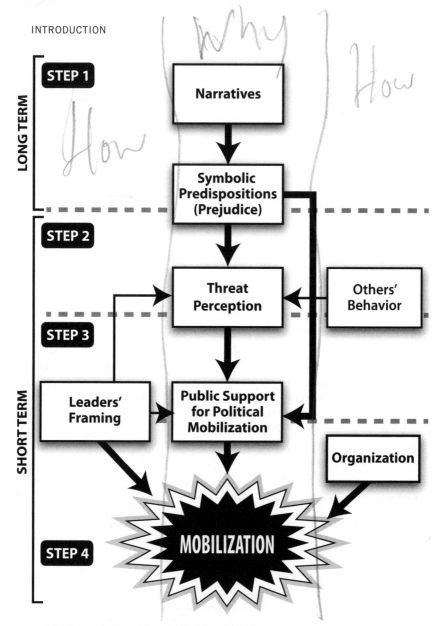

Figure I.1. The symbolic politics of (ethnic) mobilization.

of the other group promoted by the ingroup's identity narratives. The second step is *threat perception*, which depends in part on the other group's behavior but even more on people's symbolic predispositions (especially prejudice) and on whether leaders frame what is going on as a threat. The third step is *support for political mobilization*, including whether people vote for ethnically aggressive politicians. Such support depends in part on which threat people perceive to be greater: Is it more dangerous to allow the ethnic threat to go unchallenged or to mobilize and fight back against a potentially powerful enemy? Support for mobilization also depends on people's SYPs and on how leaders frame the threat. The fourth step is *mobilization* itself, the actual formation of a nonviolent movement or an army. The degree of mobilization depends on the degree to which people support it, on the leaders' framing, and on what organizational networks are available.

In figure I.1, the series of steps in the middle—narratives, SYPs, threat perceptions, and public support—traces the development of the motive for conflict. These factors, the core of symbolic politics theory, explain the degree to which group goals are in conflict and therefore *why* people support either moderate or chauvinistic ethnic leaders. The major elements on either side of that line, leadership and organization, have to do not with why ethnic groups mobilize but *how* they do so.

To further illustrate how the theory works, let us return to the question about why Sudan returned to civil war in 1983. The first key factor was the existence of strongly hostile SYPs on both sides: many northerners were fiercely racist, despising the darker southerners as "slaves" or "monkeys"; many northerners were also fervently attached to their Islamic identity. Southerners, for their part, had strong symbolic predispositions against Islamist rule after two horrific past experiences with it. The status quo after the 1972 peace deal was a politics of distribution: Numayri framed his policy as a secular leftist one aimed at pursuing economic development, appealing to both northerners and southerners and avoiding reference to ethnic SYPs to prevent ethnic threat perceptions from rising.

When economic problems arose, however, Numayri's "economic development" frame stopped working. Cultivating an image as a pious Muslim seemed to be a promising strategy to Numayri because of the strength of Islamist SYPs among northerners (which also contributed to the strength of rival Islamist politicians). Numayri therefore began framing his leadership in religious terms and allied himself with those Islamist politicians. These moves triggered southerners' SYPs against Islamism, so southerners' threat perceptions began to rise. When Numayri moved directly against southern military units, they mutinied, creating the nucleus of the rebel Sudanese People's Liberation Army, which was led by southern military officers. A politics of protection then ensued, as the threat that each side posed to the other came to dominate politics on both sides. Widespread support for mobilization followed on both sides, though its speed lagged, especially in the south, until the rebel organizations grew strong enough to widen their recruiting nets.

This theory explains why ethnic mobilization is relatively rare: because it occurs only when all or nearly all of the conditions for it exist. If members of different groups are not prejudiced against each other, they are unlikely to see the others as a threat, so ethnic politics is likely to be a politics of distribution. If prejudice is present but leaders are careful to avoid threatening the other group, then perceived threats are likely to be low, and a peaceful politics of distribution can continue. If members of any group feel overwhelmingly threatened by the state, then they will not dare to challenge it, adopting instead a politics of submission. If group members perceive a threat from another group, but chauvinist would-be leaders lack credibility, then people will not join the chauvinists' movement; moderate leaders may then still maintain a quiet politics of distribution or submission. Finally, even if group members perceive a threat and support mobilization, then even a credible chauvinist leader will fail if he is not backed by an organization that can sustain the movement.

Put more formally, the theory states that threat perceptions, credible chauvinist leadership, and effective organization are all necessary conditions for ethnic mobilization. Significant ethnic mobilization does not happen unless all three factors are present. Increases in any of them—perceptions of stronger threat, more credibility for chauvinist leaders, or better organization—increase the likely scale and intensity of ethnic mobilization. Together, these three factors are also sufficient for ethnic mobilization: if all three are simultaneously present, ethnic mobilization will occur, though violence may not erupt. While prejudice is neither necessary nor sufficient, it is a key motivating factor, at least on one side, in the vast majority of cases.

REVERSING ESCALATION: PROCESSES OF DEMOBILIZATION AND PEACE BUILDING

While figure I.1 outlines the process of mobilizing for conflict, it also gives strong clues about how to reverse the process. The key obstacle is that it is virtually impossible to reduce prejudice in the short run. Since prejudice is itself a cause of conflict and contributes to threat perceptions that further increase conflict, this is an important problem that makes peace building difficult. The other factors that lead to intense conflict are more malleable, however, and enable the pursuit of peace. One of the first things to change may be short-term behavior: if one side implements a cease-fire, for example, the other side is likely to perceive a reduction in its threat environment, allowing it to respond with de-escalating moves of its own as public support for hostile action begins to decline.

Going from an armed truce to real peace requires that leaders begin to frame the issues differently. If threat perceptions decline enough, leaders can shift from a rhetoric of fear to a more hopeful framing, promising a politics of distribution in which all sides reap the benefits of peace and the ensuing prosperity. If threat perceptions remain high—which is more typical—the leaders can reframe the threat by arguing that the threat from the other side is now outweighed by the threat posed by the conflict itself ("We just cannot go on this way"). Such reframing is not easy, but it is essential, and it must work on all the different kinds of threat. Leaders must argue not only that physical threats can be managed peacefully but also that peace will ameliorate threats to their group's status and identity. Ultimately, the reframing must lead to a change in the group's identity narrative into one compatible with peace. For example, groups often need to stop defining themselves as victims of the rival group, defining their identity and source of group status in more positive terms.[35]

Finally, leaders must use all the organizational resources at their disposal to shift their efforts from war making to peace building. Rebel movements must be converted from armies into political parties. Political parties must use their propaganda resources to promote frames and narratives that promote peace. Governments must shift resources from war to economic development, offering economic benefits such as jobs especially to former rebels. And security forces must shift from fighting to peacekeeping and policing.

Numayri's leadership in moving Sudan from war to peace in the early 1970s illustrates these processes. He reduced southerners' threat perceptions by clearly signaling his interest in peace. He reframed the identity of the Sudanese state from an Islamic identity to one focused on economic development—a frame that opened the door to an inclusive peace. Finally, he changed political institutions to maintain that inclusive peace, incorporating some rebels into the national army and creating an autonomous regional government through which southerners could govern themselves. The result was a peaceful politics of distribution in Sudan that lasted for a decade. Sudan's tragedy is that Numayri later reversed all of those actions, triggering renewed war.

These insights also suggest some tips for mediators. The most important is to pay more attention to how the leaders of the parties to a conflict are framing the issues they face.[36] The more the leaders of the rival groups frame the other group as hostile and threatening, the more they increase their followers' threat perceptions and support for continued conflict. In other words, aggressive and hostile rhetoric by a group's leadership creates a political environment that makes peace unlikely. Whether the leaders secretly want peace or not, they cannot suddenly persuade their followers to accept a peace deal if their previous rhetoric framed the enemy as unconditionally hostile: the deal itself would appear inadequate, and the leader would lose credibility by suddenly abandoning long-held positions. Therefore, when dealing with a conflict in which leaders continue to emphasize the other side's hostility, the best option for would-be mediators is to denounce those leaders' aggressiveness and intransigence instead of wasting their time convening fruitless peace talks. Anything leaders say privately in peace talks is meaningless if they will not say it publicly.

23

Summarizing the New Symbolic Politics Theory

Putting together the ideas presented earlier in this chapter allows the revamped symbolic politics theory to account in detail for when and why ethnic politics in any country is peaceful, contentious, or violent. According to this theory, each of the four patterns of politics is caused not only by different threat perceptions but also by different levels and types of SYPs, leaders' frames, and organization. The logic of each pattern is as follows.

The Politics of Submission. If state repression generates a physical threat that is too powerful to resist, that threat dominates the influence of other factors. Subordinate group members are prevented from organizing, and ethnic politicians see little alternative to submission to the dominant group. Those who try to resist are harassed, imprisoned, or killed. In such a situation, quiescence is the subordinate group's only option, regardless of levels of prejudice. The result is repressive ethnic peace. The position of South Africa's blacks in the 1960s and early 1970s is an example of this pattern; it is discussed in chapter 6.

In many cases, including South Africa under apartheid, the reason for the repression is that the dominant group perceives a threat from the subordinates. Leaders of the dominant group are practicing the politics of protection, framing subordinate demands for justice as threats to the dominant group and thereby encouraging prejudice and ethnocentrism in the public opinion of their group. The politics of repression remains peaceful until the subordinates perceive a change in the source of the main threat: if the threat from the state diminishes so that subordinates can focus on threats to their group's interests or security, they can mobilize and create a politics of either redistribution or protection.

The Politics of Protection. The politics of protection happens when people perceive a physical threat to their group. Feelings of threat cause people's attitudes to shift in a more ethnocentric and hostile direction because of the terror management effect, which prompts them to feel more loyalty to their group and to support more aggressive actions against any perceived enemy. Again, the source of threat is important: while mobilizing in support of a national government against some other threat is relatively low in risk, mobilizing to fight the government may pose more of a threat than submitting to it. The group also needs a chauvinist leader and an effective organization if it is to be able to mobilize. An example examined in this book (chapter 2) is the rebellion by Muslims in the southern Philippines in the early 1970s: strong SYPs among Muslims against the Philippine state led them to interpret President Ferdinand Marcos's introduction of martial law in 1972 as exceptionally threatening to them and motivated them to rebel, organized by the Moro National Liberation Front and led by that organization's founders.

In the politics of protection, leaders are able to get their people to "rally around the flag" by creating a threat frame depicting the conflict in terms of good versus evil and by claiming that group loyalty and violent action are necessary to defend the lives and values of the group. President George W. Bush's speech after the September 11, 2001 attacks provides a stark and powerful example of this sort of rhetoric in response to an obvious threat:

> Today, our fellow citizens, our way of life, our very freedom came under attack in a series of deliberate and deadly terrorist acts. . . .
>
> These acts of mass murder were intended to frighten our nation into chaos and retreat. But they have failed. Our country is strong. A great people has been moved to defend a great nation.
>
> Terrorist attacks can shake the foundations of our biggest buildings, but they cannot touch the foundation of America. These acts shatter steel, but they cannot dent the steel of American resolve. . . .
>
> Our military is powerful, and it's prepared. . . . The search is underway for those who are behind these evil acts. . . . We will make no distinction between the terrorists who committed these acts and those who harbor them.[37]

Bush's rhetoric needs little analysis. It is all there: the evoking of an immediate threat to lives, the depiction of a struggle between good and evil, the call for unity and resolve, and the promise of violent retaliation. This is, of course, a rhetoric of war, and similar language is used when the enemy is an internal ethnic group rather than a foreign nation.

It is worth noting that Bush used very similar rhetoric in the more ambiguous case of the war with Iraq in 2003. Iraq was neither involved in the 9/11 attack nor engaged in the production of weapons of mass destruction, but the Bush administration leveled both charges on the basis of sketchy evidence, aiming to bolster its case that Iraq posed a threat. Ultimately, the evidence did not matter. What mattered were the general atmosphere of fear, long-standing symbolic predispositions against Muslims in general and Saddam Hussein in particular, the conflation of terrorism Iraq did support (against Israel) with terrorism it did not support (9/11), and shrewd deployment of a threat frame employing nationalist and good-versus-evil rhetoric. The result was strong, if temporary, popular support for the war in Iraq.

Threat and SYPs are not enough to create a politics of protection, however. Such violent mobilization cannot happen without a credible chauvinist leader (Bush, in the preceding example) and strong political organizations that control armed forces. Also, once contending ethnic groups start mobilizing for "protection," one final process kicks in to push the clashes toward more violence: the security dilemma.[38] Each move by one side to protect itself is seen by the other side as a threat that justifies even more counteraction. Each act of violence justifies another in retaliation, and the result is an escalation to ethnic war. If one side mobilizes, as Afrikaner whites did in

25

midcentury South Africa, while the other side does not (or cannot) respond, war can be avoided; the weaker side is then forced into a politics of submission.

The Politics of Redistribution. A politics of redistribution involves mobilizing a social movement. It typically occurs when prejudice or ideological conflict is at a moderate level, leading to perceptions of social threat—that is, feelings that one's group's status, identity, or interests may be threatened. Since redistribution means taking benefits away from one group in favor of another, it is more contentious than distributing routine government benefits and results only from the rise of rambunctious social movements. Such a movement is likely to arise, though, only if the threat environment is right: not only must potential supporters feel that their group is threatened; they must also feel that it is not too dangerous for them to mobilize to protect their group. A powerfully repressive government can prevent ethnic mobilization. Gandhi's nonviolent movement in India (discussed in chapter 5) is an example of this pattern.

In addition to a favorable threat environment, a successful movement needs credible leaders who frame the issues at stake in a way that effectively appeals to the followers' SYPs, persuading them that the situation they face is unjust. Finally, the leaders need organizations, social networks, and money to turn support for a mobilization into an active social movement organization. If all of these elements are present, leaders can succeed with a political strategy of unarmed mobilization. If an ethnic group leader lacks either credibility as an aggressive ethnic champion or a credible threat to point to, or an organization to mobilize her followers, she is more likely to pursue a political strategy of accommodation, attempting to steer politics back toward the distributive pattern.

The U.S. civil rights movement of the 1950s and 1960s is a famous example of a successful strategy of nonviolent mobilization, with its ideals beautifully articulated in the rhetoric of Martin Luther King Jr. The issues are framed in terms of injustice, as King said explicitly in his 1968 "I've Been to the Mountaintop" speech: "The issue is injustice. The issue is the refusal of Memphis to be fair and honest in its dealings with its public servants." King then increased his rhetorical punch with a symbolically evocative passage from the Bible: "Let justice roll down like waters and righteousness like a mighty stream." The appeal is to common values, as he continues, "Somewhere I read of the freedom of speech. Somewhere I read of the freedom of press. Somewhere I read that the greatness of America is the right to protest for right. And so just as I say, we aren't going to let dogs or water hoses turn us around, we aren't going to let any injunction turn us around. We are going on." He was also clear about the threat to both his supporters and opponents; though he advocated nonviolence, he warned in the same speech, "If something isn't done, and done in a hurry, to bring the colored peoples of the world out of their long years of poverty, their long years of hurt and neglect, the whole world is doomed."[39]

More broadly, the U.S. civil rights movement illustrates the conditions required to create a politics of redistribution. The continuing threat posed by segregation to blacks' status and interests was obvious. King and other charismatic leaders ably articulated their demands, carefully steered their followers into nonviolent mobilization, and were backed by an array of mass organizations such as the National Association for the Advancement of Colored People (NAACP) and King's South Christian Leadership Council. An interesting subtlety is that while whites were indeed racist toward blacks, most blacks' symbolic predispositions were not so much antiwhite as simply antisegregation or antisystem. Such a stance, as we will see in the South African and Philippine cases, is not unusual among repressed peoples.

The Politics of Distribution. The most low-key pattern of politics is what happens when prejudice is low and there is little sense of group threat. In this kind of situation, ethnic identity is not salient, so it does not play a major role. Its effect is subtle: voters may prefer politicians who speak their language or share their religious faith—so the politicians may make a point of letting them know—but political campaigns and debates are typically about other things. This is a politics of distribution: voters are primarily interested in roads, schools, jobs, and other economic-related issues, so politicians address those concerns and frame issues in terms of material benefits. Leaders seek support primarily through political parties rather than social movement organizations. In this book, the case of Tanzania (chapter 7) illustrates this pattern.

When politics is distributive, politicians still use symbolic messages to appeal to people's SYPs, but the topics are the images of the candidates and parties, not ethnic identity. If politicians do mention ethnic, religious, or national pride, it is likely to be in a feel-good way aimed to get people to accept the system rather than to mobilize to change it. The political strategy that works best for politicians in this context is accommodation: engaging in political horse-trading to secure benefits for their own supporters in exchange for benefits to others'. Their organization-building efforts focus on political party building and vote seeking; they have no need to create mass-movement organizations.

A colorful example is the ethnic politics of New York City. Italian Americans in New York, celebrating Christopher Columbus's Italian origins, have turned Columbus Day into an expression of ethnic pride featuring an annual parade. Far from rallying their own groups in opposition to this display, politicians from other ethnic groups seize the opportunity to show their respect for Italian Americans by participating. For example, marchers in the 2009 parade included the African American governor, David Patterson; a Jewish American member of Congress (and later senator), Charles Schumer;

and Chinese American councilman John Liu, most of them, of course, seeking Italian American votes in future elections.[40] When assurances of mutual respect are not effusive enough—as in 2011 when New York mayor Michael Bloomberg made an ill-considered joke about "inebriated Irish" on St. Patrick's Day—the result is a ritualized pattern of group self-defense and reconciliation. Protests about the mayor's insensitivity were trumpeted in the local press, Bloomberg apologized, and the matter was set to rest, Irish honor restored.[41]

Intermediate and Unstable Situations. Reality obviously does not always fit neatly into these four patterns. Many situations contain some factors that should lead to one pattern but other factors that push toward another. For example, what happens if prejudice and threat perceptions are high, but leaders adopt political strategies of accommodation? The result is an unstable political situation, often involving some kind of power sharing. As long as the moderate leaders remain in power, politics may keep to a low-conflict distributive pattern. However, the moderate leaders are constantly threatened by the possibility that chauvinist rivals might emerge to play to popular prejudice and fears and so replace the moderates in power by creating a politics of protection. The case of Sudan in the 1970s (described earlier in this chapter and in chapter 3) is an example of just this situation.

The Plan of the Book

The rest of this book is aimed at further developing the symbolic politics theory of ethnic relations and then putting it to the test. Chapter 1 explores in detail the origins of the theory in the empirical findings of psychologists, sociologists, and political scientists. Chapter 1 also develops the theory in more detail, generating specific hypotheses that the case chapters can test. The bulk of the book is then taken up with six case studies that are selected to span the widest possible range of cultures, political systems in developing countries, and patterns of relations among ethnic, religious, racial, and national groups.

Chapter 2 considers the outbreak one of the most violent ethnic wars in post–World War II Asia: that between the Christian-dominated Philippine government and the Muslims in the southern part of the country beginning in the early 1970s. I find that, as expected, the key causes of the conflict included strong Christian prejudice against Muslims and strong feelings among Muslims in the south that President Ferdinand Marcos's 1972 imposition of martial law was an intolerable threat—even though it was not aimed primarily against them.

Chapter 3 examines the interesting case of Sudan in the 1970s and 1980s— that swung from war to peace and back again in little more than a decade, providing us with an opportunity to test the expectations of the theory for

28

both shifts. We find strong prejudices among the dominant Muslims against the "blacks" of the south playing a critical role in motivating northern repression, and that repression in turn creating the perceptions of threat that moved southerners to rebel.

Chapter 4 considers whether symbolist theory can explain not just ethnic war but also genocide, in this case in Rwanda in 1994. The theory works: Rwanda in 1994 faced a racist prejudice routinely dehumanizing the Tutsi minority as "cockroaches"; an obvious threat to the Hutu regime by the rebel Tutsi-led Rwandese Patriotic Front (RPF); and the pervasive labeling of all Tutsis as "accomplices" of the RPF. A military coup then brought to power a genocidal leadership that implemented this eliminationist ideology, using the institutions of the Rwandan state and allied extremist groups to carry out the genocide.

Chapter 5 then looks to an iconic case of nonviolent nationalist mobilization, Gandhi's nationalist campaign in India, to test whether the symbolist theory can account for that kind of nonviolent contention. Even though this is a case of *nationalist* rather than *ethnic* mobilization, the theory claims that the political dynamics should be the same. In outline, the theory holds up as a textbook case of the contentious politics of redistribution, featuring Gandhi leading tens of thousands on his famous Salt March, with millions of other Indians participating in other ways. However, the contentious political atmosphere also brought out tensions between Hindus and Muslims which Gandhi's brand of leadership, based primarily on Hindu symbolism, could do little to soothe.

The next case, chapter 6, explores another iconic case, South Africa's negotiated transition from apartheid to majority rule. This transition was much more violent than is usually understood: it was accompanied by over twenty thousand deaths in political violence in the transition years from 1985 to 1995. The case, therefore, is really one of a negotiated end to a civil war, not of a peaceful transition. The main explanation for the transition is that the politics of protection that justified apartheid lost its support as whites' prejudice and feelings of threat declined; this enabled F. W. de Klerk, the National Party leader and president of South Africa, to shift to a policy of seeking a power-sharing sort of distributive politics.

Chapter 7 anticipates one possible criticism of symbolic politics theory: the notion that perhaps prejudice is too widespread to explain variations in ethnic violence. Chapter 7 therefore examines a "healthy body politic," Tanzania, a multiethnic country that faces very little ethnic tension. I find that the reason for this pattern is mostly that prejudices and feelings of ethnic threat are low because of the concerted efforts of Tanzania's founding leader, Julius Nyerere, to build an inclusive Tanzanian national identity and weaken ethnic identities. The result is a nonethnic politics of distribution.

The Conclusion accomplishes two tasks. First, it restates and summarizes the findings of the book, highlighting the effectiveness of symbolic politics theory for explaining the full variety of ethnic relations, from Tanzania's peace to Rwanda's genocide. Second, it expands on my earlier statement that adopting symbolic politics theory amounts to a paradigm shift away from rationalist logic, providing a new way of thinking about politics that, among other things, helps us understand when other theories are most useful and when they are less so. Examples include a more practical and intuitive understanding of public opinion, voting, and elections; an account of why rational institutional analysis works well for western countries but fails to explain corrupt institutions elsewhere; and suggestions about how to transcend the international relations debate between realism and liberalism by distinguishing when each logic most applies.

CHAPTER 1

Symbolic Predispositions and Ethnic Politics

The introduction explains the basic outlines of my reformulated theory of symbolic politics. The starting point of the theory is the best available evidence from psychology about how people think and what motivates them to act. The evidence shows that in politics as in everything else, people rarely act "rationally" to pursue their material interests; instead, they act intuitively and in knee-jerk fashion on the basis of their values and biases. For example, U.S. liberals often vote for candidates who promise to raise their taxes, while U.S. conservatives often vote for candidates who propose to cut government programs that benefit them. In short, U.S. citizens tend to vote on the basis of ideology and partisan identity—their symbolic predispositions—not their material interests.

More broadly, if we want to understand or anticipate anyone's political behavior, we should not ask what we think their interests are; we should examine what their biases are. If we want to understand people's attitudes and behavior across ethnic lines, the first bias to look for is prejudice. This last proposition—that prejudice is important in interethnic relations—is so obvious only an academic could doubt it. To answer these doubters, this chapter begins with a survey of the nature of ethnic and national identities. Before we begin, however, we need to consider the nature of this "best available evidence" about human behavior—namely, that most of it comes from studies of the psychology and political behavior of U.S. citizens. Evidence that people in other countries behave similarly is less systematic. Is it a problem to generalize based on these mostly U.S. data?

I think not, for two reasons. First, it is not hard to distinguish behaviors that should in principle be universal from those that are not. All we have to do is define our focus carefully enough so we can explain why we expect that reactions to a sunny day will be fairly universal but reactions to seeing a U.S. flag will not be. To take a more relevant example, I expect that like U.S. citizens, people elsewhere vary in the degree and kind of prejudices that they

31

feel and that any strong prejudices that they have will prove politically consequential.

Second, this book goes beyond theorizing to test the resulting hypotheses in six very different cases. As with any hypotheses, we should begin with skepticism, but to the extent we find evidence that the processes predicted by the theory occurred in cases in the Philippines, in India, and across much of Africa, we can have some confidence in the theory. If people do not behave as the U.S. citizens studied lead me to expect, my hypotheses will fail when put to the test.

In this chapter, I explain in detail how I put my version of symbolic politics theory together and how the theory works. After a bit of definitional spadework, the main presentation begins with a discussion of neuroscientists' "two-systems" theory of decision making, which explores the mental tug-of-war between intuition, emotion, and reason that determines how people make decisions. I turn next to social psychological theories of group behavior, which show more specifically how factors like prejudice and feelings of threat can shape individual and group behavior. The next section examines how groups get from attitudes to action, focusing on the roles of leaders and organizations in mobilizing people for political action, whether peaceful or violent. I then put all of these pieces together into a complete statement of the theory, summarizing the factors that make ethnic politics peaceful in most times and places but contentious in some and extremely violent in a few. This chapter closes with a brief explanation of methodology and how this theory relates to other approaches, especially constructivism.

More on Definitions

Despite its distinguished pedigree going back to Max Weber, the notion of the ethnic group as an imagined family, as discussed in the introduction, has always been controversial. Scholars of ethnicity have identified three main schools of thought for explaining ethnic identity.[1] The first account, the primordialist one, emphasizes that ethnicity is usually ascriptive—people are typically born into an ethnic group—and then argues that ethnicity is more or less a fixed, family-like relationship. Instrumentalist and rational-choice approaches, in contrast, see ethnicity mostly as a political tool often manipulated by elites. Constructivism, the third approach, emphasizes that ethnicity is socially constructed, a "social fact" created by the repetition of group myths or narratives. After much debate, scholars have increasingly recognized that the three approaches are really compatible: even primordialists do not really think ethnic identity is fixed; it is an *imagined* family. Similarly, when Weber talks about a kinlike relationship, he adds, "whether or not an objective blood relationship exists."[2]

Clifford Geertz, who is often taken as the founder of the primordialist school, includes in his thinking a caveat very similar to Weber's, asserting, "As culture is inevitably involved in such matters, [a primordial attachment is based on] the *assumed* 'givens' of social existence."[3] Leading instrumentalists also agree that their theories "are all constructivist" because they accept that ethnic identities are "produced and reproduced by specific social processes."[4] Realizing that most so-called primordialists see ethnicity as *culturally* determined, not genetically fixed, therefore allows us to construct a middle ground reconciling all three schools of thought about ethnicity.

This approach also defines a middle ground on the question of how malleable ethnic identity is. On the one hand, we know that ethnic identities are changeable. Intellectuals and political leaders can reinterpret history and culture to "reconstruct" ethnic identity; in some cases, the new identity becomes widespread and established through the process of socialization. For example, Francophone elites in Quebec redefined the highly religious French Canadian identity of the early twentieth century into the more secular nationalist Quebecois identity of later decades; generations of Quebecois grew up with this new identity and felt no connection to the older French Canadian one. On the other hand, leaders cannot stray too far from existing beliefs and real group needs, or they will fail. Identities with weak cultural roots do not survive, even if, as in the case of the Yugoslav and Soviet national identities, they are promoted for decades by powerful governments. The result is that ethnic identities are usually quite stable: while people can sometimes change their ethnic identities, most of them stay with the language, religion, and ethnic identity that they are born with.

Combined through the concept of the imagined family, the three approaches to understanding ethnicity offer a convincing explanation of why it is so powerful and so widespread a political force. The contribution of the primordial approach is to note the cultural and psychological power of ethnic attachment, which comes from its kinlike appeal and importance for members' self-esteem. The instrumentalist view points out that tangible interests such as land, economic goods, and political power are also often at stake in ethnic conflicts.[5] Also, once it is formed, the ethnic identity does become a useful tool for elites to use for seeking popular support. Constructivists, finally, point out that the group is a social construction, created through not only people's beliefs but also their practices, so that if beliefs and practices change, so do ethnic identities. Additionally, the core of an ethnic identity is another social construction, the "myth-symbol complex"— the combination of myths, memories, values, and symbols that define not only who is a member of the group but what it means to be a member.[6] Thus ethnic symbolism is at the heart of this conception.

From this point of view, religious, sectarian, and racial groups can all be seen as "ethnic," as can ethnic groups distinguished by language, as long as they are imagined by their members as families. It does not matter what binds the imagined family together; all that matters is that its members believe in it, which often leads them to refer to each other as "brothers" or "sisters" and to their territory as the "fatherland" or the "motherland."

A final definitional question is what I mean by *ethnic conflict*. I begin with Lewis Coser's classic definition of conflict: a "struggle over values and claims to scarce status, power and resources."[7] *Ethnic* conflict is any conflict that is defined by those involved as pitting one ethnic group—one imagined family—against nonmembers of the group. Ethnic conflict is thus the dependent variable in this book, and it has four possible values. First, ethnic conflict may be suppressed by an authoritarian government, resulting in repressive peace. Second, it may be low, so that contests between ethnic groups are few and easily managed by political routines, resulting in an inclusive peace. Third, ethnic conflict may be moderate, with contending ethnic groups represented by clashing social movements that lead to contentious politics, perhaps involving raucous mass political rallies but not massive violence. Fourth, ethnic conflict may be extreme, leading to war or even genocide.

The Psychological Basis of Symbolic Politics Theory

Neuroscientists have identified two different processes of human decision making based on different neural systems. The first system is intuitive, and is located in an evolutionarily older portion of the brain. Its decisions are unconscious or preconscious and extremely fast; it considers information that is not even consciously noticed, responds strongly to a person's emotions, and works primarily based on learned associations between different objects. The second system, for "reflective" decision making, is more logical and is carried out by parts of the human brain that evolved later. It works consciously but much more slowly than the intuitive system, and it has much less capacity.[8] Neuroscientists consider the intuitive system so much more powerful that psychologist Jonathan Haidt refers to the relationship as one between an elephant and its rider, with the reflective rider often acting not as the intuitive elephant's controller but as its "public relations firm."[9]

Rational choice theorists focus all of their attention on the rider. I think it is wise to listen to the neuroscientists and consider the elephant first.

INTUITIVE REASONING

One of the most famous experiments in neuroscience was carried out by a team led by Antonio and Hanna Damasio. In the experiment, participants were offered two sets of cards: the red cards yielded high rewards but even higher penalties, while the blue cards offered a steadier stream of lower rewards. The Damasios found that after choosing about ten cards, people started showing stress responses (sweaty palms) to the red cards, and they unconsciously shifted toward preferring the blue cards. After fifty cards, on average, they reported a hunch that the blue cards were better; after about eighty cards, people understood the game.[10] In other words, what the Damasios found was that emotional response and reaction come first, conscious intuition second, and conscious understanding later.

The intuitive system is powerfully effective for a variety of reasons. First, the human senses collect a million times more information than is registered consciously, and the intuitive system considers it all; the reflective circuits, in contrast, rely mostly on the tiny fraction of information that is consciously noticed.[11] Second, the intuitive system is fast, reacting in some cases within one-tenth of a second.[12] The power of the emotionally charged intuitive circuit means that experiences that involve emotional content produce stronger and more vivid memories than emotionally neutral ones.[13] The intuitive system also uses emotion to evaluate experiences: if something feels good, then it is good.[14] The intuitive system therefore steers our most basic actions: it guides our attraction to food and good-looking potential mates, while preparing us to react to danger, seek social status, and pursue other needs and wants.

Some intuitive abilities are universal: people in every culture learn to read emotional expressions on other people's faces within a few months of birth, and many of these expressions are recognizable by cultures all over the globe.[15] Others are the result of training or education: art experts, for example, can often spot a forgery immediately, long before they can articulate how they can tell.[16] This is why Haidt refers to the reflective system as the "public-relations firm" for intuition: people often do not know the reasons for their decisions, though they are often good at rationalizing whatever decision they make after the fact.[17]

The way the intuitive system works is through "networks of association, bundles of thoughts, feelings, images and ideas that have become connected over time."[18] Again, emotions are critical: as Drew Westen explains, "The fact that someone or something holds any significance to us at all means that it has *emotional associations.*"[19] New networks of associations can be created in two ways, either by repetition or as the result of some traumatic experience. Either way, "neurons that fire together, wire together," so once a network of associations is created, evoking one image in the network tends to activate others as well.[20]

SYMBOLIC PREDISPOSITIONS AND BIAS

Decades ago, a few scholars recognized the huge effects these networks of mental associations had on politics. It was David Sears, as mentioned in the introduction, who defined the "symbolic predispositions" (SYPs) created by these mental networks as "stable affective responses to particular symbols."[21] In U.S. politics, he found, some of the most powerful and enduring SYPs are ideology, party identification, and racial prejudice. Later research found that SYPs toward particular leaders, institutions like the U.S. military, and specific values like human rights or feminism were also powerfully influential at times.[22] Thus the credibility of a leader will depend on people's SYPs toward that leader: if they feel favorably toward a leader, they are more likely to support him or her and his or her policies; that leader is thus said to have charisma. If people perceive a leader as likable but weak, however, they are unlikely to consider the leader a credible "protector" if they perceive a threat.

Some of the SYPs most important in politics are deeply rooted in individual personalities. For example, people who place a high value on "universalism" and "benevolence" tilt toward the left of the political spectrum, while those placing a high value on power and security prefer the political right.[23] Those who emphasize "tradition," "conformity," or "sanctity" tend particularly to support the religious right.[24]

What makes SYPs so important in politics is that they create a range of biases in judgment. An example is the "halo effect" of attractiveness: attractive advocates for any idea tend to be more persuasive than less attractive ones.[25] One study showed, for example, that essays were rated as better written if their authors were identified as attractive women in a photo.[26] This effect is widely known to advertisers, of course, which explains the prevalence of sexy women in advertisements. People are also predisposed to like others who are familiar, or whom they see as warm or similar to themselves.[27] In politics, voters tend to elect political candidates who are rated as more competent-looking in photos.[28]

In ethnic politics, of course, one of the most important SYPs is prejudice, defined as a negative attitude toward another group with three components: negative stereotypes, negative feelings, and inclinations to behave in a negative way. The study mentioned in the introduction, in which participants were more likely to mistake a tool for a gun if they were shown a photo of a black person's face first, illustrates the intuitive mind at work: it draws on the associative memory to draw lightning-quick conclusions that are sometimes unreliable.

Because symbolic predispositions are based on learned associations of feelings and ideas, they can change. One way they can do so is by "affect transfer": if I like one thing, I am more likely to feel positively about associated things.[29] The halo effect is one example: if I am attracted to a pretty woman, I will feel more positive toward her writing—or the brand of beer she is promoting. Affect transfer can even erode racial bias: during World War II, for example, U.S. citizens' dislike of the Nazis spilled over into dislike of their racist values, with positive feelings about patriotism, nationalism, and the imperative of national defense transferred to the notion of opposing racial discrimination.[30]

THE REFLECTIVE SYSTEM

Though the emotional and intuitive "elephant" is faster and more powerful than the rational "rider," rationality still plays a role. For example, it can temper racial bias. In one experiment, subjects playing a video game were told to "shoot" quickly if they spotted a person carrying a gun; if the target was unarmed, they should quickly press a "don't shoot" button. The subjects were slightly quicker to "shoot" armed blacks than armed whites, and slower to identify unarmed blacks than unarmed whites. In a second trial, the participants were given a shorter time to respond; as a result, participants became more likely to shoot black targets—whether armed or unarmed—than comparable whites.[31] Even if they did not consciously believe the stereotype, many participants still held the link between blacks and violence in their associative memory, so it influenced their intuitive reactions. But importantly, when participants had more time to respond (in the first trial), they were usually able to correct for this bias: confronted with unarmed blacks, their tendency was to hesitate but then to make the right decision, not to shoot.

Unfortunately, the reflective system is just as good at rationalizing bad decisions as it is at generating good ones. In one study, participants were hypnotized to feel a flash of disgust when reading neutral words such as "take." When these participants read that student council president Dan "tried to take topics that appeal to both professors and students in order to stimulate discussion," a third of them condemned Dan for it. Their rationalizations included "Dan is a popularity-seeking snob" and "it just seems he's up to something."[32]

Even when the reflective system is fully engaged, it is subject to a host of biases, mostly bubbling up from the intuitive system. One source is motivated bias, including a range of ways in which people tend to believe what they want to believe. Sometimes this is to salvage self-esteem: one study found, for example, that when participants were asked to try to convince a study staffer of something, the same staffers were rated as more intelligent when they agreed than when they refused to be convinced.[33] The unsuccessful participants blamed their persuasive failure on the staffer's perceived stupidity. In other cases, the bias stems from an effort to avoid having to make a tough tradeoff decision, leading to "defensive avoidance." For example, Admiral Kimmel, the naval commander at Pearl Harbor in 1941, believed that his equipment could not stand to be kept on high alert, so he and his staff distorted intelligence information to convince themselves—with disastrous results—that a low state of alert would be good enough.[34]

MASS POLITICS IS SYMBOLIC POLITICS

If symbolic predispositions are so influential, mass politics must be largely about trying either to harness or to create SYPs in individuals that favor one's own candidates or positions and tilt against the opposition's. Consider first some more implications of affect transfer. In one study, experimenters subtly manipulated people's moods by putting them in a sunny room or introducing a subtle odor into the room. The result was that participants in a good mood evaluated candidates more favorably, especially if they were unaware of the reason for their mood.[35] Yet another study found that adding appropriate mood music made political ads on television more effective.[36] Another found that people are more likely to favor politicians who are smiling or associated with a flag.[37]

Pity, therefore, the poor politician. We criticize politicians for their superficiality, always fussing about their image; yet if our first glimpse of one shows him dirty or disheveled, we are likely to dismiss him as a slob and vote for his opponent. People vote with their guts to such an extent that politicians *have* to calculate every move, smiling, waving flags, and playing stirring music because that is what actually influences votes. When politicians are trolling for votes, they have to appeal to the emotional and intuitive elephant, not the reflective rider. People do not usually *think* about politics. Rather, as George Marcus and his colleagues have argued, people usually react to political symbols by relying on preexisting beliefs—that is, symbolic predispositions.[38]

On the other hand, if well understood, these processes can be of enormous help to the politician, as they also enable charismatic leadership. If I have strong liking for a leader, I am more likely to feel favorably toward the leader's ideas. But how far I am willing to follow the leader depends on the connections in my associative memory. If the charismatic leader challenges weakly held concerns, I am likely to follow. If the leader can induce a positive mood, however short-lived, while discussing an idea, he can begin to inculcate a SYP in its favor, a SYP that can grow stronger if the positive association is repeated. A leader lacks charisma if he lacks the ability to induce these strong positive feelings and get them to spill over onto his ideas. Even with charisma, however, if a leader challenges deeply held beliefs, affect transfer is more likely to work the other way: the more the leader associates with values I oppose, the more my dislike will spill over onto the leader.

Some SYPs are deeply rooted moral and ethical values, such as those that form a political ideology. In examining issue voting in the 1976 presidential election, for example, David Sears found that such "symbolic attitudes . . . had strong effects," accounting for between 27 percent and 37 percent of vote choice, "while self-interest had almost none."[39] George Marcus found that SYPs about individuals mattered more in the 1984 presidential election: "Feelings about the candidates, rather than thoughtful assessments regarding public policies, appear to be central to the voters' choices."[40] SYPs also influenced people's factual beliefs: one later study found that most strong Democrats believed that the inflation rate had increased during the Reagan administration, while in fact it had declined by about two-thirds; Republicans tended conversely to believe that Reagan had reduced the budget deficit, when in fact he increased it.[41]

What is true of voting behavior is even truer of public opinion, especially on polarizing issues: SYPs matter; facts do not. Drew Westen found, for example, that people's views about whether President Clinton had committed impeachable offenses in the Monica Lewinsky scandal could be predicted with 85 percent accuracy based on four symbolic predispositions: feelings about the political parties, about Clinton, about infidelity, and about feminism.[42] Strikingly, Westen had measured these SYPs in a previous survey, six to nine months *before* the participants were asked about the Lewinsky scandal. In contrast to the SYPs, factual knowledge made little difference to people's views. Westen found very similar patterns on other issues, achieving 83 to 85 percent predictive accuracy about people's views of the Supreme Court decision *Bush v. Gore* and the Abu Ghraib torture scandal based exclusively on their SYPs.[43] Sometimes the effect of factual information is less than zero: one study found that after learning negative information about a candidate, supporters tended to *increase* their support for that candidate.[44]

In sum, the argument of symbolic politics theory is that when people make decisions on political issues, symbolic predispositions guide the decisions most of the time; facts and material interests matter much less. As Westen puts it, "In politics, when reason and emotion collide, emotion invariably wins."[45] Election campaigns, therefore, focus on creating, modifying, and appealing to SYPs. Candidates try to use affect transfer and similar processes to create positive images for themselves, appeal to positive images of their party, and frame their positions in emotionally pleasing ways while trying to create negative images of their opponents and the opponents' positions. The facts do not matter if candidates get the emotions right. These insights lead us back again to the basic principle of symbolic politics theory: because people make decisions based primarily on their symbolic predispositions, the way leaders gain support is by using symbols to manipulate those SYPs.

If the general rule about politics is that emotions and SYPs matter, not facts, logic, or interests, then the same rule should apply even more to ethnic politics. The implication is that what makes an aggressively chauvinistic politician popular is not the logic of the politician's arguments, but the power of the SYPs the politician appeals to. This is a proposition we can test. Are the voters prejudiced against the targeted group? Does the politician effectively appeal to related SYPs such as group pride and traditional values? Does the politician offer plausible ways to rationalize away the obvious moral and tangible costs of their policies? Is the politician personally trusted?

The expectation is that the more the answer to these questions is yes, the more successful the politician is likely to be, and the more conflict there is likely to be between ethnic groups in that society.

Group Psychology, Ethnicity, and Nationalism

Contrary to the common assumption of human individualism, people are naturally group oriented, not exclusively selfish. In Haidt's terms, humans are "ultrasocial," because we are capable of shared intentionality. It is human nature, Haidt points out, to cooperate in a way that chimpanzees cannot. According to primatologist Michael Tomasello, "It is inconceivable that you would ever see two chimpanzees carrying a log together."[46] Even when they seem to be working together, chimps make no effort to communicate with each other or to share food.

GROUP PSYCHOLOGY AND POLITICS

Some of the best evidence for how human group-thinking works comes from social identity theory, based on Henri Tajfel and his followers' famous "minimal group experiments." In these experiments, Tajfel found that people assigned randomly into groups immediately began showing signs of ethnocentrism: when given a choice of how to distribute benefits, they worked to make sure that in-group members received more than out-group members did, even if the result was worse for both. The reason, Tajfel argues, is to achieve "positive ingroup distinctiveness"—that is, to find some basis on which to say, "Our group is better than yours." The competition is for status, not material benefits.[47]

These findings suggest that there is an unconscious human tendency—a universal symbolic predisposition—to favor "us" over "them." However, some versions of the experiment did manage to eliminate the in-group favoritism effect: for example, if participants were divided into more than two groups, or if all chances were eliminated that other in-group members would reciprocate.[48] This suggests that group membership is not "inherently conflictual," as some have suggested.[49] Intergroup conflict is easy to start, but it can be avoided.

Ethnic identity is also ubiquitous in the world. In a set of studies of ethnic groups in Africa, northern Canada, and the Pacific islands, "attachment to the ingroup was found in all the groups studied."[50] In the East Africa study, members of thirty different ethnic groups seemed to have no difficulty in stating their degree of like or dislike for other groups in their country.[51] Furthermore, as one scholar noted, when an in-group is receiving favoritism in allocating limited resources, the result is discrimination against other groups even if that is not the intention.[52]

ETHNIC NATIONALISM

Of all the in-group–out-group divisions that might become salient, why is it ethnic nationalism and its cousins—racism, sectarianism, communalism, and so on—that so often take center stage in political conflict? As noted earlier in this chapter, ethnic groups are "imagined families" bound together by a believed common descent, common historical memories, and elements of shared culture such as language or religion. These elements are all tied together by a "myth-symbol complex," a set of narratives that define who is in the group and who is not; what it means to be a group member; and the symbols of group identity, usually including "chosen traumas" or "chosen glories" that are at the heart of the group's identity narrative.[53] Anthony Smith defines this as the "ethno-symbolist" understanding of ethnicity: the ethnic narratives identify group symbols and establish symbolic predispositions: to defend "our" land, language, or religion; to venerate group heroes; to defend against group enemies; and so on.[54]

Ethnic identity has existed for thousands of years, as the examples of the Jewish, Japanese, and Armenian peoples illustrate.[55] What turned ethnicity from a perennial political sideshow into the central fact of world politics was nationalism. The rise of modern democracy, with its dictum that "the people govern," demanded an answer to the question, who are the people? Whoever was inside the bounds governed by the state had to be—or at least to include—the nation, but what are the "right" boundaries for the nation? Ernest Gellner points out that the modern state, especially the bureaucratic, industrial state, needed a literate population and a common language for purposes of administration and trade, so it made sense to define the nation by its language.[56] Furthermore, the state wanted to foster patriotism—popular loyalty to itself—so it promoted a doctrine of nationalism by using public education to socialize its children into accepting national values.

If the population was not already united by language—and it never was, entirely—the state had to create linguistic unity by promoting the official language. These efforts politicized ethnic identity, making it important to ordinary people in a way it never had been before. Therefore the lines of language difference became lines of ethnic difference and political dispute. Some states, like France, managed to assimilate their linguistic minorities, ending the conflict that way, but most others, from Russia to Fiji, were not so successful. Most modern countries are therefore multilingual and multiethnic, and so face potential ethnic conflict.

The power of these national identities to break apart states and empires comes from the usefulness of identities in symbolic politics. As Jonathan Mercer points out, nationalism itself is an emotional belief, so it creates powerful symbolic predispositions that can be harnessed politically.[57] The myth-symbol complex—that is, the set of ethnic or national narratives of group identity—creates a host more, defining sacred territory, values, heroes,

41

and enemies. Furthermore, nationalism does not only harness religion; to some extent it is itself a religion. Membership in the nation offers people an eternal meaning for their life, a transcendent one that will endure after their death, giving people a reason to sacrifice their life for the nation.[58] With all of this emotional ammunition to use, ethnic nationalism has the potential for great power.

PREJUDICE

Of all the symbolic predispositions that come with ethnicity and nationalism, one of the most important and dangerous is prejudice. As mentioned earlier in this chapter, I define prejudice as a negative attitude toward another group, with three components: negative stereotypes, negative feelings, and inclinations to behave in a negative way. According to this understanding, as formulated by John Duckitt, prejudice has two key dimensions: a stereotype of the other group as superior (competent), equal, or inferior (incompetent); and a feeling about the other group as either warm and likable or cold and unlikable.[59] The result is six possible categories of feelings. If the other group is seen as likable, then a stereotype of competence leads to admiration, a stereotype of equality leads to tolerance or respect, and a stereotype of incompetence leads to paternalism. If the other group is not likable, then a stereotype of competence leads to feelings of envy or resentment, a stereotype of equality leads to feelings of hostility, and a stereotype of incompetence leads to contempt. These negative feelings are prejudices. One refinement is when a disliked group is seen as greater in power but lower in status; this leads to fear and an image of the other as barbarians.[60]

Ethnic and national narratives commonly express just these sorts of feelings and stereotypes. The old white racist narrative in the U.S. South claimed white superiority and prescribed paternalism toward submissive blacks, as in the common expression, "He's a good [Negro]; he knows his place." Traditional anti-Semitism portrays Jews as cold, calculating, and capable but hostile, inviting feelings of resentment. Armenian narratives, in contrast, typically portray Turks as genocidal barbarians, hostile, and powerful but inferior in status and culture. Mixed evaluations are common: in Eastern Europe, about two-thirds of groups are seen by neighboring groups either as immoral and competent or as moral and incompetent, yielding either envy or pity, respectively.[61] The way the in-group is defined is also important: if a nationality defines its identity exclusively, as essentialist or primordial, then the more people identify with that nation, the more prejudiced they tend to be.[62]

A few studies have documented variation in prejudice across societies. For example, while open displays of racial prejudice became increasingly unacceptable in the United States after World War II, apartheid South Africa continued to cultivate such attitudes for decades. Another example concerns anti-Semitism, which was widespread and encouraged in Tsarist Russia, including among the Romanian-speakers of Bessarabia and nearby Transnistria. After the Russian revolution, however, the new Soviet government promoted ethnic tolerance in its territories, including Transnistria, so anti-Semitic attitudes there seem to have declined during the interwar period. Romania, in contrast, had taken control of Bessarabia, and it fostered anti-Semitism. The result was that during World War II, people in Transnistria were much more likely to help Jews survive the Holocaust and much less likely to collaborate in their oppression than were people in Bessarabia, even though both areas were occupied by the fascist Romanian government at the time.[63] The tolerant attitude fostered by the interwar Soviet government remained in Transnistria even during the Holocaust.

The implication of all of these ideas—in particular that ethnic or national narratives often define stereotypes of out-groups—is that those narratives are a key source of prejudice. This is the first specific hypothesis that will be tested in this book: the more hostile a group's narratives are toward another group, the more prejudiced members of the first group are likely to be. This hypothesis is one of the main ways that symbolic politics theory crosses levels of analysis to tie psychology and constructivism together. The claim is that there is a causal relationship between a group's narratives and discourse measured at the societal level, and the SYPs of individuals within the group measured at the individual level.

Some evidence for this hypothesis—that is, for the psychological power of prejudice, especially racial prejudice—was mentioned in the preceding section. The human brain begins reacting to racial cues within one-tenth of a second, and stereotypes of the "dangerous black" automatically prime many members of other racial groups to expect aggression. Negative feelings are even more powerful: "affective prejudice" predicts discriminatory behavior even more strongly than do negative stereotypes—and we saw in the preceding section in the "shooter game" that negative stereotypes alone were enough to prompt discrimination against blacks. Unsurprisingly, then, groups that are both negatively stereotyped *and* targets of prejudiced feelings tend to be discriminated against the most.[64] When prejudice combines with group status-seeking, it leads to a particularly toxic kind of discriminatory politics. "In matters of [U.S.] public opinion," Donald Kinder notes, "citizens seem to be asking not 'What's in it for me?' but rather 'What's in it for my group?' (as well as 'What's in it for other groups?),'" yielding a politics of envy. For example, "white working-class participants in the Boston antibusing movement were motivated especially by their resentments about the gains of blacks and professionals, and less by their own personal troubles."[65]

People often do not realize that they are behaving in a discriminatory way, and they may do so even if they consciously reject prejudiced values. For example, in a jury experiment, some mock juries were given incriminating evidence that was marked as having been excluded by the judge. The result of the experiment was that juries that saw the excluded evidence tended to recommend harsher punishments if the "defendant" was black than if he was white; juries that did not see the excluded evidence punished black and white defendants about equally. It appears that the effect of the "excluded" evidence was to give jurors an excuse to act on the prejudiced feelings they denied having and were apparently trying to suppress.[66] Here is another case of Haidt's intuitive "elephant" driving the behavior of the cognitive "rider."

All of this leads to another hypothesis: the more prejudiced the members of a group are toward some out-group, the more likely they are to support hostile and discriminatory actions toward the out-group. This hypothesis is really just an alternative, more specific form of the basic principle of symbolic politics theory—that because people make decisions based primarily on their symbolic predispositions, the way leaders gain support is by using symbols to manipulate those SYPs. In this case, the relevant SYPs are ethnic prejudices, so the stronger the prejudices are, the more support leaders will gain for policies framed to appeal to them. Hostile and discriminatory policies can be framed no other way: when they are not framed explicitly in prejudiced terms, they are framed in terms of code words that still appeal to prejudice, such as anti-"welfare" messages in U.S. politics that appeal to stereotypes of blacks as constituting the majority of welfare recipients.

The effect of prejudice can occur even if the prejudiced people perceive very little threat; their aim may not be specifically hostile, but merely selfish. Alternatively, the discrimination may even be well intentioned but based on ignorance—presented in a paternalistic way as "helping" the target group. For example, in the early twentieth century, some Native American children in the United States and aboriginal children in Australia were forcibly removed from their families so they could be educated according to the values of the white-dominated societies in which they lived. The motivation for these programs—which were of course perceived by their recipients as hostile and discriminatory—probably included some degree of perceived symbolic threat to the dominant groups' values, but were explained as paternalistic efforts (drenched in racism) to replace the blacks' or Native Americans' "primitive" ways with more modern ones.

Among other factors that influence intergroup relations, two more are worth mentioning here. First is the salience of group identity: when group identity is salient, the result is usually increased group conflict. For example, when people are encouraged to compare their countries to others, those who identify most strongly with their own group tend to become more xenophobic.[67] Another factor that makes for hostile group relations is inequality. In general, intergroup inequality or discrimination makes group identities more salient and leads to negative intergroup attitudes.[68] These insights help us to understand the process of ethnic politics. Anything that raises the salience of ethnic identity, whether the stark fact of inequality or a politician or media outlet harping on ethnic difference, makes people think more in ethnic terms and rouses whatever prejudices they may hold.

THREAT PERCEPTIONS

Prejudice also influences threat perceptions: people are more likely to perceive a threat from a group if they hold negative stereotypes about that group, especially if the out-group is seen as lower in status.[69] For example, as noted in the introduction, a major reason why the Bush administration was able to persuade U.S. citizens in the aftermath of the 9/11 attacks that Iraq was an imminent threat was that most of them already had a stereotype of Saddam Hussein as aggressive and dangerous. Preexisting prejudice did much of Bush's persuasive work for him. This point is important enough to stand as another hypothesis: the more prejudiced group members are, the more likely they are to perceive a threat from the disliked group.

Threat, furthermore, comes in many forms. Since in-group favoritism leads to discrimination against the out-group, group dynamics can lead to "realistic group conflict" over access to resources.[70] Inequality would strengthen this tendency. In other cases, such as opposition to affirmative action in the United States, the out-group is seen as a threat to traditional values such as hard work, resulting in "symbolic threat."[71] In yet other cases, what is at stake is status, as denial of respect to a cultural icon or a verbal insult to the in-group can result in strong reactions against the out-group.[72] Multiple studies have shown that all three of these kinds of perceived threat, which I will call collectively "social threat," are significant in affecting attitudes toward out-groups.[73] Those effects are powerful. A perceived social threat—whether a threat to power, wealth, values, or status—raises the salience of group identity for the threatened group, and at the same time increases hostility and prejudice.[74] One study found that threat perceptions accounted for 55 percent of the variation in prejudice in the United States, Israel, and Spain.[75]

Everything said to this point, focusing still on people's attitudes, leads me to another general hypothesis: stronger ethnic threat perceptions lead to more support for hostile action against the disliked group. "Hostile" action in this case may mean discriminatory laws, forcible repression, or open violence.

Putting the last three hypotheses together, the argument is that prejudice leads to support for hostile action against the disliked group through two different pathways: by blocking empathy, and thereby promoting selfishness or in-group bias ("Let's do what's good for us; who cares about them"), and by promoting threat perceptions that encourage action in "self-defense" against the other group. For example, when Sudan imposed shari'a nationwide, including on non-Muslims, the move could be cast *either* as an inoffensive move to express the Muslim majority's identity (with non-Muslim minorities' feelings and likely reactions considered irrelevant) *or* as an answer to the social threat posed to Muslims' identity by the presence of non-Muslims in the country. The point is that even though these two justifications are mutually exclusive—either the measure was aimed against non-Muslims or it was not—both types of justifications can be presented almost simultaneously by the same person as a result of these two different effects of prejudice on people's judgment. Racism (and other prejudice) means not having to be consistent.

Furthermore, the type of threat influences the nature of the reaction. If the perceived threat is a social threat, not a physical one, the typical reaction should be social or political but not violent. We therefore get the following subhypothesis: the more group members perceive social threats to group identity, status, or economic interest, the more likely they will be to support discriminatory actions toward the other group.

When a threat concerns people's physical safety, however, the effect on political attitudes is especially powerful. According to studies of "terror management theory," priming people to have thoughts of their own mortality in the back of their minds drives political attitudes toward conservatism and ethnocentrism. People become more respectful of their own national and religious symbols, more favorable to those who praise such values, more unfavorable toward those with different values of any sort, and more punitive toward moral transgressors—that is, they become more concerned with symbolic and status threats. At the same time, people become more physically aggressive toward those who differ politically and less concerned with incidental harm to innocents.[76]

One result is that people who are anxious about death also become much more likely to support nationalist leaders and policies, as one 2004 study dramatically showed.[77] In this experiment, participants in the baseline or control condition indicated that they preferred John Kerry to George W. Bush by 57 percent to 13 percent in the upcoming election—unsurprisingly for a sample of college students in liberal New Jersey. Other participants from the same pool, however, were first asked to think about death; asked later about their candidate preference, people in this subgroup said they preferred Bush to Kerry by 46 percent to 20 percent. Background thoughts about death caused support for Bush to more than triple, and support for Kerry to go down even more.[78]

The implication of these findings suggests another subhypothesis about the effect of threat: the more group members perceive threats to their physical safety, the more likely they will be to support violent action against the threatening group, as well as nationalistic leaders who advocate such action.

Strong fear, of course, can have the opposite effect, leading to feelings of intimidation and submissive behavior if people feel their position is weak.[79] One study found, for example, that feelings of anxiety or fear led people to want to avoid risks and therefore to lower support for George Bush's antiterrorism policies.[80] This implies yet another subhypothesis: the more group members perceive a physical threat to be overwhelming, the less likely they will be to support any effort to confront the source of that threat.

RELIGION

This account of how ethnic nationalism works, and of how social threat can power ethnic conflict, also explains why conflict involving religiously defined groups works in a similar way. First, religions, like nations, have a myth-symbol complex, defining a group history full of heroes, villains, and holy symbols. Second, religion also defines a central part of any believer's identity, and the three Abrahamic religions in particular lay down strict rules about who is included in the religious community and who is excluded (even if different sects within each religion differ fiercely over what those rules are). Third, religions are generally defined by a set of values and religious laws. When there is a symbolic threat to religious values or symbols—for example, the publication of cartoons mocking the Prophet Mohammed—all of the psychological processes that drive ethnic conflict can be engaged. The result is the typical group reaction to social threat: more loyalty to the in-group, less tolerance of criticism, and more inclination to defend the in-group.

To be clear, religious difference does not necessarily lead to group conflict, and evidence is mixed about whether religiously defined ethnic groups are any more or less likely to engage in violent conflict than other groups, such as ones distinguished by language. The point here is that religious identity *can* be harnessed politically, and if it is, the resulting politics and political psychology are similar to other ethnic disputes.

ETHNIC QUIESCENCE

The other end of the spectrum of ethnic relations is the symbolic politics of quiescence discussed by Murray Edelman.[81] When groups remain poorly organized, Edelman points out, it is easy to prevent them from mobilizing by offering symbolic concessions—which are, of course, extremely cheap— even if the grievances are economic.[82] In ethnic politics, because so many ethnic group concerns are wholly or primarily symbolic—especially concerning group status and respect—this insight is especially relevant.

The ethnic politics of New York City, described in the introduction, provides one example of this kind of low-key atmosphere of mutual respect and symbolic concessions. Another example is Edward Aspinall's account of ethnic politics in Indonesia in the early 2000s:

> It has become a new political norm in ethnically diverse provinces and districts for ethnically diverse tickets to run for [executive] positions. Thus, most

tickets for the governorship and deputy governorship in West Kalimantan consist of a Malay paired with a Dayak. . . .

In describing themselves, candidates for political office across the country routinely use phrases such as *"Sahabat semua suku"* [friend of all ethnic groups], . . . or *"Keberagaman itu indah"* [Diversity is beautiful]. . . .

Syamsul Arifin, the victor in North Sumatra, who is ethnically Malay, . . . wore an *ulos*, a Batak shawl [at rallies with Batak voters, and] was given the title of *Raja Batak* or Batak Chief.

As these examples illustrate, while ethnic politics is often contentious, it does not have to be. As Aspinall notes, "in most Indonesian elections, ethnic coalition building, not ethnic outbidding, is the norm."[83] These examples also support the suggestion that perceptions of threat are a necessary condition for ethnic conflict. In Indonesia, symbolic politics is used to prevent feelings of ethnic threat from arising, so ethnic politics is cooperative, not conflictual.

From Attitudes to Action

The discussion so far has been mostly about political attitudes, which we measure and analyze at the level of the individual. However, the only behavior these hypotheses can really explain is voting behavior and to some extent politicians' rhetoric. Explaining the move from attitudes to action requires a broader focus and a different theoretical basis. Prejudice and threat perceptions are important, but they do not necessarily tell us how the groups as a whole—or the organizations and leaders acting on their behalf—are likely to behave. To explain when attitudes turn into action, and what kind of action ensues, we must incorporate some insights from other theories of ethnic conflict. One starting point is that the reasons people actively join social movements or organizations are generally different from the reasons why they might sympathize with them.[84] This is the reason for the multistep process mentioned in the introduction. First we must explain when people are likely to perceive a threat, then how political support is built—individual-level processes—and then how that support is organized and mobilized into a political movement at the societal level.

ELITES AND FRAMING

One school of thought about ethnic conflict is the elitist theory, which blames ethnic problems largely on what Michael Brown calls "bad leaders."[85] A prominent example of this school is the work of V. P. Gagnon Jr., who points out that in the case of Yugoslavia's conflicts, most of the blame belongs to Serbian leader Slobodan Milošević.[86] Milošević, Gagnon notes, did not merely exaggerate the political threats to the Serbs from other ethnic groups; he also manufactured threats to those other groups by directly organizing violence. Prejudice, Gagnon argues, was not a critical factor: though Milošević did promote a threat frame, many Serbs did not respond. Many young Serbs, in particular, chose to go into exile instead of joining the Serbian army as conscripts, and many Serbs in Bosnia, far from being prejudiced against Muslims, were instead married to Muslims.

Gagnon has made two important points here. First, leaders do play an essential role: escalating or de-escalating ethnic conflict requires a strong leader on at least one side who is capable of changing the trajectory of group relations. Second, it is not necessary that all group members, or even a majority, respond to group appeals, as long as the ruling elite has enough mass support from a large enough group—either those who are prejudiced, if the policy is escalation, or those who are not, if the policy is de-escalation. In Yugoslavia, urbanites tended to show the tolerance discussed by Gagnon; however, rural residents tended to be prejudiced, forming the base of support for chauvinist leaders such as Milošević in Serbia and Franjo Tudjman in Croatia.

The main tool leaders use to alter the course of ethnic relations is framing. As William Gamson and Andre Modigliani define it, a frame "is a central organizing idea or story line that provides meaning to an unfolding strip of events. . . . The frames suggest what the controversy is about, the essence of the issue."[87] Frames are important because people's opinions on issues can vary depending on how an issue is framed. Collective action frames are a particular type of frame that does more than shift opinion. According to Robert Benford and David Snow, they accomplish three core tasks: they identify a problem, prescribe a response, and motivate action.[88] Framing thus provides a leader with a tool that simultaneously sets the agenda (through the choice of the issue to frame), builds support for the leader's program (by framing issues in a favorable way), and can galvanize and direct the followers into a social movement.

From the point of view of symbolic politics, the way a frame works is to use symbols to appeal to specific symbolic predispositions. The abortion issue provides a clear example. Abortion can be framed in terms of the "right to life" of the fetus, appealing to SYPs of sympathy for children and the principle of the value of human life. Alternatively, the issue can be framed in terms of the mother's right to choose, appealing to SYPs in favor of personal liberty and opposed to discrimination against women.

Scholars of framing have much to tell us about the details of how symbolic politics works, especially explaining how leaders lead and why followers follow. Briefly, leaders lead by framing, and followers follow if the frame resonates with them. According to Benford and Snow, the resonance of a frame depends on the credibility of the leader and of the frame; on the frame's "salience" (its relevance for the audience's concerns); and on its "narrative fidelity," or its consonance with culture, ideology, and myth—that is, with symbolic predispositions.[89] Furthermore, leaders of social movements need to find a plausible way to link different frames focused on different issues under the rubric of a single master frame. Master frames of "injustice" are particularly useful for social movements because they offer diagnosis, prescription, and motive for a response.[90] Political opponents, however, will propose "counterframes" that attempt to infuse events with a competing meaning. The resonance of the competing frames will increase or decrease as events bolster or undercut their salience, credibility, and resonance with widespread SYPs.[91]

These insights add important details to our understanding of symbolic politics. Again, the notion that leaders use framing is another way of saying that leaders appeal to and manipulate symbols; and of course "narrative fidelity" refers to a frame's appeal to the audience's symbolic predispositions. The credibility and salience of the frame, at least in ethnic politics, boil down essentially to threat: group members are unlikely to respond to an ethnic frame for an issue unless a credible case can be made that there is some threat to the group, either a social or a physical threat. So far, framing simply *is* symbolic politics, adding specificity to the previous hypothesis about the effects of threat, suggesting the hypothesis, stronger threat perceptions lead to more resonance for more assertive frames. More specifically, perceived threats to physical safety make threat frames resonate; perceived social threats make injustice frames resonate; and absence of threat makes benefits frames resonate.

The final requirement for a frame's resonance—the credibility of the leader—adds a valuable element to symbolist theory. A self-indulgent leader, for example, is unlikely to be credible in a call for self-sacrifice, and a moderate leader is unlikely to try to mobilize his or her group. Thus if an ethnic cause lacks a leader who is sufficiently skillful, credible, and assertive, the group is unlikely to be able to mobilize.

The point about injustice frames offers another important insight. William Gamson finds that in the relatively peaceful social movements that he studies, a master frame making a claim about injustice is almost always at the heart.[92] In ethnic politics, these injustice frames refer to some kind of social threat: the injustice is to deprive "us" of economic benefits that we deserve, or to denigrate our values or threaten our group status. Put together with the central insight of terror management theory—that physical threat leads to physical aggressiveness—this point yields another hypothesis: use of assertive frames by credible leaders increases the likelihood of ethnic mobilization. We can make this hypothesis more specific by adding two subhypotheses: first, the more leaders use social threat frames when such frames resonate, the greater the likelihood and probable scale of nonviolent mobilization; second, the more they use physical threat frames when such frames resonate, the greater the likelihood and probable scale of ethnic violence.

MOBILIZATION PROCESSES

Mobilization theory offers yet another critical piece of our puzzle. The preceding hypothesis is that credible leaders using resonant frames can directly generate some degree of mobilization; however, *sustained* violence or even peaceful mobilization requires organization. Studies show that what makes most people join any social movement is not the strength of their commitment to the cause, but direct contact with movement organizers.[93] Therefore, we have to look at the role of organizations.

There are two possible sources of the organization for each party to ethnic conflict: the government and a social movement organization outside government. In my past work, I unfortunately termed the first possibility *elite-led violence*, which was misleading since the second possibility also involves elites of some sort.[94] For clarity, then, I suggest labeling the first pattern *government-led mobilization* and the second *mass-led mobilization*. The government-led process usually mobilizes a dominant ethnic group, but in some cases the government of a region declares separatist aspirations against the national government, as occurred in the former Yugoslav republics and in Nigeria's Biafran war of the 1960s.

Whether mobilization is mass led or government led, the second tool leaders have, in addition to framing, is networking.[95] The difference is roughly parallel to what U.S. political operatives call the "air war" and the "ground war" in election campaigns. The air war is the arena of framing where rival politicians appeal to symbolic predispositions that favor their side. Framing issues in terms of symbols of group identity—or, even better, in terms of threats to those group symbols—is one powerful way of pursuing the air war and is one reason why identity politics has become so pervasive in U.S. political campaigns.[96] The ground war, in contrast, is the arena of networking, where political organizations—themselves essentially networks of political associates—send out volunteers to knock on doors, but even more to recruit their friends and relatives to join in the campaign. To simplify a bit, the "air war" is mostly about building political support or sympathy for the cause; the "ground war" is mostly about mobilizing people, appealing to them one by one to join the organization.

Since prejudices are among the most powerful symbolic predispositions, "air wars" often focus on appealing to them. Slobodan Milošević, for example, was famous for his government-led air war, the onslaught of television propaganda that justified violence by Serbs against Croats and Muslims in defense of the Serbian identity. The symbols he evoked included the iconic Battle of Kosovo Field and Prince Lazar, the hero of that battle. Ethnic rebels rarely have the resources to get on television, but all rebel organizations have propaganda efforts, and most successful ones have at least a radio station whose job includes creating and invoking emotive symbols that frame the rebel effort in terms that resonate with potential followers. Similarly, both governments and rebels have political ground war campaigns, in which they send out agents to use their networks of social ties to solicit support for their side in the conflict. As in political campaigns, organizations mobilizing for ethnic war also use tangible incentives to recruit, paying some agents to join or to become full-time participants.

Symbolic politics can also involve changing symbolic predispositions, not just appealing to them. As mentioned earlier in this chapter, SYPs can change through either of two mechanisms: repetition (socialization) or shock. The easiest sort of change to foster is to add a new element to an existing narrative. For example, if people are already prejudiced against members of another group, it is easy to add new stereotypes to the existing list. This process explains, for example, the extraordinary malleability of anti-Semitism over the centuries. Jews, already disliked, could sequentially be charged with poisoning wells to cause the Black Plague; with ritual murder in the wake of unexplained disappearances; with Bolshevism in Nazi Germany; and with anti-Bolshevism in the Soviet Union. Similarly, in the aftermath of the 9/11 attacks in the United States, the already-loathed Saddam Hussein was a plausible target for U.S. outrage despite his lack of any connection to those events.

The process is particularly important, as the Nazi example implies, for explaining the symbolic politics of genocide, which always includes devaluing the target group—a process that works best in the context of existing prejudice.[97] The list of ways of devaluing hated groups is long: not only dehumanization ("dogs" or "snakes") but also outcasting, trait characterization ("aggressors"), political labels ("Zionists," "Communists"), group comparison ("Vandals," "Huns") and demonization ("embodiment of evil").[98] If such a discourse is repeated over years as the first hypothesis suggests, prejudices change—in this case, hardening to the point that they are "eliminationist," so that the most extreme measures, such as ethnic cleansing or genocide, come to seem justifiable.[99]

These "air war" dynamics determine political support at the level of attitudes, but they do not determine recruitment into an organization or an armed group. As noted earlier, that requires organizations to engage in a mobilizational "ground war." Obviously, in government-led cases the institutions of the state can make this happen, but even then effective mobilization cannot be taken for granted. Attitudinal mobilization is still necessary, especially in cases of genocide. In peacetime, most armies would respond to orders to commit genocide with incredulity or revulsion. Studies of genocide show that such orders are carried out only in cases of both very high perceived threat and intense prejudice.[100]

Personal contact is important in recruiting activists for a number of reasons. First, personal appeals can get the attention of people who might ignore general "air war" appeals. A second reason is "affect transfer": if the recruiter is a friend or relative, she can try to exploit the tendency for friends to transfer liking for each other into affection for each other's causes.[101] Another reason is the compliance effect: people often have an impulse to comply with requests, especially ones made in person. A related reason comes from what psychologists call the Hawthorne Effect—in this case, personally asking someone to join a group makes the recruit feel important, in a way that a general "air war" appeal does not.[102] Finally, there are also "solidary benefits": recruits can enjoy the association of the group if they join, but if they exclude themselves, then they are distancing themselves from the group. The emotional benefits of belonging are powerful, so they constitute an important SYP that a political ground war exploits.

The main difference between U.S. election campaigns and ethnic warfare, of course, is that coercion is also used on both sides in ethnic warfare, so that the ground war eventually becomes a literal and not just a metaphorical war. The government can amass resources by using its taxing power, it can recruit soldiers by conscripting them, and it can extract information from enemy sympathizers by threatening or torturing them. Rebel groups can take parallel actions, taxing supporters, seizing goods from opponents, recruiting coercively, and generally gaining supporters through violence. But again, for both sides, it is cheaper and ultimately more reliable to persuade rather than coerce supporters to join, so the psychological mechanisms of persuasion and recruitment remain at the heart of the matter of mobilization.

Since rebels typically lack the organizational muscle of the state, people usually have to choose to join the movement, making the ground war a more challenging task. Traditional authority structures can be pivotal where they remain intact. For example, one study of 1960s villages in Indonesia found that the most influential men in each village determined village loyalty, following their personal ties either to rebel leaders or to government officials.[103] Key to these mobilization efforts is "brokerage," the process by which "brokers" bring together previously separate social networks.[104] Religious leaders may mobilize their followers, educators may recruit their students, clan leaders may recruit their kin, and industrial managers or labor leaders may mobilize workers. Organized crime networks may also be recruited.[105]

One important lesson here is that even if prejudice and stereotypes are important in creating attitudes that support ethnic confrontation, ordinary members of armed groups will not necessarily be the more prejudiced individuals, though local leaders often are. In other words, patterns of individual or small-group recruitment may not be closely connected to the causes of the conflict, beyond the fact that in an ethnic conflict, at least one side is ethnically defined. While some fighters will take up arms for reasons of ethnic identity, most will do so on the basis of more immediate social attachments. All that matters to make ethnic war happen is that when ethnic elites wish to mobilize their followers, they have not only attitudinal support and tangible resources but also a source of recruits whom they can mobilize.

These considerations lead to one final hypothesis: Since recruitment of movement activists or fighters is based on organization more than attitudes or leadership, the stronger the organizational network supporting an assertive leader, the greater the degree of social mobilization (violent or nonviolent) that leader can achieve.

OPPORTUNITY AND ETHNIC MOBILIZATION

As noted in the introduction, ethnic groups not only need the means and motive to mobilize politically; they also need the opportunity. As was also noted, some good studies have been done of what provides such an opportunity, especially in ethnic civil wars. First, territorial concentration is important, making it much easier to organize a rebellion by an ethnic group.[106] Second, poverty matters: civil wars are virtually unknown in rich countries since 1945, but the less economically developed a country is, the more likely it is to experience civil war, ethnic or otherwise.[107] Third, new, weak, or unstable states are more likely to suffer ethnic civil war than strong ones.[108] Fourth, exclusion of the ethnic group from the political system increases the likelihood of ethnic civil war by shutting off peaceful political alternatives.[109] Fifth, high levels of government repression reduce the likelihood of ethnic civil war, as potential rebels lack the political space to mobilize. Finally, foreign support for rebels—weapons, money, and so on—increases the chance of ethnic civil war.[110]

To simplify my list of variables, I have included these considerations in the context of how they influence organization and threat perceptions. Anything that makes group mobilization easier—territorial concentration, government weakness, foreign support—matters only if it produces better organization. Political exclusion is important because it increases the perceived social threat: such exclusion threatens the group's status and material interests; the result is a greater willingness to support action to achieve inclusion. Individuals' personal wealth, of course, would work in the opposite direction: the notion of joining a rebellion or other risky political behavior would be seen as an economic threat, which has also been shown to trigger shifts toward political conservatism. Strong government repression, finally, should make joining in any antigovernment effort scarier and therefore deter people from joining.

INTERACTIONS BETWEEN GROUPS

So far, my focus has all been on what happens within groups: their symbolic predispositions, threat perceptions, organization, and leadership. The central question we want to ask is what leads ethnic conflicts to escalate, and what leads them to de-escalate or remain calm. As explained earlier in this chapter, perceptions of social threat—threats to wealth, status, or values—

tend to arouse hostile feelings between groups and may cause conflict to escalate politically. According to terror management theory, physical threats
have an even more powerful effect in promoting ethnocentrism and intergroup hostility and are a core cause of ethnic war.

Such threat perceptions are especially likely to lead to violent conflict if
martial values are an important part of the group's myth-symbol complex.
While few studies focus on this point, anecdotal evidence suggests that many
of the groups engaged in violent identity conflict—most famously the Chechens in Russia and Pashtuns in Afghanistan and Pakistan, but also Serbs,
Philippine Muslim groups like the Tausug, and Herzegovinian Croats—are
self-consciously warrior peoples. This can be explained psychologically
because people's attitudes often vary with their perception of in-group stereotypes.[111] If in-group stereotypes foster a martial image, the result is
likely to be symbolic predispositions toward violence in response to threats
to the group. Any references to group identity are likely to make those
predispositions—and thus violent political alternatives—salient in the public's mind.

If perceptions of physical threat are what cause groups to mobilize for potential violence, then *mutual* threat is what causes them to escalate their efforts. This is the situation known in international relations theory as the security dilemma, and it has been widely applied to explain ethnic war as
well.[112] Once the two sides begin organizing for self-defense, and especially
once they begin arming, each "self-defense" move by one side constitutes a
real threat to the other; the result is a spiral of increasing threat perceptions,
increasing ethnic aggressiveness, and escalating violence. As I have argued
elsewhere, security dilemmas in ethnic conflicts tend to be driven by predatory motives: what really makes the moves of each side so threatening to the
other is that at least one of the sides defines its security needs to require dominance over the other group.[113] If the other group rejects subordination, then
the two sides' security needs are incompatible, and violence is more likely.
On the other hand, if both sides have moderate definitions of their security
needs, it is much easier to head off the security dilemma spiral before it results in war.

A Theoretical Restatement: Patterns of (Ethnic) Politics

The symbolic politics theory laid out here is a recasting of the original ideas
of symbolic politics laid out by David Sears, Murray Edelman, and other
scholars decades ago. This newer version of the theory is updated to account
for more recent findings in psychology and broadened to include the insights of mobilization theory and other strands of scholarship. It functions
to integrate these alternative perspectives into a single, coherent account, instead of pitting them against each other.

This account of ethnic politics starts with the group narratives that define the group and also characterize neighboring groups. The more these narratives are repeated over years and decades, the more strongly they convey stereotypes of the other groups that can harden into prejudice. This is the first step in the process. In the second step, the stronger the prejudice is at any given time, the greater the likelihood that the disliked group's behavior will be perceived as threatening. Greater threat perceptions and stronger prejudices encourage leaders to frame issues in terms of threat, resulting in the third step, public support for aggressive action against the perceived threat. Finally, if they have the support of public opinion and effective organizations, these aggressive leaders can take the fourth step, mobilizing their groups either for peaceful contention or for war.

The type and degree of mobilization depend largely on the nature and degree of perceived threats. Threats to physical security allow politicians to take an aggressive, chauvinist stance by deploying powerful threat frames; indeed, the stronger the threat perceptions, the more politicians who do so are rewarded with political support. If these leaders are backed by strong organizations, the result is a politics of protection that can lead to violent conflict. Social threats—threats to economic interests, group status, or values—lend themselves to leaders' assertive use of injustice frames; in these cases, an effective organization can produce a politics of redistribution involving the relatively nonviolent clash of protest movements. In the absence of any perceived threats, politics is focused mostly on tangible goods discussed in terms of "benefit" frames. There is less need for mass organization, and the successful politicians are accommodative, engaging in a low-conflict politics of distribution.[114] Finally, the presence of severe repression generates perceptions of overwhelming threat which intimidates the targeted population and persuades them to submit to state authority.

Table 1.1 illustrates this logic. In this table, variables in **bold italics** are strongly causal, those in *italics only* are intervening variables, and those in **bold** are outcomes. Each row summarizes the causes of a different pattern of politics. The first step in figure I.1 (see introduction), the influence of group narratives on prejudices, is omitted, since it is a longer-term process that occurs before everything else. The other three steps are summarized: first the effect of prejudice on threat perception; then the influence of threat on the degree of support for mobilization in public opinion (an intervening variable); then finally the influence of leadership, organization, and public support (public opinion) on the degree of mobilization that results.

Table 1.1 shows, in the first row, that the perception of an overwhelming threat from the state makes other variables irrelevant. Subordinate group leaders and public opinion alike are forced to be submissive, so their prejudices cannot be expressed. The only organizations such a regime would allow the subordinate group would be either apolitical or state controlled, so

Table 1.1 Patterns of politics

Level of Prejudice	Main Threat Perceived	Leadership	Public Opinion	Type of Organization	Pattern of Politics (Outcome)
Any	Overwhelming physical threat	Submissive	Submissive	Apolitical or state-run	**Submission (repressive peace)**
Any	Obvious physical threat	Chauvinist (threat frame)	Aggressive	Armed forces or militias	**Protection (violence or war)**
High	Ambiguous physical threat				
Moderate	Social threat	Assertive (injustice frame)	Competitive	Social movement	**Redistribution (contentious politics)**
Low	Minimal threat	Accommodative (benefits frame)	Materialist	Political parties	**Distribution (inclusive peace)**

the resulting pattern of politics would be one of submission, resulting in a repressive peace.

The row for a politics of protection is partially split in two because it can occur in two different ways. It begins with the other group's behavior: either an obvious physical threat to the group (such as an armed attack) or a more debatable and ambiguous threat viewed through the lens of a high level of prejudice, which predisposes people to perceive others as threats. In either context, chauvinist leaders can use threat frames to elicit the terror management effect, which in the next step drives public opinion toward support of aggressive action against the perceived enemy. If both sides turn to forming armed forces or militias, such a politics of protection leads to a security dilemma and ethnic war in the final step.

The third row begins with a moderate level of prejudice, which typically leads in the first stage of the process to perceptions of social threat, as in the kinds of U.S. racism that perceive threats to white economic interests and social values in social welfare programs from which African Americans benefit. In the context of a perceived social threat, ethnically assertive leaders are likely to emerge, framing the socially threatening policy or trend as unjust. Such framing further raises the salience of ethnic identity, eliciting (as prejudice theory tells us) a popular tendency to think in terms of ethnic competition, turning politics into a zero-sum competition for positional values such as status. This tendency in public opinion yields support for mobilizing in defense of the group; if the assertive ethnic leaders then succeed in building social movement organizations, a contentious politics of redistribution is the result.

The bottom row depicts the conditions that lead to a routine politics of distribution. Typically emerging in a situation in which prejudice is low, this pattern begins with a perception of minimal group threats. In these conditions, political leaders have little incentive to engage in ethnic competition. Rather, because public opinion focuses on material needs rather than identity concerns, even politicians representing subordinate ethnic groups have an incentive to be accommodative toward leaders of other groups, seeking through cooperation to secure economic goods that they can distribute to their constituents. If their bid in this direction succeeds, the result is the relatively noncontentious politics of distribution: pork-barrel spending, logrolling, and in general the routine distribution of government largesse.[115]

The theory overall suggests a hierarchy in the power of alternative frames. Because frames suggesting physical threat call on such a powerful mixture of psychological mechanisms, especially the "terror management" effect, they are the most powerful frames, and are likely to dominate other frames if they are credible. Injustice frames do not evoke the "terror management" effect, but they do evoke a number of other psychological effects (such as prejudice effects) that make them very effective at promoting social mobilization. Only when threat and injustice frames do not resonate can leaders successfully resort to a "benefits" frame by credibly promising tangible gains to their constituents.

As mentioned in the introduction, reality does not always line up neatly with the scenarios depicted in the rows of this table. Each row depicts a situation in which all factors point toward the same resulting pattern of politics, but it often happens that different factors point in different directions. One example is the politics of a peace process after an ethnic civil war. A peace process typically involves, on the one hand, perceptions of physical threat ("they killed our people!") and high levels of prejudice; on the other hand, if the peace process makes any progress, it must feature an accommodative leadership wielding a political party, not an army.

According to the theory as summarized in table 1.1, such a situation is unstable. On the one hand, the physical threat and high prejudice create an atmosphere in which public opinion is primed to be aggressive. In these conditions, a moderate leader is likely to face a powerful hard-line opposition movement promoting a threat frame and opposing steps toward peace; a likely outcome is the replacement of the moderate by the hard-liner, and a stalemate or collapse in the peace process. However, there is also the possibility that a moderate leader with a strong political organization and a base of strong, favorable symbolic predispositions among the public—that is, with charisma—may successfully strike a peace deal and begin to implement it. If the deal holds, threat perceptions will decline and prejudice will become less salient as peace continues. Thus the unstable pattern of the peace process will stabilize in either a return to a hostile politics of protection or a transition to a peaceful politics of distribution.

Ontology, Methodology, and Case Selection

CONSTRUCTIVISM OR POLITICAL PSYCHOLOGY?

Academic readers are likely to notice that the symbolic politics theory outlined in this book is largely consistent with a rich tradition of international relations constructivism that focuses on the importance of cultural narratives, values, and leaders' rhetoric in explaining political outcomes.[116] I have claimed that the constructivist understanding of ethnicity is the consensus view. This means that ethnic (or racial, or national) identities are social facts created by people, primarily through telling and retelling the stories and narratives that define the group, praising group heroes, blaming group enemies, and so on. Prejudice, I argue, is a product (over the long term) of the stereotypes and attitudes that are communicated in such narratives. Furthermore, I suggest that the way leaders lead is primarily through framing their arguments to resonate with just such narratives, and the more effective a politician is at "selling" such framings, the more successful he or she will be.

Another constructivist idea that fits to some degree with symbolist logic is the idea of co-constitution. From the perspective of constructivism, for example, hostile group narratives do not simply cause prejudice; rather, hostile narratives and prejudice constitute each other, evolving together as narratives shape prejudices and prejudices shape narratives. Similarly, most of the other factors in symbolic politics theory have the same dynamic of mutual influence. Thus while prejudice may encourage the perception of threats, an enduring threat is likely to create or harden prejudice. Also, while leaders are influenced by existing group narratives and symbolic predispositions, drawing on them as they frame their policies, their frames may over time work to alter those narratives. Finally, leadership and organization also influence each other: leaders' framing of issues influences the development of the organizations they lead, while the needs of the organization influence leaders' framing. If we add these mutual influences (and some others I lack the space to detail) to the relatively simple figure I.1, the result is the more complicated, but also more complete, picture illustrated in figure 1.1.

On the other hand, I have also consistently claimed that the theory is social-psychological in character, deriving my hypotheses whenever possible from theories of individual and social psychology that have been well attested in laboratory studies. Thus two of my central assertions are that physical threats to the group evoke the terror management effect, leading to popular support for aggressive action against rival groups; and that social threats combined with prejudice lead (according to prejudice theory) to support for discriminatory action, and often thence to social movements framing either the discriminatory action or its failure as unjust. In arguing

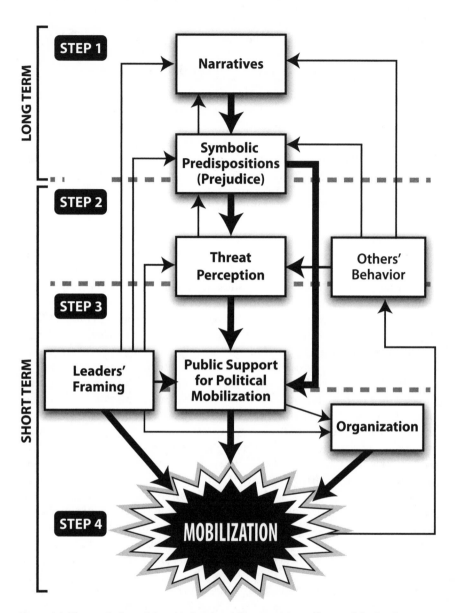

Figure 1.1. The symbolic politics of (ethnic) mobilization: Main effects and feedback processes.

this, I differ with those constructivists who argue that rhetoric's power comes from its grammatical structure; instead, I assert, rhetoric's power comes from its *emotional* appeal, which derives from its resonance with symbolic predispositions.[117] Still, constructivists should have little problem with the logical chain I posit, which they would interpret as noting primarily that threat is socially constructed and that contemporary rhetoric is more effective to the extent it fits with familiar narrative tropes.

Yet other readers might see this argument as sociological, largely compatible with mobilization theory. Along with mobilization theory, I assert the critical importance of leaders' framing of issues and the indispensable role of social organizations in moving from rhetoric to political action. I even affirm the importance of opportunity structure, reframed in terms of its effect on organization and threat perception. But to sociologists, as to constructivists, I still assert that while prejudice is the result of discourse over the long term, rock-ribbed racism—or tolerance—in the present is an independent factor that often remains untouched by rhetoric; leaders must sometimes choose between riding the chauvinist tiger and being consumed by it.

This last point is the reason why I make a causal argument in this book instead of a constructivist argument about co-constitution. If we give too much emphasis to the co-constitution of narratives and prejudice in the long run, we lose sight of the very powerful constraints that prejudice (and other symbolic predispositions) create in the short run. At any given time, prejudiced people are more likely than unprejudiced ones to see a disliked out-group's behavior as threatening, and to agree with leaders' efforts to frame out-group behavior as a threat. A crisis or an election campaign does not typically afford enough time for leaders to try to use discourse to moderate followers' prejudices or group narratives; they must act within the context of narratives that are already familiar and prejudices that are long held and resistant to change. Therefore, it makes sense to me to think of most of the upward-flowing arrows in figure 1.1 as feedback effects instead of evidence of co-constitution. In the long run, prejudice and narratives can be changed by leaders' (and cultural elites') framing and by out-group behavior, but in the short-run processes that I focus on in this book, the influence runs the other way and feedback effects are typically weak.

My plea here is not for interdisciplinary tolerance, but for intellectual fusion. The psychologist in her lab documents many specific effects of prejudice and bias but has no overall theory of their social effects. Those who theorize about broad social patterns, however, often do so on the basis of flimsy assumptions about how rhetoric might influence the individual people of which any crowd is comprised. One scholar has asserted a "psycho-cultural" perspective but did not provide a rigorous framework for tying disparate theoretical ideas together.[118] The aim of this book is to begin the process of marrying the psychological microfoundations of how ideas and SYPs influence people with the sociological and political macroprocesses that lead to quiescence, contention, or war. The aim is to ensure that any theory based on assumptions about human psychology derive those assumptions wherever possible from psychological evidence about human behavior and similarly to base claims that any psychological process matters on studies that show how it works sociologically—that is, how what happens in individuals' heads translates into group action. In sum, when any field of study has compiled good evidence on an issue related to a theorist's work, that theorist is obligated to take it into account. I invite readers who are willing to accept this effort to label me as they will.

METHODOLOGY AND CASE SELECTION

Having outlined the symbolic politics theory of ethnic politics, the rest of the book will test its validity primarily using the process-tracing method for the six cases discussed in chapters 2 through 7.

To restate, the hypotheses being tested, in order of logical progression, are as follows:

1. The more hostile a group's narratives are toward another group, the more prejudiced members of the first group are likely to be.
2. The more prejudiced group members are, the more likely they are to perceive a threat from the disliked group.
3. The more prejudiced group members are, the more they will support hostile and discriminatory actions toward the disliked group.
4. Stronger threat perceptions lead to more support for hostile action and more resonance for more assertive frames. Specifically,
   a. The more group members perceive a physical threat to be overwhelming, the less likely they will be to support any effort to confront the source of that threat.
   b. The more group members perceive (nonoverwhelming) threats to their physical safety, the more likely they will be to support provocative and violent action against the threatening group, and the more threat frames should resonate.
   c. The more group members perceive social threats to group identity, status, or economic interest, the more likely they will be to support actions that disfavor the other group, and the more injustice frames should resonate.
   d. The less group members perceive any threat, the less salient group identity will be, and the more benefits frames should resonate.
5. Use of assertive frames by credible leaders increases the likelihood of ethnic mobilization. Specifically,
   a. The more they use social threat frames when such frames resonate, the greater the likelihood and probable scale of nonviolent mobilization.

    b. The more they use physical threat frames when such frames reso-
nate, the greater the likelihood and probable scale of ethnic violence.
  6. The stronger the organizational network supporting an assertive leader,
the greater the degree of social mobilization (violent or nonviolent) that
leader can achieve.

Finally, as noted earlier in this chapter, Hypothesis 3 is really just a specific
version of the basic principle of symbolic politics theory, that because people
make decisions based primarily on their symbolic predispositions, the way
leaders gain support is by using symbols to manipulate those SYPs. In those
cases in which frames appeal to symbolic predispositions other than prejudice, the appropriate hypothesis to test is this one, not the more specific
Hypothesis 3.

Strictly speaking, with six independent variables (narratives, prejudice,
threat perception, frames, leader credibility, and organization) and only six
case studies, what follows cannot be considered a full and rigorous test of
the symbolic politics theory outlined here. What is possible, however, is to
apply a qualitative research design using process-tracing methods to put the
hypotheses to the test in a less formal way, looking for evidence supporting
or infirming each of them. Furthermore, what the process-tracing evidence
allows me to do is not only to show that A and B covary in the way expected
but also to show that the influence follows the expected process or mecha-
nism. For example, when Tutsis began slaughtering Hutus in Burundi in
1993, increasing threat perceptions in Rwanda, previously moderate Rwandan Hutu politicians formed "Hutu Power" factions that began articulating
the chauvinist threat frames promoted by the extremists (and future *genocidaires*). This sequence of events provides strong evidence that the rising
threat perceptions did make threat frames more resonant—more people
started repeating them.

Additionally, more hypotheses or "testable implications" from the theory
give us more ways to test the theory.[119] Each time a hypothesis "works" in a
case, we have one more bit of evidence in the theory's favor; each time one
fails, we have a bit of evidence against the theory. The mode of inference
we are using here is not typical statistical logic, but Bayesian logic, which is
more appropriate in a situation with small numbers of rich nuggets of
information.

The way I put the hypotheses to the test in the case chapters is as follows.
After opening with historical background, most chapters begin by examining the group narratives that define the identity of each group and that
articulate the group's relationship with other groups. Theoretically (Hypothesis 1), these narratives should be found to have influenced the symbolic predispositions of group members toward other groups; each chapter therefore
has a section considering evidence about those SYPs. The next section typically examines evidence about group members' threat perceptions both

before and during key events under examination, allowing consideration of the effects of SYPs on threat perceptions (Hypothesis 2). In most cases, the method used will be qualitative discourse analysis, as evidence of symbolic predispositions and threat perceptions is typically anecdotal even in otherwise well-studied cases. We typically do not *know* how ordinary people felt or what they feared, but I scour what evidence can be found, including from interviews conducted either by me or by other researchers.

In principle, symbolic predispositions, threat perceptions, and political preferences are quantifiable and subject to statistical analysis: all that is required is to employ standard survey research techniques. Unfortunately, because so many scholars dismiss the notion that prejudice matters, it is rare that survey research about racial or ethnic attitudes is done in developing countries, and doubly rare that it is done before or during the sorts of dramatic events studied here. One major exception to this rule is South Africa, which was conducting regular survey research among all racial groups during the transition to majority rule. Uniquely in this case, therefore, I am able to run statistical tests of my hypotheses (nos. 2, 3, and 4), using responses to survey questions that serve as reasonable proxies for measures of symbolic predispositions and threat perceptions, as well as policy preferences and attitudes toward key leaders.

The true process tracing occurs in later sections of each case chapter as attention turns to leaders, their rhetoric and framing, and types of organization, allowing tests of Hypotheses 3, 4, 5, and 6.[120] The nature of the evidence used varies across cases. In the Philippines case, for example, I have interview data collected by myself and other scholars in which participants in the Moro National Liberation Front (MNLF) rebellion directly explain either how they recruited fighters or why they joined, in either case shedding light on the role played by framing and organization in the mobilization process (Hypotheses 5 and 6). In Tanzania, in contrast, the absence of mass social movements is obvious; much of the key evidence examined is the frames used by political candidates (Hypothesis 5) and evidence about how well different frames resonate.

A key methodological question for studies of this kind is whether the hypotheses are falsifiable. What would constitute evidence that these hypotheses are wrong? The following is a list of some examples:

1. If, in interviews, conflict participants admit to politically consequential prejudice that their group narratives do not promote, this would infirm the hypothesis that hostile narratives tend to underlie prejudice.
2. If conflict participants admit to prejudice but deny feeling threatened, this would infirm the hypothesis that prejudice increases threat perceptions.
3. If participants in a conflict support hostile action against the other group but deny prejudice, this would infirm the hypothesis that prejudice

tends to underlie ethnic violence. (If prejudice is normatively accepted, interviewees should feel no compunction about articulating it.) If they admit to prejudice but oppose hostile action, the hypothesis would be more strongly infirmed.

4. If participants in ethnic mobilization claim pure economic motivation, this would infirm the hypothesis that perceived status and identity threats are key motives for contention.

5. If fighters in a violent ethnic conflict claim pure economic motivation, this would significantly infirm the hypothesis that physical threat is what motivates ethnic war.

6. If mass mobilization occurs in the absence of leaders asserting threat frames, this infirms the hypothesis that mobilization tends to result from such framing.

7. If mass mobilization occurs in the absence of strong group organization, this infirms the hypothesis that organization tends to underlie such mobilization.

A final question concerns case selection: Why were these particular cases chosen for this study? Several criteria were used. First, since most theorists agree that politics in wealthy countries is fundamentally different from that in developing countries, the sample includes only developing countries, where most of the ethnic violence in the world takes place. Cases were selected from among developing countries according to the "most different systems" logic.[121] Cultural variation is achieved in part by diversity of regions, with cases from Southeast Asia, South Asia, and Southern, Central, and East Africa. Religious cleavages play an important role in some cases (Sudan, Philippines) but very little in others (Rwanda, South Africa). The three high-violence cases include one that was a democracy before the war (1960s Philippines), one that had a prewar system of authoritarian power sharing (1970s Sudan), and one with an authoritarian, ethnically exclusive prewar system (1980s Rwanda). A theory that stands up well in such different settings has a strong claim to credibility.

Next, since the theory posits conditions that lead variously to ethnic quiescence, contention, and violence, cases were selected across the spectrum of possible outcomes, to maximize variation on the dependent variable. There is also within-case variation, so cases of ethnic quiescence include not only the durably stable Tanzania but also the temporary peace of 1970s Sudan, and the peace in the Philippines that had lasted a half century before the outbreak of war in the 1970s. Violent cases were selected to include some of the most extreme cases of ethnic violence worldwide in recent decades. Finally, the Indian and South African cases were included because they are considered iconic, but both are widely misunderstood, so their ostensible lessons need to be reconsidered.

The Muslim Rebellion in the Philippines

In the early 1970s, ethnic politics in the Philippines changed from a politics of distribution to a politics of protection, as the Muslim minority in the southern part of the country launched a rebellion against the Christian-dominated central government led by President Ferdinand Marcos. The resulting civil war killed between 50,000 and 100,000 people and displaced over one million in the 1970s, during its most intense phases.[1] A separate rebellion by the Communist New People's Army escalated a few years after the Muslim one. Both conflicts would drag on for decades to come, though the 2014 signature of a "Comprehensive Agreement on the Bangsamoro" may prove to have marked the end of the Muslim rebellion.

Attempting to apply opportunity theory to explain these events gives us an illustration of the strengths and weaknesses of that theory. In overview, the case seems to fit the theory. Just as opportunity theory would expect, the Philippines was a poor country with a weak government, rough terrain in which rebels could hide, natural resources that rebels could exploit, and potential sources of external aid for both rebel groups. But on closer examination, the logic of the theory does not work. The main problem is that the government was so weak, and opportunity to rebel was so obvious—private armies controlled by politicians were common in many parts of the country—that opportunity theory cannot explain why rebellions were not even more frequent and widespread. Furthermore, the Muslim rebellion in particular did not fit the expected pattern. It did not break out in the inaccessible mountains of Mindanao, but in the highly populated lowlands, and the rebels did not try to exploit the region's natural resources to enrich themselves as the theory would postulate. The theory also cannot explain why Marcos's 1972 imposition of martial law—which narrowed rebel opportunity—caused the Muslim rebellion to escalate while political violence elsewhere in the country declined.

The case is, however, a textbook example of how symbolic politics theory can make ethnic wars of this kind comprehensible. Philippine politics until the late 1960s followed a pattern of distributive politics in which elites of all ethnic groups had access to state resources. Marcos, however, tried to shift to the politics of protection, proclaiming martial law and attempting to unify Filipinos against an alleged Communist threat. Filipino Christians generally went along with this shift, but Muslims felt Marcos's repressive measures to be so threatening that they answered with their own politics of protection against him.

In this chapter, I examine in detail the causes of the ethnic war in Mindanao, assessing how much support (or disconfirmation) each of the symbolist theory's hypotheses receives from the evidence. After a brief background section, the chapter examines the group narratives, symbolic predispositions, and threat perceptions among both Muslims and Christians that set the stage for violent conflict. The first three symbolist hypotheses are assessed in this section. There were long-standing narratives justifying hostility, with both Muslims and Christians portraying Philippine history as an enduring struggle between them. These narratives in turn generated vicious prejudices, with many Christians carrying stereotypes of Muslims as violent and fanatical, and Muslims expressing symbolic predispositions in favor of violent resistance to an oppressive Christian government. In the context of such SYPs, efforts by Marcos's local clients to use political violence to expand their power caused the people of Mindanao to perceive severe threats that Filipinos elsewhere did not. Put differently, Marcos's policies reawakened Christian-Muslim hatreds and fears that had lain dormant for decades. Thus prejudices led both religious communities to perceive the other as increasingly threatening, and increasingly to support violent action against the other group.

After examining these hostile narratives, prejudices, and threat perceptions, the chapter turns to tracing how ethnic mobilization and war occurred. First, as threat perceptions increased, so did the resonance of aggressive frames. Thus among Christians, violence blamed on Muslims led to election victories for politicians with tough, anti-Muslim images who used the police and private armies to repress Muslims violently, resulting in repeated massacres. This pattern illustrates Hypotheses 4 and 5: greater perceived threats made more aggressive frames resonate, and the success of these aggressive frames empowered the hard-line leaders to use their private armies violently. Among Muslims, a late-1960s call to countermobilize failed, as it came from a leader who lacked credibility. However, as Christian violence continued, calls for Muslim self-defense resonated more strongly with increasingly threatened Muslim communities, as we would expect from Hypothesis 4. The result (Hypothesis 5 again) was growth in Muslim militia groups promising to defend their communities.

In this atmosphere, Marcos's imposition of martial law in 1972 paradoxically caused the Mindanao conflict to escalate, even as it successfully repressed violence elsewhere in the country. Dissident Muslim leaders had already managed by 1971 to form the Moro National Liberation Front

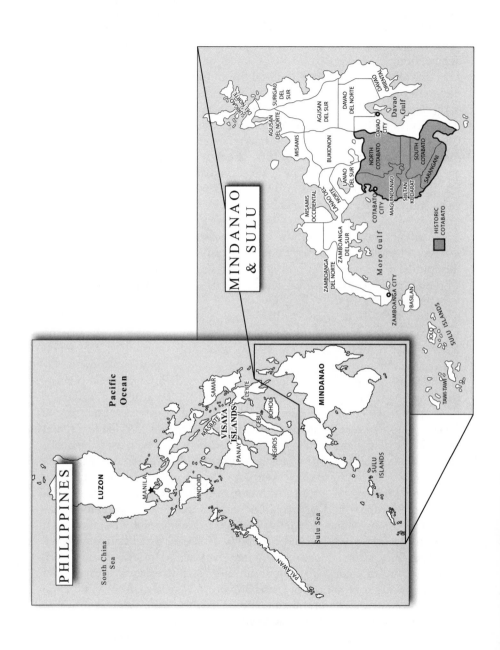

(MNLF), tying together traditional elites, rising new ones, and their follow-ers into what became the main rebel organization and forging ties with for-eign sponsors providing arms and training. As we would expect from Hy-pothesis 6, this stronger organization enabled Muslim mobilization on a much larger scale. Marcos's announcement of martial law increased Mus-lim threat perceptions enough to generate a massive increase in popular Muslim support for the rebels, powering the explosion into full-scale war. The conflict would continue for another four decades in large part because Christian prejudices continued to bias Philippine government policy through-out that period.

As explained in the conclusion to this chapter, the Mindanao conflict was a tragedy unintended by the politicians who caused it. But the atmosphere of hostile group narratives and vicious prejudices led local Christian elites, and later Marcos, to see brutal repression as wise, and it encouraged Chris-tian communities to support it. Those same prejudices blinded Christian leaders and followers alike to the fact that, far from making them more secure, these hostile moves were acting like lighted matches in a powder keg, touching off a decades-long rebellion by an already-hostile Muslim population.

Background of the Mindanao Conflict

GEOGRAPHY AND ETHNIC GROUPS

The sprawling Philippine archipelago consists of over seven thousand is-lands. Luzon, the biggest and most populous island, is in the north; a group of smaller islands, the Visayas, is in the center; and in the south are the second-biggest island, Mindanao, and the smaller Sulu island chain to its southwest. Linguistically, there is no majority: in 2000, the largest ethno-linguistic group, the Tagalogs of Luzon, constituted only 28.1 percent of the population.

About 90 percent of Filipinos are Christian; most of the rest are Muslims and animists, who have historically been disadvantaged in government pol-icy. For example, over 80 percent of Muslims in the early 1980s were, by one estimate, landless tenants. Muslim-majority provinces consistently rank among the poorest in the Philippines, and infrastructure and educational opportunities even within those provinces go disproportionately to serve Christian areas. Much of this is a legacy of a previous lack of education and other opportunities: in 1957, for example, there were reportedly 1,546 Chris-tian educators in the Muslim heartland province of Cotabato but only thirty-seven Muslim ones; there were 144 Christian business proprietors and only six Muslim ones; and so on.[2]

Muslims, constituting about 5 percent of the Philippine population, and animists (known as Lumads) are clustered primarily in central Mindanao and the Sulu Islands. The Muslim population is further divided among thirteen ethnolinguistic groups, but four of those groups—the Maguindanao, Maranao-Ilanun, Tausug, and Samal—account for over 90 percent of the Muslim population.[3] Of these, the Maguindanao and Maranao are concentrated in central Mindanao—the Maranao in the former province of Lanao, and the Maguindanao in the former province of Cotabato (Lanao was later divided into two, and Cotabato eventually into five smaller provinces). The Tausug and Samal live primarily in the Sulu Islands.

HISTORICAL BACKGROUND

Most political organization in the precolonial Philippines was restricted to village communities under the leadership of a local big man, or *datu*. There was some indirect political influence from India via Indonesia, with some political leaders taking the title of rajah. This influence took on an Islamic character in the sixteenth century, leading to the emergence of sultans of Sulu and of Maguindanao, and of a Muslim rajah of Manila.

Ferdinand Magellan pioneered Spanish expansion in the Philippines, arriving in 1521, but he was soon killed in a clash on the island of Mactan. In 1565, however, a new Spanish expedition under Miguel López de Legazpi established a base in the Visayas and then conquered Manila in 1571, establishing a Spanish colony in the islands, which were named the Philippines after the Spanish king Philip II. Early Spanish efforts against Mindanao and Sulu were less successful, however, and Spain abandoned all of its posts there before the end of the century.[4]

These events set the pattern for the following centuries. In Luzon and the Visayas, Spanish control was weakly contested and most of the populations were quickly Christianized. The Muslim sultans of the south, however, resisted successfully for centuries, often collaborating with each other and aided by foreign powers.[5] The tide finally began turning in the mid-eighteenth century, when the Spanish managed to divide, weaken, and later conquer the Maguindanao sultanate. In the late nineteenth century, it was the turn of the Sulu sultan to be reduced in stages to a Spanish vassal. Finally, at the end of the century, a Spanish expedition defeated the leading Maranao sultans.

The Muslims were never quite subdued, however. The Maranao, located in Mindanao's inaccessible interior, never ceased guerrilla warfare against the Spanish. The Tausug of Sulu, more exposed on their smaller islands, turned to a more desperate measure. The Tausug *ulema* (Muslim clergy) declared a holy war after the Sulu sultan's surrender in 1878, sanctifying attacks by suicidal warriors whom Spaniards called *juramentados*—fighters who dedicated themselves to kill as many Spaniards as possible before being killed themselves.

After the Spanish-American War of 1898, the Philippines passed to U.S. rule. The United States ruthlessly quashed both a Filipino nationalist revolution on Luzon and all Muslim resistance in Mindanao and the Sulu Islands.[6] The subsequent U.S. policy of economic development and of the cultivation of local datus in governing the south successfully stabilized the region, but at the cost of entrenching the authority of the datus.[7] At the same time, a centerpiece of economic policy was the encouragement of large-scale migration of Christian settlers from Luzon and the Visayas to relatively underpopulated Mindanao. As a result, between 1903 and 1939, the Muslim portion of the population of Mindanao declined from 76 percent to 34 percent.[8] Protesting this peaceful invasion of what they considered their territory, Muslim leaders repeatedly asked that Mindanao and Sulu be made separate from the Philippines before it was granted independence, but to no avail.

The Christian immigration into Mindanao spawned conflict in part because it resulted in a massive transfer of land from Muslim to Christian control, resulting in the displacement of many Muslim peasants.[9] As Peter Gowing reports, "in some cases powerful business interests or wealthy Christians, taking advantage of Muslim ignorance of, or indifference to, Philippine land laws, cheated them out of large tracts of their best lands, in collusion with corrupt Government officials."[10] In other cases Muslim farmers were displaced as a result of the sale of lands by their own datu landlords.

After the Philippines gained its independence, Christian migration to the Muslim heartland of Cotabato and Lanao continued. As a result, land disputes also grew, as did disputes over political power between Muslim datus and Christian settler leaders.[11] By 1980, Muslims had been reduced to only 23 percent of the population of Mindanao, including 26 percent in what had been Cotabato province (the Maguindanao heartland) and 54 percent in the two Lanaos (the Maranao heartland).[12]

MARCOS'S POWER GRAB

State structures in the Philippines were weak, based more on the personal support networks of local elites than on neutral, formal institutions.[13] In this context, many local and regional leaders throughout the Philippines were able to maintain their own private armies, including one built by Marcos opponent Benigno Aquino Jr. in the 1950s, and militias maintained by large sugar growers in the Visayan Islands.[14] After his election as president in 1965, Marcos attempted to change this situation by consolidating his own power. He therefore made a concerted effort to sideline any local elites who did not support him, expanding the use of private armies to aid his clients' election campaigns, and even deploying police forces for that purpose. As a result, the 1967 congressional election campaign was "the bloodiest election in

Philippine history," involving over one hundred killings, most attributed to police or government paramilitaries.[15]

The 1969 campaign, when Marcos was running for reelection, was worse, with private armies reportedly operating in nineteen of the sixty-six provinces in the Philippines, from the motorcycle-riding "Suzuki Boys" on Batanes in the far north to the "Barracudas" guarding pro-Marcos candidates in Lanao del Norte on Mindanao. More than two hundred people were killed in the resulting election violence, as opponents hired their own goons to counter those of Marcos's clients.[16] After the balloting, Marcos falsified the vote count, claiming an absurd 74 percent of the popular vote for himself and 78 percent of seats in the House of Representatives for his supporters.[17] Public outrage led to protests against the bogus results and ended in rioting that rocked Manila, adding further to the increase in political violence in the country.[18] This atmosphere of political violence would significantly influence the threat perceptions that motivated Mindanao's ethnic war in the following years, with the Barracudas playing a key role in escalating the conflict.

Hostile Narratives, Symbolic Predispositions, and Threat Perceptions

This historical background produced narratives among Christian Filipinos that were strongly hostile to Muslims, which in turn generated strong symbolic predispositions to dislike and fear Muslims, just as Hypotheses 1 and 2 would lead us to expect. Muslims, for their part, also had anti-Christian group narratives, as well as narratives glorifying violent resistance to the Philippine government; the result was a strong symbolic predisposition to distrust and fear the Philippine government, and ultimately to support rebellion against it (Hypotheses 1 through 3). Each of these tendencies is detailed in the following sections.

CHRISTIAN FILIPINO NARRATIVES

While Christian Filipinos often identify more with their ethnolinguistic group (as Tagalogs, Ilonggos, Ilocanos, Cebuanos, etc.) than they do with the Filipino nation, most are also proud of their Philippine identity. One of the factors that bind them together is a shared historical and religious identification with the Spanish colonizers of the Philippines: to a large extent their history is the history of the Spanish colony of the Philippines. For example, a standard 1951 history text asserts that the Spanish defended their sovereignty in the colony "backed by the loyalty of the Filipinos."[19] Furthermore, this Filipino Christian identity essentially excludes the Muslims of the south. The period of Spanish colonial rule in the Philippines from the sixteenth through the nineteenth centuries was, in this view, "three centuries of Moro-Spanish warfare." The Spanish goal in these wars was to Christianize the Muslims of the Philippines, aiming to stamp out their "accursed doctrine." Muslims were not part of the nation; they were the national enemy.

According to Peter Gowing, writing in 1969, just before the renewal of war, "The major legacy of three centuries of Moro-Spanish warfare was the 'Moro image'—the picture of the Moro as a cunning, cruel, treacherous savage, a pirate, a raider, a slaver. That image, to this day, is operative in the minds of many, if not most, Christian Filipinos, whose ancestors after all bore the brunt of the Moro jihad."[20] Relatedly, tales of nineteenth-century *juramentados* created "in the minds of many Christian Filipinos the worst imaginable form of the 'Moro image' as a wild fanatical *juramentado* who delights in chopping heads off of Christians and looting Christian homes."[21] This hostile mythology survived among Christian Filipinos in part "through the cultural institutions of the 'moro-moro,' a form of folk theater in which Christian heroes battled Moro villains, who were depicted as cruel and barbarous pirates."[22] Survey research in the 1960s also showed that "in Luzon and the Visayas, the word 'moro' (with all its derogatory implications) is a mother's household weapon of social control for misbehaving children."[23]

For educated Christians, these images were sometimes reinforced in school. In the 1951 history text cited earlier, for example, the bulk of discussion of Muslims in the Philippines comes in a description of the Moro wars, which emphasizes Spanish victories in those conflicts and also mentions "Moro raids" on Christian areas. Remarkably, in the list of "things to identify" at the end of the relevant chapter, the only Muslim listed is an eighteenth-century sultan of Sulu who—in an extremely rare case— converted to Christianity along with his family.[24] Not noted is the fact that this sultan converted under duress, while a captive in Manila, and went back to practicing Islam after his eventual release.[25] The improbable policy prescription implied by this story is the oft-expressed belief that peace is possible only if the Moros convert to Christianity (the resolution also promoted in the standard moro-moro tale).[26]

MUSLIM NARRATIVES

A 1954 Philippine government report on the "Muslim problem," though in many ways a reflection of Christian myths, also accurately characterized a central element of the identity of Muslims in the Philippines: "As an individual the Muslim refuses to concede that he is a part of the entire Filipino citizenry."[27] This view of a separate identity stems in part from Muslim myths of origin: the Tausug, for example, believe that their ancestors, migrants from the south, were unrelated to the people who populated the rest of the Philippines.[28] Partly as a result, one 1967 report by a sociologist in a rural Muslim region reported, "Identification with the Philippine nation is practically nil" among Muslims.[29]

Muslims' primary identification tends to be with their ethnolinguistic group—Maranao, Maguindanao, Tausug, and others[30]—but their origin myths share an emphasis on their conversion to Islam as foundational moments. Thus the founders of the Tausug are taken to be the fifteenth-century Rajah Baguinda, who came to Sulu from Sumatra, and Sultan Sharif ul-Hashim, who introduced Islam, married Baguinda's daughter, and established the Sulu sultanate.[31] Similarly the Maranao have a folk epic, the Radia Indarapatra, about the emperor who led the settlement of their homeland around Lake Lanao and established the Maranao line of royal descent.[32] These epics are important in part because they establish both Islam and the hereditary elite of sultans and datus as essential aspects of the groups' identities. According to one expert, Maranaos "consider the normative social condition to be one of being ruled," so they as a matter of course follow the leadership of datus.[33]

Another story explicitly identifies all of the Muslims of the region as an imagined family, linking the founders of three major sultanates in the area: "A . . . tradition still heard in Sulu is that three brother *sharifs* founded the sultanates of and introduced Islam to Brunei, Sulu and Maguindanao."[34] This story illustrates the fact that "Muslim" is itself an important identity category.[35] This common identity was strengthened after World War II, when Muslim education and practice surged: hundreds of new mosques and madrassas were built; Philippine Muslims went abroad to study Islam; and foreign Muslim teachers came to Mindanao and Sulu. "The total effect of this resurgence of Islam," missionary Peter Gowing reports, was "to make the Moros ever more self-consciously Muslim."[36]

Muslim traditions in the Philippines justify not just hostility to Christians but also violence more generally. All of the main Muslim groups share a notion of honor—called *maratabat* by the Maranao—which, if besmirched, is expected to be defended violently. The result is a family or clan feud, which can be settled by the payment of blood money but may drag on indefinitely. As a result, according to anthropologist Ruth Moore, "war is the eventual expectation of every Tausug male."[37] One feud between leading Tausug families in 1990 escalated to the point that the two sides exchanged mortar fire in Jolo, the capital city of Sulu, killing seven and injuring more than forty people.[38]

The value of bravery and war in these cultures is reinforced by many myths, stories, and cultural practices among Tausug and Maranao. As one Tausug informant described it, Tausug children learned epics of fighting the Spanish, Americans, and Filipinos through oral history and even lullabies.[39] One such tale tells the story of a girl who is abused by a Spanish officer. Seeking revenge, she, her fiancé, and her mother sneak into Jolo and kill the officer, along with nearly forty other Spanish soldiers, before being themselves killed. The three, in short, become *juramentados*, nineteenth-century suicide guerrilla fighters.[40] Maranao epics such as the "Darangen," tales of the legendary Prince Bantugen—a great warrior with godlike powers—similarly glorify war. The Maranao origin myth, the Radia Indarapatra, also concerns a warrior-king, the emperor Indarapatra.[41]

Beyond prescribing behavior for Muslims, these myths also attribute specific qualities to Christians. Gowing reports, "There is also a . . . negative 'Christian image' in the minds of the Moros: the Christian is a coward, a cheat, a bully, a land-grabber who, if he could, would destroy Islam."[42] Of course, the perception that Christian authorities in the Philippines wished to destroy Islam is true: that was long the explicit goal of the Spaniards and the implicit goal of the U.S. and independent Filipino authorities.

CHRISTIAN SYMBOLIC PREDISPOSITIONS TOWARD MUSLIMS

According to Hypothesis 1, the Christians' narratives about Muslims should have generated anti-Muslim prejudice, and this is exactly what happened. Anthropologist Thomas McKenna offers an illustration: "Voiced attitudes of local Christians [in Cotabato City] toward indigenous Muslims tend to oscillate between paternalism and apprehension, either expressing condescending tolerance for a benighted folk or betraying anxiety about 'uncivilized' (and thus unpredictable) neighbors."[43]

Survey research confirms how widespread those attitudes were among Christian Filipinos. For example, a survey of Christians in the early 1970s found among respondents a strong attitude of rejection of Muslims, regardless of the respondent's level of education or the region where they lived. The authors' assessment was that Christian narratives about Muslims (as summarized earlier in this chapter) had translated directly into stereotypes and prejudice:

> Christian prejudice toward Muslims in the Philippines is not a new phenomenon. It is one of the legacies of more than three hundred years of Muslim-Christian hostility perpetuated under the Spanish colonial rule and a half century of American public policy wavering between separatism and integration. The Muslim-Christian hostility is perpetuated to this day by an ignorant and biased media aided by some members of the educated elite. There is ample evidence that Christians today continue to measure out of their fertile imagination an image of the Filipino Muslims as "brutal," "treacherous," "bandits" and "pirates."[44]

A nationwide survey a few years later demonstrated the problem in more detail. When asked to describe Muslims, most of those who responded made unfavorable comments in accordance with Muslims' image in the narratives, typically describing Muslims as "fierce," "treacherous," or "killers." Notably, those offering such answers were especially likely to be members of Visayan groups such as Ilonggos and Cebuanos—groups, that is, that were historically the targets of Muslim raids, and more recently the providers of the lion's share of Christian settlers in Mindanao. One of the few favorable comments, offered by 20 percent of respondents, was that Muslims are "brave," which of course also reinforces the violent image. More broadly, the study concluded "the Muslim image is exclusively negative for all nine traits [measured, with Muslims seen] . . . as unreliable, hostile and proud people, and [who] lead all other ethnic groups in being [seen as] extravagant, non-progressive, lazy, hostile, unreliable, poor, proud, conservative and stingy."

In sum, according to this survey, "To non-Muslims, the Muslim-Filipino is a fierce and troublesome character who cannot be trusted."[45] This survey was conducted after the outbreak of war in Mindanao, so these feelings of hostility are probably stronger and more widespread than they would have been beforehand. However, the fact that these attitudes accord so perfectly with the Moro stereotype of Christian Filipino myth suggests that they existed before and were only strengthened by the new outbreak of fighting.

Such attitudes infused Philippine government policy long before that fighting. A 1955 special committee on "the Moro Problem" argued, for example, "In their ignorance and in their trend toward religious fanaticism, the Muslims are sadly wanting in the advantage of normal health and social factors and functions."[46] The committee claimed that this "ignorance" was the reason for poverty in Muslim areas.

MUSLIM SYMBOLIC PREDISPOSITIONS TOWARD CHRISTIANS

It is surprisingly difficult to find evidence of Muslim prejudice against Christians in the Philippines; instead, hostile Muslim narratives seem to have created symbolic predispositions to distrust and oppose the Muslim government. For example, anthropologist Ruth Laura Perry Moore records meeting "young [Tausug] males for whom being Muslim is synonymous with being in militant opposition to the Philippine government."[47] As Hypothesis 2 would project, this hostile SYP increased Muslims' tendency to perceive the government as an enemy. Thus as T. J. S. George explains, violence by Christian militias known as Ilaga provided "the confirmation of Muslim suspicions that the government was hostile to them."[48]

At the same time, Muslim narratives had also cultivated a general symbolic predisposition favoring the use of violence. The Tausug, according to Moore, exhibited "a dominant cultural idiom of violence" in which "all forms of interaction are between potential aggressors."[49] Writing on the basis of fieldwork done in the mid-1960s, anthropologist Thomas Kiefer agreed: "To be Tausug is to be capable of fighting," he noted, and "physical force is encountered at every turn."[50] Along with these attitudes toward violence was a strong gun culture among many Muslim groups.[51] As one of Moore's informants told her, "A [Tausug] man would rather sleep with his gun than with his wife." Such a willingness to resort to violence is also common among Maguindanaoans: one Muslim administrator told me that he could not consider laying off excess (Maguindanao) workers because he would expect to be killed if he did so.[52]

CHRISTIAN THREAT PERCEPTIONS

Given the Christian stereotype of the Muslim as unusually violent and at worst a savage, cruel pirate, the logic of Hypothesis 2 suggests that Christian Filipinos should be especially prone to perceive Muslims as a threat— an effect presumably stronger in those whose mothers used the myth as a "household weapon of social control." The tough image projected by traditionally reared Muslims, illustrated by what Moore labeled "the Moro mask," should have contributed to such feelings of threat. Additionally, some Christian settlers on Mindanao were victimized by Muslims engaged in extortion or terrorism in response to the loss of their land, which should have further increased fears.[53]

The evidence supports this hypothesis. Ruth Moore reports that in the mid-1970s—at the height of the war—the "genuine physical fear" among Christians was strong and visceral. She quotes one woman as saying, "Muslims believe that they will go to heaven only if they have killed a Christian. . . . You cannot trust any of them, even the children. They are all fanatics." Moore reports, however, that this symbolic predisposition toward fear of Muslims predated the fighting: in 1968, she asserts, the "Christian reaction to the MIM announcement [of the formation of the prewar Muslim Independence Movement] was hostile panic."[54] The fear remains pervasive today, with ordinary Filipino Christians frequently expressing fear at the notion of anyone visiting Mindanao.

The idea of mobilizing armed groups in response to this perceived threat was plausible because, just as we would expect from Hypothesis 4a, local Christians would not be confronted by overwhelming power from the state if they did so, since private armies were common in the Philippines. If a politician's opponent was backed by Marcos, that politician and his supporters did face a significant threat—not from the state, but from extralegal political violence. This perceived threat further motivated some Christian elites in Mindanao to sponsor their own private armies; the perceived threat from state institutions was too small to deter them.

MUSLIM THREAT PERCEPTIONS

Feelings of threat among Muslims were long-standing. These were usually feelings of social threat—threat to economic values and group identity—but they sometimes including feelings of physical threat. Thus Gowing, writing before the outbreak of violence in the 1970s, noted, "In the confrontation of Islam and Christianity in the Philippines, the Moros . . . have been, and still are, threatened with psychological death"—that is, the death of their identity.[55] The overt Spanish goal of Christianizing them set the tone for this perception, which was reinforced by later U.S. and Philippine government policies premised on the need to change the "backwardness" of Muslim culture to advance development in the region. These policies, varying from land laws, marriage laws, educational initiatives, and so on, were seen cumulatively as an assault on the Moros' entire way of life, not to mention their livelihoods. The perception was reinforced by frequently expressed Philippine government views that Moros' "religious fanaticism" was to blame for their poverty and by the frequently stated Christian Filipino insistence that they follow the "wrong religion" and should convert.[56] The influx of Christian settlers into Muslim areas further reinforced these fears.[57]

Muslims were left with few alternatives for maintaining their culture. In the late 1960s, Gowing reported, "Most [Muslims] simply maintain themselves in relative isolation from the mainstream of Philippine society" as a way of resisting these pressures at assimilation and "cultural death."[58] Furthermore, explicit (if unofficial) efforts to suppress Islam had not ended. The creed of the early 1970s Ilaga (Christian militia in Mindanao) proclaimed, "If the Muslims in the Philippines are poor and backward, it is because of their wrong religion and ideology, Islam . . . [which] has brought poverty, ignorance and darkness."[59]

Christian settlement of traditionally Muslim areas added another dimension to this fear: feelings of economic and social threat. In the common Muslim narrative illustrating this threat perception, Christian settlers were "land grabbers," leading to the bitter joke that "Ilaga" was really an acronym for "Ilonggo Land Grabbers' Association."[60] Bishop Hilario Gomez reports, "Psychologically, to the aggressive Maranaos, Christian settlers are a real threat to their existence in Lanao del Norte. . . . The Maranaos felt they would become second-class citizens in their own homeland."[61] This threat was exacerbated, of course, by the threat to the power of the traditional Maranao leadership in the politics of Lanao del Norte, as the province became increasingly Christian in political leadership as well as demography.

This threat perception led directly to Muslim support for hostile action against the Christian settlers, as Hypothesis 4 would lead us to expect. In particular, Gomez reports that some Christians expelled by Barracudas (Muslim militiamen) in Lanao del Norte in 1971 were told that it was "time for the Christians to go back to the Visayas and Luzon—swim . . . if necessary." Underlying this behavior, Gomez suggests, was a "desire to assert political dominance in the province," based on the belief that the Maranao are the "owners" and "masters" of Lanao even if they had become the minority in the province.[62] In other words, the Barracudas' motivation was a combination of economic and status threats.

Widespread Muslim mobilization for violence did not occur, however, until these perceptions of social threats were supplemented with physical threats. Talk of a campaign of genocide against Muslims in the early 1970s was so widespread that an international delegation of eight Muslim ambassadors was prompted to visit Mindanao to investigate the charge (which it concluded was unfounded).[63] The significance of this talk, as Gomez recognizes, was that Muslims "were expressing only their strongest fear in Mindanao, namely, the fear of a genocide that they believed the Philippine Government and the Christian Filipinos have lately been doing." Many individuals who were involved in the Muslim movement confirm in interviews that such fears were important in motivating them. For example, a former Muslim guerrilla commander told me, "In our mind their intention [was] to wipe out all Muslims in Mindanao."[64] Finally, as was true for Christian politicians, Muslim politicians also saw little risk in raising private armies; doing so was tolerated at the time.

Symbolic Mobilization in the Mindanao Conflict

The background conditions for ethnic war in Mindanao were of long standing. Hostile narratives and prejudice had existed for centuries, with both Christians and Muslims feeling social threats from the other side. Yet Christian-Muslim relations in Mindanao in the 1960s were mostly peaceful, as they had been for more than half a century. Politics remained distributive in nature: democratic on the surface, thoroughly corrupt and dominated by rich elites in fact, but relatively peaceful and ethnically inclusive. What were required to turn this uneasy peace into war were three factors: adding perceived physical threats to the social threats, the emergence of credible leaders using aggressive ethnic frames, and the growth of mobilizing organizations. It was Ferdinand Marcos who inadvertently set the stage for these to emerge.

THE JABIDAH MASSACRE AND MOBILIZATION FAILURE

In March 1968, twenty-eight Muslim recruits to the Philippine armed forces were secretly executed without investigation or trial.[65] Though the full truth of this incident, known as the "Jabidah Massacre," was never made clear, the basic fact of the deaths quickly emerged. The Jabidah Massacre had a galvanizing effect on Muslim opinion; in Manila, it sparked student demonstrations that continued for a year.[66] One of the student-demonstrators, Nur Misuari—a member of the first generation of Philippine Muslims to gain broad access to secular higher education—was already a founder of a Muslim Nationalist League, and later claimed that the Jabidah Massacre inspired him to become a leader of the Moro separatist rebellion.

In Mindanao, one leader tried to mobilize a movement in response to this incident: Datu Udtog Matalam, the erstwhile moderate governor of Cotabatao province who had lost his post to his own former (Muslim) ally the year before. Disgruntled at his political isolation and anguished over the death of his son at the hands of a policeman, Matalam seized the moment and established the Muslim (later Mindanao) Independence Movement (MIM) just two months after the massacre.[67] He used an "injustice" frame to articulate the reasons for his action, asserting broad government mistreatment of Muslims. Thus the MIM's constitution states, "The policy of isolation and dispersal of the Muslim communities by the government . . . has been detrimental to the Muslims and Islam," adding, "It is the duty and obligation of every Muslim to wage Jihad physically and spiritually." It asserts an Islamic rather than an ethnic or nationalist identity for the victim group: the MIM constitution states, "Islam being a communal religion and ideology, and at the same time a way of life, must have a definite territory of its own for the exercise of its tenets and teachings, and for the observances of its Sharia."[68] Consequently, as the MIM's program, Matalam demanded the creation of a separate Islamic state of Mindanao and Sulu.

This framing of a response to the Jabidah Massacre did not resonate with the public, apparently dismissed as a stunt by a disgruntled politician.[69] One problem was that while most of the Jabidah victims were Tausug from Sulu, Matalam was a Maguindanaoan based in Cotabato. Thus Matalam's own supporters did not feel as strongly about the incident, while he lacked both credibility and an organizational base among the Tausug who were more concerned.[70] Furthermore, Matalam's actions were restrained: though he seems to have controlled a private army of "Blackshirts," who later joined the MNLF-led rebellion, he did not attempt to use it to engage in rebellion in the late 1960s; MIM did little more than issuing manifestoes.[71] Still, for at least one young man who later became an MNLF leader, the formation of MIM was an "eye-opener" pointing out the possibility of national liberation for Philippine Muslims.[72]

The failure of MIM illustrates an important point: despite volatile popular emotions caused by mutual prejudice and suspicion, Mindanao was not a bomb set to explode at the first spark into full-blown ethnic warfare. Supporting one aspect of Hypothesis 5, a key reason was the absence of credible chauvinist leaders.

LEADERSHIP, ORGANIZATION, AND THREAT PERCEPTION IN THE ILAGA-BLACKSHIRT WAR IN COTABATO

While MIM did not initiate violence, its creation set off a wave of panic in Christian communities in Cotabato province: within a month, reports began circulating that Christians were fleeing Muslim areas. The result was mobilization for violence in a way that precisely follows the pattern Hypotheses

4 through 6 would lead us to expect. The rising threat perceptions led to increased support for violent action (Hypothesis 4b), so other Christians in Cotabato began forming self-defense groups that came to be known as "Ilaga" (the Ilonngo word for "rats"). They were aided, according to one source, by some church groups and business interests.[73] The organization of armed groups accelerated when rumors spread about young Muslims receiving military training in the Middle East and nearby Muslim countries.[74] Into this volatile environment stepped a group of unscrupulous politicians, mostly Christian at first, who began using threat frames to mobilize support in their election campaigns (Hypothesis 5). Harnessing the Ilaga groups in their efforts (Hypothesis 6), these politicians ended up starting what became known as the "Ilaga-Blackshirt War."[75]

An incident in Upi, Cotabato, in March 1970 is usually considered the first violent clash in the conflict. The Upi clash pitted an armed gang of Tirurays (a Lumad group) led by a Christian Ilonggo, Feliciano Luces, nicknamed "Commander Toothpick," against a gang of local Muslim outlaws. Six were killed in the clash. Later that year, a group of Christian mayors and mayoral candidates called the "Magic Seven" was said to have employed Luces's and other Ilaga (Christian militia) gangs to terrorize supporters of their Muslim opponents.[76]

The case provides a good example of how the framing, and therefore perceptions, of the Mindanao conflict evolved from a frame of social or political violence to one of ethnic violence. Early newspaper reports framed Luces as a sort of Robin Hood figure defending the poor against exploitative elites (who happened to be Muslim). Later reports framed his actions as political, associating him with former Constabulary captain Manuel Tronco, a (Christian, pro-Marcos) candidate for Upi mayor who was running against the incumbent representative of the local (Muslim) datu clan, the Sinsuats. Later still, Luces's violent and brutal exploits, presumed to have been in the employ of Tronco or other Christian politicians, the rumored "Magic Seven," earned him "quasi-legendary status as a ferocious and fanatical anti-Muslim."[77] The violence was now framed as Christian versus Muslim.

Local Christian politicians generally focused on the criminal backgrounds of the violent groups, framing the conflict as a simple matter of law and order. The most important of them was Carlos Cajelo, Cotobato Province's constabulary commander, who in 1971 was running for governor of the province. His "law and order" framing of the conflict resonated with Christian constituents in part because they were concerned with personal security. At the same time, though, the "law and order" appeal was also a coded identity appeal: as Ruth Moore reports, "Christians tend[ed] to associate all criminal activity with Muslims."[78] The continuing violence helped Cajelo, who cruised to victory against the previously popular incumbent, Simeon Datumanong. The violence in Cotabato then stopped for a time.

While direct proof is lacking, this pattern of events led to widespread suspicion that Cajelo was among the sponsors of groups like Luces's, aiming to provoke Muslim violence which Cajelo could promise to oppose.[79] Datumanong, Cajelo's rival for the governorship of Cotabato, was similarly likely responsible for much of the violence on the Muslim side. On the Christian side, it seems that President Marcos himself acted as a broker, forging ties to regional political elites like Cajelo who in turn took control of local Philippine Constabulary units as well as private armies to pursue their political goals. Marcos even hosted Feliciano "Toothpick" Luces at the presidential palace in a gesture suggesting approval of his actions.[80] Luces's folk hero status was later given an additional boost with the production of a Filipino-language film, entitled *Commander Toothpick*, that memorialized his exploits.

The violence of this campaign, however, went far beyond what was politically helpful for its original backers, and it eventually escaped their control. On the Muslim side, the conflict came to be explicitly framed as a religious war and even a war of survival between the Christian Ilaga gangs, often backed by the Constabulary, and Muslim Blackshirts. The violence continued to escalate until the middle of 1971 before tapering off. Ilaga groups terrorized Muslims in the Cotabato Valley in this period: one Muslim activist compiled a list of a dozen Ilaga "massacres" in Cotabato between September 1970 and August 1971, three of them with death tolls of sixty or more.[81] In their most shocking attack, an Ilaga group massacred sixty-five Muslim men, women, and children at a mosque in the village of Manili in June of 1971.

Muslims could hardly have framed such an attack as anything but a religious assault on Muslims. In this context, any Muslim would be credible in using a frame of physical threat to the Muslim community. The violence was widespread enough to be salient for virtually all Muslims in Mindanao, and of course the religious war frame resonated with Muslims' narratives of Christian hostility and with their symbolic predispositions to expect it. Traditional Muslim leaders therefore responded with the traditional prescriptive element of the religious war frame: they "began their call for a quasi-*jihad* against the Ilagas who, by this time, were perceived as a threat to the Moros' survival."[82] By the end of 1971, the government estimated that 1,566 people had been killed, 56 percent of them Muslims; the number of displaced persons in Mindanao was estimated at more than one hundred thousand.[83]

Even in this context, however, the Muslim side was careful in defining the enemy. In keeping with preconceptions that it was the government that was the enemy, Blackshirt leaders were trained to stick with this view. The Blackshirt stance was that they had no quarrel with the Christian community, but only with the soldiers and Ilaga militias who were attacking their people.[84]

Even so, the scale of violence had by now exceeded what was in the interests of its sponsors. Regarding the Manili mosque massacre, T. J. S. George writes, "The outstanding feature of the Manili Massacre was its meaninglessness. There was no big political, [economic,] or religious issue at stake. . . . Revenge was the only explanation people could think of—revenge against the purported killing of Christians in some earlier incidents in the vicinity."[85] While Christian politicians like Cajelo benefited from the atmosphere of violence, such large-scale killing of Muslims risked (and ultimately sparked) outright communal war, upending the very law and order Cajelo was promising to bring.

LEADERSHIP, ORGANIZATION, THREAT PERCEPTION, AND THE ILAGA-MARANAO CONFLICT IN LANAO

Simultaneous with the Ilaga-Blackshirt War in Cotabato was a separate fight in Lanao del Norte Province, where violent escalation followed a pattern similar to that in Cotabato, except that Muslim rather than Christian militias seem to have driven it. The political context was the collapse of an alliance between (Maranao Muslim) Congressman Ali Dimaporo and (Christian) Governor Arsenio Quibransa. Dimaporo, a Marcos ally, maintained a private army of Barracudas and at first controlled the local Constabulary force through a relative, who was its chief. In the 1971 gubernatorial elections, Dimaporo backed a Muslim ally, Vice-Governor Mamalig Umpa, against Quibransa. Political violence escalated rapidly, peaking in late October—ten days before the election—when a Barracuda unit wiped out a Constabulary force of seventeen men, prompting a Constabulary counterattack that left an estimated sixty-six Muslims dead around the town of Magsaysay.

As in Cotabato, such violence in a context of hostile narratives and prejudice led to rising perceptions of *ethnic* threat (Hypothesis 2) and increasing resonance of hostile ethnic frames (Hypothesis 4), turning what had been political violence into ethnic violence. The powerful organizations of these two well-established politicians enabled them to escalate the violence quickly (Hypothesis 6), even as its relevance to immediate electoral motivations declined. Thus Christians in the region talked about an "Operation Bawi" in the summer of 1971, a Maranao drive to expel Christians from farmland in the province—that is, an ethnic cleansing campaign—which may not have been initiated by Dimaporo's Barracudas but does seem a likely response to the stereotype of Christians as land-grabbing threats to the Muslim community. This was the context in which Maranao attackers were said to have told their victims it was "time for the Christians to go back to the Visayas and Luzon—swim . . . if necessary." The Philippine army later intervened, permitting the Christian settlers to return, but one result was that ordinary Christians countermobilized in self-defense.

Even after the gubernatorial election, political violence continued in Lanao del Norte, where a special election for a senate seat was held a month later. The violence climaxed on November 22, voting day, when thirty-nine

Muslim would-be voters were massacred in the town of Tacub while on their way back from a nearby polling place.[86] This massacre, like the one in Manili, had no definable political motive. The election was between two Christian candidates: Alejandro Almendras, the strong man of nearby Davao, and Manuel Elizalde, a champion of the animist Lumads with a personal connection to Marcos. Muslim support was split, with some clans backing Almendras and others Elizalde. Furthermore, the victims were killed on their way *from* the polls—most of them having been prevented from casting their ballots—and after voting was completed, thus after it was too late to intimidate voters of any description.[87] The only plausible motive, again, was revenge, presumably further retaliation for the earlier Barracuda attack in Magsaysay. But this time, the perpetrators were not just gang members; they were aided by soldiers in uniform. The lesson for Muslims was chilling: the Philippine army was not merely hostile to them, but capable of being actively murderous. When Muslims made efforts to protect themselves in response, of course, those actions looked like threats to the government.

Considered this way, Cotabato and Lanao had been plunged into a security dilemma, raising threat perceptions on both sides even further. Muslims distrusted both Christian civilians and the government, since both the Ilagas and government security forces had been involved in massacres. In a "Consensus of Unity" document issued in 1971, Muslim leaders made these suspicions explicit, and, asserting "threats to the existence of the Islamic community in the Philippines," they threatened violent reaction if the government did not protect them.[88] They also took concrete action, secretly arranging for three hundred Muslim men to receive military training abroad. Christians, already fearful of Muslim gangs and of the violent "Moro image" of Muslims, could only have been further threatened by this Muslim stance. Recruiters for armed groups on both sides were already using the recruiting pitch: the other side is organizing, so we must do so as well.[89] The mistrust on each side thus enhanced the possibility of potential conflict and escalated levels of destruction.

The role of Christian feelings of threat is clearest in the way it fed escalation of the violence once it had begun. For Christian victims of Muslim attacks in Lanao, for example, flight left them threatened with starvation. This situation shifted their perceptions of risk, yielding new slogans: "Our cowardice is all spent, it is bravery that is left" and "It is better to die full, than to perish with an empty stomach."[90] Mobilizing for violence now seemed less dangerous than failing to do so.

THE EMERGENCE OF AGGRESSIVE MUSLIM LEADERS AND ORGANIZATIONS

The lasting significance of MIM was less in its own activities than in the network of Muslim leaders it fostered. The critical broker was Datu Udtog

Matalam, whose longtime associate was Congressman Rashid Lucman, a Maranao datu from Lanao del Sur. Lucman seems to have become radical-ized in part because he lost his seat in Congress in 1969 to a Marcos ally from the Dimaporo clan, his longtime rivals.[91] MIM brought together under its umbrella traditional leaders like these, along with younger, more educated leaders such as Nur Misuari (a leftist Tausug from Sulu) and Hashim Sala-mat (an Islamist Maguindanaoan from Cotabato).[92] An offshoot or parallel organization was known as Ansar al-Islam, which proved to be more active. Family ties played an important role: Matalam and Salamat, for example, were related by marriage.[93]

Pivotally, Lucman also had a connection to Tun Datu Mustapha Harun, the Muslim governor of nearby Sabah, Malaysia—who happened to be an ethnic Tausug and with whom Lucman arranged for the first foreign mili-tary support for the Muslim cause. Under the umbrella of Ansar al-Islam, a first group of three and a second group of ninety Muslim men were sent to Sabah for military training, starting in 1968 and late 1969, respectively.[94] In 1970, Lucman set up a separate, more radical (though also short-lived) orga-nization, the Bangsa Moro Liberation Organization (BMLO) as an umbrella group to coordinate Muslim political action.[95]

By 1971–1972, however, Misuari and Salamat had split away from Lucman, becoming the leading figures in what became the MNLF, which Misuari founded at a special assembly in Zamboanga City in mid-1971.[96] Educated young leaders like Misuari, in turn, were able to link up with radical stu-dent groups across Mindanao to broaden the movement's leadership, and they established a network of local and provincial organizing committees.[97] As Hypothesis 6 suggests, the creation of this organization was a vital step in escalating Mindanao's conflict into full-scale war. Having established the connection to Tun Mustapha and through him to foreign supporters and sup-pliers like Muammar Gaddafi, the MNLF was for the next decade able to monopolize foreign military aid, and therefore to emerge as the leader of the Muslim military effort. This foreign aid was another critical enabling factor in the escalation of ethnic violence.

The government of Malaysia had its own motive in allowing this action: the Philippine government was pursuing a territorial claim in Sabah based on the sultan of Sulu's traditional overlordship in that area; the Malaysian government naturally wished Marcos to desist.[98] Gaddafi, for his part, rarely needed extra motivation to support foreign radical movements of all kinds, but there is no reason to doubt his claim that in this case he was impelled to act at least in part as a response to the appalling Manili Massacre.

In mobilizing Muslims in what became the MNLF, existing elites in the different ethnic groups played different roles. Among the Maranao, the initial mobilization was top-down, as the prominent and powerful Rashid Lucman played a central role in organizing militant opposition to the Ilaga. Among the Maguindanaoans, in contrast, the datu class seems to have played primarily a permissive role. At the top, Datu Udtog Matalam established the initial umbrella of leadership, but it was soon seized by educated nonaristocrats like Hashim Salamat. Many of them, including Salamat himself, were the beneficiaries not of a secular education, but of an Islamic one from al-Azhar University in Cairo or other foreign institutions. At the local level, one local commander reported that while Cotabato datus were the "entry point" for Blackshirt and later MNLF fighters into local Maguindanao communities, the datus provided their blessing but not their leadership in the effort.[99]

Recruitment seems to have spread through family networks: as one informant put it, when one family member joined the movement, the family did.[100] This included women, who were mobilized and trained as paramedics, fund-raisers, intelligence personnel, and even in some cases combat soldiers. In some cases, recruitment of women was carried out coercively by family members. To raise funds, MNLF fund-raisers tapped into the Muslim tradition of obligatory charity, or *zakat*, as donations to the MNLF were considered *zakat*.[101] In some cases, family networks extended to mobilizing clans or villages to form MNLF units.[102]

Among the Tausug, the key role seems to have been played by nontraditional elites like Nur Misuari himself, a poor Tausug who had managed to receive an advanced education.[103] One of my informants described a relative who worked as an MNLF recruiter among Tausug: the recruiter had to work behind the backs of local datus who did not support his efforts.[104] Again, as Samuel Tan's data show, some of them joined largely because relatives were members.[105] But the mobilizing effort extended far beyond families; according to one source, even before 1972 the MNLF had provincial and local organizing committees in Sulu.[106]

In late 1971 and early 1972, violence in Lanao and Cotabato died down, but tensions did not. In May 1972, Iligan City, the mostly Christian capital of Lanao del Norte, imposed an economic boycott on Marawi City, the mostly Muslim capital of Lanao del Sur, until marines dispatched by the Philippine Constabulary reimposed order. Such economically self-destructive behavior makes sense only as identity conflict mobilized symbolically. In July, violence flared up on the Zamboanga Peninsula in western Mindanao, with one clash resulting in the death of the Christian mayor of the Zamboanga town of Dimataling.[107]

GOVERNMENT LEADERSHIP, FRAMING, AND ORGANIZATION FROM 1972

The Mindanao violence of the early 1970s might well have died down had Marcos not provoked further escalation by declaring martial law on September 21, 1972. Marcos's motive was maintaining power: proclaiming martial law gave him an excuse to cancel the upcoming elections, in which he was not eligible to run. Marcos was, in short, engaged in diversionary conflict. The frame he used to justify his action was the threat of Communism: in the text of his official proclamation of martial law in September 1972, over 80 percent of paragraphs focused on the Communist insurgency.[108] The violence in Mindanao was an afterthought, mentioned in fewer than 5 percent of paragraphs in the text. Marcos chose the anti-Communist frame in the hopes that it would act to unify his population across ethnic lines; it also appealed to his foreign sponsor, U.S. president Richard Nixon. Furthermore, it had some credibility: there was a large and growing Communist insurgency which he had been blaming for violent attacks all over the Philippines.

Marcos quickly followed up the martial law decree with a program of confiscating privately held firearms. In many respects, these measures worked. In the six months after martial law was proclaimed, homicides declined 49 percent nationwide. Almost half a million firearms were confiscated from civilians before the end of 1972, further pacifying most of the country.[109] Marcos himself benefited enormously: thousands of people were arrested and imprisoned (including many of his opponents), the mass media were silenced, and the Philippine Congress was abolished. With backing from the United States and from conservative domestic elites, Marcos managed to remain in power and rule as dictator for an additional fourteen years.

All of this suggests, however, that Marcos was *not* looking for a fight with the Muslims in Mindanao. He did *not* frame these measures primarily in anti-Muslim terms. Thus the idea of a diversionary conflict fits the later rise of the insurgency of the Communist New People's Army (NPA), but it does not explain why the anti-Communist Muslims also rebelled. Ironically, Marcos's actions backfired against both enemies, as both the Communist insurgency and the Muslim one escalated dramatically in the following years.

Marcos's problem in Mindanao was that the anti-Communist frame did not resonate. Christians in Mindanao were more concerned about a perceived Muslim threat. For Muslims, on the other hand, the imposition of martial law itself represented an urgent threat to their existence as a group, worse than any threats experienced in the previous decades. They especially objected to the compulsory disarmament of private citizens, which ordinary Muslims perceived to be a direct threat to their communities. In interviews my respondents repeatedly pointed to this disarmament order, and efforts to enforce it, as a key motive for their resistance to the regime.[110] Songs sung by Muslim rebel fighters also reflected this insecurity frame.

Marcos later added an additional frame, calling for the building of a "new society," asserting goals of fighting corruption and launching a "crusade" for unity, "social conscience," and economic equity.[111] In Mindanao, Marcos promoted this framing by offering economic development programs and political autonomy for Muslims, and offering generous bribes to MNLF commanders to switch sides and support the regime. This policy helps to explain how he was later able to lure Muslim leaders to defect from the rebel coalition and accept his promises of economic development programs (as well as personal benefits) in exchange for their loyalty.

The government's organizational efforts or "ground war" requires little analysis; it was simply the product of the government bureaucracy. The Philippines had a conscript army, so government forces were recruited by legal compulsion. Regular forces were supplemented by local militia groups organized by the military into "Barangay Self-Defense" units (BSDU). According to the general who commanded the government forces, the BSDU at first consisted largely of retired World War II veterans armed with 1940s-era weapons.[112] Still, the lesson is that even a relatively weak state commands organizational resources more than adequate to mobilize troops for ethnic civil war.

MUSLIM LEADERS AND ORGANIZATION FROM 1972

The MNLF mobilized its supporters beginning in 1972 using a master frame of threat, including a range of physical and social threats. In the MNLF's framing and the view of many Muslims, even Marcos's notion of a "new society" was threatening. From the MNLF viewpoint, "The declaration of martial law and the concomitant programme of creating a 'New Society'" added up to an attempt at imposing "a 'Christian' totalitarian social order" that would destroy Muslims' traditional religion, culture, and way of life and impose Christian culture on them.[113] Ordinary Muslims came to share this perception, leading many young men to turn to armed resistance. McKenna interviewed a number of Muslim rebel fighters in Maguindanao areas and reported the following explanation to be "typical: 'The rise of the Ilaga caused young Muslims such as me to join the front to defend the people as fighters, to protect the people and Islam.'" While this formulation sounds clichéd, it is supported by multiple streams of evidence. As discussed earlier in this chapter, I repeatedly heard similar statements in my own interviews with leading MNLF figures and former local commanders. As one of McKenna's informants put it, "There was no place safe during the trouble at that time," so joining an armed group may actually have appeared to be a rational act of self-defense.[114]

McKenna's analysis of the rebels' songs and ballads turned up the same theme. It is clear that these songs do not represent the "approved" MNLF message, as the object of defense in these songs is not the "Bangsa Moro," the Moro nation for which the MNLF was named and for which it struggled. Rather, more typically the songwriters wrote of defending their local community, rather than the Bangsa Moro or even their ethnic group.[115] This is the refrain also in MNLF commanders' reports of the appeals they used to recruit fighters: the theme was, "We are here to defend you, join us."[116] Other recruiting pitches appealed to social norms. Maranao, for example, were recruited with the pitch, "A man who has lost his *bangsa* [nation] has no *mara-tabat* [honor or status]," and "a man without *maratabat* is nothing."[117]

The motives of Sulu Islander rebels (mostly Tausug and Samal), as reflected in Samuel Tan's account of interviews with thirty-four former MNLF rebels from the Sulu Islands, were a bit different from the Maguindanao and Maranao reasons. The most common motives Tan's ex-rebels reported—over one-third of all reasons offered—were framed in terms of injustice: to oppose "exploitation of Muslims" or "injustice to Muslims," sometimes with a focus on a specific ethnic group such as "discrimination against the Yakan tribe." A related set of reasons had to do with social threats—threats to group status and group interests—such as a "threat to Islam" or a desire to oppose the government's "oppression of Muslims" or to fight against government efforts to convert Muslims. Physical threats were mentioned about one sixth of the time, typically defined in terms of fighting "military abuses against Muslim women" or "the defense of Muslims harassed by the military." A final relatively common theme was reference to the legitimacy of the Muslim cause, typically defined as a desire to "fight for Muslim freedom in . . . the Bangsamoro homeland," or more generally to defend "the cause of Islam."[118] A related theme I heard was references to past Muslim states in the region, especially the Sultanate of Sulu, for whom Suluans' ancestors "fought with invaders."[119]

Based on all of these motives, Muslim mobilization escalated quickly after the martial law proclamation. In October 1972, a month after the declaration of martial law, an armed Muslim group called Ikalas—a community group, not a student group—occupied the entire Marawi City campus of Mindanao State University.[120] Through the university's radio station, the Ikalas sought to appeal to other Muslims, claiming the need to wage jihad against the state. That particular uprising was quickly suppressed by the Philippine armed forces, after which the MNLF quickly emerged as the main umbrella group for Muslim resistance and the primary funnel for foreign support. The most intense period of the MNLF's struggle followed.[121] An estimated sixty thousand civilians were killed in the period 1972–1975; by 1977, between five hundred thousand and one million people had been displaced, not counting an additional two hundred thousand who fled to Sabah.[122] The Philippine government and the MNLF signed a peace deal in 1976, but this did not end the fighting: Hashim Salamat broke away to form the Moro Islamic Liberation Front (MILF), which would not finally agree to peace until 2014.

As mentioned earlier in this chapter, the MNLF combined the injustice, identity, and threat frames into a master frame of generalized threat. For example, the MNLF's 1974 "Manifesto on the Establishment of the Bangsamoro Republik" opens with reference to the Philippine government's "terror, oppression and tyranny," its "usurping our land," "threatening Islam," and "murdering our innocent brothers, sisters and old folks."[123] A number of the ex-rebels Tan interviewed specifically mentioned being convinced by such themes of MNLF propaganda.

In the late 1970s, however, MNLF chief Nur Misuari developed a new framing: the conflict as a "national liberation struggle" of the Bangsa Moro (the Moro nation) against a colonialist regime in Manila and its "war of genocide." In this view, the Muslims of the Philippine south were not an assortment of a dozen different ethnic groups, but a single nation that had been waging an anticolonial struggle for centuries. In naming this nation the Moros, Misuari was attempting to transform the old Spanish pejorative term into a symbol of group pride.[124] Not all Muslims accepted this notion of a Bangsa Moro, but many did.[125]

Social networks remained critically important in generating recruits for the rebels' armed groups. Family ties were often important, with people being motivated to join the fight because an uncle or brother had already joined. The move by Hashim Salamat and his supporters to form the rival MILF exposed the continuing role of ethnic ties: most Maguindanaoans followed (the Maguindanaoan) Salamat into the new MILF, while most Tausug remained with (the Tausug) Misuari in the MNLF.

Conclusion

The Mindanao conflict is complex, but the logic of symbolic politics theory explains its causes well. The first set of reasons for the conflict begins with Hypothesis 1: widely known hostile narratives contributed to strongly hostile symbolic predispositions among both Muslims and Christians. The narratives focused on differences between Muslims and Christians, and portrayed the conflict between them as unremitting and centuries long. As a result of these narratives, Christians widely accepted the "Moro image," stereotyping Muslims as violent, uncivilized, and dangerous. Christians were therefore inclined (Hypothesis 3) to support hostile and discriminatory policies toward Muslims. Muslims, for their part, saw the Christian-led government as invaders and land grabbers who wanted to eliminate Islam. Additionally, identity narratives among the key Muslim groups— Maguindanao, Tausug, and Maranao—promoted warrior self-images and therefore some predisposition to violent resistance. All of these factors interacted to lead to strong feelings of threat on both sides, just as Hypothesis 2 would predict: Muslims felt threatened by government repression and violence, and the government and local Christians felt threatened by the Muslim rebellion that resulted.

These feelings were politically quiescent until they were harnessed by aggressive leaders backed by effective organizations. On the Christian side, in accordance with Hypothesis 5, violent mobilization required credible leadership using assertive frames—first from local and provincial politicians, and then overtly in Marcos's imposition of martial law. The ethnically tinged "law and order" frame used by politicians like Cajelo resonated with the Christian population for the reasons proposed by Hypothesis 4: threat perceptions led to support for hostile action. Cajelo was harnessing the terror management effect, and his background as a Constabulary commander made his use of this frame credible. Then, as Hypothesis 6 would predict, these politicians used existing coercive organizations (such as the police) and also created militia organizations to expand the scale of violent mobilization. Later, of course, Marcos used government machinery to mobilize the army to suppress the MNLF rebellion. Finally, Marcos's clever use of the "new society" frame lured some Muslim leaders into abandoning the rebellion; this helps to explain the later de-escalation of the conflict.

Evidence from the Muslim side also tends to confirm Hypotheses 3 through 6. The failure of Matalam's MIM is easily explained in terms of that leader's lack of credibility on the Jabidah issue (Hypothesis 5) even though Muslims' SYPs inclined them to distrust the government (Hypothesis 3). The MNLF, in contrast, was more credible, appealing not only to Muslim SYPs (Hypothesis 3) but also to rising threat perceptions after events like the Manili Massacre (Hypothesis 4). The MNLF also boasted a more diverse and credible leadership (Hypothesis 5) than MIM, and it built an extensive organization through leaders' networking and grassroots recruiters' efforts. Foreign support played an important role, but the key motivation for young men to join the movement was a self-evident need for family and group self-defense. Interestingly, the new MNLF narrative of the Bangsa Moro—a Moro *nation*—did not resonate, but it did not have to. Rank-and-file fighters more often reported that they were fighting for their religion and the (local) Muslim community against the martial law regime. It was the general symbol of "Islam," not the newfangled MNLF ideology, that provided the main rallying cry for most.

The rebel "ground war" began with social networks, but these grew into a set of organizations. The MIM experience helped to create an elite network that tied together younger educated leaders like Misuari and Salamat with traditional Muslim leaders like Matalam and Lucman and with commanders of the Blackshirt and Barracuda militia groups. Contacts with Tun Mustafa in Sabah, and later with Gaddafi in Libya, provided these rebels with the resources to train a corps of guerrilla leaders and then to equip a rebel army. Thus the informal network at the core of MIM grew into the organization of the MNLF, with branches reaching all of the main Muslim ethnic groups. As we would expect from Hypothesis 2, the growth of this organization enabled Muslim mobilization on a larger scale. Later Salamat, a religiously oriented Maguindanaoan, parted ways with the secular Tausug Misuari, turning his faction into the MILF.

All of these circumstances created a security dilemma in Mindanao, but one driven by predatory motives. Local Christian politicians initiated violence in Cotabato by creating the Ilaga militias, seeking to create fear for electoral gain. The Ilagas were so threatening to Muslims, however, that they provoked a violent countermobilization by groups like the Blackshirts, which in turn prompted army and police crackdowns. Marcos's later imposition of martial law, though not primarily aimed against the Muslims, was seen by Muslims as a truly existential threat, propelling further mobilization to full-scale war on both sides.

The Mindanao conflict, in sum, was a tragedy unintended by Marcos and the Mindanao politicians who provoked it. However, the same factors that made the political appeals of people like Cajelo work—the prejudices and hostile narratives, Muslim groups' violent SYPs, a weak state that permitted them to have private armies—were the factors that touched off the fighting. By using aggressive threat frames in their election campaigns and sponsoring armed groups like the Ilaga gangs in the conditions that prevailed in Mindanao, these politicians were metaphorically starting campfires in an oil refinery. Once they caused the explosion, rebels like Misuari and his supporters were pleased to come back at them with flamethrowers—which foreign backers like Gaddafi were happy to provide.

The North-South War in Sudan

In late 1982, Sudanese dictator Jaafar al-Numayri gave orders that three bat-talions of his troops be transferred from their southern garrison towns to new bases to the north. Numayri knew that this move was risky: these troops were former southern Anyanya rebels who had been included in the Suda-nese army—and promised basing in the south—as a result of the Addis Ababa peace agreement that Numayri himself had signed with the Anyan-yas in 1972. Such southern troops had initiated short-lived rebellions sev-eral times in previous years on much less provocation than this.[1] A similar transfer order given to southern troops in 1955 had triggered a mutiny that led eventually to the 1962–1972 Anyanya rebellion, and in the mid-1970s a low-level guerrilla insurgency had been started by groups calling themselves Anyanya II.[2]

Predictably enough, some of the southern troops refused the 1982 trans-fer order. Numayri responded by ordering northern troops to attack the mutinous southern troops in May 1983, impelling the southerners to flee to Ethiopia, where they established a guerrilla base. Numayri followed up his provocative moves with two more. In June 1983 he announced the dissolu-tion of the autonomous government in southern Sudan, replacing it with three regional governments wholly subordinate to central authorities—that is, to Numayri himself. Three months later Numayri instituted shari'a by de-cree on a nationwide basis, including in the formerly autonomous—and mostly Christian and animist—south. All of these actions violated key terms of the 1972 Addis Ababa peace accord, and they defied explicit warnings from southern leaders that such actions would result in civil war.[3] When Nu-maryri persisted, southern military leaders responded by forming the Su-danese Peoples Liberation Army (SPLA) and its political wing, the Sudanese Peoples Liberation Movement (SPLM), and then battling the government in a civil war that would last twenty-two years. The costs to Sudan of that war included an estimated two million people dead, four million driven from their homes, and the secession of the south as the independent state of South Sudan in 2011.[4] Even the 2005 peace agreement ending the north-south war

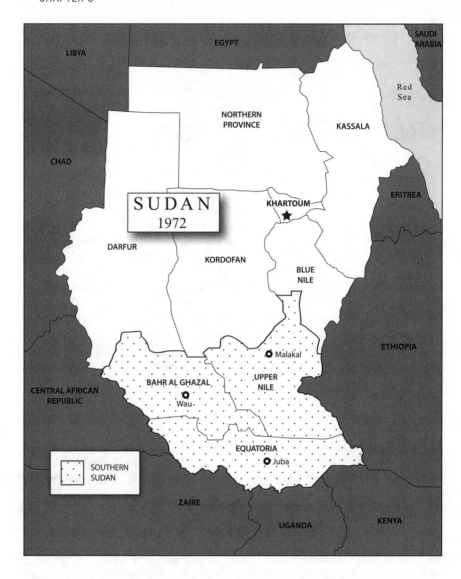

proved costly, leading directly to the outbreak of a new civil war in the western Sudanese region of Darfur.

From the point of view of opportunity theory, the pattern of multiple civil wars in Sudan makes sense. Sudan was the largest country in Africa, and very poor, with a GDP per capita of only about $382 in 1983.[5] Furthermore, Sudan's non-Muslims were concentrated in the south, easing problems of mobilization, and neighboring Ethiopia was a reliable supplier of assistance and bases to southern Sudanese rebels. The trouble is that this approach cannot explain why peace was achieved in 1972. And if we try to apply the related rationalist theory to the outbreak of war in 1983, the questions multiply. How could it have been rational for Numayri to provoke this war? According to one account, Numayri's motivation was to monopolize the revenue from the oil fields that had been discovered at Bentiu in the south in 1976.[6] If true, this was a spectacular miscalculation: the fighting prevented any oil production in the region for years to come, at an estimated cost of over $300 million annually.[7] Furthermore, the cost of the war itself would rise to an estimated $450 million per year by the late 1980s—or more than the annual value of all of the oil that might have been pumped. The alternative "rationalist" explanation is that Numayri's war policy was an effort to seek popularity and maintain his power, but this idea begs the question, why would so costly a policy be popular?

Symbolic politics theory provides an answer, starting from the observation that what happened politically was a change in Numayri's ruling strategy from a low-conflict politics of distribution to a high-conflict politics of protection. After the 1972 Addis Ababa peace agreement, Numayri had allied himself with a coalition of technocrats, the army, and southerners, uniting his backers into a single ruling party, the Sudan Socialist Union, whose creed was state-led economic development. This was the politics of distribution—an effort to maintain political power and legitimacy by delivering economic growth. However, this governing model began to fail when economic growth stalled.

Trying to maintain power, Numayri turned to symbolic identity politics, allying himself with Islamist elites and fostering an image as the vindicator of Islam. This turn cost Numayri the support of his southern allies, so he turned on them, initiating a jihad to spread Islam in the south. Ironically, Numayri's tactics failed in maintaining his power: he was overthrown by a military coup in April 1985. His identity politics outlived him, however, as popular prejudice, fear, and hostility toward the south prevented his short-tenured civilian successors from accepting a compromise end to the war before they were overthrown in another military coup in June 1989. The new military dictatorship of General Umar al-Bashir continued to practice the symbolic politics of Islamic identity and prosecuted the war in the south at heightened intensity for more than another decade.

Symbolic politics theory explains this pattern. The reason Islamism was popular in the north—the reason Numayri and his successors turned to that ideology—was because Islam was at the heart of northern narratives of Sudanese identity, strengthening (Hypothesis 1) prejudices against southerners. Those prejudices, in turn, encouraged northerners to see non-Muslim southerners as not only inferior but threatening (Hypothesis 2) and therefore to support discriminatory policies toward the south (Hypotheses 3 and 4) such as the imposition of shari'a. Because of the terror management effect, those same threat perceptions made it difficult for moderates to gain support for peace initiatives. As a result, every peace initiative by northern politicians in the later 1980s was stymied by opponents' charges of selling out. Southerners, on their part, recognized northerners' prejudice and hostility and so were relatively easily roused to return to self-defensive warfare once Numayri's betrayal was clear (Hypotheses 2 through 4 again).

It was this context that made Numayri's use of aggressive ethnic frames potentially effective (Hypothesis 5), and his control of the Sudanese government gave him the organizational base to pursue war (Hypothesis 6). Numayri lost power because he personally had lost credibility, but the war continued because popular hostility and fear left his successors with little choice: identity and threat frames resonated with a hostile and fearful northern public opinion, while benefits frames supporting peace did not. The southerners were able to fight back because ex-Anyanya leaders and their troops provided the leadership and organization necessary for a sustained rebellion (Hypotheses 5 and 6 again).

The details of this explanation are laid out in the rest of this chapter. After a brief background section on the groups and their histories, the next section details the group narratives, symbolic predispositions and threat perceptions among northerners and southerners. The following two sections respectively examine the roles of leadership and organization in the north and in the south. The final two sections explore the nature of Sudan's security dilemma and sum up the findings.

The Groups and Their Histories

Accounts of Sudan's ethnic warfare focus on the broad conflict between the Muslim, Arabized north and the Christian and animist black African south, and on the separate conflict in Darfur. There are, however, many other layers of identity in Sudan, including by some accounts as many as six hundred ethnic groups, and this diversity is important in understanding the dynamics of both the north-south and Darfur fighting.

NORTHERN GROUPS

The historically most powerful groups in Sudan have been the "Arabs" in the northern part of the Nile River valley, many of whom claim descent from migrants from the Arabian Peninsula. Distinct from them are traditionally nomadic and politically marginalized "Arab" groups such as the Baqqara, who are actually Arabized descendants of more recent African immigrants.[8] There is also a sectarian split among different Sufi orders, especially the Ansar led by the al-Mahdi family and the Khatmiyya led by the al-Mirghani clan. These sects were historically the basis of Sudan's two leading political parties: the Ansar's Umma Party and the Khatmiyya's Democratic Unionist Party (DUP).

Also among the northerners are non-Arab Muslim peoples, including the more than fifty ethnic groups of the Nuba Mountain region of southern Kordofan Province. Darfur in the west is the traditional home of sedentary farmers such as the Fur and Masalit, as well as the nomadic Baqqara Arabs and the non-Arab Zaghawa nomads. The Darfur conflict of the early 2000s primarily pitted the Baqqara Arabs, backed by the Sudanese government, against rebel groups among the Fur, Zaghawa, and other non-Arab ethnicities of the region.

SOUTHERN GROUPS

The largest ethnic group in the south is the Dinka, who speak a western Nilotic language and are dominant in Bahr al-Ghazal region. Upper Nile region inhabitants include Dinka and also Nuer—cattle-herding western Nilotes like the Dinka who are nevertheless traditional Dinka enemies.[9] Neither Dinka nor Nuer have an overarching ethnic leadership, and both are divided into subgroups that have often fought each other. The capital of the Upper Nile region, Malakal, is located in the territory of the Shilluk, another western Nilotic group who have historically been adversaries of the Dinka.[10] Thus while Sudan's conflict was an ethnic war, it was a coalition war, with the Arabs of the north and the Dinkas of the south leading shifting coalitions of ethnic groups and subgroups against each other.

The third and southernmost region of the south, Equatoria, is most diverse of all. Important groups in eastern Equatoria include the Latuko and Acholi, speakers of distantly related Nilotic languages. Western Equatoria is home to the Azande (among others), whose language is a member of the unrelated Sudanic language group. Many of these groups are also divided on sectarian lines, with Catholic groups like the Latuko pitted against smaller groups like the Fajulu, who are more commonly Protestant.[11]

HISTORICAL BACKGROUND

Sudan's history begins with the Nubians, who were at different times the enemies, subjects, and rulers of Pharaonic Egypt.[12] Successively Christianized and then Islamized in the medieval period, northern Sudan was united in 1504 under a Funj kingdom, a polity whose economy was based on the slave trade.[13] Further expansion of the Funj was blocked by the Keira sultanate in Darfur and the Shilluk kingdom in the south.[14] This period also saw wars among the Shilluk, the Dinka, and the Nuer.[15]

In 1820, the Funj kingdom was conquered by Muhammad Ali's "Turco-Egyptian" regime in Egypt. This new regime introduced shari'a and extended the previous pattern of slave raids farther into the south, east, and west.[16] Its leading local collaborators were the Mirghanis, the leaders of the Khatmiyya Sufi order.[17] In 1881, however, a Sufi sheik named Muhammad Ahmad ibn Abdallah declared himself the Mahdi, or redeemer, launching an Islamist rebellion that overthrew the Turco-Egyptian administration in Sudan. The Mahdi built a political-religious coalition, later called the Ansar, uniting Baqqara Arabs in the west, Nile River valley Arabs, and non-Arab Muslims among the Nuba farther south.[18] His movement, the Mahdiyya, captured Khartoum in 1885, but the Mahdi himself soon died. The next thirteen years were a period of constant warfare, including civil war within Sudan and external war with all of the Mahdiyya's neighbors—the Anglo-Egyptians, the Fur, and others.[19] The Mahdiyya was finally ended by a British invasion and the establishment of the "Anglo-Egyptian Condominium," a polite term for rule by a British governor-general, in 1899.

In the northern two-thirds of Sudan, the British established a system that was friendly to Muslim religious concerns and included shari'a courts for settling some disputes. Ansar leader Abd al-Rahman al-Mahdi pledged loyalty to the British and by the 1930s was the most powerful indigenous leader in Sudan.[20] In the south, however, the British set up a separate colonial administration that excluded Arab traders and Muslim law; instead, they encouraged Christian missionaries to operate in the area. The British also created a local military force in the south, composed of Equatorian troops with British officers.[21] When Sudanese independence approached after World War II, the southerners requested separation or at least autonomy from the Muslim north. They were promised autonomy and other safeguards, most notably at a 1947 conference at Juba, but never received them. Thus when Sudanese replaced British bureaucrats in the 1950s, only six of about eight hundred government positions went to southerners, leaving northerners dominant.[22]

The first Sudanese Parliament did have nearly one-quarter of its members from the south, but the southerners were excluded from any real power. Instead, Khartoum quickly took a coercive tone: facing a restive south in 1955, transitional prime minister Ismail el-Azhari asserted, "The government must use all its force and strength" to deal with the southerners.[23] Sudan gained independence in 1956; by December 1957, it had been declared a unitary state, with Arabic the official language and Islam the official religion—all policies obnoxious to the south. Repression of the south intensified after a 1958 coup brought General Ibrahim Abboud to power. The first in a series of southern rebel movements emerged in 1962 and began military operations the next year; Abboud cracked down even more viciously, employing widespread arbitrary arrest and torture.[24] Abboud's overthrow in 1964 brought only a short respite, as elections in 1965 were dominated by Islamist parties—the sectarian Umma (Ansar) and DUP (Khatmiyya), and the Muslim Brotherhood–backed Islamic Charter Front.[25] Over the next four years, civilian prime ministers continued fruitlessly to pursue military victory in the south.

The 1969 coup by Numayri and his "Free Officers Movement" quickly led to a peace initiative, but peace was slow to come.[26] Instead, the Ansar rose in revolt in early 1970, triggering a brutal crackdown that killed twelve thousand people, including the al-Mahdi clan leader, and sent the surviving Ansar leader Sadiq al-Mahdi scuttling into exile.[27] The next year, Numayri's Communist allies attempted a coup, forcing yet another regime purge and further narrowing Numayri's political base. At the same time, a flow of Israeli arms allowed Anyanya leader Joseph Lagu to turn that rebel group for the first time into a united and militarily effective organization, apparently convincing Numayri that military victory would be impossible.[28] This was the context in which Numayri appointed the southerner Abel Alier vice president and minister for southern affairs, and sent him to conclude the Addis Ababa Agreement with the Anyanya, which he did in March 1972.

Narratives, Symbolic Predispositions, and Threat Perceptions

HOSTILE NARRATIVES IN THE NORTH

The most widespread northern Sudanese narrative claims an Arab and Muslim identity for its adherents. Many northern subgroups cultivate a narrative of descent from Arab ancestors (and for one group, kinship with the Abbasid caliphs) as a way of claiming membership in the Arab world and a distinction from the "Africans" of the south. The reason for such claims is "to enhance pride and self-esteem," as Francis Deng puts it; but as Ahmad Sikainga notes, this narrative also creates "an attitude of racial and cultural superiority."[29] G. P. Makris sums up the narrative as one of an "imagined Arab community . . . defin[ed] as the realm of freedom, humanity, Islamic tradition and heroic history . . . [which] constructed its exact opposite; the realm of the pagan African slaves."[30]

The social history of the region was one in which "races and religions were ranked, with Arabs and Muslims respected as free, superior, and a race of slave masters, while Negroes, blacks, and heathens were viewed as a legitimate target of slavery, if they were not in fact already slaves."[31] This traditional ranking was legally established by Arab rulers as early as the seventh century. A tenth-century Arab writer "described black Africans as cannibal, pagan and primitive" with "little understanding or intelligence." Later, the usually insightful medieval geographer Ibn Khaldun asserted, "Negro nations . . . have little that is human and possess attributes that are similar to those of dumb animals."[32] Racism has a long pedigree in Sudan.

Another element of northerners' nationalist narrative is a proselytizing brand of Islam. While northerners feel superior to the "primitive" peoples of the south, many also view southerners as "eligible for salvation through Islam." Indeed, Khatmiyya leader al-Mirghani in 1957 "declared that his sole ambition and desire was to see Islam spread throughout the Southern provinces."[33] Likewise, Ansar sect leader Sadiq al-Mahdi reportedly remarked, "Islam has a holy mission in Africa and southern Sudan is the beginning of that mission."[34] A third northern official remarked, "The problem of the south will be solved when Islam will be propagated [there]." The media often echoed these views.[35]

Other northern narratives glorify the aggressive use of force. For example, Deng reports, "In a flood of tribal songs [from central Sudan, the 1960s dictator General] Abboud was exalted for his 'manhood,' and power was said to belong now to those with the force of arms."[36] Deng quotes one song from the period as declaring, "Ours has become a country held by force of the arm / Our Great leader, Abboud, hold our country." Similarly, in some Arabized tribes, "becoming a warrior is a routine feature of later youth and early manhood, not a specialized occupation, since it is one that every man follows during a defined period of life. . . . During this period of warrior-hood, such attributes of the male role as valor and aggressive virility are emphasized." In these tribes, boys who display these virtues are lauded by girls in praise-songs.[37]

In the mainstream northern narrative, the father of Sudanese nationalism was the Mahdi, progenitor of the Ansar. The Mahdiyya established an early equation between Sudanese national identity and fundamentalist Islam. Further, the Mahdiyya was a violent jihadist fundamentalism, which some northern intellectuals long continued to justify—for both past and current purposes—as necessary to achieve desirable revolutionary change. As M. W. Daly puts it, "In retrospect the Mahdiyya assumed the quality of a nationalist myth, . . . and its ideology of xenophobia and Islamic rectitude became an exclusive heritage of the North."[38]

NORTHERN SYMBOLIC PREDISPOSITIONS AND FEARS

If Hypotheses 1 and 2 are correct, these hostile narratives should have sown widespread antisouthern prejudices and other negative SYPs in the north; those prejudices in turn should have fostered perceptions that southerners were threatening to the north. The evidence supports these expectations. Even after the notion of a racial pecking order was no longer enforced by law, the related symbolic predispositions—especially racist beliefs and attitudes—remained influential. In 1955, for example, a government report on disturbances in the south stated that southern Sudanese were "one of the most primitive peoples in the world"; a typical northern policeman at that time called southern children "monkeys."[39] Looking back on the 1950s, Any-anya leader Joseph Lagu would recall, "The Northern officials looked down upon Southerners, openly discriminating against them and on the whole treated them as a subject people. . . . They kept on insulting and abusing us, often using the word *abeed* (slaves) when referring to Southerners."[40]

A second set of symbolic predispositions promoted fear and hostility. For example, many northerners said of southerners who had migrated to the north, "If we don't keep these people at a distance . . . they will soon run the Nile Valley."[41] Educated Arabs shared this prejudice: for example, one Arab schoolmistress remarked to her southern students in 1962, "Out of your black skins we shall make soles for our sandals."[42] Repeating another common stereotype, Ali al-Mirghani, then prime minister as well as leader of the Khatmiyya sect and of the DUP, remarked in 1967, "The only language the southerners understand is force."[43] In response to the fear of southern refugees, the Khartoum government responded at times with policies of forced repatriation of southern (and western) migrants out of the Khartoum area.

Observers note a distinct feeling of social threat underlying northern assertions of superiority, rooted in the tendency of non-Sudanese Arabs to dismiss northern Sudanese as Africans, not Arabs.[44] Other Arabs thus project onto northern Sudanese the very identity northern Sudanese deny about themselves but attribute to southerners—the "African" identity that implies inferiority and slave status. In historical terms, the non-Sudanese Arabs are right: the practice of slavery in northern Sudan allowed the children of slaves to assimilate with their Arab owners, so many contemporary "Arab" Sudanese are in fact the descendants of black "African" slaves. The implication is that any claimed "racial" distinction in Sudan is highly questionable; the conflicts in Sudan are primarily between those local groups who adopted an "Arab" identity in recent centuries and those who adopted competing identities.

Ansar leader Sadiq al-Mahdi has articulated the link between northerners' anxieties and the push for Islamic rule. "This nation will not have its entity [sic] identified and its prestige and pride preserved," he has stated, "except under an Islamic revival."[45] This is a claim about a social threat that some northerners raise to an existential level: if southerners' idea of an African identity were to become the official one in Sudan, then northerners' Arab identity would be extinguished (they fear) even if they were physically unharmed. The implication was that Sudanese Arabs' pride and group identity required, in their view, forcing their identity and religion on the southerners.

As a result of these narratives, prejudices, and fears, Islamist policies are perennially popular in Sudanese politics, as Hypotheses 3 and 4 project. As early as 1957, the "two Sayyids," al-Mahdi and al-Mirghani—the leaders of the Umma and DUP parties—had called for an "Islamic constitution." And when democracy returned to Sudan in 1965, the same parties reemerged; they had just agreed on a constitution for an Islamic state in 1969 when Numayri took over in his military coup.[46] Talk of an Islamic state was thus a familiar and widely popular symbol in northern Sudan in Numayri's time.

HOSTILE NARRATIVES IN THE SOUTH

Like many of the northerners' narratives, southern Sudanese narratives identify slavery as a key element.[47] In the southern narratives, however, the south is the land not of slaves but of those who resisted Arab slave raids. As southerners see it, the early nineteenth-century conquest of the south by the Turco-Egyptian government just eased the slavers' jobs: slave raids became *more* intense after the south came under the rule of the Arab north. In one case, a prominent Arab slave trader gained so much power that he was appointed a regional governor.

The Mahdist government that followed allowed not only intensified slave raids but also degenerated into a Hobbesian state of violence so severe that by one estimate, Sudan's population fell by more than one-half in thirteen years. Dinka tradition, Deng reports, vividly remembers the period as equivalent to "the total destruction of the world."[48] Deng continues, "The Dinka refer to the Turk-Egyptian and Mahdist periods as the time when 'the world was spoiled,' an abomination of which they speak with consistency and vividness." He reports "extensive interviews" with Dinka chiefs recounting how the Mahdists "destroyed the country" and "captured our people and sold them."[49] According to southern mythology, such violence and oppression are the meaning of Islamic law. As Amir Idris sums it up, the "southern nationalist narrative contends that the shared experience of slave trading and colonialism unified various ethnic groups in the South."[50] A song sung by the Dinka illustrates this attitude:

> The feud of the Southerners with the Northerners
> Our feud will never end . . .
> We shall avenge the evils of the past . . .
> We are the Dinka of Bahr al-Ghazal.[51]

Even if the particular song is new, the memories it preserves are old. As another song declares, "This feud began with our ancient leaders / When Arob Biong . . . met with the Mahdi."[52]

SYMBOLIC PREDISPOSITIONS IN THE SOUTH

Systematic evidence on southern symbolic predispositions before 1983 is difficult to find, but the anecdotal evidence available generally supports Hypothesis 1: hostile southern narratives do seem to have led to hostile symbolic predispositions. Among the Nuer in the Upper Nile region, for example, some remembered and were motivated to rebel in the 1960s by a nineteenth-century prophecy that they would fight Arabs.[53] Another indication comes from the testimony of a southern official, Elijah Malok, who reports that ex-Anyanya personnel in the 1970s were strongly predisposed to dislike and distrust the government. The former rank-and-file soldiers gained little from the Addis Ababa Agreement, so thousands of these men were left homeless, "perpetual beggars" who felt that "the Agreement had been a sham and thus the struggle for national liberation should be re-staged." Many former middle-ranking Anyanya officers agreed: "full of contempt for the Regional institutions . . . [they] vowed to destroy the accord."[54] Such contempt for institutions is an important symbolic predis-position.

Resentment of northerners and their mistreatment was widespread. Scopas Poggo records some of the lasting memories from the Anyanya strug-gle.[55] Some were of the efforts at forced Islamization: Christian mission schools were nationalized in 1957, and Koranic schools were subsequently built. In 1960, southern chiefs were forced to convert to Islam or resign, and Friday replaced Sunday as the day of rest in the south. Knowledge of Ara-bic was made a requirement for school admission, so most pupils even in the middle schools in Juba in the far south were northerners. Christian stu-dents still in school were flogged for attending church.

Another set of southern memories was of violent repression by northern-ers.[56] After the famous Torit mutiny of 1955, many of the southern muti-neers surrendered on a promise of fair treatment, but three hundred of them were quickly executed, creating a lasting memory among their fellow Latuko. Subsequent repression included "burning, prison, public execution and arbitrary arrests" as well as torture and arbitrary shootings, with those tar-geted including all tailors in the south. Northerners reportedly raped southern women with impunity. July–August 1965 saw massacres in all three southern provinces as northern troops sought to eliminate southern politicians: in Juba, capital of Equatoria, an estimated 1,400–2,000 civil-ians were indiscriminately killed, while in Wau, the capital of Bahr 'al Ghazal, seventy-six men including the deputy governor of the province were mas-sacred at a wedding. All teachers in the province were also reportedly arrested and killed. Later in the decade, "collectivization" and "peace vil-lage" programs forced the resettlement of southerners, leading to many deaths as a result of inadequate food and other material support. In 1971, the government blocked international aid that was offered to treat a cholera epidemic in the south.

According to anthropologist Sharon Hutchinson, the lingering feeling of this repression among Nuer was symbolized by the concept of slavery. Hutchinson quotes one Nuer warrior as saying, "The peace of the slave is not worth it." Another complained, "The Arabs called us dogs and slaves and said that we were no better than the dirt under their feet."[57] A related theme emphasized by Francis Deng, especially among Dinka, is victimiza-tion. One chief reported of the behavior of northern troops, "They would proceed to destroy the camp [for arbitrary reasons]. Children would die and women would die. The chief would only stand holding his head. If you tried force, you fell a victim. Whatever you tried, you fell a victim." According-ing to another chief, "The terrible things that have happened in this area, if I were to take you . . . around to the whole South, to see the bones of men [women and children] lying in the forest, to see the houses that were burned down . . . you would . . . not ask me a single question." A third chief reported that he had himself been imprisoned and tortured; when he responded by joining the Anyanya rebels, his children were killed and his wives burned to death.[58] While strictly speaking these stories are narratives, not statements of symbolic predispositions, it seems clear that their telling is an indication of resentment and other hostile SYPs. These inclinations were complicated by the fact that many southerners also felt hostile SYPs toward each other—Catholic against Protestant, Dinka against Equatorians, and so on.[59] These cross-pressures led some groups of southerners to side with the north against their local adversaries.

Another important symbolic predisposition among southerners is toward violent resistance. Writing in 1963, anthropologist Godfrey Lienhardt observed, "The Dinka and Nuer are a warlike people, and have never been slow to assert their rights as they see them by physical force."[60] Deng elaborates that these southern groups, like many northern ones, shared a "warrior tradition," leading to "the mutuality of the predisposition to engage in military action." As Deng observes, "Both the state and the SPLM-SPLA have also found in these traditional military values a ready . . . framework for recruitment and morale-raising among their fighting men."[61]

Leadership and Organization in the North

Numayri was the dictator of Sudan until 1985; leadership of the government, of course, came from him. The key question we must answer is why his political strategy shifted from a master frame and policy focused on economic development to an Islamist master frame and policy focus. In order to explain the strategy's failure—that is, the fact of Numayri's ouster in 1985—we must also examine the interaction of those frames with Numayri's organization-building and coalition-building strategy.

NUMAYRI'S NEW FRAME AND POLITICAL STRATEGY

The first reason for Numayri's shift to a new master frame was that he failed to produce economic growth, so the old economic development frame lost credibility. Early in his tenure, Numayri began suspecting the technocrats in his government of disloyalty, so he sidelined them; the result was "the relentless disintegration of the Sudan economy" as a result of corruption and mismanagement.[62] Unable to keep up payments on its foreign debt, Sudan began defaulting on loans in 1978, while domestic mismanagement caused exports to decline. The World Bank extended aid in 1978 but insisted on tough conditions that caused inflation to soar and the standard of living of poor Sudanese to plummet.

In order to bolster his flagging popularity as the economy weakened, Numayri began pursuing a symbolic politics of image manipulation, cultivating an Islamist image for himself and framing some of his policies in Islamist terms. As early as 1972 Numayri told the People's Assembly that shari'a should be "the principal source of legislation," and the next year he initiated an annual Holy Qu'ran Festival.[63] He publicly performed the Friday prayers every week, and in 1976 he ordered all members of his cabinet to stop drinking and gambling.[64] He began publicly campaigning for "the Islamic Way" in 1977 and approved establishment of an Islamic bank in the same year. Similarly, "Numayri began to dress in Arab garb, with all the outward symbols of an Islamic sheikh or imam."[65] In 1980 he published a book entitled *The Islamic Way: Why?*, which advocated a Sudanese recommitment to Islamic values. Numayri merged the previously separate secular and shari'a courts that same year.

However, he was far from consistent. As late as 1981, for example, a major Numayri address to the leadership of the Sudanese Socialist Union (SSU) was couched almost entirely in the quasi-Communist jargon of glorifying the May Revolution in which he took power; his main themes were national unity and economic development. The movement toward political Islam merited only a single sentence in a twenty-five-page speech.[66] The speech, full of details on policies for regional autonomy and economic development, included no details on how to implement this "Islamic Trend." Addressing the National People's Assembly the following year, Numayri emphasized his conciliatory policy toward the south—the scheduling of fresh elections—and did not mention the "Islamic Trend" at all.[67] Also in 1982, he personally acted to overturn a ban on alcohol in the city of Omdurman.[68]

This was the context in which Numayri decreed the imposition of full Islamic law in September 1983—laws that were swiftly, strictly, and publicly enforced.[69] Not only was consumption of all alcohol banned, even the local *marissa* beer, but thousands of gallons of Scotch whiskey and other alcohol were poured into the Nile or crushed by bulldozers in a public spectacle. With *hudud* (the traditional Koranic criminal code) given legal sanction, public executions and amputations began within months.[70]

An Islamic orientation suddenly permeated Numayri's speeches, remaining prominent for the rest of his time in power. A typical formulation was, "The Islamic avenue is the paramount pillar of the comprehensive political program."[71] Pursuing this theme, Numayri criticized one crowd for their supposed sexual promiscuity and attacked striking workers in another speech for being "adverse to striving in the cause of Allah." He expanded on his ideas in a widely publicized May 1984 address to the cabinet. In this speech, he asserted, "The application of Islam is unconquerable," and he attributed opposition as "aimed at aborting enlightenment, the correct path, belief and Islam." He directed his ministers to lead their employees in prayer. Even here, however, his self-interested goals were obvious: most of the speech was focused on the economic crisis of the period, and the strikes and political disruptions that it spawned. His response, amid fierce denunciations of the strikers and other opponents, was to emphasize "how much we needed pure faith and steadfastness by which we could encounter hardships"—that is, the population should be good Muslims and suffer economic distress quietly.[72]

Summing up Numayri's political strategy, Simone explains, "The excision of limbs for crimes of thievery, flogging for alcohol consumption, and stoning for adultery were imbued with great symbolic value," as progress toward the ideal Islamic society.[73] Numayri was, however, an unconvincing Islamist, indulging in what Collins describes as "public displays of profanity from a foul-mouthed Imam," and "comparing himself to the Prophet Muhammad to the point of heresy."[74] This lack of credibility would be a key reason for Numayri's overthrow in 1985. A second problem was that he was using the wrong frame: in the context of a civil war with the south (Hypothesis 4), frames of physical and identity threats were likely to be most resonant; identity frames that did not focus on such threats were not very powerful.

ORGANIZATION AND NUMAYRI'S COALITION STRATEGY

Another reason for Numayri's political weakness in the 1980s was (Hypothesis 6) his weak organizational base: he never built the SSU into a mass political party. As a result, he always relied on coalitions with other elites who did lead mass organizations. After his initial coalition partners, the Communists, turned on him in 1971, Numayri was forced to seek new allies—among them the southerners he co-opted through the Addis Ababa Agreement. Even before that agreement, however, Numayri was seeking accommodation with northern Islamists as well. Thus while Numayri had imprisoned most Muslim Brotherhood leaders in 1969 for opposing his rise to power, he freed them in 1971 and allowed them to reenter politics. Numayri shortly began bringing leaders of the smaller Sufi orders into the ruling SSU, eventually garnering the political support of virtually all of them.[75] In 1974, one of these Sufi sheiks, Sharif Abdalla, was installed as grand mufti of the presidential palace, and the formerly hard-drinking Numayri began abstaining from alcohol.[76]

These moves were not enough to shore up Numayri's power base, however. In 1976 a coalition of Islamists led by Ansar members launched a coup attempt with support from Libya. Numayri barely survived assassination, so though he defeated the coup, he decided to conclude a "National Reconciliation" deal with the Islamists in 1977, taking Ansar leader Sadiq al-Mahdi into the SSU leadership. Numayri had discovered that "the only ones who could mobilize people beyond the tribal level were the sectarian [and other religious] figures."[77] After 1978, there were no more southerners in Numayri's cabinet.[78] While the reconciliation with al-Mahdi and Ansar never took root, Numayri forged a strong link with the Muslim Brotherhood, appointing Brotherhood leader Hassan al-Turabi to head a "Committee for the Revision of Sudanese Law on Islamic Principles"; Turabi was made attorney general in 1979.[79]

By one account, Numayri's only supporters by 1980 were the Muslim Brotherhood, the army, southerners, the SSU, and the police. Of these, only the Brotherhood was able to mobilize large numbers of followers on the streets, based on its predominant position in student organizations and affiliated organizations for Islamist women, youth, clerics, artists, and others. The Brotherhood also had strong influence in the Islamic banking sector and many labor and professional unions. But this influence was not useful for Numayri: regardless of the Brotherhood's position, student activists organized extensive protests *against* the regime in 1981–1982, followed by Brotherhood-supported labor unions in 1982.[80]

In this context, Numayri's proclamation of shari'a was probably aimed at strengthening his organizational base of support in several ways. First, and most obviously, it was an effort to co-opt the power base of his Islamist rivals—though a fruitless one, since he lacked an organized network of supporters who could have secured that base. Second, it was an attempt to manipulate religion to strengthen elite support for him, since declaring shari'a also provided an opportunity for him to declare himself imam and demand "the *bay'a* from the senior members of his government, as had Muhammad Ahmad al-Mahdi."[81] There was also a short-term motive: by one account, a mid-1983 strike by doctors and judges had left Numayri seeking a new tool of social control—by controllers who would be pleased to be turned against such secular elite groups.[82] Numayri's turn to the Brotherhood to staff his new shari'a courts did achieve that goal.

This last point highlights another dimension of Numayri's organization-building effort: a series of government reorganizations intended to strengthen his control over the state apparatus. Already in 1975, Numayri had pushed through a constitutional amendment that, at least in his interpretation, gave him unlimited dictatorial powers. Even his "National Reconciliation" deal with Ansar was aimed at securing his power, not sharing it: Ansar leader Sadiq al-Mahdi was given a seat on the SSU Politburo, but not a cabinet post where he had any effective authority. Similarly, Numayri sponsored a "Regional Government Act" in 1980 that allegedly increased autonomy in the regions of Sudan's north but in fact increased his control by giving him the power directly to appoint regional governors. In 1982, Numayri decided to dispense even with his own political party, dissolving all SSU structures, simultaneously firing the entire cabinet and twenty-three high-ranking military officers.[83]

Numayri's efforts in 1982–1983 to curtail the autonomy of the south can be seen in this light, as part of a general strategy of strengthening his power within the government. Thus his attempt to transfer southern military units to the north and west can be seen as aiming to undo a concession that he had made from weakness a decade before. If he had succeeded, he would have substantially reduced the danger of a southern rebellion. (He miscalculated; the officer he sent to woo one rebellious unit was John Garang, the soon-to-be commander of the SPLA.)[84] Similarly, the dissolution of the south's autonomous government was of a piece with his reorganization of northern regional government, ostensibly yielding to demands for more local control while actually increasing his power over the regions.

Numayri's actions in 1982–1983 were far from the first time he had intervened in the politics of the autonomous south. At first, his actions were relatively benign, appointing the Dinka lawyer Abel Alier as interim head of the autonomous southern government in 1973, and permitting free elections in January 1974 that Alier won.[85] In 1979, however, Numayri persuaded Alier to step aside in favor of former Anyanya military chief Joseph Lagu, who had been charging Alier with fostering "Dinka domination."[86] Numayri's intervention now became chronic: he replaced southern leaders three times in the next three years, typically alternating Alier and Lagu in power, before finally dissolving the southern government by decree in June 1983.[87]

SYMBOLIC POLITICS IN THE NORTH AFTER 1983

Numayri's two major policy moves of 1983—to revoke southern autonomy and implement his version of Islamic law—both had the same result in the south, increasing southern incentives to launch a new rebellion. Numayri must have anticipated this; his expectation was apparently that cooperation with the Islamists and picking a fight with the southerners would enable him to increase his political support through elite-led chauvinist mobilization. The idea was to rally the northern population behind the key symbols of Sudanese nationalism—shari'a, jihad against the south, and the status of religious leader for Numayri himself. The southerners, given their beliefs, would obviously fight back, but taking them on helped Numayri portray himself as an Islamic hero. Tim Niblock summarizes Numayri's strategy this way: "The political arena . . . became a theatre where the president could arrange spectacles . . . designed to distract the population from immediate economic problems and to weld together a shifting basis of proclaimed yet insubstantial support." Regarding the Islamist program, Khalid Duran notes, "Shari'a, most of which had long since fallen into oblivion, was turned by [the Muslim Brotherhood] into a chimerical remedy of all ills, a kind of Aladdin's wonderlamp."[88]

Numayri's support was "insubstantial" for the reasons we would expect from symbolic politics theory: because he was using the wrong frame for the situation (Hypothesis 4), he personally lacked credibility (Hypothesis 5), and he lacked a loyal organizational network. Certainly the foul-mouthed, formerly whiskey-swilling politician who had negotiated the peace was not plausible as a leader for jihad and symbol of Islamic piety. Tactical mistakes now eroded his position further. The September decree was drafted by radicals among his Sufi advisers, who ignored the draft that Attorney General Turabi's committee had been working on. Numayri thus alienated his allies in the Muslim Brotherhood without gaining any additional support. Sadiq al-Mahdi announced his opposition to Numayri's hasty move, resulting in his imprisonment and heightened opposition to Numayri among the Ansar.[89] Even Sudan's usually rubber-stamp Parliament, stocked with Numayri's erstwhile core supporters, refused to endorse the September Laws. Numayri was thus forced to declare a state of emergency in April 1984, and to put the Muslim Brotherhood in charge of special courts to implement the new Islamic laws.[90]

This increased reliance on the Brotherhood further weakened Numayri's position. The Brotherhood judges' attacks on corrupt high-ranking officials, in particular, undermined Numayri's support within his own government administration even as it gained popularity for the Islamist cause. Thus a 1984 march to welcome an International Islamic Conference turned into a demonstration for the Brotherhood in which Numayri was sidelined; one million people are estimated to have participated.[91] Numayri tried to exploit the initial popularity of the war against the south, using the official media to characterize the war as a jihad, but with limited success.[92] By the time he turned on the Brotherhood in 1985, sacking Turabi, Numayri had no supporters left; his own defense minister announced his ouster. Ultimately Numayri, the ersatz chauvinist, was outmaneuvered and replaced by real ones.

For our purposes, this last point is the key one: none of Numayri's successors—not the interim military regime, the subsequent civilian government, or General Bashir's long-lasting military dictatorship—reversed his policies toward shari'a and the war until two decades had passed. Some civilian politicians did try in the late 1980s, but the symbolic politics of Islam and protection against the south proved insurmountably powerful. These were the continuing effects projected by Hypotheses 2 through 4: prejudice increasing threat perceptions, and both prejudice and threat yielding support for hostile policies toward the south.

The long-term effect of Numayri's Islamist policies was to strengthen the intolerant strain in Sudan's identity narrative and the corresponding symbolic predispositions of many Sudanese. As Abdelwahab El-Affendi explains,

> The second phase of the implementation of Shariah in the context of the special courts gave Ikhwan [the Muslim Brotherhood] a major political and psychological boost. As Shariah was seen to be implemented with full seriousness, people knew that they had to reconcile themselves to it. . . .

Many turned to the study of Islamic texts. This compulsory Islamic education finally turned the language Ikhwan kept speaking in relative solitude
into the language of the majority, and . . . a great number of secularist (and
even left-wing) intellectuals started announcing their conversion to the path
of Islam.[93]

As soon as Numayri was gone in 1985, it quickly became apparent that
the Islamists had the upper hand. The Muslim Brotherhood was the first to
organize political rallies after Numayri's ouster, attracting thirty thousand
to forty thousand people to two rallies four days apart. One fiery speaker
shouted, "We will not make any compromise on the application of the *Shari'a*
and, if need be, we are prepared to die fighting to defend Islam!" A slogan
shouted by the crowd was, "No alternative to God's law!" In an interview,
Brotherhood leader Turabi directly threatened the interim regime: "The street
protests which overthrew Numayri can also topple anyone who tries to abolish the *Shari'a*"—though it is not clear that the Brotherhood had had much
to do with those protests.[94] Still, according to one analysis, "the threat to
northern cultural identity posed by the SPLA, including opposition to *shari'a*
demands, swelled the ranks of the NIF [National Islamic Front, led by the
Muslim Brotherhood]."[95]

Heeding the message, interim military leader Siwar al-Dhahab took the
position that "the Sudanese people had welcomed the Islamic laws except a
minority of southerners who had showed some reservations." Secularist pressure did not budge the interim leadership on this issue.[96] Though Ansar leader
Sadiq al-Mahdi made efforts to project a moderate image, substantively he
took the same line: "We call for the implementation of Islamic law in a correct
way." Khatmiyya sect leader Mohammed al-Mirghani took a similar view:
what was needed was "to correct the misconceptions in the *Shari'a* laws."[97]

By the time new elections were held in April 1986, the Islamist parties were
dominant, winning a combined total of 83 percent of seats in Parliament.
Sadiq al-Mahdi's "modern" Islamist appeal, combined with his base in
Sudan's largest religious sect, earned his Umma Party the biggest share of the
vote, gaining it 39 percent of seats. Next were Mirghani's DUP with 24 percent
of the seats, and the Muslim Brotherhood's NIF with 20 percent. Regional
parties won the rest, except for the Communist Party's 1 percent take.[98] This
evidence is not precise: the election system was first-past-the-post, so well-
organized and large parties were overrepresented, while smaller parties were
underrepresented, and most of the south was unable to vote at all. But one
conclusion is clear: virtually the only victors were those who made identity
appeals, either Islamist or regional.

Symbolic politics around Sudan's Arab identity was also important. After
the ouster of Numayri, it was revealed that his government had cooperated
with Israel in evacuating Ethiopia's Jews, the Falashas, to Israel. The revela-
tion provoked a political firestorm: the Sudanese News Agency launched a

detailed investigation of this "dirty operation," and the transitional government launched a legal probe.[99] Sadiq al-Mahdi denounced it as "high treason," asserting that the issue of Palestine was the most important issue for all Arabs.[100] An ex–foreign minister went further, averring, "The Sudanese people will never forgive the deposed Numayri for his pan-Arab treason."[101] Considering the complex issues of regime transition facing Sudan at the time, it is striking that so much attention was devoted to this purely symbolic issue.

Most importantly, however, the politics of protection proved an insuperable obstacle to a quick end to the war in the south, despite prominent efforts toward peace. In March 1986, the secularist National Gathering for the Salvation of the Homeland sponsored a meeting between northern and SPLM leaders that resulted in the so-called Koka Dam Agreement, which provided for a compromise peace and the repeal of the September Laws.[102] The Umma Party endorsed the agreement, but Umma leader Sadiq al-Mahdi refused to push through a true repeal, which was vehemently denounced by the DUP and the NIF. Instead, al-Mahdi pushed through a mild revision in keeping with his idea of a "correct" Islamic law, for which he was denounced by left and right: southerners complained that the revisions did nothing to address their concerns, while the Brotherhood repeated its slogan, "No replacement for God's legislation!"[103]

Faced with this storm, al-Mahdi quickly tacked to the right, appointing Brotherhood leader Turabi to draft a new revision of the Islamic legal code, whereupon DUP leader Muhammad Uthman al-Mirghani tacked the other way. Abandoning his previous opposition to the Koka Dam Agreement, Mirghani cut his own deal with the SPLM in November 1988.[104] Upon his return Mirghani was proclaimed a hero and given strong popular support; one of the slogans in his favor said simply, "Against hunger . . . against war."[105] However, the NIF mobilized some one hundred thousand people to protest against Mirghani's agreement to freeze application of shari'a.[106] Prime Minister al-Mahdi dithered, unwilling to abandon his NIF allies; when he finally bent to the pressure and stopped the move toward shari'a, he was answered by riots by NIF supporters screaming for "God's Law." When that pressure failed to stop the move toward peace and suspension of the September laws, the NIF sponsored the June 1989 coup led by Brigadier General Umar al-Bashir.[107] The prospect for peace was dead for a decade.

Mobilization Processes in the South

ORGANIZATION AND THE SPLA'S GROUND WAR

Since the southern rebellion began secretly, as a mutiny, the south's political ground war began before its air war. As we would expect from Hypothesis 6, the spread of the conflict largely followed the expansion of the SPLA's organizational network. The first serious trouble in the south led to the 1975 start of the Anyanya II rebellion, but there had been aborted mutinies even in 1973–1974. By 1980, the ragtag Anyanya II rebellion had gained significant strength as a result of backing from Ethiopia.[108] Serious planning for the new war seems to have begun when Anyanya II leader Akwot Atem got in touch with key southern officers still in the Sudanese military. Atem's key co-conspirators included Colonel John Garang, who had recently returned from studies in the United States, and Major Kerubino Kuanyin Bol (also a Dinka), a commander in the southern 105th Battalion, as well as leaders of previous aborted uprisings such as Samuel Gai Tut (a Nuer), who had been forced out of the military. It was these leaders, linked by their experience serving together in the previous war, who planned and executed the May 1983 mutinies that marked the real start of the second war. As part of the planning, Garang had secretly formed the SPLM the month before and written its manifesto.[109]

Ironically, the persistent Sudanese government discrimination against southerners even in peacetime made the rebels' task of expanding their organizational network easier in some ways. For example, with somewhere between one-sixth and one-third of the country's population, the south had only about 7 percent of secondary schools by the 1980–1981 school year, and for seven of the eight years from 1976 to 1983, fewer than 1 percent of students admitted to Khartoum University were from the south.[110] Southern military officers were similarly excluded: while the Addis Ababa Agreement had promised one-third of all admissions to Sudan's Military College would be southerners, the actual total between 1974 and 1982 was only 5 percent.[111] These facts meant that on the one hand, the educated elite among southerners was a relatively small group bound together by a relatively dense network of social ties—they all went to one of a few schools. On the other hand, southern elites—civilian or military; Dinka, Nuer, or Equatorian— shared a similar experience of mistreatment that motivated them to join the SPLA and SPLM once contacted by others in their social network.

The SPLA's ground war, a literal one starting in 1983, escalated with the aid of arms from Libya and material support from Ethiopia. Critically, the support from Ethiopia included promoting—some said imposing—a unified leadership on the SPLM-SPLA, with Garang ending up on top, and Atem and Gai Tut marginalized because of Ethiopian opposition to their secessionist goals.[112] After some initial small military actions, the SPLA sent out recruiting expeditions widely across the south, especially in Upper Nile Province near their Ethiopian bases. The organization also claimed a network of local cells across the south that aided in its organizational efforts. Moving beyond that base of support, the SPLA also embarked on a systematic campaign to persuade the various factions of Anyanya II across all three southern provinces: most heeded the call, but a few switched sides and began backing the Sudanese government.[113]

According to the analysis of Douglas Johnson and Gerard Prunier, the SPLA's strength was at first concentrated in areas most opposed to the division of the south, especially Nuer around the oil region of Bentiu, and Dinka and Nuer areas in eastern Bahr al-Ghazal and eastern Upper Nile. However, dissident Dinka politicians were successful in keeping it out of some areas in Bahr al-Ghazal, while in Upper Nile Province, the mid-1980s governor D. K. Matthews worked with his own Gaajak Nuer supporters and with dissident Anyanya II groups to oppose the SPLA. In Equatoria Province, which had supported division of the south, the SPLA did not gain a significant foothold until the late 1980s. It was only increasing brutality by the government army that slowly persuaded the peoples of Equatoria that the SPLA was the lesser evil.[114]

THE SPLM'S AIR WAR

Garang and the SPLM leadership understood that they needed foreign support and that they would not get it for a separatist cause. They therefore framed their cause in their July 1983 manifesto as "the liberation of the whole Sudan, . . . the unity of its people and its territorial integrity." Other key points in that manifesto were explicitly liberal, calling for "a democratic Sudan in which equality, freedom, economic and social justice and respect for human rights are . . . concrete realities." Similarly, it called for secularism; regional autonomy; equal economic development; and opposition to racism, tribalism, and provincialism. Garang's more emotive points included denouncing the government's policy of forcibly repatriating internal migrants back to their areas of origin in the west, south, and elsewhere; and a stated determination that "Sudan shall never again be the sickly and degenerate dwarf of the Arab world nor the starving bastard child of Africa."[115]

Garang and the SPLM also used, as we would expect from Hypothesis 5, frames of social and physical threat to justify their rebellion, often playing to major themes in southern national narratives to get their symbolic appeals to resonate. One of the main themes was southern victimization, which the SPLM recast into a broader threat frame depicting victimization of all Sudanese peoples by corrupt regimes. Garang justified armed resistance by arguing, "Peaceful struggle has always been met with ruthless suppression and callous killing of our beloved people." He sometimes highlighted the southern experience, for example, noting, "The general exploitation, oppression and neglect of the Sudanese people . . . took peculiar forms in the southern third of our country."[116] Garang's colleague Joseph Oduho expanded on this theme in a 1984 radio broadcast, denouncing discrimination in Numayri's development policy: "All this money [for development] is concentrated in the already over-developed parts of the Sudan. Not a bit of this money has been given to raise the standard of living . . . of the people of western Sudan, of eastern Sudan and even for south Sudan for that matter."[117] As a contrast, the SPLM's program emphasized equal development and "libera-tion." In his statement at Koka Dam, Garang gave a homely illustration of what he meant: "In our villages, people have to walk over twenty miles to bring water in tins carried on the head . . . if we reduce this distance . . . to some few yards, we call this liberation."[118]

While SPLM rhetoric did not refer explicitly to slavery, many of its themes are best understood against the background narrative of past resistance to northern discrimination. For example, two of the four slogans Garang men-tioned in a March 1984 speech were "autonomy" and "religious freedom"; the next year, he emphasized "liberation," "equality," "freedom," "respect for human rights," and the need to "fight racism." In the 1985 speech he sim-ilarly asserted, "The SPLA is determined to fight for a democratic and new Sudan where social justice, freedom and human dignity for all flourish," and for a Sudan "free from racism."[119] Garang expanded on the theme of oppo-sition to racism in his 1986 Koka Dam statement. Contesting a statement by Sadiq al-Mahdi, accusing the SPLA of wanting a "Sudan of negroid non-Arab origin," Garang replied, "Negroid origin and non-Arab origin, we are a good mix of people; Arab blood runs in some of us. Let us make this cocktail into a viable country, Sudan."[120]

A third theme in SPLM rhetoric, amplifying the key issue of social threat, was resistance to shari'a and forced Islamization. In a 1984 radio interview, for example, Kerubino Kuanyin Bol charged that Numayri "has made himself [into] a Muslim fanatic." In contrast, Kuanyin asserted, "Our ide-ology and our principle are clear; that everybody in the Sudan is indepen-dent in his own religion. Nobody forces a religion." His colleague Joseph Oduho amplified both points in a broadcast the next day. First, he asserted, "Shari'ah law was not, as Numayri claimed, established to purify the Sudanese society. Shari'ah law was actually intended to facilitate and to intensify . . . the Islamisation of non-Muslim areas." In contrast, he said, "The SPLM aims at . . . guarantees for freedom of religious beliefs and right of worship for all Sudanese. . . . Abolish the Shari'ah law and re-establish the Sudanese secular law."[121] After al-Mahdi became prime minister, Garang had a clearer target on this issue, denouncing al-Mahdi's assertion, "The southern Sudan will inevitably be Islamized and Arabized." In response to another northern politician's offer to discuss which aspects of shari'a he agreed or disagreed with, Garang responded pithily in the same speech: "We don't agree with any of it, plain and simple."[122]

Shari'a remained a key symbolic issue for the SPLM, and its repeal a ma-jor demand.[123] Indeed, it was probably the strongest motivation for south-ern resistance and for southern unity. For example, even Joseph Lagu, whom Numayri had made vice president, denounced its introduction, noting in December 1983, "The proclamation of Islamic law has brought the South together. . . . There are no differences on this issue."[124] Oduho agreed, commenting, "Equatoria . . . was quite unwilling . . . to join the war on the problem of division [of the South] alone, because Equatoria said it wanted division." However, "Equatoria is the most Christian province . . . in the Sudan," so "when the Shari'ah law was also introduced . . . they felt very strongly against" it, ultimately joining the rebellion.[125]

In pursuing his politics of protection, Garang was very clear in calling for war to protect his people. His 1983 manifesto stated,

> In proclaiming and pursuing the objectives I have just mentioned, we have no illusions about the abhorrent nature of the regime we are fighting. We are fighting a one-man rule, a dictator who is clinging to power by means of use of savage repression, torture, . . . and murder of innocent citizens. . . . We are aware that our objectives can neither be asked from nor negotiated with the minority and decaying regime in Khartoum. We are mentally and physically prepared to *fight a long war* [emphasis in original] in order to completely destroy all the institutions of oppression.

Garang repeatedly returned to this effort at demonizing the Numayri regime, accusing it of a "morbid campaign of hate and distortion," of "evil intentions," and so on. He concluded, "I assure the Sudanese people that the SPLA-SPLM shall never let them down."[126]

Subsequent speeches by Garang and his SPLA colleagues emphasized the theme of protection by celebrating SPLA military victories, attempting to hammer home the point that the SPLA-SPLM was actively working to protect people from the regime's depredations and that the Sudanese people should join the fight. Kuanyin, for example, began his November 1984 radio interview with an account of military victories won by his battalion, and concluded with this call: "It's better that all the Sudanese nation get up and fight for their rights to be free people like other people in different parts of the world."[127]

Southern leaders explicitly recognized the importance of symbolic mobilization to build popular support for their cause. As one southern leader, Peter Adwok Nyaba, phrased it, "The minds and hearts of the people of South Sudan . . . will only be stirred into action by fundamental ideas, images and feelings rooted deeply in their past."[128] Garang's rhetoric embodied a sophisticated strategy to do so, using terms such as *liberation, equality,* and *freedom* to function simultaneously as code words for anti-Arab sentiment in the south and as a basis for building a broader coalition for a "New Sudan" in other regions.[129]

Security Dilemma in Sudan

By 1983 a security dilemma had emerged in Sudan, but it was of the sort that Jack Snyder and Robert Jervis identify as a predation-driven security dilemma.[130] Numayri provoked the war by attempting to subjugate the south politically, breaking up the southern autonomous region, imposing shari'a, and trying to disarm and transfer southern military units. Unwilling to surrender on all of these issues, many southerners felt compelled to defend themselves and returned to guerrilla war.

Given that Numayri had been trying for two years to break up the autonomous southern region and had been moving toward shari'a even longer, there is little reason to believe that southerners were uncertain about his intentions by 1983. Neither is there evidence to suggest that they expected a quick victory; Garang's speeches instead expressed determination to persevere in a long struggle.[131] Similarly, after his experience negotiating the 1972 Addis Ababa Agreement—and after a series of small mutinies by southern troops in the years that followed—Numayri can have been in little doubt about the near-certainty of a violent southern response. Once Numayri's predatory motives became clear, the security dilemma went into operation for the southerners—anything they did to protect themselves merely provoked Numayri more. Southern soldiers began refusing orders, Numayri sent northern troops to suppress them, and the southerners returned to guerrilla war.[132] Having fought in the previous war, Numayri can hardly have expected a quick victory in this one. Thus while there was a security dilemma in Sudan, it was driven not by uncertainty but by southern certainty about northern hostility.

Conclusion

It is tempting to blame Sudan's civil wars on bloody-minded military leaders. Savage repression by General Abboud's regime in 1958–1964 was what provoked the start of the Anyanya rebellion in the early 1960s, and Colonel Numayri's revocation of the south's autonomy and imposition of shari'a were what sparked the emergence of the SPLA in the mid-1980s. Furthermore, Numayri's actions—his "reconciliation" with al-Mahdi and Ansar, his alliance with the Muslim Brotherhood, and his subsequent efforts to steal the constituency of both—were transparently aimed at increasing and securing his own power. On the southern side, the core of each rebel group was formed by dissident southern soldiers and officers who mutinied before the start of each rebellion. At first glance, therefore, the "bad leaders" theory of ethnic war seems to explain the case.

What this theory does not explain, however, is what came after each rebellion began. In both the mid-1960s and mid-1980s (especially the earlier case), the military dictators were succeeded by interim military regimes that temporarily softened policy toward the south. It was the 1964–1965 interim regime, for example, that closed General Abboud's torture centers in the south. More importantly, in each case the transitional military regime was succeeded after one year by a popularly elected civilian government that then escalated the conflict further. If the problem was bloody-minded soldiers, why did not elected civilians improve the situation? Furthermore, why did Numayri—who had settled the first war by negotiating the Addis Ababa Agreement—turn into the bloody-minded soldier who provoked the second one? Why did he think that, if his power was tottering in large part because of a calamitous economic situation, that power could be stabilized by initiating a bloody and expensive civil war?

Symbolic politics theory can provide the answer, starting with the narratives and symbolic predispositions that underlay Sudanese politics in both north and south (Hypotheses 1 and 2). In the north, political discourse was traditionally Islamist discourse, and nationalism was defined in terms of an Arab and Muslim identity. Symbolic predispositions toward the south were hostile, framed in terms of either a racist sense of superiority or a sense of religious obligation to redeem the south from its pagan ignorance. Southerners' expression of a different identity was seen as a threat either to northerners' identity or to Sudan's unity. These feelings of hostility and threat motivated support for discriminatory policies (Hypotheses 3 and 4) like the imposition of shari'a and pursuit of war against the south.

In this context, leaders in the north consistently acted on the assumption that Hypothesis 5 was accurate—that is, that maintaining public support required adopting assertive frames in accordance with those public sentiments. Control of the state and of the army provided a constant temptation for them to do so, while the Islamists' control of mass organizations created a strong incentive (Hypothesis 6). In rural areas, the only real mass organizations were sectarian ones belonging to Ansar and Khatmiyya; in the cities, the Muslim Brotherhood consistently out-organized leftist rivals, in large part because of the resonance of their identity appeals.

All of this fed into southern inclinations to fight back. Southerners shared historical memories of past victimization by northerners, which (Hypothesis 1) seem to have fostered SYPs hostile to the north. Those SYPs led southerners to quickly identify the threat posed by Numayri's imposition of shari'a and support countervailing action (Hypotheses 2 through 4). Rebellion was feasible because of the organizational assets the rebels possessed: the ex-Anyanya military structures, social ties among southern elites, territorial concentration, and foreign support (Hypothesis 6).

This background of narratives, symbolic predispositions, and organization explains not only why military leaders like Abboud and Numayri initiated civil wars but also why civilian successors like al-Mahdi were unable to halt them. During the mid-1960s period, for example, Abel Alier later recalled, "The fever for an Islamic constitution was high. . . . Even leaders . . . who had long looked for a secular state, were impelled to support the demand."[133] Needless to say, this push impeded the peace efforts of the time. Twenty years later, Numayri's economic hopelessness made a turn to symbolic Islamist appeals his only option for maintaining power—by first allying himself with Islamists, then trying to steal their supporters.

Yet once the war had begun and shari'a had been imposed, Numayri's successor al-Mahdi was trapped. A religious leader himself, he was unwilling to be seen as the man who repealed Islamic law, especially when faced with pressure from Islamist opponents. After five years of civil war, an exhausted public was prepared by 1988 to support Mirghani's proposed peace deal with the SPLM, but even then the Brotherhood's organizational edge and ideological power—"no alternative to God's law!"—enabled it first to delay the repeal of shari'a and then to derail peace by supporting Bashir's military coup. The mid-1980s prominence of the issue of past aid to the Falasha Jews further illustrates the importance of symbolic politics: Sudanese had more important things to worry about at this time, notably a war and a collapsing economy, yet this issue of "pan-Arab treason" nevertheless grabbed the nation's attention.

The south, for its part, was repeatedly offered only the cruelest of options. Not consulted at the nation's founding, it was quickly subordinated to the northern Arab riverine elite. General Abboud's forced campaign of Islamization and Arabization could be answered only by submission or violent resistance; the result was hundreds of thousands of dead. The Addis Ababa Agreement allowed for peace, but many southern leaders approached it with deep doubts about the reliability of their northern partner—doubts that would be more than amply justified in 1983. External aid made it possible for southern armies to fight government soldiers to a stalemate, but often not to protect civilian southerners from war's violence. In that context, when the politicians failed, southern soldiers did what soldiers do: they fought. Northern brutality, past and continuing, made it easy for rebel leaders to gain political support from their battered people, even when their own brutalities began to rival those of the northerners. In the end, the result was independence for South Sudan, but even that did not guarantee a happy ending as ethnic violence soon flared between the new state's largest ethnic groups, the Dinka and the Nuer. Those two groups' mutually hostile SYPs had been reinforced, not attenuated, by savagery of decades of war during which Nuer, especially, could often be found on both sides.

Ethnic War and Genocide in Rwanda

Even considered decades later, the Rwanda genocide remains shocking. Sparked by the April 1994 death of President Juvenal Habyarimana, a depraved group of coup plotters hijacked the Rwandan government and army under the noses of a UN peacekeeping force and carried out a carefully planned mass slaughter of unprecedented speed. In only about three months, somewhere between half a million and one million people were brutally massacred, many of them hacked down with machetes by their own neighbors or even spouses. While the bulk of victims were members of the minority Tutsi ethnic group, killed merely because of their ethnic (or, as Rwandans said, "racial") label, upward of one hundred thousand members of the Hutu majority were also killed. In its rate of killing, the Rwandan genocide surpassed even the Holocaust.[1]

It is impossible to ignore the stunningly ineffective international response to these events: instead of reinforcing its peacekeeping force, the United Nations chose to withdraw most of it as the killing accelerated. Nevertheless, the focus of this chapter is on the causes of the genocide itself and of the ethnic civil war that led up to it. The Rwandan case presents in an especially stark way the question of why ethnic violence happens. Besides being glaring examples of human evil, genocides are usually self-destructive as well. The Armenian genocide during World War I, for example, prompted the U.S. ambassador to wonder why the perpetrators, the Ottoman Turkish government, were acting in ways that seemed almost willfully to undermine their war effort. The Holocaust similarly deprived the Nazi state of valuable human capital in wartime and diverted scarce resources of manpower, railroad capacity, and materiel from their life-and-death struggle against the Soviet army and other opponents.

Yet even in comparison with these earlier cases, the Rwandan genocide stands out as being uniquely suicidal. The genocidaire leaders knew that their civil war enemy, the Rwandan Patriotic Front (RPF), was militarily stronger than their own army, yet they still carried out the genocide in defiance of RPF warnings. In fact, they scattered most of their army around the

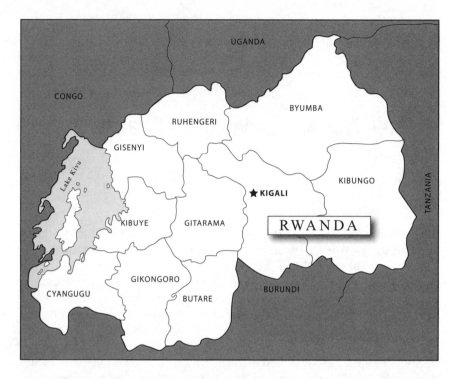

country to carry out the genocide while the RPF rebel advance rolled ahead. In just three months, the RPF had forced them and their supporters into exile in squalid refugee camps. What possessed these people to focus on the slaughter of harmless innocents while their main enemy was destroying their regime? Why did the army and the civilian administration carry out their insane orders? How did these murderous local officials gain the collaboration of the majority of the population, inducing many to wield machetes against their neighbors?

The best way to think about this question is from the perspective of symbolic politics. The most important factor that made the genocide possible was the symbolic predispositions of the population, and even more of the ruling elite. Rwandan culture had for decades been pervaded with narratives that promoted stereotypes of Tutsis as evil and dangerous; it also offered previous examples of the massacre of Tutsis as a response to social threats. The result was strong prejudice that was turned in a genocidal direction by openly racist propaganda in the early 1990s. The factors that turned the possibility of slaughter into a program were the threat from the Tutsi-led RPF, and the organizations the extremist leaders created to carry out their plans. In sum, the genocide happened mostly because Rwanda's Hutu leaders were maddened by prejudice and fear, and they controlled organizations that could implement their insane ideas.

All other considerations are details that follow from this basic insight. For example, the opportunity perspective focuses on the facts that the RPF leaders saw the chance to invade in 1990, and the genocidaires saw the chance to launch a coup and carry out genocide, so both groups seized their opportunities.[2] This is of course true, but the reason the RPF existed in the first place was because prejudiced Rwandan governments had for thirty years refused to allow Tutsi refugees to return home, so forming the RPF and launching an armed invasion was the Tutsis' only option. The related rationalist explanation is that the genocidaires saw genocide as a "rational" policy to achieve their goals, especially holding on to power.[3] But this is true only according to an absurdly broad definition of rationality: obviously the genocidaires believed this, but only because they were blinded by fear and prejudice as well as greed for power. The genocide was only "rational" to someone convinced that unarmed and unorganized Tutsi civilians posed a more urgent threat than a superior RPF army poised to attack. Both were merely the "Tutsi" enemy, *inyenzi* in the Kinyarwanda language, or cockroaches, and wiping out as many as possible was ultimately more important to the genocidaires than staying in power. If this is "rational," it is so only if one accepts insane preferences as rational.

A better argument is that of Lee Ann Fuji, who takes a mobilization approach, showing that the way the genocide played out on the ground was the result of organizational factors—the local ties on which grassroots organizations were built and the group dynamics that animated them. This also is true as far as it goes, but Fuji rejects any role for prejudice or fear, writing, "Proponents of the ethnic hatred and ethnic fear theses expect ordinary people to participate in campaigns of mass violence out of overwhelming fears or hatreds of the targeted group."[4] Fuji is wrong here: as we have seen, the effects of prejudice and fear are not to overwhelm people with emotional passion, but to bias their thinking in favor of supporting aggressive or hostile actions toward another group, and there is a great deal of evidence that such biases were operating in Rwanda, motivating people to join or support extremist organizations.

The symbolic politics argument is that all three of these arguments are right and that they make the most sense together—with due attention to leaders' frames added—because they all explain different parts of the process. Hostile ethnic narratives and prejudices were widespread, leading to pervasive prejudice against Tutsis. The RPF invasion and other events raised Hutus' threat perceptions. Extremist national leaders then promoted racist propaganda that stoked popular hostility toward Tutsis, including the view that all Tutsis were "the enemy" and that genocide was the proper response. The prejudice and fear were important in making those extremist frames resonate, motivating more and more elites and ordinary people to join the growing extremist camp. Later, the extremist leaders took power in a coup, giving them control of the national-level organizations that powered the genocide. It was this combination of prejudice, fear, and national leadership that created the context in which Fuji's local-level organizations acted to carry out the genocide.

The chapter proceeds as follows. The first section provides background on the two main groups and their histories. The next section details the extraordinary collection of hostile group narratives developed by Tutsis and Hutus against each other and the hostile symbolic predispositions and threat perceptions that resulted. The following section traces in detail the path to war and genocide, considering the rise of extremist leaders and the growth of extremist organizations on both sides, shifts in threat perceptions and SYPs, the genocidaires' hostile framing in their "air war," the organizational muscle deployed in their genocidal "ground war," and the nature of the security dilemma that resulted from all of these factors. The conclusion summarizes the insights this approach gives us into the horrific puzzle of genocide.

The Groups and Their Histories

Rwanda's population is divided into three groups, the Hutu majority (historically about 87 percent of the population), the Tutsi minority (12.5 percent), and the Twa (0.5 percent). All three groups speak the same language, profess the same range of Christian religious beliefs (mostly Catholic), and share the same culture in most other respects; thus they lack the distinctions that mark off most ethnic groups. There is a stereotypical physical difference, with Hutus seen as typically shorter and stockier, and with broader noses, than the Tutsis, and both much taller than the Twa. Many Rwandans do not resemble their ethnic stereotypes, however, and any difference in height between Hutus and Tutsis is attributed by some experts to diet, not different ancestors. If the Tutsis were later migrants to the region, as the standard narrative claims, no one knows when they arrived, with estimates ranging from the tenth century to the fifteenth.[5]

What is certain is that the Rwandan monarchy had existed and entrenched itself long before the European colonialists arrived. According to one estimate, the first Rwandan king or *mwami* probably ruled a small part of Rwanda in the fifteenth century, and the kingdom's military expansion began two centuries later.[6] During the better-attested reign of the centralizing mwami Kigeri Rwabugiri, starting around 1860, the mwami "began, or consolidated, a process of ethnic polarization" based primarily on cattle and land ownership—that is, on wealth, not race: the rich and powerful cattle-owners were codified as Tutsi, most others as Hutu.[7] Rwabugiri also imposed a system of corvee labor, requiring all Hutus to work for their chiefs for one day out of every five. The administrative system for each area included a Hutu chief who controlled and taxed the land and the Hutus, a Tutsi chief who controlled and taxed the Tutsis and the cattle, and a military chief. By this time, social mobility between Hutus and Tutsis was minimal.[8]

German colonialists arrived in the 1890s and helped the mwamis to expand their power in exchange for their loyalty to Germany. The mwami became the "sole proprietor of cattle and land."[9] The aristocratic German officials admired the "proud reserve" of the Tutsis so, applying the European racist thinking of the time, they defined the difference between Hutus and Tutsis as one between an inferior and a superior race. Belgian rule after World War I was even more hierarchical, solidifying both the Belgians' own control and the Tutsis' control over Hutus. The Belgians replaced the three-headed administrative system in each region with a single Tutsi chief, increased the demand for corvee labor from one day out of five to two or even more, and replaced the mwami in 1931.[10] At the same time, the Belgians promoted western education among the Tutsi while sharply limiting access for Hutus: as late as 1945, there were forty-six Tutsi students at the Astrida college in Butare, but only three Hutu students.[11]

After World War II, under UN pressure, the Belgian authorities did an about-face, instituting policies to "end feudalism" and introduce democratic institutions.[12] A more sympathetic set of clergymen offered education to ambitious Hutus, and also gave them access to the clerical press. These changes enabled the publication in March 1957 of the Bahutu Manifesto, penned by Gregoire Kayibanda, which denounced Tutsi domination and called for democracy and the promotion of opportunity for the Hutus. Political change, however, was slow until 1959, when the Belgians announced plans to turn Rwanda into a constitutional monarchy and to hold elections.

Political parties now began forming, primarily pitting hard-line royalists against Kayibanda's Party of the Movement for Hutu Emancipation (Parmehutu). Violence erupted in November 1959, as a few royalist attacks on Hutu leaders sparked a massive backlash led by Parmehutu activists. This atmosphere of violence and polarization set the context for local elections in June–July 1960, which Parmehutu won massively, if not freely or fairly. The abuses of the Hutu burgomasters who now took power motivated all the other parties to form a "communal front" against Parmehutu's "racist" and "dictatorial regime" in November 1960, while royalist leaders in exile began launching terrorist attacks.

Fearing the rising backlash against them, Parmehutu leaders seized power in the "Coup d'État of Gitarama" in January 1961, forming a new government led by Kayibanda as prime minister, who went on to sweep national elections in September 1961. Extremist royalist émigrés now stepped up their military efforts, pledging to be as numerous and difficult to stamp out as cockroaches (*inyenzi*). Their biggest effort, however, the December 1963 "Bugesera invasion," quickly failed and sparked a series of massacres in which about ten thousand Tutsis are estimated to have died. Another wave of Tutsi refugees now fled the country, while the Hutu majority united behind the previously ramshackle regime. The opposition politicians in government were shot, and the government became a one-party state. Overall, the violence of the independence period is estimated to have resulted in some thirty thousand Tutsis being killed and over three hundred thousand driven into exile.[13]

The next round of violence began in mid-1972, in response to the massacre of between one hundred thousand and two hundred thousand Hutus in neighboring Burundi, "the first clear genocide since the Holocaust."[14] Kayibanda organized vigilante committees to protect against any Tutsi resurgence in Rwanda, trying to unite the Hutu majority behind himself. Few Tutsis died, but many fled in yet another wave of refugees. The tension eased when the army chief, Major General Juvenal Habyarimana, led a military coup that displaced Kayibanda. Habyarimana, a northerner, now created a new regime that would channel economic benefits to his own and his wife's home districts in northern Rwanda, reversing the flow that had previously gone to Kayibanda's political base in the south. The new regime made the policy of discrimination against Tutsis slightly gentler—they were permitted to prosper in private business—but more systematic. Tutsis were barred from the military, and allowed only 9 percent of places in school, reflecting the regime's claim about their share of the population. Intelligence agents investigated the backgrounds of candidates for responsible jobs to ensure that no Tutsi succeeded in "passing" as a Hutu.[15]

Habyarimana also systematically discriminated against Tutsis in refugee policy, welcoming Hutu refugees from Burundi in 1988 and 1993 but steadfastly refusing to allow Tutsi refugees from Rwanda to return. When Ugandan dictator Milton Obote forcibly expelled a group of Tutsis back to Rwanda in the 1980s, the Rwandan government kept them in guarded camps, eventually forcing them back into Uganda.[16] Habyarimana's rationale was that Rwanda was too overpopulated and did not have room to accommodate the Tutsi exiles.[17]

Narratives, Symbolic Predispositions, and Fears

TUTSI GROUP NARRATIVES

Experts differ about the nature of the difference between the Hutu and the Tutsi. German and Belgian officials called it a "racial" difference, the scholar Rene Lemarchand defined them as "castes," and some other scholars see them more as social classes. Without disagreeing with any of those labels, however, the Hutu-Tutsi distinction also fits my definition of an ethnic distinction, especially because both groups adopted narratives asserting that they were separate "imagined families," and there was evidence of "extensive endogamy" among Twas and elite Tutsis.[18] And because the government treated the difference as not only inherited but unchangeable, the notion of a "racial" difference became a social fact, in exactly the same way that Jews were defined as a racial group in Nazi Germany.

The belief in a "racial" distinction was reinforced by a profusion of myths and narratives asserting Tutsi superiority. As Lemarchand notes, "Rwanda is unique in the sheer abundance of traditions purporting to show the superiority of the Tutsi over other castes." Many of these myths define Rwanda's three groups as imagined families by referring to eponymous ancestors of each. According to one of them, Rwanda's first king, Kigwa, who had descended from heaven, had three sons, Gatwa, Gahutu, and Gatutsi. He decided to test them by assigning them each to watch over a pot of milk for a night. Gatwa drank his milk, and Gahutu spilled his; only Gatutsi carried out his father's instructions. As a result, the story goes, the king made Gatutsi his successor, Gahutu the serf, and Gatwa a pariah—a divinely established social order.[19]

An alternative Tutsi myth denied even this asymmetrical kinship, asserting instead a Tutsi right of domination earned through conquest. According to a Tutsi text from the 1950s, for example, Kigwa's Tutsi ancestors "conquered the lands of the Bahutu by slaying their kings and have thus enslaved the Bahutu."[20] Another myth bluntly asserts Tutsi superiority by claiming that when God invited all the people to drink from a pitcher of beer that provided intelligence, the king drank the most, followed by Gatutsi, who left little of the beer remaining. Gahutu then finished the pitcher, leaving none for Gatwa or the women.[21] Racist and sexist ideals such as these were taught in Rwandan schools in the 1920s and 1930s.[22]

As Lemarchand observes, "kingship was the focal point around which mythical imagery clustered" in Rwanda.[23] The mwami was surrounded by elaborate ceremonies. The central royalist claim was that the Rwandan social structure was divinely ordained, as demonstrated in the myth of the divine king Kigwa and the pots of milk. The king was portrayed as the incarnation of a god, so any rebellion was not only treason but sacrilege as well. The less savory aspects of Tutsi domination, and its origins, were illustrated by a key symbol of the king's power: the *Kalinga*, a ceremonial drum decorated with the testicles of defeated Hutu princes.[24]

Europeans developed their own pseudo-scientific racist theories that dovetailed cleanly with Tutsi beliefs. The most important of these was the "Hamitic hypothesis," named for the biblical son of Noah. According to this notion, African kingdoms such as Rwanda's were founded by a superior race of conquerors (the descendants of Ham) who came from Ethiopia or even farther north and "conquered the Hutu and the Twa because of their superior civilization akin to Europe's."[25] The Belgian administrator Pierre Ryckmans, for example, wrote matter-of-factly, "The Batutsi were meant to reign," and referred to the Hutus and Twas as "inferior races."[26] All Rwandans educated under colonial rule learned this Hamitic hypothesis, and the Rwandan priest Alexis Kagame wove it into the narrative of his book, *The Triumphant Kalinga*, which glorified the monarchy.[27] As a result of this education, "even the 'small Tutsi,' who did not benefit from the system in any way, started to believe that they were indeed a superior race."[28] What they gained was status.

For those Tutsis who fled into exile after the Hutu takeover, their Rwandan Tutsi identity became even stronger in exile, as social barriers distinguishing different Tutsi social groups evaporated. Their mythology mellowed into a reinterpretation of precolonial Rwanda as a harmonious society with substantial social mobility between poorer Hutus and richer Tutsis, into which ethnic divisions were inserted by the colonialists.[29]

HUTU GROUP NARRATIVES

On the Hutu side, leaders of the 1959 "democratic revolution" did not reject the Tutsi Rwandan ideology; instead, they "merely inverted its sign." Thus they agreed that the Tutsis were invaders from afar, but took that to mean the Tutsis were aliens whose presence was illegitimate. "Traditional" Tutsi rule, in this mythology, was a "cruel and . . . oppressive tyranny" that had enslaved the Hutus. Thus Gregoire Kayibanda, the future Rwandan president, wrote in the "Bahutu Manifesto," "The problem is basically that of the political monopoly of one race, the Mututsi . . . which condemns the desperate Bahutu to be for ever subaltern workers."[30] To the Hutus, the *Kalinga* drum, with its decoration of Hutu testicles, was a particularly effective symbol of what Tutsi rule meant: bloody emasculation.

Reversing the logic of the "natural" Tutsi right to rule, the new Hutu elite suggested that it was legitimate simply because it was Hutu. The denigration of the Tutsis soon escalated into dehumanization: the label that the Tutsi guerrilla fighters in the 1960s had adopted, *inyenzi*, or cockroaches, was used against them to suggest that the Tutsis deserved to die. During the December 1963 crisis, the local prefect in Gikongoro was reported to have said, "We are expected to defend ourselves. . . . How? [The Tutsis] must be killed."[31] Five thousand of them were killed in Gikongoro alone at this time, among the ten thousand killed nationwide. Kayibanda protected the guilty officials from punishment, and this murderous prefect was elected to the National Assembly in 1965.[32] In the aftermath of the violence, Kayibanda asserted that it was "caused by the . . . *inyenzi*. . . . If you resist the wisdom of democracy, you can blame no one."[33]

In the aftermath of the 1963–1964 violence, the central regime narrative became one glorifying the revolution as embodying the benefits of democracy and the end of feudalism. Anasthase Makuza, then president of the National Assembly of Rwanda, articulated this narrative as follows:

As soon as the Hutu became aware of the atrocities perpetrated in Bugesera, they understood the great danger of returning to prior circumstances. They remembered the abuse they had endured under feudal rule. They glanced at the scars the Tutsi regime had left on their bodies. They remembered hard labour, the contempt they withstood and the practice by which a Tutsi could ask another to lend him a Hutu to murder. They then felt a great anger . . . intensified by the fact that the former servant had, for four years, experienced the flavourful treats of democracy.[34]

After the violence receded, the threat narrative was used less often, but a system of discrimination against Tutsis was put into place. Kayibanda thus shifted from a violent politics of protection to a politics of nonviolent mobilization for ongoing redistribution.

Under Habyarimana, at least before 1990, overtly hostile rhetoric was replaced by the use of code words to refer to Tutsis. For example, Habyarimana stigmatized job-seeking Tutsis as people with a "feudal mentality" and "those who refuse to work," the latter playing on stereotypes of Tutsis as capable but lazy.[35] Additionally, school curricula in the Habyarimana period still "painted the Tutsi as natural enemies of the Hutu. . . . This systematic preaching of racial ideology served to keep alive racial hatred."[36] The discriminatory politics of redistribution continued.

SYMBOLIC PREDISPOSITIONS

While it is difficult to know how much the Rwandan population absorbed these hostile narratives before 1990 and turned them into prejudice, there is strong evidence that many did, as we would expect from Hypothesis 1. According to one source, hating Tutsis was the (Hutu) Rwandan "lifestyle" by the late 1980s, even though the school curriculum guide was no longer overtly discriminatory.[37] Another expert detected "the longstanding and deeply ingrained racism of Rwandan society" as a major factor. He continued, "The image of the Tutsi as inherently evil and exploitative was, and still is, deeply rooted in the psyche of most Rwandans."[38] One bit of statistical data in this direction comes from the work of Omar McDoom: when he asked Hutus in interviews about people's beliefs about the origins of Tutsis, the majority agreed with the statement, "Most people thought Tutsis came from outside Rwanda originally." The narrative of Tutsi alienness was widely believed.[39]

A set of popular proverbs recounted by Twagilimana gives a strong indication of the kinds of stereotypes that were widespread in Rwandan society. One asserts, "If you polish the teeth of a Tutsi, tomorrow he will bite you." Another, self-explanatory, is, "You let a Tutsi sleep in your living room and during the night he invades your bed [for your wife]." These proverbs combined with the royal mythology produced two different sets of Tutsi stereotypes: on the one hand, they were seen as intelligent, refined, and courageous; on the other hand, they were considered to be arrogant, cruel, and greedy. Later government propaganda efforts to dehumanize Tutsi succeed to the point that Twagilimana reported, "I personally heard people in Ruhengeri [in northern Rwanda] who said that the Tutsi grew horns on their heads."[40]

Here is one account of the nature of Hutu prejudice against Tutsis before the 1990s, according to an ordinary Hutu:[41] "Basically, Hutus and Tutsis had been playing dirty tricks on one another since 1959. . . . They called the Tutsis weaklings, too high and mighty. . . . After 1959 the oldsters jabbered in the cabarets about eliminating all the Tutsis. . . . A Hutu could certainly choose a Tutsi friend . . . but he could never trust him. For a Hutu, a Tutsi might always be a deceiver." Another person who lived through this period recounted, "Hutus had always reproached Tutsis for their great height and for trying to use this to rule. Time has never dried up that bitterness. . . . For example, on the first day of school the teacher had to call out the background of every pupil, so that the Tutsis would feel timid about taking their seats in a class of Hutus." McDoom also found an important role for schools in reinforcing ethnic distinctions, with 43 percent of his Hutu respondents and 33 percent of his Tutsi respondents reporting that they first found out their ethnic identity in school.[42]

One Rwandan offered this backhanded admission of prejudice: "Actually, Hutus did not detest Tutsis as much as that. Not enough to kill them all, anyway." Another added, "Maybe we did not hate all the Tutsis, especially our neighbors, and maybe we did not see them as wicked enemies. But among ourselves we said . . . we did not want them anywhere around us anymore, and that we had to clear them from our land. It's serious, saying that—it's already sharpening the machete." According to a third, "It is awkward to talk about hatred between Hutus and Tutsis, because words changed meaning after the killings. Before, we could fool around among ourselves and say we were going to kill them all, and the next moment we would join them to share some work or a bottle. Jokes and threats were mixed together. We no longer paid heed to what we said. . . . Since then we have seen: those words brought on grave consequences."[43] All of these statements are anecdotal, but together they provide substantial evidence for Hypothesis 1: hostile narratives did lead to anti-Tutsi prejudice.

One more symbolic predisposition is important to mention: obedience to authority. Claims that Rwandan political culture was somehow uniquely authoritarian are controversial for good reason. Stanley Milgram's famous experiments that showed that most people can be obedient to authority to a frightening degree in the right circumstances seem to offer an instant refutation of this notion.[44] But Rwanda was unusual in one respect: Rwandan peasants were accustomed for generations to respond, reluctantly but reliably, to the requirement to supply corvee labor to their rulers, a practice the Habyarimana regime revived in the form of the *umuganda* service requirement. Thus when called to engage in literal exercises in "brush clearing," Rwandans were predisposed to go along because doing so was habitual—and resistance was reliably punished. They were thus much easier to mobilize for government-approved mass action than are most people in nontotalitarian societies.

TUTSI EXILES' FEARS AND THREAT PERCEPTIONS

The war in Rwanda was started in 1990 by Tutsi exiles, primarily in Uganda, organized in the Tutsi-dominated and Ugandan-based RPF. Therefore, it is fear or threat perceptions among those Tutsis that is most relevant to understanding the start of the war.

Many Tutsis who had fled to Uganda in the 1960s or earlier came to consider themselves Ugandans; they were therefore shocked when they began to face oppression there in the early 1980s. Many young Tutsis responded by joining the Ugandan rebel movement led by Yoweri Museveni. By the time Museveni's forces took power in Kampala in 1986, some three thousand of their fourteen thousand–man army were Rwandans, almost all Tutsis. One of them, Fred Rwigyema, was subsequently appointed deputy minister of defense in Museveni's new government; another, Paul Kagame, became acting chief of military intelligence. However, the prominent place of Rwandans spurred a backlash of prejudice among indigenous Ugandan ethnic groups. Responding to its ethnic base, the Museveni government reneged on promises to give Ugandan citizenship to the Rwandan Tutsis, and in 1988 Rwigyema lost his position in the Defense Ministry. Ugandan citizens were increasingly successful at dispossessing Tutsis of lands they had acquired, branding them as noncitizens.[45] By 1990, then, the position of Rwandan Tutsis in Uganda was increasingly under threat. At the same time, the door to peaceful return to Rwanda remained locked tight. Thus Hypothesis 4 applies to the RPF invasion of Rwanda, but in an indirect way: it was threats to the Tutsis' position from Ugandans that motivated them to take hostile action in Rwanda.

1980S HUTU FEARS AND THREAT PERCEPTIONS

On the Hutu side, the threat of enslavement was at the core of the ethnic mythology: if the Tutsis returned to power, it was claimed, they would return to the repressive policies of the past. As Peter Uvin has put it, Hutu ideology claimed that the Hutu-led government was "the sole defense against the Tutsi's evil attempts to enslave the people again."[46] According to Hypothesis 2, the resulting prejudice should have encouraged Hutus to perceive

Tutsi rule as threatening. Such fear was made highly plausible by the continuation of Tutsi rule in neighboring Burundi, and even more by the waves
of violence that swept Burundi in 1965, 1972, 1988, and 1993, each time cul-
minating in government-inspired massacres of Burundian Hutus and waves
of Hutu refugees fleeing to Rwanda.

It is important to distinguish, however, the real threat of external Tutsi organizations from the powerless and unorganized Tutsis in Rwanda. The
measure of the power of Hypothesis 2 is the extent to which Rwandan Hutus failed to make that distinction, identifying all Tutsis as equally threatening. Rene Lemarchand noted that this was true in the late 1960s: "internal
opposition to the regime became so closely identified with the external menace as to make them almost indistinguishable."[47] Interviews by McDoom
found that Hutus continued to believe this decades later: 91 percent of Hutus interviewed said that they identified the enemy during the 1990s conflict as being all Tutsi, not merely the RPF rebels.[48] This, of course, was the
prejudiced, essentializing view that justified the genocide. The fact that virtually all Hutus still believed it, and told an interviewer so, even after a
decade of postwar Tutsi rule aimed at breaking down those prejudices, is
significant.

The Path to War and Genocide

ORGANIZING EFFORTS BY THE RPF

The emergence of the RPF was the result of a chauvinist symbolic politics—
though ironically, it was initially on the government's side. As noted earlier
in this chapter, the RPF's Tutsi supporters were in exile because of the particularly exclusionary nature of Hutu ideology, which claimed that Tutsis did
not really belong in Rwanda. Successive Rwandan governments therefore
refused to let the Tutsi refugees return. Had the refugee problem been resolved, even on terms favorable to Habyarimana's government, there could
have been no RPF.

At the same time, and in accordance with Hypothesis 4a, the Rwandan
government's repressive power meant that Tutsis inside Rwanda could not
mobilize; therefore, any organized Tutsi challenge could only come from
abroad. Thus Ugandan backing for the RPF was a critical cause of Rwanda's civil war of the early 1990s, and it was events in Uganda that largely
dictated the timing of Rwanda's war.[49] As tensions between Rwandan refugees and indigenous Ugandans grew and Museveni increasingly sided
against the Rwandan Tutsis, the Tutsi exile community had to rethink its
options. Led by officers who retained powerful positions in the Ugandan
military, Tutsi refugees organized themselves to form the RPF in December

1987. As Tutsi soldiers were purged from the Ugandan army, they flocked to the RPF, often with their arms and equipment. By thus enabling the RPF to launch its attack into Rwanda, Museveni was solving two problems at once: giving the Rwandan refugees someplace to go and responding to Ugandans' demands that they leave. RPF leaders, of course, made the same calculation: increasingly unwelcome in Uganda and blocked from returning peacefully to Rwanda, they saw no alternative but to try to force their way back. As Hypothesis 6 points out, organizing themselves into the RPF was a necessary step in enabling themselves to make the attempt.

The global social network of Tutsi exiles then began functioning as the RPF's recruitment network. Motivated in part by their parents' narratives about Rwanda, young Tutsi exiles flocked to join the RPF even after its severe initial reverses, and even if they had bright prospects in exile: Gerard Prunier estimates that the RPF was "the best-educated guerrilla force the world had ever seen."[50] Older exiles, Tutsi businessmen in Europe and North America, donated the funding.[51] It is hard to imagine that educated Tutsis came even from Brussels and New York to join the RPF because they calculated their individual prospects to be better with the guerrillas than in their places of exile. Since the RPF had few selective incentives to offer—it permitted its soldiers relatively little looting, for example—the only explanation that fits for explaining its successful recruiting efforts is symbolic politics, and especially Hypothesis 5: the charisma of RPF leaders Fred Rwigyema and Paul Kagame and the myth-based identity they appealed to were the factors that moved them.[52] Lemarchand reports that RPF cadres saw themselves as a nonethnic organization whose members would be liberators from a corrupt dictatorship.[53]

The RPF invaded Rwanda with about 4,000 fairly well-equipped troops on October 1, 1990. It advanced quickly at first, but things soon started going wrong.[54] Its charismatic leader, Fred Rwigyema, was killed on the second day of the operation. Then, with support from France, Belgium, and Zaire, the Rwandan army recovered from its initial shock and put the RPF troops to flight by the end of the month. Paul Kagame took command of the tattered remnants of the RPF, now down to two thousand men, and regrouped them in the mountainous border region between Uganda and Rwanda. With aid from Uganda, Kagame reorganized and expanded his force, which grew to fifteen thousand men by mid-1991. Over the next months, the RPF launched a new offensive, capturing a swath of territory in northern Rwanda about twenty miles wide even though the Rwandan army had grown in size even more quickly than the RPF had: the quality of the rebel troops was simply better. As the RPF advanced, the overwhelmingly Hutu population of northern Rwanda fled. By the time the RPF troops had completed an advance into the northeastern Byumba region in 1992, some 350,000 Hutu civilians were refugees.

REGIME LEADERSHIP AND ORGANIZATIONS

In Rwandan society, leaders traditionally drew their key followers from members of their lineage, but Habyarimana came from a very weak one. While he did have a few cronies from his home region of Ruhengeri, therefore, Habyarimana was forced to rely more on members of his wife Agathe's very high-ranking lineage from the neighboring northern prefecture of Gisenyi.[55] Some of these people were given high official posts, such as one brother of Agathe who was named prefect of Ruhengeri; others simply used their connections to amass wealth and power in private business. This "clan de madame" formed the core of Rwanda's ruling elite, which was known as the *akazu* (or "little house"); it had the capability, through its access to government, party, and private resources, to organize massacres and other political events even outside of official government policy.[56] It used that ability unsparingly.

Given its degree of internal control, the only restraint on Rwandan government power was foreign leverage, which was significant, especially after the Rwandan economy nearly collapsed in the late 1980s.[57] The international price of coffee, Rwanda's biggest export crop, declined drastically after 1985, and the country's previously lucrative tin mine had to close soon after. A series of droughts depressed food crop yields at the same time. As a result, GDP per capita declined 27 percent from 1983 to 1990, while food production declined from a bit over 2,000 calories per capita per day to barely 1,500–that is, from subsistence quantities to starvation rates. Rwanda became dependent on foreign aid for 22 percent of GNP by 1991, with France contributing the lion's share of the assistance.[58] The government was also forced to increase demand for *umuganda* labor from the hard-pressed peasantry, while being forced to cut its budget 40 percent, with social services absorbing most of the cuts.

With foreign donors holding his government's purse strings, Habyarimana was vulnerable to international pressure, forcing him to allow the emergence of opposition parties. Similarly, it was foreign pressure that would force Habyarimana to sign and begin to implement the Arusha peace accords with the Tutsi-led RPF rebel group in the early 1990s. However, foreign pressure was extremely weak on the issues of the preparation for genocide: France steadfastly supported the Rwandan government with military aid before and even during the genocide, and the UN peacekeeping force, the UN Assistance Mission in Rwanda (UNAMIR), was handcuffed by great-power reluctance to intervene and by UN officials' timidity.[59]

This context helped to shape Habyarimana's reaction to the RPF invasion, which was to exaggerate the RPF threat to justify a turn to a politics of protection. One of his first moves, a few days after the initial attack, was a propaganda move: the Rwandan army staged a fake RPF attack on the outskirts of the capital, Kigali. Habyarimana used this event as an excuse to round up between eight thousand and ten thousand alleged "accomplices"—mostly Hutu political opponents—and detain them for about eight months before releasing the survivors. Over the following months, regime supporters also organized a number of massacres of Tutsis in its northern stronghold regions of Gisenyi and Ruhengeri, killing hundreds of people.[60]

An ongoing civil war is not a promising time to promote democratic reforms, but Rwanda was under strong international pressure to do just that, so President Habyarimana began unevenly to comply. He began allowing the creation of opposition parties, the most important three of which appeared in the summer of 1991.[61] All three primarily represented the southern Hutu elites who were disgruntled about northerners' monopoly of power; they were also more tolerant toward Tutsis than the regime was. To counter these groups, the akazu encouraged creation of another party in early 1992, the Coalition for the Defense of the Republic (CDR), which consisted of northern extremists who would later spearhead the push for genocide. The ruling National Revolutionary Movement for Development (MRND), now called MRNDD (the additional "D" ironically standing for "Democracy") refused to permit the creation of an opposition radio station and began sponsoring violent attacks to try to intimidate the opposition.

Still, the opposition was popular enough that it managed to mobilize fifty thousand people to protest against the government in January 1992. The regime responded by claiming the opposition was planning a massacre of Hutus by Tutsis, and called for Hutus to attack first in "self-defense." This is Hypothesis 5 in operation: the regime was using a frame of physical threat to justify violent mobilization in a politics of protection. The result was another massacre of Tutsis—this time in southern Rwanda, in the Bugesera area, the southernmost part of Kigali prefecture. Another three hundred people died. Habyarimana then changed tack again, agreeing later that month to opposition demands for a power-sharing government, including a prime minister from an opposition party, with a majority of cabinet seats held by opposition groups. CDR, not yet organized, was not included, but the ruling party kept control of the Defense and Interior Ministries, and it created a network of death squads supervised by a revived clandestine police. Still, the opposition ministers managed to initiate some reforms. One, for example, replaced the ethnic quota system for government hiring with a fair system of civil service examinations. Furthermore, the defense minister was a relative moderate who sidelined some—but not all—of the more extremist military officers, including one of Mrs. Habyarimana's brothers. The akazu now became more radical and began considering the possibility of a coup.

Parallel with both the war and the democratization process was an internationally mediated peace process. Habyarimana had agreed to open negotiations with the RPF as well as the opposition in March 1992, and actually did so in May. A combined delegation of opposition leaders met separately with the RPF, which responded with a pledge to stop fighting and shift to a purely political struggle. The regime signed a cease-fire with the RPF in July at the official negotiations in Arusha, Tanzania. After months of talks, the government negotiating team reached agreement with the RPF in January 1993 on a new "Broadened Base Transitional Government" that would include the RPF as well as the ruling MRND(D) and the Hutu opposition parties. The reaction of the extremists was to launch a new round of massacres, killing an estimated three hundred people in late January. The RPF retaliated by launching an offensive in February, easily sweeping aside a disintegrating Rwandan army and conquering new territory before it stopped about twenty miles north of Kigali and declared a new cease-fire.[62]

This RPF offensive, which involved the killing of over two hundred civilians, weakened the Hutu opposition, driving some opposition politicians to back Habyarimana and condemn the RPF.[63] Still, moderates managed to get the negotiations back on track, and in the summer of 1993 Habyarimana finally signed agreements at Arusha that, among other things, included the return of Tutsi refugees and a plan for integrating RPF fighters into the Rwandan army. As the talks proceeded, however, the moderate Hutu president Melchior Ndadaye of Burundi was murdered in October 1993 by extremist Tutsi military officers who then took power in a coup. This set off a wave of violence that left fifty thousand dead in Burundi and 150,000 Burundian Hutu refugees in Rwanda.[64] The shock of that event radicalized Rwandan politics. As one analyst explains, the CDR was a marginal group before the killings in Burundi; afterward, several of the previously moderate opposition parties split, with many of their leaders forming "Hutu Power" factions allied with the CDR and endorsing its genocidal ideas.[65]

Foreign pressure on Habyarimana continued to mount however, pushing him to implement the Arusha accords; UNAMIR peacekeeping troops began arriving in Kigali in November 1993. Finally, on April 6, 1994, Habyarimana went to another negotiating session in Arusha and promised again to implement the accords.[66] His returning plane was shot down on its approach to Kigali Airport. The genocide began within hours.

FRAMING AND THE GENOCIDAIRES' AIR WAR

The 1990 RPF invasion of Rwanda had motivated the akazu to drop their subtle use of discriminatory code words about Tutsis and resort instead to framing Hutu-Tutsi relations in blatantly racist and dehumanizing terms. Again as Hypothesis 5 would lead us to expect, this use of assertive frames that resonated with Hutu SYPs made them more favorable to mobilizing against the Tutsis. The akazu's first weapon in this effort was the newspaper *Kangura*, which famously published the "Hutu Ten Commandments" in December of that year. The first three of these "commandments" emphasized that any Hutu who married a Tutsi woman, or even hired one as a secretary, was a "traitor." The fourth asserted, "The Tutsi are incapable of honesty in business. They only work for the supremacy of the ethnic group. Consequently, any Hutu is a traitor who associated with the Tutsi in business." The next three advocated discrimination against Tutsis in government, business, education, and the military. Number 8 said simply, "The Bahutu must cease to have pity for the Batutsi."[67]

The extremist propaganda campaign became more intense over time, invoking all the symbols of Hutu mythology to justify elimination of the Tutsis. Going beyond racism to dehumanization and demonization, *Kangura* asserted in 1993, "A cockroach cannot give birth to a butterfly"—that is, Tutsi are inherently evil and cannot change. As a result, "the unspeakable crimes of the *Inyenzi* [cockroaches] of today . . . recall those of their elders [in the 1960s]: killing, pillaging, raping girls and women, etc." Additionally, the extremists claimed that the Tutsi goal was at best to impose a "feudalism" approximating slavery and enforced with the whip. The *Kalinga* drum, the old king's symbol of bloody emasculation of Hutu, was also revived as a symbol in Hutu propaganda: "No more *Kalinga*!" was one slogan, though the object in question had been absent from Rwandan politics for thirty years.[68] One shocking cartoon portrayed Burundian president Ndadaye being crucified and his genitals being cut off and hung on the *kalinga*, all with the encouragement of RPF leader Paul Kagame.[69] By December 1993, *Kangura* was already hinting at genocide, asking, "What weapons shall we use to defeat the *inyenzi* [cockroaches] once and for all?"[70]

The extremists also spread their racist message in party meetings and rallies. One infamous example was a November 1992 speech by MRND(D) ideologue Leon Mugesera asserting that all of the opposition parties "have plotted to let the prefecture of Byumba fall in the hands of the enemy"; he called for them to be executed. He continued, "You know very well that there are accomplices [of the RPF] in this country. They send their children to the RPF. . . . Why don't we decimate those families?" Furthermore, he argued, "If you allow the serpent to bite without it being bothered, it will soon be your turn to be exterminated."[71] This speech helped inspire the massacres of Tutsis in northern Rwanda that occurred in the following months. It exemplifies how Hutu propaganda had become explicitly genocidal. "We must act forcefully!" Mugesera urged; "Get rid of them!"

The official Radio Rwanda station played a similar role in promoting genocidal action. For example, in early March of 1992, Radio Rwanda repeatedly broadcast a report claiming that the opposition Liberal Party was planning to kill twenty-two Hutu leaders. It was in response to this report that a group of *Interahamwe* militiamen traveled to Bugesera to carry out the massacre there in the following days.[72]

The akazu's last entry in the propaganda war was the hate radio station "Radio-Television Libres des Milles Collines" (RTLMC), which began broadcasting in July 1993. It was fiendishly effective because "it knew how to use street slang, obscene jokes and good music to push its racist message." It was even popular with Tutsi troops.[73] One of the most popular singers was Simon Bikindi, who would later be tried for crimes against humanity. In one evocative song Bikindi sang, "Carrying chiefs, servitude, the whip, the lash, and forced work that exhausted the people, that has disappeared for ever. You, the great majority . . . remember this evil should be driven as far away as possible, so that it never returns to Rwanda."[74] After the genocide began, RTLMC cast away what little restraint remained in such songs, broadcasting assertions like this one: "The Tutsis, *inyenzi-inkotanyi* [cockroach-warriors], these are bloodthirsty men that kill in a cruel manner. . . . They even would go and eat them. There is no doubt . . . that's why we can't even find the corpses."[75]

Prunier explains the overall appeal of these extremist messages as a clear exercise in symbolic politics, featuring claims of economic, physical, and symbolic threats:

> They presented the situation in terms of almost biblical urgency. To the fear of losing one's privileges (rational level) they added the fear of losing one's life (visceral level) and the fear of losing control of one's world (mythical level).Their radio station, RTLMC, poured out a torrent of propaganda, mixing constant harping on the old themes of "majority democracy," fears of "Tutsi feudalist enslavement" and ambiguous "calls to action." A monstrous answer to a monstrously misrepresented problem was beginning to be turned into a deliberate, organized, cold-blooded political programme . . . [for] a "final solution."[76]

In sum, these extreme frames of physical and social threat—which did resonate with existing SYPs and threat perceptions—should, according to Hypothesis 5, have contributed to extreme ethnic violence. They did so, contributing ultimately to the genocide.

HUTU THREAT PERCEPTIONS AFTER 1990

Events in the early 1990s increased Hutu feelings of threat. As we would expect from Hypothesis 4, this rising threat perception gave extremist politicians' symbolic appeals more traction. The RPF's initial invasion in 1990 marked the first major shift, meriting perceptions of physical threat. McDoom found that among the 265 Hutus he interviewed, 72 percent reported that during the war they feared they would be killed if the RPF won. Furthermore, these feelings of threat translated directly into interethnic tensions: over 40 percent of McDoom's respondents reported that interethnic relations deteriorated after the outbreak of war in 1990, with the effect twice as strong in the north, near the fighting, as in the south.[77]

The RPF military offensive of February 1993 generated even more fear. RPF atrocities were magnified in Hutu propaganda as representing the RPF's violent intentions. These arguments gave even moderate Hutus qualms about giving the RPF a share of power, including in the army. The October 1993 murder of Burundian president Ndadaye and the subsequent massacres and Tutsi-led military coup there then drove Hutu fears to the boiling point. Extreme accusations against the Tutsis now became more common: that the Tutsis planned genocide, for example. While such charges were not initially believed by ordinary Hutus, they came to be believed after months of repetition, and against the background of the reality of events in Burundi.[78] Extremist propaganda repeated that the necessary reaction was preemptive genocide. Mugesera's speech continued to be widely circulated on audiotape, and his prescription reiterated that Hutus should "rise up" and "exterminate the scum."[79]

The death of Habyarimana raised fears still further. One reluctant participant in the genocide reported that by this time neighbors were "spreading the rumour that the Tutsis in our area had had a meeting and were planning to kill the Hutus."[80] One of Scott Straus's informants went further, asserting, "What pushed us to kill the Tutsis was the death of Habyarimana. . . . You could say his death made everyone crazy; it was like a poison that spread in the population." Again, however, this perception was primarily the result of regime propaganda. As another informant said, "*The authorities said* our president had just been killed, that he was liked by many people, that you have to kill the Tutsis, that they are our enemy."[81] McDoom's data also show the importance of Habyarimana's death and the subsequent propaganda: the majority of McDoom's respondents from southern Rwanda, relatively far from the early fighting, told him that only at this time did interethnic relations in their area deteriorate.[82]

Combined with strong prejudices, these intense feelings of threat were critical in motivating the genocide. As a young Rwandan summed it up, his neighbors "hear over and over again that the Tutsis are out to kill them, and that is the reality. They act not out of hate as fear."[83] This young man is only half right, however: the alarmist propaganda was plausible, and therefore provoked fear, largely because of the preexisting anti-Tutsi SYPs—the beliefs that Tutsis were dangerous and not to be trusted.

SYMBOLIC PREDISPOSITIONS AFTER 1990

When the regime began beating the drum of the "Tutsi feudalist threat," it managed at first to get a response only in its traditional base of support in northern Rwanda, where the threat was most immediate and where prejudice toward the Tutsis was the strongest. But years of the kinds of savage propaganda quoted in the preceding section finally had its effect. Straus's evidence demonstrates the effectiveness of the propaganda line that all Tutsis are RPF "accomplices": the most common term for killing unarmed Tutsi civilians was "fight[ing] the enemy." McDoom's finding was even clearer: 91 percent of his informants said that they identified all Tutsis as the enemy (with about 20 percent of them including moderate Hutus as well).

One participant summed up the attitudes and the responses to leaders' frames that led to genocide as follows:

> I think the possibility of genocide fell out as it did because it was lying in wait. . . . There was never any need to talk about it among ourselves. The thoughtfulness of the authorities ripened it naturally, and then it was proposed to us. As it was their only proposal and it promised to be final, we seized the opportunity. We knew full well what had to be done, and we set to doing it without flinching, because it seemed like the perfect solution.[84]

Another participant explained the mixture of feelings this way:

> The radios were yammering at us since 1992 to kill all the Tutsis; there was anger after the president's death and a fear of falling under the rule of the *inkotanyi*. But I do not see any hatred in all that.
>
> The Hutu always suspects that some plans are cooking deep in the Tutsi character. . . . He sees a threat lurking in even the feeblest or kindest Tutsi. But it is suspicion, not hatred. The hatred came over us suddenly after our president's plane crashed.

While this respondent disclaims "hatred" as a long-standing attitude, like most of Straus's informants, the views he describes certainly include all three elements in the definition of prejudice: negative stereotypes, negative feelings, and a predisposition to negative action. Even while arguing that hatred was unimportant, Straus admits that his respondents overwhelmingly reported the prejudiced attitude that all Tutsis were enemies.[85] Thus Rwandan Hutus were certainly prejudiced against Tutsis; I contend that *hate* is also an appropriate term. Regardless of the label used, it is clear that these symbolic predispositions did contribute to support for discriminatory action, as expected according to Hypothesis 3.

Another participant describes the prevailing attitude during the genocide as closer to despising Tutsis than hating them:

> When we spotted a small group of runaways trying to escape by creeping through the mud, we called them snakes. Before the killings, we usually called them cockroaches. But during, it was more suitable to call them snakes, because of their attitude, or zeros, or dogs, because in our country we don't like dogs; in any case, they were less-than-nothings.

As this quotation shows, the extremists' propaganda effort to promote prejudice and dehumanize Tutsis in the eyes of Hutus was very effective with this man's associates: the practice of calling Tutsis "cockroaches" had become widespread even before the genocide began. Significantly, this report is from Nyamata district in southern Rwanda—that is, an area that was previously less prejudiced than the north. Furthermore, this informant is explicit about the role of radio propaganda in promoting these attitudes: "The radios exaggerated to get us all fired up. 'Cockroaches,' 'snakes'—it was the radios that taught us those words."

Here is clear evidence in support of Hypothesis 5: the extreme threat frames being purveyed by the extremist media was increasing ordinary Hutus' inclination to mobilize and attack. Since their violent propaganda now resonated with their audience's fearful mood, the extremists—based in the government and using its resources—were now able to create a political movement and mobilize supporters. By reinterpreting Hutu ideology as explicitly eliminationist, the extremists were able to make their genocidal program accepted as part of the normal political landscape. With the most extreme version of Hutu mythology now publicly prominent in the radio "air war," with Hutu popular fears at a fever pitch, and with their control over government and militia organizations, the genocidaires were finally able to act. In the new mood of fear and hostility, RTLMC's predatory logic of "kill-first-not-to-be-killed could be developed into a general feeling shared by large segments of the population."[86]

THE GENOCIDAIRES' GROUND WAR

As extremist government leaders moved toward the decision to commit genocide, they built the organizational capacity that (Hypothesis 6) would enable them to carry it out. They sponsored the extremist newspaper *Kangura* and the hate radio station RTLMC to lay the propaganda groundwork. To do the dirty work of killing, the governing party, the MRND(D), created the *Interahamwe* militia in 1991; the akazu also aided the extremist CDR and its militia, the *Impuzamugambi*. These militia groups often set up checkpoints on major roads well before the genocide, checking identity cards to block Tutsis and opposition party members from traveling across the country, all without hindrance from the police or army.

As early as the fall of 1992, extremists were already drawing up hit lists. At the same time, the military purchased twenty thousand new rifles for local police units. In 1993–1994, about half a million machetes were also imported by a close friend of Habyarimana.[87] The extremists also carried out a campaign of assassinations aimed against Hutu opposition figures: for example, the founder of one opposition grouping, Emmanuel Gapyisi, was murdered in a well-planned hit in May 1993; these examples prompted some moderates, such as Defense Minister James Gasana, to flee into exile.[88]

Another part of the mobilization plan was continuing massacres of Tutsis in outlying regions: Human Rights Watch counted seventeen episodes of massacres in 1990–1993, fourteen of them in the northwest.[89] The March 1992 massacres in the southern Bugesera region represented one innovation: the first time the *Interahamwe* militia played an important role in Rwanda's mass murders. Another round of massacres in January 1993 was the extremists' response to the signing of the third Arusha Agreement, killing an estimated three hundred people across the northwest in six days.[90] Bits of the government apparatus, including the Presidential Guard, increasingly went over to the extremists, as did factions from most of the moderate Hutu parties.

What followed was, on one level, an ordinary coup led by the genocidaire leader, Colonel Theoneste Bagosora, secretary-general in the Ministry of Defense. Bagosora allegedly phoned "Army Chief of Staff General Déogratias Nsabimana—who opposed Bagosora's genocidal plans," telling him that President Habyarimana had ordered him to join Habyarimana's trip to Arusha. This "order" contradicted Habyarimana's policy of always leaving his chief of staff in Rwanda when he himself traveled abroad, but Nsabimana followed "orders" and joined the trip. According to a "Committee of Experts" appointed by the postgenocide Rwandan government, Bagosora then used his contacts with the Anti-Aircraft Battalion at Kigali Airport, a unit he had previously commanded, to order them to shoot down the president's plane.[91]

While some analysts believe the genocidaires' claim that it was the RPF that downed the plane, I consider this unlikely, in large part because of the speed of the genocidaires' reaction (as well as Bagosora's maneuver to put his boss on Habyarimana's plane). Within hours of the president's death, the genocidaires sprang into action. Military units in Kigali and in the provinces murdered the top government leadership, including those slated to join the interim government, and conspirators seized power in the capital. They then co-opted or swept aside nonconspirators at lower levels of government. The genocide that followed was organized by government officials, enforced by army troops, and carried out by activists, militiamen, and ordinary citizens. I do not believe these actions could have been taken so quickly if the genocidaires had not previously given orders for their troops to begin preparations.

Oddly, even though the RPF was militarily superior, the genocide plan called for the Rwandan army to scatter its troops around the country— including the most reliable units—to lead the implementation of the genocide, even as the RPF attacked.[92] As a result, implementing the genocide led to quick and permanent military defeat for the genocidaires. While the regime's military, logistical, and political attention was focused on massacring unarmed and harmless Tutsis, "there were very few government troops facing the guerrillas and they tended not to put up much of a fight . . . [except in] the cities of Kigali and Ruhengeri."[93] So the RPF overran the country and the interim regime was ousted in little more than three months.

That is *what* happened. But why did the coup leaders choose a self-defeating—indeed, insane—policy of massacring harmless civilians while provoking their most dangerous enemy, the RPF? Their desire to hold power is understandable, and their extreme distrust of the RPF is equally so. But if the akazu had wanted only to hold onto power, a coup without renewed war or genocide would have served better. The RPF's successful February 1993 offensive had shown unambiguously its military superiority over the Rwandan army; the extreme peril of provoking a new war with them should have been clear.[94]

Perhaps the coup leaders felt that they had to provoke a renewal of the war so they could use the fighting to justify abrogating the power-sharing deal and as a cause to rally popular Hutu support for their new regime. Even in this case, however, they would still have been better off if they had not carried out the genocide. They would have had a better chance of getting outside military aid, which was their only chance of avoiding quick military defeat. Also, they could have focused their military efforts on the decisive battle with the RPF instead of diverting their best troops to slaughter Tutsi civilians. The genocide is simply not explicable in rational terms as a regime-saving strategy. Rather, as Mahmood Mamdani sums it up, the motivation for genocide was in madness and despair. "Faced with a military defeat that seemed to sound the very death knell of Hutu power," he writes, "the *genocidaires* chose to embrace death itself as an alternative to life without power."[95]

Symbolic politics theory provides an explanation for the nature of that madness. First, the Hutu mythology and the resulting prejudice were central in motivating the genocide (Hypotheses 1 through 3).[96] The genocidaires were implementing a program that made sense to them in the context of their ethnic symbolic predispositions and the fears they convinced themselves and their followers to feel. As Prunier notes, any explanation of the genocide "presupposes one absolutely basic thing: the total dehumanisation of the Evil Other."[97] An ethnic mythology that characterizes the "other" as "cockroaches" achieves that dehumanization. Ultimately, in a process Jack Snyder labels "blowback," the genocidaires fell victim to their own propaganda, accepting that ordinary Tutsis were as big a threat as the RPF.[98]

The second reason was threat (Hypothesis 4). Sharing power with the RPF was threatening to the akazu in every way. It posed a physical threat because it meant making Tutsi RPF troops 40 percent of the army and 50 percent of the officer corps—and some of those troops had massacred Hutus. It posed a symbolic and status threat because it required them to abandon their ideology of Tutsi illegitimacy and therefore their position as politically superior to Tutsis. And it posed a threat to their material interests—losing not only power but also the economic gains they had been reaping. As a result, the terror management effect had its usual influence on akazu thinking, prompting them to be more aggressive and punitive toward the out-group, less sensitive to humanitarian concerns, and more likely to reject outsiders' criticisms. Because the threat was extreme, the terror management effect was similarly severe, and it coupled with the akazu's already-extreme prejudices to convince them their mad program of genocide made sense.

The next key question is, why did the followers follow? How did the conspirators motivate their network of supporters, including in the military, to implement their insane campaign of murder? And why did local and regional officials not part of their network carry out such bloody orders from a recently installed and dubiously legitimate regime? Prejudices combined with threat perceptions (Hypotheses 2 through 4) and the bloodthirsty akazu propaganda (Hypothesis 5) created the political mood in which genocide was thinkable. But what turned predisposition into action was organization (Hypothesis 6).

First, since they quickly gained control of the army, the genocidaires were able to use coercion when necessary. As Human Rights Watch reports, "soldiers and national police directed all the major massacres throughout the country," and they coerced those Hutus who tried to resist the slaughter.[99] Second, because they controlled the government apparatus, they could order local and regional officials to carry out the genocide. When the time came for the killing, local people could be assembled for routine "sensibilization" sessions organized by the local leadership but addressed by an "important person" from Kigali with the messages outlined earlier in this chapter. Later, the people would be called up for a "bush clearing" *umuganda*, now employed as the euphemism for murder.[100] Officials who refused to carry out such orders were replaced, at gunpoint if necessary, with others who were willing.

At the local level, as reconstructed by Omar McDoom, the genocide was organized and carried out by a mixture of people acting for different reasons. Among the core actors were those whom David Lake and Donald Rothchild have called "ethnic activists."[101] These were typically people who were strongly committed to the anti-Tutsi ideology—that is, people who were strongly prejudiced. For example, in one locality in the northern prefecture of Ruhengeri, "the man who would emerge to lead the anti-Tutsi campaign . . . was Gervais Harelimana, a locally well-known businessman, politician and bigot" who was a local leader of the CDR. Similarly, in another locality in the southern prefecture of Butare, the man who led the killing was Emmanuel Karimunda, "a butcher . . . well-known for his bigoted views on Tutsi and his violent temper." Karimunda, in particular, was a vicious bully reported to have stood out in his community for his propensity to harass and intimidate Tutsis even before the genocide.[102] For this critical group of actors, then, symbolic predispositions—prejudice—were critical in motivating the genocide.

Other participants had other motives. Many local "political entrepreneurs" were simply opportunists, going along with the genocide when they saw it as necessary to keep power, or useful as a way to seize power. Others, such as Emmanuel Rekeraho, a former soldier and local opposition party representative in the southern Butare prefecture, seem to have become radicalized by the events of the time, the constant repetition of extremist narratives, and finally the shock of Habyarimana's death.[103] At the lowest level, as Fuji also found, preexisting social ties heavily influenced who became involved: the ethnic activists recruited relatives, neighbors, and friends to help them to organize the massacres. Thus, for example, the businessman-activist Harelimana in Ruhengeri prefecture had his younger brother and a neighbor as his key aides, while Karimunda, the extremist butcher in Butare, had a brother and a nephew as his key henchmen.[104] Another SYP, partisan sympathies, may also have played a role here: according to Straus's analysis, the violence began first in areas where support for the MRND(D) was strongest.[105]

The appeal to *umuganda* is a final piece of the puzzle. Rwandan peasants were used to being called up to perform this community service work, so they were socialized into a predisposition to go along. This SYP developed in response to both the regime's ideological justification (to promote economic development) and its ability to enforce its demands. The presence of special speakers and armed men, as well the real nature of the "work," all made clear that this was not the usual kind of *umuganda*. Yet at the same time, the soldiers and militiamen made clear that to refuse was to risk death. The genocidaires had cleverly harnessed both the machinery and the practices of routine Rwandan government for their murderous purpose.

Why so many ordinary Hutus participated in the genocide is summed up by an elderly man quoted by Prunier: "I am ashamed, but what would you have done if you had been in my place? Either you took part in the massacre or else you were massacred yourself. So I took weapons and I defended the members of my tribe against the Tutsi." Prunier comments, "Even as the man pleads compulsion, . . . he agrees with the propaganda view (which he knows to be false) by mythifying [the victims] as aggressive enemies."[106] In short, ideology, prejudice, fear, and compulsion were all necessary to get most Hutu to participate in genocide. The compulsion, in turn, was dependent on greater ideological fanaticism in the militia and the army leadership.

RWANDA'S PREDATION-DRIVEN SECURITY DILEMMA

A final reason for what happened in Rwanda was the particular kind of security dilemma it faced. The situation is best summed up by Bruce Jones: "Security fears, real and constructed, were tools more than causes of war." In fact, he notes, in many cases " 'fears' were indistinguishable from greed and predatory motives."[107] The most important fears were those of the Hutu extremists, who feared losing power if the Arusha Agreement were implemented. Even the problem of trust makes sense only in the context of the ethnic mythologies, as uncertainty over RPF intentions made the extremist ideology seem credible to some, splitting the Hutu opposition into moderate and hard-line factions and strengthening the akazu by giving it allies outside its northern home base.

This security dilemma was, of course, manufactured: the akazu had instigated the January 1993 massacre of Tutsis and stalled the Arusha negotiations in the hope of provoking just such an RPF attack. And that is Jones's point: the one unambiguously predatory group, the akazu, provoked violence as a tool to force the RPF and some opposition Hutus to line up on opposite sides of the fight. Later, immediately after Habyarimana was killed, a large portion of the army tried to oppose the coup leaders, but once its commanders received word of renewed fighting with the RPF, they ceased their opposition and united with the extremists. Thus in one stroke, the extremists ensured both the short-term success of their coup (by winning army support) and its long-term failure (by committing it to genocide instead of fighting the RPF).

Conclusion

The mistake many scholars make in trying to understand the Rwanda genocide is to assume that it is explicable only if it was "rational." Benjamin Valentino, for example, argues that the akazu had tried all lesser means than genocide, and all failed: "This was the cold logic that led Colonel Bagosora to . . . [conclude], 'The only plausible solution for Rwanda would be the elimination of the Tutsi.' "[108] As I have shown, however, that conclusion does not represent "cold logic" at all; it was illogical and self-defeating. These leaders certainly did not view an RPF-ruled Rwanda as an acceptable outcome, but that was where their actions led.

Another rationalist analysis, that of Rui J. P. de Figueiredo and Barry Weingast, recognizes that the extremists' strategy was self-defeating if their aim was to hold onto power. To save their assumption of rationality, they posit that the extremists had a different goal: to kill their opponents' supporters so that they themselves could later make a comeback after having been driven from power.[109] The trouble with this assumption is that they provide no evidence for it at all. This unsupported assertion illustrates the problem with the axiomatic assumption of rational behavior: when it does not work, its adherents stray further and further from the evidence in search of some logical premise from which the observed behavior can be judged rational. They thereby make rationalist theory unfalsifiable, denying that any behavior is irrational. And if all behavior is "rational," regardless of its illogic, then the "rational" label is meaningless.

The fact is that the Rwanda genocide was irrational—indeed, insane; not only self-defeating but also depraved. But it was not inexplicable. The madness of Bagosora and his akazu colleagues can be explained through the prism of symbolic politics theory. As with most people, the behavior of the genocidaire leaders was driven by their symbolic predispositions. The most important of these predispositions was intense racialized prejudice against Tutsis, a deep-seated belief in the illegitimacy and sinister nature of the Tutsi presence in Rwanda. The other key SYP of the genocidaire leaders was the common African elite determination to hold onto power at any cost. Had they been more flexible toward the Tutsis, they could have safeguarded their power in the 1980s by accepting the return of Tutsi refugees in exchange for foreign aid. Habyarimana's claim that Rwanda was too overpopulated to accept the refugees was only a flimsy excuse; he and the akazu were simply incapable of accepting the notion that the refugees' return might be both legitimate and nonthreatening. Therefore instead of adjusting its strategy of distributive politics, the regime shifted to a politics of protection aimed against the Tutsi "threat."

When the situation changed in the early 1990s, these predispositions to keep power and keep out the Tutsis created more and more unrealistic thinking by Habyarimana and the akazu. The combination of the RPF military threat, the international economic and diplomatic pressure, and the rise of the Hutu opposition parties made it impossible for them to achieve both goals, but their biases prompted wishful thinking that led them to pass up every opportunity to share power and thereby keep a generous portion for themselves. Habyarimana did finally negotiate a bargain with Hutu opponents and the RPF alike, but his relentless bad faith frequently disrupted the talks, leading ultimately to less favorable results for himself. The akazu, in contrast, stubbornly insisted on trying to monopolize power at all costs, leading them to undermine every bargain and ultimately, perhaps, to kill Habyarimana himself.

The extremists' commitment to genocide after the death of Habyarimana represents the ultimate result of their extreme SYPs, made even more extreme by the scale of the threat they faced. Genocide can have made sense to them only if they believed their own propaganda that unarmed Tutsi civilians ("collaborators") represented just as much of a threat as did the armed forces of the RPF. Otherwise, they would have followed their coup by reinforcing their military position against the RPF, instead of weakening it to carry out the genocide. This is a unique contribution offered by symbolic politics theory: only a focus on Hutu extremists' symbolic predispositions—which lumped all Tutsis together as warriors, accomplices, or cockroaches— allows us to explain why they chose a genocide policy that was morally horrendous, irrelevant for addressing the biggest threat to them (the RPF army), and destructive of their ability to defend themselves against that threat. The extremism of those SYPs is what explains the extremism of their policy choice; the distorting influences of prejudice and the terror management effect are the psychological processes that explain their choice of a policy so self-defeating and so monstrous.

The Rwandan Hutu population and lower-level officials followed the orders of the genocidaire leaders for reasons similar to the leaders' own. Like their leaders, they had a background of long-inculcated prejudice and had been exposed to years of the same eliminationist propaganda. Rwandans themselves typically denied feeling "hatred," but the evidence of prejudice is unmistakable, with negative stereotypes of Tutsis widespread, along with strong negative feelings (especially suspicion and distrust) toward Tutsis, and predispositions toward negative actions illustrated by the pervasive "joking" about killing Tutsis.

This popular prejudice was activated by a combination of the obvious RPF threat and the ambiguous "threat" from Tutsi civilians, resulting in the terror management effect. The most bigoted of ordinary Hutus took the lead in organizing the killing on the local level, aided initially by relatives and other close associates. Furthermore, those who resisted participation in the genocide could be killed. Finally, ordinary Rwandans were called out in accordance with the familiar practice of *umuganda*. The "work" of genocide resonated with their prejudices and fears, was justified by regime ideology and propaganda, and was enforced with the muzzle of a gun. Most Rwandans therefore did what they were told.

We need all of the elements of symbolic politics theory to understand this story because each element explains a different piece of the puzzle. The extreme levels of prejudice and fear were the essential motivating factors, explaining why the genocidaire leaders chose to organize genocide (Hypothesis 2 through 4). Put differently, both extreme prejudice and extreme threat perceptions were necessary conditions for the Rwanda genocide—and, I suspect, all ethnic genocide. Long-established bigoted narratives, in turn, help explain the source of that prejudice (Hypothesis 1). Adding the extremist frames promoted by the media to the prejudice and fear explains why ordinary Hutus found that course a plausible one (Hypothesis 5), as the participants' accounts show. Finally, both war and genocide required organization, so attention to the role of organizations (Hypothesis 6) is necessary to explain how the genocide was carried out and who was swept up in its implementation—including why rank-and-file participants were often not the most bigoted individuals, while grassroots leaders often were.

The initial outbreak of the war, on the other hand, fits less comfortably with symbolist logic. Hostile narratives, fears, and threat perceptions on the side of the Hutu government (Hypotheses 1 through 4) did set the stage for confrontation, motivating the policy of refusing to allow the return of Tutsi refugees. However, anti-Hutu hostile narratives and ethnic prejudice among Tutsis do not seem to have played a role in motivating the formation of the

RPF, whose ideology was a kind of inclusive Rwandan nationalism, not ethnic chauvinism. If there were hostile SYPs here, they were at first directed against the government, not against Hutus as a group (though later RPF war crimes imply that prejudice may well have grown among its personnel during the war). Hypotheses 4 through 6 still do apply: threat perceptions, assertive frames, and organization were the key elements motivating the RPF's initiation of the war. But it was the government's ethnic hostility, not the RPF's, that made this an ethnic war.

The only good news in this story is that it illustrates why genocide is so rare. An eliminationist ideology is a necessary condition for genocide: no one convinces himself or herself that genocide is a thinkable policy unless they dehumanize the other group to a point that justifies its annihilation. Additionally, such an ideology is activated only in the context of both an obvious threat that creates a wartime environment of fear and the ambiguous threat of an apparently threatening (but actually defenseless) internal "enemy" that is the target of the prejudice. Finally, genocide is not attempted unless the genocidaires control the government and are so fanatical as to overlook the fact that genocide is almost always self-destructive for those who order it. Fortunately, not too many situations contain all of these elements.

Gandhi's Nonviolence, Communal Conflict, and the Salt March

Michael C. Grillo and Stuart J. Kaufman

Starting in 1919, Mohandas Gandhi encouraged, organized, and led a series of protest campaigns against British imperial control over India. It was a classic case of using symbolic mobilization for a politics of redistribution, but unusually it led a nationalist campaign in nonviolent directions, focused on confronting the injustice of British rule using strikes, boycotts, marches, and civil disobedience. In his salt campaign of 1930, for example, Gandhi himself led tens of thousands in a march to the sea to defy Britain's salt tax and inspired a broader resistance movement that drew the involvement of millions. When Gandhi's campaigns did erupt into violence, most notably in 1919 and 1921–1922, Gandhi famously stopped the campaigns. One question this chapter asks is, how was Gandhi able to use symbolic politics to mobilize people for a nationalist cause so effectively without it resulting in massive violence against the British?

Gandhi's efforts also pose a second puzzle, however. Gandhi often spoke and wrote about the need for Hindu-Muslim solidarity—"heart-unity," he called it. To prove his sincerity to Muslims, he threw himself into the early 1920s "Khilafat" movement defending the Turkish sultan's spiritual role, and Gandhi also devoted his term as president of the Indian National Congress in 1925 to the goal of Hindu-Muslim unity. Yet despite these efforts by the most popular political leader of the time, the 1920s was a period of rising Hindu-Muslim tensions and increasing communal rioting. By the time he put together the 1930 salt campaign, Gandhi had essentially given up on Hindu-Muslim unity, cutting his ties to long-standing Muslim allies while mending fences with Hindu revivalist groups. The eventual result of the ever-widening Hindu-Muslim split was the violent 1947 partition of India that created Pakistan, accompanied by riots that killed hundreds of thousands and displaced millions. So our second question is, how was Gandhi

able to mobilize his followers so successfully for nonviolent struggle against the British, while at the same time failing to prevent the rise of Hindu-Muslim violence?

This case is important because it presents the dilemma of ethnic or nationalist mobilization in a stark way: if even Mahatma Gandhi was unable to keep his nationalist movement united and nonviolent, who could? What went wrong in this case? At the same time, we must also understand what went right. How did this strange man and his ideas of nonviolent confrontation come to dominate the drive for Indian independence? He returned to India from South Africa in 1915 with no political base in the country, and he was, according to journalist William Shirer, "no orator."[1] Can symbolic politics theory explain both Gandhi's success in mobilizing people for his campaigns of nonviolence and his failure to prevent massive communal violence in the same period?

The answer lies in reframing the question: How do we understand both Gandhi's success in mobilizing people for his campaigns of nonviolence and his rivals' successes in mobilizing people for confrontational acts that repeatedly led to communal violence? The same set of factors explains both. Gandhi succeeded in mobilizing people for his campaigns but also contributed to the conditions for communal conflict, because of the particular kind of symbolic politics he engaged in. Gandhi's appeal was primarily religious; his charisma came from his aura as a Hindu holy man. Though he preached tolerance and inclusion, the language and the symbols Gandhi used generally left Muslims cold, while some of those ideas worked to strengthen the hand of the Hindu revivalists who ultimately killed both Indian unity (aided by Muslim inflexibility) and Gandhi himself.

From the point of view of symbolic politics theory, Gandhi's mistake was to promote "Hindu-Muslim unity" instead of *Indian* unity. Indians needed to create an Indian national identity with a set of narratives that included all religious groups equally. Gandhi occasionally wrote about this, but as a Hindu holy man he never really pursued the idea. The omission was crucial, because by always speaking about Hindus and Muslims as different and sometimes conflicting groups, Gandhi was raising the salience of that communal split, making it easier for rival leaders to appeal to the prejudices and other hostile symbolic predispositions associated with those competing identities. It was not until Nehru's efforts after independence that the work of constructing a unified Indian national identity would truly begin.[2]

In exploring these issues, we begin with some background on India's ethnic diversity and the political setting of colonial India. The next section discusses the context of narratives, SYPs, and popular fears in which Gandhi and his rivals worked. The focus is primarily on the Hindu side of the divide—the primary target audience for both Gandhi and the Hindu revivalists—though some attention to the Muslim side is also essential. The following section explores the symbolic politics behind both Gandhi's rise and that of Hindu revivalists in groups such as the Hindu Mahasabha in the 1920s, showing the interdependent roots of both movements. Next comes a detailed analysis of the symbolic politics of the 1930 salt campaign. Each section explores the degree to which the hypotheses of symbolic politics theory are either supported or infirmed by the evidence.

Ethnic Groups and Political Setting

ETHNIC GROUPS IN INDIA

India in the early twentieth century was one of the most diverse societies in the world. Religiously, about one-quarter of the population was Muslim, and most of the rest were Hindu; this "communal" divide would be India's pivotal ethnic divide of the twentieth century and beyond. Minorities of Sikhs, Buddhists, Jains, and others were also present, but in much smaller numbers. Hindu society was further divided by its famous caste system, with a particular conflict between a priestly Brahmin class dedicated to excluding millions of Untouchables and a growing social movement to end untouchability. Hinduism itself, furthermore, is more a broad religious tradition than a single religion, as different cults emphasize worship of different gods: Vishnu for some (usually in his incarnation as Krishna or as Rama), Shiva in others, and so on.

India was also divided linguistically. In northern India, Hindus promoted the use of Hindi at the expense of the closely related Urdu, which was associated with Muslims. Millions of others spoke distantly related regional languages that were also in the Indo-Aryan language family, such as Bengali, Gujarati (Gandhi's native tongue), Marathi, and Punjabi. Farther south were millions of speakers of Dravidian tongues unrelated to the Indo-Aryan ones, including Telugu speakers in what is now Andhra Pradesh and Tamil speakers in contemporary Tamil Nadu, among others.

POLITICAL SETTING

Ruling over this vast subcontinent were the British imperialists. The crushing of the 1857 "Mutiny" had eliminated any chance of restoring the pre-British order in India, and modern mass nationalism did not yet exist when Gandhi returned in 1915. The Indian National Congress, founded in 1885, was little more than an annual convention of part-time publicists, and in 1916 it rejected a push to build it into a mass political party.[3] Congress was also divided into two rival factions: Moderates led by G. K. Gokhale, who believed only in verbal appeals to liberal Britain's conscience; and Extremists led by B. G. Tilak, who favored mass actions such as boycotts of British goods, "national" education, and development of indigenous (*swadeshi*) industry while also defending if not organizing violence. The Moderates usually controlled the Congress, but neither faction had a significant mass base, and very few leaders had any appeal beyond their home regions.

Yet there was much unrest in India if the nationalists could find a way to harness it. Repeated famines had led to tax strikes in Maharashtra and Gujarat in the later 1890s. Unrest was also of long standing among the indigo growers in parts of Bihar province.[4] Most notably, the 1905 British decision to partition Bengal province—seen as a bid to divide and rule Indians by pitting mostly Muslim East Bengal against the mostly Hindu West—sparked unprecedented resistance. Congress briefly adopted the Extremist platform of boycotting British goods and promoting local industry (*Swadeshi*) and "national" schools. Mass resistance quickly collapsed, however, in part because the wealthy upper-caste leaders' ideas offered little to poor peasants and workers. Hindu revivalism in organizations such as the Hindu Mahasabha and Arya Samaj was more popular in many areas, even though their activities (and those of their Muslim counterparts) sometimes led to Hindu-Muslim riots.

In 1915, the year Gandhi returned, a few extremists tried to incite a mutiny among Indian troops, but the British discovered the plot and energetically suppressed it. This British action eliminated what might have been the nationalists' best violent option. That same year, established Indian politicians finally turned to mass politics, with the English-born activist Annie Besant and Extremist leader B. G. Tilak both forming Home Rule Leagues to agitate for Indian self-government, though neither league was active for more than a few years.[5]

When Gandhi arrived in India, therefore, the situation was favorable for peaceful mass political action. Neither the Moderates' genteel persuasion nor the fringe groups' terrorism had achieved much, while the best military option, mutiny, failed. Indians lacked the organization and resources to rebel, and there was no foreign support for any such efforts. Meanwhile, the initial success of the new Home Rule Leagues demonstrated that the opportunity existed for creating mass social movement organizations, and the leagues themselves were ripe to be co-opted by capable new leaders.

Narratives, Symbolic Predispositions, and Threat Perceptions

In an overwhelmingly illiterate society like British India, the narratives and symbols to which leaders can appeal come primarily from religious images and oral traditions.

HINDU NARRATIVES AND SYMBOLS

We cannot begin to summarize here the universe of Hindu mythology, but two points are important for our purpose. First, Hindu stories and texts are rich in messages that can be used either to promote violence or to promote love and nonviolence. Second, while there were few prominent historical narratives justifying hostility to the British, there were more justifying hostility and violence toward Muslims. This is hardly surprising—Muslims had been present in India for a millennium before the British arrived—but it is consequential, helping to explain why mass violence by Hindus was more often directed against Muslim than British targets.

An outstanding example of the first point is the Bhagavad Gita, which forms part of a larger Hindu epic, the Mahabharata.[6] One of the most important Hindu religious texts, the Gita chronicles a conversation between the god Krishna, believed by Vishaiva Hindus to be the incarnation or avatar of the supreme being Vishnu, and his disciple Arjuna.[7] The story takes place on the battlefield before the start of a war, where Krishna guides Arjuna through the moral dilemma of having to fight against his own kin. Krishna explains to Arjuna the virtues that are required of him—namely, that he as warrior and prince was obligated to fight, even against his own kin if necessary.[8] This portion of the Gita obviously can be, and has been, used to justify violence in some circumstances.

There is, however, another side to the Gita: Krishna as the people's god and the god of love. Hindu mythology holds, for example, that Krishna was born into royalty and had supernatural powers yet lived a simple village life among the poor. Artistic renderings of Krishna often place him among cattle and children, which signify his compassion toward the weak. Furthermore, Krishna promoted love as a way to achieve salvation, or *moksha*. According to Krishna, *moksha* is achieved by rising above one's selfish desires, abandoning all worldly possessions, and engaging in a life of service to others. This teaching embodies the notion of dharma, which Hinduism describes as the natural moral law of the universe.[9] Many ancient gurus considered compassion to be the root of dharma.[10]

Another key Hindu text is the *Ramayana*, the tale of Lord Rama, an earlier avatar of Vishnu (according to the Vishnaiva tradition). The *Ramayana* is a rollicking tale of royal virtue and usurpation and of battle against evil demons and monsters, in stark contrast to the philosophizing and law-giving of the Gita. Still, the images from two scenes were to prove potent in Gandhian lore: early in the book, when Rama tamely retreats to the forest to avert civil war after his brother's usurpation; and later, when he embarks on a war against the demon king of the island of Lanka, who had abducted his wife.

Another set of symbols from Hindu mythology important in understanding Gandhi's success concerns the traditional holy man and the ashram. While the most famous of India's "saintly renouncers" was Siddhartha Gautama, the sixth-century BCE Buddha, Hinduism and Jainism also traditionally revere the saintly holy man. This tradition was revived by Swami Vivekananda (1863–1902).[11] Gurus are often associated in Hindu tradition with ashrams, religious hermitages or monasteries. In Hindu mythology, the sage would become a *rājaguru*, or royal teacher, in times of crisis. A common theme in many Hindu folktales is that of the troubled ruler who finds solace, wisdom, or military training in the guru's ashram.[12]

Another element of Hinduism that was central to Gandhi's message was ahimsa, or nonviolence, a doctrine common to Hinduism, Buddhism, and Jainism that prohibits killing or injuring living beings. The earliest references to the idea date back to the eighth century BCE.[13] While the extent to which ahimsa should be applied is contested, it is widely held to be a component of dharma and is closely connected to the notion that all kinds of violence yield negative karmic consequences.[14]

Narratives justifying hostility and violence, however, were also present. One key narrative is that of Shivaji Maharaj, the seventeenth-century Hindu king who successfully fought the Mughal emperor Aurangzeb to establish the independent Maratha Confederacy. Aurangzeb makes for an ideal villain: notoriously religiously intolerant, he came to power by supplanting his older brother and imprisoning his father, the builder of the Taj Mahal. Shivaji, in contrast, already a hero in popular ballads and other folklore in Maharashtra, came increasingly to be interpreted as the founder of Indian nationalism, vindicator of Hinduism, and scourge of Muslims.[15] Extremists led by Tilak played up an episode in the Shivaji narrative in which Shivaji assassinated an opposing Muslim general, thereby promoting not only hostility toward Muslims but also assassination as a tactic.[16] Tilak promoted the Shivaji cult more broadly by sponsoring a popular Shivaji festival celebrating the hero's accomplishments—a festival that frequently sparked communal violence.

There were, of course, also narratives that could be used to justify hostility toward the British. The most potentially powerful of these concerned the brutality of British repression after the 1857 Mutiny. Particularly noted in collective memory were the cases of ritual defilement imposed by the British on the condemned men. Thus, Hindus were forced to eat beef, Muslims' bodies were smeared with the fat of pigs, and different castes were forced to eat together in prison mess halls.[17] Such stories were remembered, but more in some regions than others. According to a British observer in 1925, "The Mutiny . . . means little in South India. Nor does it yet mean a great deal in Bengal. . . . But from Bihar to the Border the Mutiny lives."[18] Thus across a large swath of northern India, such collective memories were available as bases of mobilization.

HINDUS' SYMBOLIC PREDISPOSITIONS AND THREAT PERCEPTIONS

In the absence of polling data, the only evidence we have about ordinary Indians' early twentieth-century values and biases is indirect. Yet some facts are clear enough, starting with the central importance of religious values. As one observer noted in 1929, "for the mass of the people religion still holds a far larger interest than politics."[19] For example, the walls of many Indian homes were adorned with pictures of Krishna, and millions of Hindus routinely turned out for festivals celebrating Ganesh and other popular deities.[20] What this meant for politics was that the most effective way to mobilize large numbers politically was to use religious symbolism to appeal to religiously based symbolic predispositions. An example is the concept of *darshan*, the blessings that were believed to flow from the sight of a holy or auspicious person, of whom Gandhi was seen as one. The "belief in Gandhi the demi-god," David Arnold notes, "drew many thousands of peasants to his meetings or caused them to gather in huge crowds at railway stations to catch a glimpse of him, to have his *darshan*."[21] This symbolic predisposition was a pivotal source of Gandhi's charismatic authority.

Of course, not all religious symbols had such benign effects: Muslim slaughter of cows—which are of course sacred to Hindus—frequently touched off riots by offended Hindus in early twentieth-century India. Similarly, Hindu religious processions, accompanied by loud music and often taking place around mosques, were offensive to Muslims and also touched off violent confrontations with distressing regularity. As one foreign observer noted, "each community . . . seems often at pains to choose the route which causes the largest amount of public inconvenience."[22]

Another symbolic predisposition among Hindus was an anti-Muslim bias that shaded into a strong tendency to fear Muslims. Here is a clear example of Hypothesis 1: popular narratives shaped the development of (hostile, in this case) symbolic predispositions. According to David Hardiman, "the image of the supposedly cruel, fanatical and belligerent Muslim was a relatively recent construct" in the late nineteenth century, but it was widespread nevertheless.[23] This bias was visible even in Gandhi's own writings. For example, in a 1924 article entitled "Hindu-Muslim Tension: Its Cause and Cure," Gandhi characterized Islam as having "become gross and fanatical here," even while conceding "that we have had no small share in making it so." Echoing popular stereotypes, he added, "The Mussulman as a rule is a bully, and the Hindu as a rule is a coward."[24]

Since this particular SYP is based on a stereotype of Muslims as threatening, the unsurprising result was evidence for Hypothesis 2: this type of prejudice encouraged heightened threat perceptions by Hindus. The Hindu revivalist Swami Shraddhanand reported hearing an extreme example of this threat perception among poor Hindus of Gujarat: "When Swaraj [independence] comes, it will be the Musalmans who will rule," these peasants suggested, and "the musalmans can destroy the Hindus if they want to."[25] The result, in turn, was a predisposition to believe a wide range of accusations against Muslims. For example, in 1929, strikebreaking Pashtun workers in Bombay were accused of kidnapping Hindu children, a rumor that resulted in a riot.[26] More broadly, according to Hardiman, "large numbers of caste Hindus came to accept the notion that their religion was under demographic threat, to the extent that it became a form of Hindu 'common sense.'" Narratives promoted by the Hindu Mahasabha portrayed Islam and Christianity as explicitly hostile and dangerous to Hinduism: one song published in 1911 asserted, "To eat us alive the Quran and the Bible are hissing [like snakes]." The remedy, it was held, lay in reversing the conversions through a counter-proselytisation, which would culminate in the public performance of *shuddhi* (reconversion).[27]

A related symbolic predisposition among Hindus was the notion that Muslims did not regard India as their home, so they were not truly Indian but rather a dangerous foreign element who could not be loyal to India.[28] Hindu Mahasabha leader B. S. Moonje, for example, argued that Indian Muslims had a "one-sided Nationalism," indeed an "Islamic Mission," that was incompatible with Indian nationalism.[29] The Hindu chauvinist M. S. Golwalkar later pushed this notion to an extreme, asserting, "The non-Hindu people in Hindustan must either . . . learn to respect and hold in reverence

Hindu religion . . . in a word they must cease to be foreigners, or they . . . [may] claim nothing . . . not even citizen's rights."[30]

Yet another prejudice among some Hindus was an anti-Western bias. At the mass level, for example, there was an anti-British riot in Bombay in 1921 which turned against "anyone wearing Western clothes."[31] Yet this attitude, too, existed also at the elite level. When the writer Rabindranath Tagore gave a lecture in Madras a year or two later, "every criticism of anything Western was roundly applauded," even though "the real extremists boycotted the lecture."[32]

MUSLIMS' SYMBOLIC PREDISPOSITIONS
AND THREAT PERCEPTIONS

There were similarly powerful anti-Hindu biases among Muslims, an indication that narratives helped to shape Muslim prejudice (Hypothesis 1). One high-ranking British official observed, "To the Muhammadan the Hindus are not merely idolaters, they are the descendants of a race which his own ancestors have conquered and ruled, and he regards them less as fellow Indians than as an inferior race which he would subjugate to his service if free to do so."[33] Even educated and moderate Muslims showed this tendency: Gandhi's ally Mohamed Ali, for example, was quoted as saying, "Gandhiji is a good man, but I believe an adulterous and drunken Musalman to be his better, inasmuch as the latter has 'iman' (faith)."[34]

Muslims' prejudices, in turn, motivated them to demonstrate hostility to Hindus, as anticipated by Hypothesis 3. For example, Muslim rituals were altered in ways that were specifically offensive to Hindus. As one scholar observed, "In particular the slaughter of cows as a ritual act by Muhammadans at the Idu'l-azha festival, which is regarded as a commemoration of Abraham's willingness to slay his son Isaac, is strongly resented" by Hindus.[35] Yet as the Aga Khan noted in the 1920s, the Koran does not mention cow slaughter in this connection; rather, animal sacrifices in that book, and as practiced in other Muslim countries such as Saudi Arabia, typically involve sheep, not cattle.[36]

These prejudices also led to threat perceptions among Muslims, as expected according to Hypothesis 2. Swami Shraddhanand's reconversion campaign was a particular source of anxiety, with one member of the ulema charging that the Swami aimed "either to extirpate the Mahomedans in India or to drive them out of India."[37] Indian nationalists' campaign for self-rule was also a source of fear, with one Muslim journalist asserting in 1924, "When Swaraj comes . . . they will drive Musalmans out of India."[38] "Better," the journalist concludes, "that India may not get Swaraj." The Muslim politician Yakub Hassan took a similar position five years later, arguing that India should seek dominion status, not independence, because "common allegiance to a non-Indian king can alone keep Hindus and Mussalmans from aggression" against each other.[39] According to another Muslim leader, Hakim Mohamed Jamil Khan, this issue confronted Muslims with a "life and death struggle."[40] Moreover, many Muslims believed that independence would result in the creation of a Hindu religious state, which is why Gandhi's rhetoric of noncooperation was viewed with suspicion.[41]

The Symbolic Politics of Gandhi's Rise and the Hindu-Muslim Split

EXPLAINING GANDHI'S RISE: SYMBOLIC SOURCES OF A LEADER'S CREDIBILITY

Mohandas Gandhi first gained prominence as a leader of the Indian community in South Africa; starting in 1912, his association with G. K. Gokhale, the Moderate leader in India, helped raise his stature there as well. While in South Africa, he also began developing his philosophy of satyagraha (literally "firmness in truth," but translated by Gandhi to mean "soulforce"), which came to include his signature embrace of nonviolent political and social activism. Gandhi thereby established himself "as a spiritual and moral leader" who had also managed to achieve some minor concessions on improved rights for South Africa's Indians.[42] He returned to India in 1915 with a unique personal stature.

Gandhi's method was to turn his life into a well-documented experiment that used all aspects of Indian culture and daily life for their symbolic significance—especially symbols that resonated with Hindu mythology. Gandhi's ascetic lifestyle established his saintly image in accordance with traditional tropes of the Hindu holy man: the limited diet, the celibacy, the loincloth, and the mixture of simple speech with incomprehensible philosophizing all worked to elevate him to that status. Gandhi's establishment of ashrams further strengthened this status as a sage, giving Gandhi the image of a *rājaguru* to whom conventional politicians could be expected to turn for guidance. At the same time, exploiting the image of the ashram as a school of warfare (as in the *Ramayana*), Gandhi made his ashrams also into places of training for his acolytes in the spiritual warfare and nonviolent confrontation of satyagraha.[43]

Digging deeper into Hindu scriptures, Gandhi made the Bhagavad Gita into his touchstone text, and he elevated Krishna, to whom he repeatedly referred in his commentaries as "the Divine One," into his great hero.[44] To justify his interpretations of ahimsa, which lean toward Jainism, to his predominantly Hindu audience, Gandhi interpreted the Gita's great war as an allegory. In Gandhi's telling, the battlefield in the Gita represents the soul, while Arjuna represents man's impulse to reject evil and do what is righteous.[45] This interpretation justified Gandhi's embrace of the Jainist idea that because all life is sacred, any violence toward humans, animals, or even plant life that is not used for sustenance is prohibited. In Gandhi's view, if violent, coercive, and unjust means were used to achieve a goal, then the ends produced would reflect the unjust means that were used.[46]

Gandhi also molded his own life story and ideology to imitate the narrative of the life of Krishna. For example, while Gandhi was like Krishna in that he was born to high status, he chose to identify with the masses and lived among the poor and lower castes, speaking and dressing with great simplicity. Similarly, Gandhi promoted ahimsa as a way to peace and freedom, in parallel with Krishna's lesson about love as the path to salvation. Gandhi was given the title "Mahatma," which means "great soul," while Krishna's title was "Paramatma," or "super soul." In his visual imagery, Gandhi mirrored the Krishnaist motif in numerous photographs where he was often seen, like Krishna, with cattle and children.[47] Gandhi even hinted, for example in a 1913 letter to a cousin, that he might be a divine avatar.[48]

The means that Gandhi used to promote his message also echoed those of Krishna. Krishna used songs and dance to mobilize the masses for action; similarly, Gandhi mobilized people with songs and prayer. Krishna used the discus (*Sudarshan Chakra*) to vanquish evil and promote righteousness; Gandhi used the spinning wheel—the term (*Charkha*) is similar to that for "discus"—to spin his own cloth as a symbol of self-sufficiency and independence. Gandhi also associated the spinning wheel with the *Dharma Chakra*, the Hindu "wheel of righteous action," which would later be emblazoned on the Indian flag. Lastly, Krishna revealed himself in his universal form (*Vishwarupa*) to open people's hearts, while Gandhi sought to do the same with satyagraha.[49]

Gandhi's cultivation of his image as saintly holy man and acolyte of Krishna was astoundingly successful, becoming his greatest source of power, as even his adversaries admitted. Thus when Gandhi left South Africa, his opponent J. C. Smuts sardonically commented, "The saint has left our shores, I sincerely hope for ever."[50] Ordinary Indians agreed, as many hung pictures of Gandhi in their homes alongside their portraits of Krishna.[51] So strong was this association that soon after Gandhi's return to India, rumors began spreading that he had divine powers. Those who doubted or opposed Gandhi were said to face bad luck, while those who showed devotion to him could expect miracles, such as the refilling of a drying well.

It was this saintly image that provided the most important motivation for the *satyagrahis*, most of whom passionately believed in nonviolence as a creed, but had little understanding of the religious or philosophical basis of the doctrine.[52] Thus in interviews, many satyagrahis stated that nonviolence could never fail when you have Gandhi as a leader; comparisons of Gandhi to Krishna or Krishna's acolyte Arjuna were not uncommon. When asked if they participated in Satyagraha because of faith in ahimsa or faith in the leadership, 76 percent replied that Gandhi was the primary reason for their participation.[53]

In addition to his appeals to Hindu myths and symbols, Gandhi also elevated simple products used by poor villagers to symbolic status. These included not only the *Charkha* (spinning wheel) but also the white cloth cap, the half-*Dhoti* garment made of khādī (homespun) cloth, and the mud house, all of which symbolized self-reliance, self-employment, and a mixture of humility and cultural pride.[54] Gandhi used all of these items himself and pressed his followers to do likewise. At public meetings Gandhi often spun khādī as he spoke. As Gandhi put it, "My life is my message."[55] The potency of these symbols was enhanced by the idea that these common items would be used to liberate all of India.[56] Weapons were not easily available, but the spinning wheel and khādī cloth were available to all. Moreover, when Gandhi employed these materials, he kept their appearance as plain as possible so that they would have a universal appeal, avoiding the local affiliation that ornamentation would give them.[57]

In sum, while preaching his message of nonviolence, self-reliance, and communal living, Gandhi adopted a lifestyle that was symbolic of the simple life that most Indians lived. Moreover, he never asked people to do anything that he was unwilling to do, such as fasting or associating with untouchables.[58]

Finally, salt itself, the issue of the 1930 march, was easy to raise to symbolic status. Indians relied on adding salt to their food to stay hydrated in their hot climate, in addition to using it for other purposes such as food storage.[59] Salt could be found easily in dried mud flats and salt beds on the coast and in marshlands and salt mines. Additionally, salt could be made by boiling seawater. However, the British government made it a crime for people to make their own salt; they had to buy it from the government, which imposed high taxes on it. For the majority of Indians who lived hand to mouth, the salt tax was a major burden.[60]

GANDHI'S RISE

Gandhi's political rise in India began in 1917, after an activist from the Champaran district in Bihar persuaded him to investigate the oppression of indigo workers in his area. Gandhi patiently launched a detailed investigation, defying an order by local officials to leave. Attracting a cadre of young professionals to assist him, he documented and publicized the peasants' mistreatment so effectively that the government felt compelled to retreat, addressing the peasants' grievances in a new law. This episode was notable in two ways. First, it was very unusual for a politician of national stature to involve himself so deeply in the pragmatic concerns of ordinary peasants, especially in so remote a region as Bihar.[61] Second, having done so, Gandhi was remarkable in that he had managed to use his celebrity to achieve some quick practical results.[62]

Fresh from this success, Gandhi was drawn into another peasant dispute in 1918, this time in the Kheda district of his home region of Gujarat. The issue in Kheda was excessive taxation in a context of poor harvests and wartime inflation. Assisted by local activists from Annie Besant's Home Rule League, Gandhi organized a true satyagraha campaign, persuading the peasant cultivators to withhold their tax payments en masse. The framing was religious symbolism: Gandhi's chief local organizer, Vallabhbhai Patel, told villagers "that their land had been made holy by Gandhi's presence," while Gandhi himself appealed to dharma.[63] It was their duty, he told the richer peasants, to make sacrifices in support of their poorer neighbors.[64] Gandhi's success in recruiting participants was spotty and short-lived, but he still achieved some partial success: the district collector agreed to suspend tax payments by the poorer peasants. A simultaneous effort to mediate a labor dispute in nearby Ahmedabad, ultimately featuring a hunger strike by Gandhi himself, similarly resulted in a compromise settlement. The effect of these two campaigns together was to make Gandhi the "most powerful politician in Gujarat."[65]

The next year, 1919, Gandhi moved to make himself the most powerful opposition politician in India. The provocation was the Rowlatt Act making wartime restrictions on civil rights permanent after World War I had ended. This act left Indian nationalists, who had been expecting increased civil and political rights after the war, sputtering in outrage. But only Gandhi came forward with a plan for a significant mass response: a call for an all-India *hartal*, a modified general strike. To organize this effort, Gandhi worked through the Home Rule Leagues, some pan-Islamist groups, and an organization called Satyagraha Sabha which he had just created.[66] The *hartal*, scheduled for April 6, was again unevenly observed. But the overall process matches the expectations of symbolic politics theory: social threat (to status) leads to resonance for Gandhi's assertive framing (given Gandhi's personal credibility), but the reliance on new and spotty organizational effort yields uneven turnout.

The government reacted to the *hartal* by restricting Gandhi to the Bombay Presidency and removing him from a train when he tried to go to Delhi. When word spread that Gandhi had been mistreated, widespread violence erupted, including massive riots in Ahmedabad and Lahore. The worst violence came in Amritsar, where British troops opened fire on a crowd without warning, killing an officially estimated 379 and wounding over a thousand.[67] Ordinary Indians responded with more violence, including in Gujarat. Gandhi therefore called off the satyagraha, blaming himself for a "Himalayan miscalculation"—not about British savagery, but about the failure of his own followers to adhere to nonviolence in the face of it.[68]

After the Amritsar Massacre, General Dyer, the officer responsible, was recalled to Britain, and British occupation policy shifted toward the minimum use of force. The provisions of the Rowlatt law were never invoked.

Instead, the December 1919 Government of India Act expanded the opportunities of Indian politicians to participate in legislative councils more meaningful than any in the past and gave voters the opportunity to elect these councilors.[69] The first round of elections was to be held in November 1920.

Instead of seizing this opportunity, Gandhi persuaded his followers to challenge British rule through more boycotts and other mass campaigns. He first threw himself into the Khilafat campaign—the campaign of Indian Muslims to protest the threatened Allied deposition of the Ottoman sultan, who was simultaneously the Muslim caliph. This movement accomplished nothing tangible but did give Gandhi a position as the Indian politician best placed to transcend the Hindu-Muslim divide.

Next Gandhi mobilized his supporters to take over the Congress at its 1920 meeting, getting it to ratify his noncooperation program and reorganizing it into a mass political party with an established structure. Gandhi's rhetoric included symbolic references to the *Ramayana*: referring to Rama's defeat of the demon Ravana in that tale, Gandhi spoke about replacing contemporary "Ravanarajya" (demonic British rule) with "Ramarajya" (God's rule). Lest this appeal seem too obscure, he also explicitly labeled British rule "Satanic."[70] He promised Swaraj (independence) within a year if his strategy was followed.[71] Gandhi's success in mobilizing people at this time again accords with symbolist theory: it was based on an injustice frame employed by a credible leader and focused on social threats that were widely perceived by the public (Hypotheses 4 and 5) and backed a large organizational network centered around the Indian National Congress (Hypothesis 6).

Though Gandhi gained a remarkable amount of support for this noncooperation campaign, that support fell far short of what was needed for it to achieve its aims. What Gandhi was asking his followers to do was in many cases to abandon their livelihoods or career prospects. Politicians were to refuse to run for office; lawyers were to close their practices; civil servants and policemen were to resign their posts; students were to quit school. The point was to make British rule unworkable by refusing to cooperate with it in any way, but too many ignored Gandhi's call. For example, the elections in November 1920 featured races for 637 legislative seats, but only six of the seats were left unfilled because candidates refused to step forward. More effective were a boycott on British-made goods and an anti-liquor campaign, both of which cut into British revenues, but the impact fell far short of achieving *swaraj* within a year.[72]

SYMBOLIC MOBILIZATION BY THE HINDU RIGHT

Ironically, one of the campaign's most important legacies was to embitter relations between Muslims and Hindus. The year 1919 had seen the peak of Hindu-Muslim cooperation, with the *Arya Samaj* leader Swami Shraddhanand, after denouncing the British for the Amritsar Massacre, being invited to preach in favor of Hindu-Muslim unity at a prominent mosque in Delhi.[73] In 1920, 118 leading ulama endorsed a fatwa requiring "Muslim participation in the Non-cooperation movement as a religious duty."[74] Unfortunately, intercommunal relations quickly went downhill from there.

One reason for Gandhi's inability to keep the Hindu-Muslim alliance together was that his religious language and symbols tended to alienate Muslims, especially because Hindu nationalists used them as well. Ram Raj, for example, is a Hindu myth about a golden age that Gandhi associated with his goal of Swaraj (independence). However, Ram Raj was depicted as a time of peace because according to the myth, lower castes and non-Hindus were vanquished.[75] In using this imagery Gandhi alienated Muslims while reinforcing the imagery used by anti-Muslim Hindu revivalists. By the 1920s, the symbol of Ram Raj was a centerpiece of hard right Hindu politics, as nationalists evoked appeals to Ram Raj when they attacked mosques.[76] Similarly, Gandhi often referred to "Mother India," but that idea was popularized in Bankim Chandra Chatterji's nationalist novel *Anandamath* (*The Abbey of Bliss*), which celebrated a sect that aimed to eliminate all evidence of Muslim influence in India.[77] Even Gandhi's adoption of the loincloth as his typical garment offended many Muslims, who believed he was wearing it to promote Hinduism.[78]

Muslims were also increasingly suspicious of Gandhi in the 1920s because he repeated, and seemed to believe, negative stereotypes about them. As we noted, one of these stereotypes was the image of Muslims as violent bullies. At different times Gandhi wrote that Muslims were "too free with the knife and pistol," that centuries of dominance over India made them tyrants, and that they were comparable to bull terriers.[79] Gandhi also suggested that Muslims are outsiders to India, asserting, "Mussulmans take less interest in the political life and advancement of the country because they do not yet regard India as their home." Gandhi did not see Muslims as a separate community, but as Hindus who had left their faith.[80]

However, the main reason Gandhi's communal alliance came apart was the rise of communal violence in the 1920s, the result of the rising popularity of communalist appeals on both sides. In the worst violence in the period, the Muslim Moplahs in the Malabar region of southern India initiated a rebellion in August 1921, killing not only British officials but also Hindu landlords. Here we have a case of Muslim prejudice overriding their national leaders' strategy of intercommunal cooperation; some Hindus responded in kind by aiding the British in suppressing the revolt. The Moplahs responded with further atrocities, including killings and forced conversion. In total, an estimated six hundred Hindus were killed and 2,500 were forcibly converted; thousands of Moplahs were also killed when the British suppressed the revolt.[81] In their reactions to these events, Indian nationalist leaders split along communal lines as a result of the terror management effect: the physical threat of intercommunal violence trumped the social threat of continued

British rule. Gandhi denounced the "Moplah madness." However, his message was inconsistent. In some instances, he placed blame on the British; in others the Moplahs; at other times Hindus were answerable.[82] Moreover, Muslims regarded Gandhi's criticisms of the Moplahs as an indictment of their religion.[83]

The Moplah rebellion was followed by violence in other areas. Riots involving Hindus, Muslims, and Parsis in Bombay led to the deaths of fifty-eight people in November 1921. Finally, and most disturbingly for Gandhi, a mob in northern India, after being fired on by local police, killed seventeen policemen and torched the police station at Chauri Chaura in February 1922. For Gandhi, this was the last straw: after consulting with the Congress Working Committee, he announced the suspension of the noncooperation campaign, and he fasted for five days to atone for the violence he had inadvertently unleashed.[84]

Muslim leaders, however, were incensed, as they had been pushing the other way, demanding the abandonment of nonviolence in their December 1921 Congress.[85] This was perhaps the most important obstacle to a Gandhi-led alliance of Hindus and Muslims. While for Gandhi nonviolence was a fundamental principle, Muslim allies like Mohammed Ali endorsed it only for tactical reasons; Ali's brother Shaukat Ali argued that tyrannicide should be considered service to God.[86] This tactical agreement could not last: while Gandhi repeatedly pulled back when his campaigns led to violence, Muslims wanted to press forward. Furthermore, while Gandhi consulted his Congress allies, he had not consulted his Muslim friends when he decided to suspend the campaign after Chauri Chaura—even though Gandhi, a Hindu, lacked the authority to cancel the fatwa in favor of noncooperation that those friends had procured.[87] Gandhi's relations with his Muslim allies had suffered a serious blow.

Gandhi's subsequent arrest and imprisonment for two years temporarily removed him from the political scene, leading to the abandonment of his policies. Moderates in Congress, recognizing the failure of efforts to boycott council elections, formed the Swarajist Party to take part in the 1923 legislative council elections and try to effect change from within the empire's institutions.

Meanwhile, Swami Shraddhanand, who had loudly denounced the "brutal and inhuman atrocities [that] were perpetrated on Hindus by Moplas in Malabar," began arguing "that if they did not organize . . . and also did not undertake reclamation [reconversion of Islamized Hindus] to prevent further deterioration in their numbers, the future of Hinduism was gloomy."[88] Acting on this argument, he began to employ his signature ceremony of *shuddhi* (rededication) for just such a campaign. In the process, Shraddhanand helped to redirect two communalist Hindu organizations, Arya Samaj and the Hindu Mahasabha, in an explicitly anti-Muslim direction. The Mahasabha ideologist V. D. Savarkar, who like Shraddhanand had previously been an advocate of Hindu-Muslim unity, also promoted this turn, publishing *Hindutva* ("*Hinduness*"), a new book glorifying Hindu civilization and branding Muslims as essentially outsiders.[89] A third Hindu communalist organization, Rashtriya Swayamsevak Sangh (RSS), was founded by K. B. Hedgewar in 1925, further contributing to the growing anti-Muslim mood among Hindus. Hindu communalist organizations like these—or, more often, their local affiliates—along with their Muslim counterparts now increasingly provoked violent riots, further increasing communal tensions. The Hindu Mahasabha, led by Lala Lajpat Rai, further capitalized on the situation by establishing a special fund to aid Hindu victims of communal riots—a very clever use of a threat frame—among other efforts.[90]

Here we have the main answer to the question about the rise of communal tensions: all of the conditions for violent communalist mobilization, especially on the Hindu side, were present at a time when Gandhi was in prison. Anti-Muslim prejudice was already widespread because of hostile narratives (Hypothesis 1), leading Hindus to perceive Muslim actions as threatening (Hypothesis 2); these prejudices and threat perceptions in turn encouraged many Hindus (Hypotheses 3 and 4) to support provocative action against Muslims, such as trying to convert Muslims to Hinduism. Communalist leaders such as Shraddhanand, Lajpat Rai, and others exploited this situation by articulating assertive communal frames playing on existing hostile narratives, SYPs, and fears (Hypothesis 5) and rebuilt or created organizations to mobilize their supporters for action (Hypothesis 6).

GANDHI'S ABANDONMENT OF "HEART-UNITY"

Gandhi emerged from prison in 1924 into this changing environment. Soon after his release, an exchange of religious insults in the Kohat region of Northwest Frontier Province led to violence, resulting in the deaths of 155 Hindus, with most of the rest of the area's Hindu population driven out and resettled. Gandhi embarked on a fast to promote peace and unity, and he joined with his ally Shaukat Ali to investigate, but their opposing conclusions just illustrated how far apart they were. Ali argued the anti-Hindu violence was exaggerated, while the Muslim League focused on the religious provocation. On the Hindu side, Gandhi denounced the "Muslim fury on 10 September [that] knew no bounds." Hindu Mahasabha leader Lala Lajpat Rai posed the poignant question, "Even admitting that the Hindus were at fault, was their fault such that it deserved the punishment inflicted on them?"[91] The answer is probably Hypothesis 3: it was most likely anti-Hindu prejudice, not the Hindus' actions, the led the Kohat rioters to decide that indiscriminate violence against Muslims was the proper response to religious insult.

Elected president of Congress for 1925, Gandhi tried to patch up the growing split, making the heartfelt plea in his presidential address: "Hindu-

Muslim Unity . . . is the breath of our life."[92] He also convened an all-parties conference in January 1925. The conference foundered, however, on the question of guarantees for Muslim rights and influence: Muslim leaders demanded special provisions, such as having one-third of all seats in a future nationwide legislature reserved for Muslims, though Muslims were only one-quarter of the population. Hindu Mahasabha leaders and young Congress radicals such as Jawarharlal Nehru, on the other hand, not only denounced such special privileges but increasingly favored a centralized (rather than federal) system that offered little autonomy for the provinces at all. Gandhi, himself flexible on these issues, proved unable to broker a compromise. In 1928, a committee led by Motilal Nehru (Jawaharlal's father) articulated a refined version of Congress's proposal, called the Nehru Report, but the committee rejected the amendments requested by Muslim League spokesman Mohammed Ali Jinnah, in spite of Gandhi's support for Jinnah. Jinnah told a sympathetic Congress colleague that this was "the parting of the ways."[93]

Fatefully, Gandhi now essentially gave up on cooperation with his former Muslim allies, turning his attention instead to improving ties with Congress leaders and the Hindu right. When Swami Shraddhanand was killed in December 1926, and again when Lajpat Rai died in November 1928, Gandhi went out of his way to memorialize these controversial Hindu communalist leaders, brushing aside the role they had played in increasing Hindu-Muslim tensions.[94] Lajpat Rai's "last will and testament" had been a speech opposing "even the most modest demands of the Muslims" demanded by Jinnah at the meeting in 1928—that is, Lajpat Rai had just helped to prompt Jinnah's "parting of the ways" with Congress.[95]

Gandhi himself had become so pessimistic about communal relations that he made this comment in April 1928: "My solution to the problem is so different from what is generally expected. I am more than ever convinced that the communal problem should be solved outside of legislation and if, in order to reach that state, there has to be a civil war, so be it. Who will listen to a proposal so mad as this?"[96] Thus when Shaukat Ali wrote to Gandhi in October 1928 to protest the handling of Jinnah's proposed amendments to the Nehru Report, Gandhi simply brushed off his concerns, then followed up with a letter denouncing a speech by Shaukat as an "unequivocal indictment against the Hindus."[97] In doing this, Gandhi was "effectively ending his relationship with" this longtime ally and friend.[98] Then, to unify an increasingly Hindu-dominated Congress, Gandhi published an article endorsing the Nehru Report, ignoring Muslim concerns about fair representation.

Around the same time, Gandhi restarted his program of mass activism with a return to his roots: a 1928 satyagraha protesting a land tax increase in the Bardoli district of Gujarat. This campaign, led by Gandhi's longtime aide Vallabhbhai Patel, succeeded in stopping the tax increases.[99] Gandhi's motive in taking this step, Kathryn Tidrick argues, was that he was "determined to have power thrust upon him," as Congress leaders, frustrated with continued British recalcitrance, began to turn back to Gandhi's brand of activism.[100] Gandhi succeeded in December 1928, when Congress recalled him to lead. Gandhi laid down conditions: Congress's support for prohibition of alcohol, for promoting homespun (khādī), and for vague language against untouchability. Promoting Hindu-Muslim unity was no longer on his list. A year later, having run out of patience with British delaying tactics, Congress endorsed a new civil disobedience campaign to be led by Gandhi and aimed at complete independence.[101] But Gandhi would move forward in this campaign without most of his previous Muslim allies.

The logic of Gandhi's actions was the logic of Hypotheses 3 and 4. Anti-Muslim prejudice and threat perceptions among Hindus, encouraged by the hard-line rhetoric of communalist leaders like Lajpat Rai and Savarkar, were generating support among Hindus for confronting Muslims, not for making concessions to them. Seeking to build support for his anti-British campaign, Gandhi saw no alternative but to praise men like Lajpat Rai to bolster positive symbolic predispositions among Hindus toward himself, since his own charisma was his key weapon in mobilizing followers. Not only did popular Hindu prejudice block Gandhi's efforts at promoting Hindu-Muslim unity, but Gandhi's own anti-Muslim prejudices had a similar effect, prompting him to resign himself to the growing possibility of civil war.

The Salt Campaign

GANDHI'S FRAMING OF THE ISSUES

After some hesitation, Gandhi decided in early 1930 to focus his new satyagraha campaign on the issue of the salt tax Britain had imposed on India. As we would expect from Hypothesis 5, he used highly assertive frames to mobilize support for this effort. One of them was the master frame of injustice: he depicted the struggle on the salt issue as part of an overarching struggle between good and evil. Salt was a necessity used by all Indians, Gandhi noted. He argued that the tax was wicked because poor Indians could not afford to pay it, so the tax deprived them of a necessity that could be widely available. Gandhi asserted that it was the birthright of every Indian to be able to make salt in their own homes, as their ancestors did.[102] The second frame Gandhi used concerned the consequences of violating the law: he applied Hindu religious principles to frame the punishments for violating the salt laws as a form of purification. This second frame was primarily used within the ashrams to motivate the satyagrahis.

Gandhi's personal focus in this campaign would be on a march from his Sabarmati ashram in northern Gujarat to Dandi on the coast, where the marchers would make salt. In the months leading up to the march, Gandhi worked hard to articulate the master frame of injustice, often referring to the salt tax campaign as a "life and death struggle" and a "holy war" pitting good against evil.[103] Gandhi proclaimed that Dandi would be "the battle-field of satyagraha" that was "not chosen by man, but by God." He urged that during the month-long march no one should utter any untruths or engage in any sinful acts, as Dandi was to be a sacred place of pilgrimage for Swaraj. He branded the tax as a satanic law that encumbers women, children, and the impoverished, violating the sacred laws of Hinduism, Islam, Christianity, and Zoroastrianism. In other words, he was arguing that the salt tax was an egregious injustice that was forbidden by all of the world's religions. Building on this notion, Gandhi implored his followers to pray to God for the destruction of the British Empire, whose laws were the epitome of evil.

In theoretical terms, Gandhi was pointing to a wide range of social threats. At the most obvious level, the salt tax was a threat to economic interests, especially for India's vast population of the poor. Additionally, the tax threatened Indian values of justice, just as the British Empire it represented threatened Indian values and cultural traditions. Finally, the salt tax also represented a status threat, the British Empire's continuing subordination of all Indians under their claim of racial superiority. His aim in all of this was to raise the salience of Indians' common identity as Indians, to move them to unite against British oppression. The success of this campaign, primarily among Hindus, is consistent with Hypothesis 5: Gandhi's assertive frames were a key factor in mobilizing Hindus for the salt campaign.

To motivate his satyagrahis, who would bear the brunt of British force, Gandhi used another set of frames. In the ashrams, Gandhi often appealed to the Gita and its teachings on the importance of selflessness and detachment. Building on these ideas, Gandhi preached that satyagrahis should welcome suffering and even death as a means of purification. For the devout satyagrahi, the endurance of suffering for the sake of truth brings one to a state of power and self-realization similar to that of *moksha* (salvation). In preparing to break the salt laws in Dandi, Gandhi told his satyagrahis to not let go of the salt when the police tried to snatch it regardless of the cost, asserting that there is no defeat for those ready to die and suffer.[104] By submitting to violence and even death, satyagrahis would offer their lives as the ultimate sacrifice for truth.

MOBILIZING PROCESSES

Theoretically (Hypothesis 6), the success of the salt campaign should have required Gandhi and his followers to use organizations and social networks to mobilize followers. To a large extent, this was true. Two overlapping sets of networks were especially important: those of the Indian National Congress and those connected to Gandhi personally. The greatest mobilization successes should have come where both networks were in operation, with moderate success where only one was operating, and minimal success in the absence of both. The two networks were, of course, closely connected, but they did not always overlap.

Since a key part of Gandhi's strategy in the salt campaign was to fill the jails, we can use the number of jail-going satyagrahis in each province as a rough measure of mobilization success in those provinces. According to Jawaharlal Nehru, four provinces generated the most jail-goers, between ten thousand and fifteen thousand each: Bengal, Bihar, United Provinces, and Punjab.[105] Seven more provinces or cities generated between two thousand and five thousand jail-goers: Northwest Frontier Province, Bombay City, Delhi, Gujarat, Tamil Nadu, Andhra, and Central Provinces. What were the networks activated in these cases?

Bengal, Bihar, and United Provinces had, as expected, both strong Congress and strong Gandhian networks. Bengal was one of Congress's earliest strongholds, but it was also the location of Gandhian ashrams (Bankura and Arambagh), which contributed substantially to organizing the campaign. Bihar includes Champaran, the location of Gandhi's first big campaign in India; thus it was the site of Gandhi's earliest personal network, including again a Gandhian ashram (in Bihpur) as well as a subsequently built Congress network. United Provinces, finally, was the base region of the Nehru family and the location of strong organization building by Congress going back to 1921. The partial exception among the "success stories" was in Punjab, which had a large Congress presence but less of a Gandhian one after Gandhi's break with his Muslim allies.[106]

This pattern also offers some support for Hypothesis 3, that prejudice (and other negative symbolic predispositions) increases support for hostile action. As noted earlier in this chapter, the strongest anti-British narrative concerned memories of the 1857 Mutiny, and those memories were strongest across the swath of northern India from Bihar through United Provinces to Punjab. It seems likely that the resulting anti-British SYPs help explain both the organizational strength of the Congress and Gandhian networks in those areas, and their strong support for the salt campaign. Similarly, it was Bombay—in Bengal Province, the fourth area of strength for the salt campaign—that experienced anti-Western riots and anti-Western intellectual sentiments in the early 1920s. Again, this fits the pattern: strong support for hostile action in an area where there is evidence of negative SYPs.

Returning to the pattern of organizational strength, the provinces where mobilization generated moderate numbers of jail-goers were generally those with networks personally connected to Gandhi. The most obvious example is Gujarat, Gandhi's home province and the base of his lieutenant Villabhbhai Patel, which generated not only thousands of jail-goers but also numerous resignations by local officials and a highly successful tax strike.

Bombay City, to which many Gujaratis had migrated, was similarly under strong Gandhian influence, led by a protégé of Patel. Tamil Nadu was the base of another of Gandhi's key acolytes, Chakravarty Rajagopalachari, who took control of the Congress organization in the region to organize a salt march in imitation of Gandhi's, among other activities.[107] Rajagopalachari took over the presidency of Congress the following year, at Gandhi's instigation.

The most colorful example of Gandhian network ties is Northwest Frontier Province, which alone among Muslim areas responded to Gandhi's 1930 call under the leadership of the Pashtun leader Abdul Ghaffar Khan. Ghaffar Khan had met Gandhi years before, and emulated him to the degree that he came to be called the "Frontier Gandhi," improbably succeeding in gaining numerous recruits for nonviolence among his traditionally warlike people.[108] At the time of the 1930 actions, Gandhi sent his son Devdas to Northwest Frontier Province, presumably to coordinate actions with Ghaffar Khan.[109] After Ghaffar Khan's arrest, tribal groups launched a series of raids in the region, demanding the release from prison of Ghaffar Khan and "the naked fakir" Gandhi.[110]

Andhra and Central Provinces represent two quite different patterns. Coastal Andhra was a longtime Congress stronghold which dutifully organized several salt marches following Gandhi's lead, but a strong personal connection to Gandhi was lacking. In Central Provinces, in contrast—and in Maharashtra and Karnataka—there was little organization either by the Congress structure or by Gandhi's personal network, but there was nevertheless strong participation in the civil disobedience campaign. In all three of these provinces, "forest satyagraha"—civil disobedience of laws governing the use of forest resources—became widespread, with one event reportedly including one hundred thousand participants. In these cases it was to a large extent Gandhi's charisma, the magic of Gandhi's name, that created "an elemental and near-millenarian fervor," much like the enthusiasm Gandhi's first nationwide campaign had stirred up a decade before.[111] The leaders were local people, not members of any nationwide network. In these cases, mobilization was primarily the result of symbolic politics, not of social networks activated by national leadership.

What is striking about the salt campaign is that it was not a response to any specific external event. Congress's demand at the time was for complete independence; even Gandhian allies like Nehru were initially bewildered by Gandhi's focus on the salt issue.[112] The salt tax was not a prominent issue at the time; it became so only as a result of Gandhi's brilliant symbolic politics—the framing of the tax as "inhuman," and especially his ability to connect it to the general question of British legitimacy.[113] Thus the campaign swiftly became less about salt than about challenging British rule and exposing its brutality. External events to bolster the frame's credibility were unnecessary.

GANDHI'S SALT MARCH

The way Gandhi organized his Salt March to Dandi illustrates the unique mix of assertive symbolic framing and organizational muscle that he employed (Hypotheses 5 and 6 again). He first used his organizational power, arranging to have Congress give him full authority to launch a protest campaign as and when he wished.[114] He then kept the opening act under the tightest possible control by mobilizing his closest followers, inmates of his Sabarmati ashram, many of whom had been with him since his time in South Africa and who had long been in training for just such action.[115] The initial marchers, then, were those most strongly affected by Gandhi's charisma and most personally dedicated to him and to ahimsa. Gandhi used students from a nearby university he had founded, Gujarat Vidyapith, to scout out the march route for him.[116]

Gandhi's march began on March 12, 1930. Among the participants were seventy-eight of his followers from the ashram, including two Muslims and one Christian.[117] His wife applied a *tilak*, the dot on the forehead that symbolizes the "third eye" associated with Hindu gods, which is rarely worn by men other than Hindu priests. Gandhi's follower Mahadev Desai later commented on the leave-taking, illustrating the resonance of Gandhi's actions with Hindu mythology: "I beheld in Gandhiji an ideal Vaishnav, Lord Rama on his way to conquer Sri Lanka. But more than this I am reminded of Lord Buddha's Great March to attain divine wisdom." Gandhi's own rhetoric was martial: "We shall face the bullets with our backs to the wall." He increased the drama by publicly predicting his early arrest. During the march he worked hard to maintain the saintly image of himself and his followers, publicly rebuking them for such lapses as bringing in vegetables from nearby Surat. The speech was effective: "His words pierced our hearts," one reporter present wrote.[118] When the marchers reached the sea, they "purified" themselves by bathing in the sea. Gandhi then stooped to pick up some salt that had accumulated on the shore, commenting, "With this I am shaking the foundations of the British Empire," by beginning a "religious war of civil disobedience."[119]

The logic of Gandhi's actions here is the logic of the basic principle of symbolic politics theory: moving beyond appeals to prejudice, Gandhi was using an assortment of frames that appealed to a wide range of Hindu symbolic predispositions in his bid to mobilize support. Wearing the *tilak*, symbolic of divinity if associated with Hindu men, he reminded his followers of Rama or the Buddha. Promoting his own concept of satyagraha, and demanding self-sacrifice of his followers, he was appealing to millennia of traditions of asceticism among Hindus, Buddhists, and Jains, while his martial rhetoric appealed to the quite separate tradition of righteous warfare associated with both Rama and Krishna. And of course, couching his overall appeal in terms of an injustice frame provided his supporters with the motivation to act (according to Hypothesis 5).

Gandhi shrewdly arranged the march so it would grow as it proceeded by exploiting his organizational base (Hypothesis 6). The early part of the route ran through the Kheda district, the site of his 1918 antitax campaign, where his followers quickly swelled the ranks of the marchers. More joined later, so that thousands were marching by the time they reached the sea. Gandhi made a point of stopping the march frequently, holding public meetings in villages to encourage listeners to join.[120] At the same time, activists in Kheda began expanding the nature of the civil disobedience campaign, as local headmen began resigning their posts, and the district began a tax strike that was, as noted earlier in this chapter, to spread widely.[121] The march was thus a triumph both of Gandhian symbolic politics and of Gandhian organizing skill.

SALT WORKS RAID

The Dandi Salt March culminated with Gandhi violating the Salt Laws by producing his own salt on April 6, 1930. Gandhi's act of defiance sparked widespread civil disobedience, with Indians across the country breaking the Salt Laws. Shortly after the march, Gandhi alerted the media and the British viceroy of his plan to raid a government-controlled salt depot in Dharasana. This led to Gandhi's arrest. The raid itself was led by three of Gandhi's associates: the poet Sarojini Naidu, Imam Bawazeer, and Gandhi's son Manilal.[122] Prior to beginning the raid, Naidu roused the protesters by stating that while "Gandhi's body is in prison his soul goes with you."[123] On May 21, the satyagrahis breached the barbed wired fence of the salt works, prompting the police to attack with clubs. Having been trained by Gandhi in his ashrams, the satyagrahis did not defend themselves and accepted the punishment inflicted by the authorities, who beat them with steel-tipped lathis.[124] Webb Miller, a U.S. journalist who witnessed the beatings, noted how none of the marchers resisted. In Miller's depiction,

> Those struck down fell sprawling, unconscious or writhing in pain with fractured skulls or broken shoulders. In two or three minutes the ground was quilted with bodies. Great patches of blood widened on their white clothes. The survivors without breaking ranks silently and doggedly marched on until struck down. When every one of the first column was knocked down stretcher bearers rushed up unmolested by the police and carried off the injured to a thatched hut which had been arranged as a temporary hospital.[125]

Miller's account of the raid would later appear in over one thousand newspapers worldwide. The publicity attracted by the incident would cause many to question the legitimacy of British rule, which was increasingly seen as brutal and oppressive.

To some extent, this story is explicable in terms of pure symbolic rhetorical politics: Gandhi was engaged in the politics of redistribution, stirring up indignation about unjust social threats to Indians' identity, status, and economic interests to generate nonviolent mobilization (Hypothesis 5). Gandhi's personal credibility, his organizing success, and his framing of the Salt Laws as a grave injustice that violates the natural right of Indians all contributed the effectiveness of his appeal. Given his stature, his defiance of the Salt Laws was a highly potent symbolic action that triggered an emotional response in Indians across the subcontinent, helping to convince the Indian masses to hope—to believe that the idea of obtaining freedom from British rule through satyagraha was a realistic possibility. Gandhi argued, "As long we accept the presence of God's hand behind all things, we may believe that the abolishment of the tax is a certainty."[126] Therefore, the mere defiance of the Salt Laws would undermine their existence and signal their imminent end.

The motivation of the satyagrahis, especially for the raid at Dharasana where hundreds were beaten by Indian soldiers under British command, was more complex. The participants in the raid included trained satyagrahis from Gandhian ashrams, college students, and government clerks from Gujarat, many from Gandhi's base district of Kheda.[127] While these Gandhian acolytes were motivated by hope for freedom, like ordinary Indians, they were also driven by a hope for self-awareness, or *moksha*. As Gandhi taught his students in the ashrams, selflessness and suffering are a means of purification that can bring one to obtain self-realization. Therefore, for the satyagrahis, there was also the hope of their actions yielding spiritual rewards for them. This, again, is the logic of the basic principle of symbolic politics and of Hypothesis 6. First, Gandhi's lieutenants were harnessing the core Gandhian symbolic predispositions, such as the values of satyagraha, to motivate his core followers to take on the most dangerous challenge of the salt campaign. At the same time, they were using the strongest Gandhian organizations, the ashrams, to help organize the effort. The case shows that mass nationalist mobilization can succeed by appealing to symbolic predispositions other than prejudice—even if prejudice at the same time blocked achievement of Gandhi's previous goal of Hindu-Muslim unity.

Conclusion

The first question of this chapter was how and why Gandhi succeeded in getting the Indian masses to follow him in nonviolent resistance to the British. One answer is Hypothesis 4a: violence was not an attractive option because of the overwhelming threat from British organizational power. While there were narratives justifying hostility, especially communal memories of

British brutality after the 1857 Mutiny, efforts to expound on them were systematically suppressed by the British, as were efforts to cultivate military mutinies.[128] Anti-British riots did occasionally occur, as in Bombay in 1921, but they could turn against "anyone wearing Western clothes"—a frightening prospect for India's westernized elites.[129] Faced with these constraints on mobilizing mass violence, Indian Moderates confined themselves to persuasion in their anti-British activities, while communalists focused on promoting Hindu-Muslim conflict. Everyday frictions between Hindus and Muslims were in any case more frequent, and therefore more salient as issues, than frictions between British and Indians, while Muslims were also easier and more ubiquitous targets of violence. Fostering communal hatred was easier also because the British did not interfere, seeing such trends as assisting their divide-and-rule tactics.

When Gandhi arrived on the scene in 1915, therefore, there were mass communal tensions, but there was no mass anti-British movement. Gandhi began with the asset of a strong image and charisma as a holy man: he was called "Mahatma" as early as 1915, and he began to attract crowds eager just to see him—to receive his *darshan*—around the same time.[130] He built and maintained this image through symbolic politics, by cultivation of an aura not only as *rājaguru* but as avatar compared variously to Krishna, Rama, and the Buddha. By using his celebrity first to help ordinary people engaged in local disputes, in Champaran, Kheda, and elsewhere, Gandhi added the image of practical leader to that of religious sage. These were Gandhi's key tools: it was Gandhi's credibility as a leader that enabled his political success.

Thus Hypotheses 4 and 5 are central to explaining Gandhi's success: he was brilliant in defining frames of social threat that resonated with Hindu SYPs and leveraged his personal charisma to promote mobilization. Drawing on themes of Hindu philosophy defining love as a combination of compassion and selflessness—his unique interpretation of the message of the Gita—Gandhi drew on religious themes not only to justify his approach, but to foster a sense of pride among his satyagrahis. Gandhi again and again insisted that he was engaged in religious activity, and he was right: the satyagrahis were convinced, among other things, that following Gandhi was their path to personal salvation (*moksha*). Ordinary Indians who lacked this total dedication could still participate in Gandhi's movement by pursuing more homely activities—spinning, wearing khādī cloth, observing *hartals*, and so on. Even such simple acts as gathering salt were invested with the symbolism of righteousness, as Gandhi framed resistance to the Salt Laws as a matter of good resisting evil. Building on his other favorite Gita theme, Gandhi convinced his followers that this resistance was their religious duty—again, therefore, a step toward *moksha*. Here is Gandhi's use of the basic principle of symbolic politics, appealing to a wide range of popular symbolic predispositions to mobilize support for his cause.

At the same time, Gandhi's rhetoric of nonviolent combat and his fierce denunciations of British rule also resonated with anti-British symbolic predispositions among many Indians. While the evidence is sketchy, it seems to support Hypothesis 3: the most support for Gandhi's movement was found in four northern provinces especially known for anti-British sentiment.

Gandhi's success also varied with the strength of his organizational base in different regions, as Hypothesis 6 would lead us to expect. His early efforts in Champaran, Kheda, and elsewhere built the start of a personal organizational network that would support his later moves. His ashrams provided a smaller pool of dedicated and trained followers fully prepared to walk nonviolently into bloody confrontation and death, as at the Dharasana salt works. And his takeover of Congress beginning in 1920 converted that organization into a mass movement that did swing into action, if a bit unevenly, for the 1930 civil disobedience campaign. It was the combination of Gandhi's personal network with the organizational muscle of Congress and Gandhi's charismatic leadership that made the 1930 campaign so large, even if it yielded few fruits in the short term.

The parallel success of communal appeals—and the resulting communal violence—was attributable first of all to the factors identified in Hypotheses 1 and 2: mutually hostile group narratives, and the resulting prejudices and threat perceptions. Communalist leaders like Tilak had for decades been promoting narratives like that of Shivaji, portraying Muslims as hostile to Hindus and violent resistance as laudable. Both religious communities had modified their rituals to be explicitly obnoxious to the other, with Muslims making cow-slaughter into a ritual while Hindus organized noisy celebrations outside mosques. As a result, members of both groups, and even Gandhi himself, were prejudiced against the other, expressing stereotypes based on the hostile narratives. This prejudice encouraged Hindu communalists to fear for the future survival of Hinduism based on their belief in demographic decline. These prejudices and threat perceptions, in turn, left members of both communities inclined to support hostile action against the other (Hypotheses 3 and 4). In these conditions, credible leaders like Swami Shraddhanand and Lala Lajpat Rai, as well as their Muslim counterparts, found it relatively easy to make assertive frames resonate (Hypothesis 5), and with just a little organization (Hypothesis 6) such leaders found it easy to spark ethnic rioting. Gandhi could not prevent the violence, in short, because he could not prevent Hindu (or Muslim) communalists from mobilizing their supporters.

He did try. Gandhi often repeated that Hindu-Muslim unity was essential to the achievement of true freedom. Recognizing that his personal appeal was primarily to Hindus, Gandhi made a point in the early 1920s of promoting the Khilafat campaign as a way to gain credibility with Muslims, and of allying himself with popular Muslim leaders such as Shaukat Ali and his brother Mohamed. When communal riots broke out, he tried to stop them: he fasted, he investigated, and he was often generous in admitting Hindu failings. When Hindu and Muslim leaders fought over constitutional provisions for power sharing, Gandhi often pushed for accommodation even of demands like reservation of parliamentary seats in excess of the Muslim share of the general population.

However, Gandhi's efforts did not lead to a lasting improvement in Hindu-Muslim relations. Muslims were highly suspicious about Gandhi's intentions because his use of Hindu myths and symbols—references to the Gita, to Ram Raj and "Mother India"—not only left them cold but also strengthened the appeal of Hindu chauvinists using similar imagery. Gandhi's repeated and forthright insistence that he was a religious leader—a Hindu religious leader, though he did not say that—inevitably cast Muslims as outsiders in his movement. No matter how courteously Gandhi invited Muslims in, they could hardly be moved by his primary reliance on Hindu religious symbols. Gandhi's references to anti-Muslim stereotypes as violent bullies hardly helped, nor did Muslims' skepticism about nonviolence.

By the time Gandhi began preparing for the Salt March, he had put aside his efforts at Hindu-Muslim unity so he could regain command of the Congress and restart nonviolent resistance. When the call came to launch the new satyagraha, Gandhi insisted that his followers first renew their commitment to the spinning wheel; he did not insist that they first reach a constitutional bargain with Muslim leaders. Instead of renewing his ties to Muslim leaders like Shaukat Ali, he escalated his quarrel with them to the point that Ali simply disappears from his biographies after that point. In short, Gandhi's appeal was essentially communal, so it never provided a viable way to transcend communal identities. And in 1929 and 1930, he subordinated the problem of Hindu-Muslim relations to his anti-British effort. The problem, of course, was never solved, and culminated in partition and the bloodbath of 1946–1947.

What Gandhi tended to overlook was that even his name for the problem was part of the problem. Symbolist theory suggests that his goal should have been not Hindu-Muslim unity but *Indian* unity. Gandhi occasionally recognized this, for example, in a rebuke to Hindu Mahasabha leader B. S. Moonje: "Why do you expect Mussalmans to be Hindus in Hindustan? . . . For the service of India, Mussalmans, Jews, Christians should be Indians even as Hindus should be Indians."[131] The obstacles to achieving such unity were legion, beginning with the fact that the linguistic contest between Hindi and Urdu reinforced the religious divide. But Gandhi never really grappled with how to achieve it; his reliance on Hindu symbology meant that he could never be a truly national leader who transcended the communal split. More focus on what Indians had in common would have helped, by increasing the salience of their common identity and decreasing the salience of identity differences; but Gandhi never worked out how to do so. A focus on nonviolent tactics was not enough in the absence of a strong unifying identity.

The End of Apartheid in South Africa

The lasting popular image of South Africa's transition from apartheid is of a "miracle" that enabled the country to achieve a peaceful shift to democracy under the benign leadership of Nelson Mandela.[1] This image is wrong, however; the transition was not peaceful. South Africa experienced a decade of civil war in 1985–1995, resulting in the deaths of over twenty thousand people, with the worst of the violence occurring while negotiations were ongoing—most of it between Mandela's African National Congress (ANC) and other black nationalist organizations.[2] The fighting subsided in 1995—about a year after Mandela's election as president—with the ANC in control of most of the country, but with its rival Inkatha still the majority party in its base region of KwaZulu-Natal.

To understand the end of apartheid in South Africa, therefore, we must reframe the question: it is not how South Africa achieved a peaceful transition, but how its people managed to settle their civil war and negotiate a changeover to majority rule. As of 1985, the ANC was committed to "armed struggle," a violent revolutionary overthrow of the apartheid regime, while the government was equally committed to violent repression. The question, then, is what explains both sides' decisions—adopted by most leaders and followers alike—to reverse their positions and accept a negotiated settlement in the early 1990s. My argument is that symbolic politics theory offers a wide-ranging answer.

First, the politics of apartheid was a textbook example of the symbolic politics of protection. Afrikaners had long cultivated a narrative that glorified their own nation as divinely chosen, and denigrated blacks as enemies of civilization; the result was strong racial prejudice. This prejudice led Afrikaners to exaggerate the threat South Africa's black majority posed to them, believing their very existence as a group was endangered. These prejudices and threat perceptions, in turn, were the underpinning of white support for the brutal policies of apartheid. Apartheid leaders like Hendrik Verwoerd kept their supporters mobilized electorally behind this policy by framing the issues in just such apocalyptic terms, and they were supported by a power-ful coalition of pro-apartheid organizations.

The story of the end of apartheid is first of all the story of the unraveling of this pattern. Prejudice declined, and perceptions of threat shifted as the collapse of world Communism removed that threat from whites' portfolio of nightmares. Therefore, when F. W. de Klerk came to power along with a new generation of moderate National Party (NP) leaders, they were able to develop moderate frames that resonated with existing threat perceptions and symbolic predispositions. Building on the remarkably strong party loy-alty of NP supporters, they also exploited the positive image of de Klerk him-self to maintain a powerful base of support. They also reframed the threats facing South Africa's whites, arguing that the biggest threat to whites' status and economic well-being was the isolation from the international community that continuing apartheid would guarantee. At the same time, they addressed fears connected to the loss of power by emphasizing the constitutional guarantees they had secured, but even more by emphasizing their goal of achieving a power-sharing arrangement, which was the one potential out-come about which whites were optimistic. Finally, superior organization also contributed to de Klerk's defeat of hard-line opponents, as the big busi-ness community, the churches, universities, and other white groups had al-ready concluded that apartheid must end.

The ANC's path to compromise was perhaps more difficult and conten-tious. The saving grace in the ANC's revolutionary narratives was that while they were violent, they were political rather than racial, always making clear that the enemy was the apartheid system. This bit of moderation in the narrative was echoed in the symbolic predispositions of most black people, who tended to reject prejudice and discrimination against whites and saw little threat from white people per se. Indeed, black public opin-ion was much more moderate than was the ANC leadership. None of this meant that assertive injustice frames were ineffective; they worked, yielding massive protest marches, as the gross injustice of apartheid was beyond dispute among blacks. While the ANC's organization was much looser and less disciplined than the NP's, it did quickly build enough capacity within the country to mobilize its supporters.

What made the transition period so violent was that hard-line sentiments remained strong among minorities on both sides, so extremist leaders needed little organizational strength to generate disproportional violence. On the government side, the biggest problem was rogue elements within the police and military forces, the so-called third force, who seemed to believe that by fostering violence they could discredit the ANC. They did not realize that they were only discrediting themselves and weakening the hand of the gov-ernment. On the ANC side, the biggest problem was the "revolutionary" practice of killing black collaborators with the regime. Extremist leaders

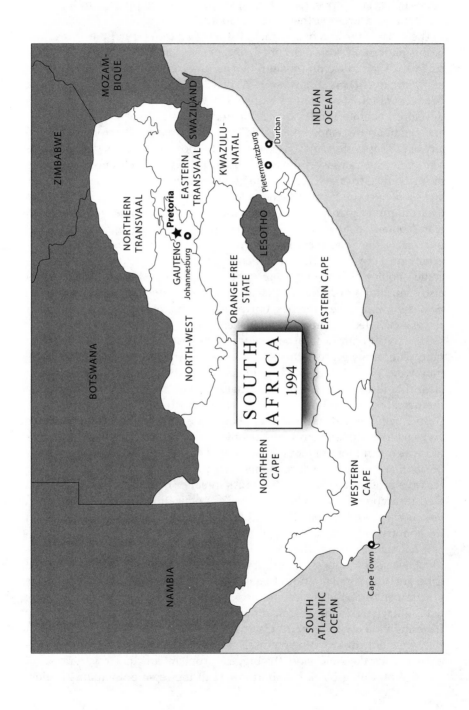

SOUTH
AFRICA
1994

like Harry Gwala combined the anticollaborator rhetoric with physical threat frames to generate the politics of protection ("We kill warlords") that fed the war between the ANC and Inkatha. Inkatha leaders were equally aggressive, so both used their party organizations to build armed militias as well.

In these conditions, neither Mandela nor de Klerk had the ability to prevent violent action by their more extremist constituents. Both mobilized the majority of their communities in favor of accommodation, but both had radical rivals who were able to appeal to those with more extreme SYPs, and to mobilize some of them for violent action. Both leaders might have done more. Mandela, in particular, could have done more to oppose violence by his own supporters; instead, he cynically blamed it on de Klerk, weakening de Klerk's bargaining leverage—but leaving a legacy of civil disorder on South Africa's streets that continues to haunt it today.

The rest of this chapter explains this story in detail. The background section focuses on South Africa's complex racial and ethnic demography and sketches some historical context. The next section explores both hard-line and moderate narratives on both sides and explains how apartheid leaders harnessed the apartheid narrative to justify their policies. The following section explores the symbolic politics of accommodation, analyzing how white attitudes and threat perceptions shifted in the early 1990s. A key focus of analysis is the pivotal 1992 referendum in which white voters overwhelmingly endorsed de Klerk's policy of negotiations; I examine how moderate elites cleverly framed the issues to persuade whites essentially to vote to give up power. The next section examines the symbolic politics of resistance, especially on the ANC side, examining black SYPs, threat perceptions, and the competing narratives deployed by Mandela and other black leaders. These latter two sections are enriched by the availability of polling data from the period, which I am able to analyze to perform some statistical tests of some of the hypotheses proposed in this book. The final section considers the implications of my findings.

The Groups and Their Histories

SOUTH AFRICA'S ETHNIC GROUPS

Apartheid South Africa legally distinguished between four racial groups—blacks, whites, coloreds (people of mixed race), and Indians or Asians. In 1991, blacks constituted an estimated 76 percent of the population, whites 12 percent, coloreds 9 percent, and Asians 3 percent.[3] There is, however, a great deal of diversity within these groups, especially by language. The largest black ethnic groups are the Zulus (24 percent of the population in 2001), who are concentrated in what is now KwaZulu-Natal Province; and Xhosas (18 percent of the population), most of whom live in the Eastern Cape. Afrikaans is the third most widely spoken language, as the mother tongue of white Afrikaners and of most coloreds. The next three most widely spoken African languages are members of the Sotho language group: Pedi or North Sotho, South Sotho, and Tswana, each spoken by about 8 percent to 9 percent of the national population—that is, about a quarter of the population combined. South Africa's richest province, Gauteng—which includes Johannesburg, Pretoria, and the gold fields—is a melting pot containing significant numbers of Zulus, Sothos, and English- and Afrikaans-speakers.

HISTORICAL BACKGROUND

The Afrikaners trace their origins to the establishment of Cape Town by the Dutch East India Company in 1652. The Dutch colonists, known for centuries as "Boers," soon clashed with the local Khoikhoi and San peoples, eventually assimilating them into the population of "colored" servants. The Dutch Cape colony was annexed by the British in 1806. Thirty years later, dissatisfied with British policies, many Boers decided to leave the British Cape colony and embark on a Great Trek into the interior.[4] Some of these Voortrekkers were killed in clashes with the local inhabitants, especially Zulus, but they ultimately succeeded in defeating Zulu attacks and establishing the two independent—"free" but slaveholding—republics of the Transvaal and Orange Free State. After the discovery of gold in the Transvaal, the Boer republics became too rich for the British to ignore. The result was the 1899–1902 Boer War, after which the British Empire incorporated both Boer republics.

Ironically, what the Boers lost on the battlefield, they won through negotiations: with the establishment of the Union of South Africa in 1910, the Boers formed a voting majority, and so they won political leadership of the state for the next eighty-four years. Until 1948, their leaders were ex-Boer generals such as Jan Smuts, who were surprisingly pro-English but still fostered the development of the Afrikaans language. These leaders instituted a system of rigid racial discrimination aimed largely at keeping a steady supply of cheap black labor available to the mines, reserving all political power and skilled and supervisory jobs for whites.

After the hard-line National Party won election in 1948, it deepened this policy of discrimination into the program of apartheid, aiming both to improve Afrikaners' cultural and economic position and to maintain the subordination of blacks. Its crowning vision was "grand apartheid," a plan to maintain white dominance in South Africa by forcing all blacks to accept citizenship in a series of small ethnic "homelands" which were to receive independence. The largest of these homelands was the Zulu one, KwaZulu. Black workers were to be treated as noncitizen migrant laborers, and racial segregation of cities and towns was enforced with increasing strictness.[5]

The black majority tried to resist the increasing discrimination. The organization that would become the ANC was established in 1912, led by the small black intelligentsia who protested through letters, petitions, and public meetings. They were ignored. Their successors' effort to organize a popular "defiance campaign" in the 1950s was equally unsuccessful and ended in the ANC being banned. Another protest effort led to the 1960 Sharpeville Massacre in which police killed sixty-nine unarmed protestors. Nelson Mandela, allied with the small South African Communist Party (SACP), responded by setting up the ANC armed wing, Umkhonto we Sizwe, whose first activists were quickly caught and jailed. In 1976, when black schoolchildren launched a mass protest against educational discrimination, white police fired on the crowd, resulting in rioting that killed twenty-three people. In the ensuing Soweto Uprising, some seven hundred blacks died.

Apartheid worked in improving the status of Afrikaners, but by the 1980s the system faced a political and economic crisis. Prime Minister P. W. Botha responded with a program of "reform apartheid": creating toothless local councils to administer black townships; establishing a tricameral Parliament with separate, subordinate chambers for coloreds and Indians; and increasing domestic repression. Many coloreds and Indians joined with the black majority to reject the new system, forming the ANC-allied United Democratic Front (UDF) to resist it. The UDF's young supporters in the black townships used intimidation and violence to enforce compliance with their strike and boycott campaigns; they murdered those they saw as regime collaborators; and they launched outright rebellions in a few local areas. Their most infamous weapon was "necklacing"—chaining a rubber tire around the victim's neck and burning him or her to death. An estimated 399 people were "necklaced" to death in the late 1980s, along with 372 others who were burned to death in other ways.[6] At the same time, the ANC unleashed an ineffectual campaign of terrorism. Over two thousand people were killed in this political violence in 1985 and 1986.[7]

While Botha's "securocrats" managed to crush the rebellion by declaring a nationwide state of emergency, the episode had lasting effects on the thinking of both sides. First, regime supporters were out of reform ideas; they increasingly recognized that apartheid had failed to bring lasting stability. Second, even relatively conservative National Party politicians, like the future president, F. W. de Klerk, learned to moderate their racial views as a result of the contact they had with colored and Indian members of the tricameral Parliament.[8] Third, the ANC learned that the regime remained too powerful to defeat in a violent uprising. After his health broke in 1989, Botha was forced to step aside for his successor, de Klerk, and the way was prepared for apartheid's endgame.

Group Narratives, Symbolic Predispositions, and Threat Perceptions

Underlying South African politics were clashing political narratives on all sides. Among blacks, two ANC narratives were particularly important: the liberal Rivonia one, and the Revolutionary one. (The rival Black Consciousness narrative associated with Steve Biko was also prominent, but I lack the space to discuss it here.) Afrikaners were similarly torn between the apartheid narrative and a liberal one. Though neither ANC narrative promoted antiwhite prejudice, both Afrikaner narratives were more or less racist, encouraging very high rates of racial prejudice among whites. Feelings of group threat were important on both sides, constituting a key obstacle to peace that leaders on both sides would have to overcome.

THE ANC'S RIVONIA NARRATIVE

The original ANC narrative was liberal, with the organization's first president identifying racial inequality—the "color bar"—as the group's concern "first and foremost"; its demand was for blacks' rightful "privileges as the subjects of the Queen."[9] The ANC's 1955 Freedom Charter expanded on these ideas, asserting the goal of "a democratic state" that operated "without distinction of colour, race, sex or belief." Throughout this period, ANC resistance was based on the principle of nonviolence.

In 1961, however, in the aftermath of the Sharpeville Massacre, the ANC approved Nelson Mandela's creation of an armed wing, Umkhonto. In his statement at the famous Rivonia trial, Mandela explained his reasons.[10] First, all lawful protest acts were made illegal, he noted, and then nonviolent illegal action was met with a "show of force to crush opposition." Mandela continued that Umkhonto "had behind us the ANC tradition of non-violence and negotiation," insisting, "We did not want an interracial war, and tried to avoid it to the last minute." Mandela's approach was minimum violence, with Umkhonto initially limiting itself to sabotaging economic targets because it "did not involve loss of life."

Another theme of this Rivonia narrative was a unified South African—but primarily black—nationalism. As Mandela also said at Rivonia, "Elders of my tribe [told] of wars fought by our ancestors in defence of the fatherland. The names of Dingane and Bambata, Hintsa and Makana, Squngthi and Dalasile, Moshoeshoe and Sekhukhuni, were praised as the glory of the entire African nation."[11] Mandela thus cleverly created the idea of a single (South) African nation by ascribing to the elders of his (Xhosa) ethnic group an equal respect for the historical leaders not only of the Xhosas but also of the Zulus (Dingane and Bambata), the South Sotho (Moshoeshoe), and the Pedi (Sekhukhuni)—heroes of each of the largest black ethnic groups in South Africa. Notably, most of these men were warrior-chiefs who were leaders of rebellions or wars against the British imperialists; Squngthi was a leader of Mandela's own Thembu subgroup of Xhosas. Mandela was, in short, defining as *national* heroes a group of leaders of resistance to white domination, and putting one of his ancestors among them.

This, then, is the Rivonia narrative. After Mandela's release from prison in 1990, he increasingly added another element to it: reconciliation. In this effort he was building on the humanitarian concept of *ubuntu*, which Archbishop Desmond Tutu had been promoting for many years. Tutu explained the idea this way: "We speak of inner *'Ubuntu'* . . . it refers to gentleness, to compassion. . . . If we could but recognise our common humanity, that we do belong together, that our destinies are bound up with one another's . . . that we can be human only together, then a glorious South Africa would come into being."[12] For Tutu and Mandela, reconciliation based on *ubuntu* was a critical means to achieving the goals of the Rivonia narrative.

The Rivonia narrative therefore generates two opposed symbolic predispositions. Its main theme is defiance: it encourages its supporters' willingness to struggle for liberation and, if necessary, to die or to kill for it. On the other hand, its *ubuntu* theme encourages compassion and reconciliation. Neither strand encourages racial prejudice against whites.

THE ANC'S REVOLUTIONARY NARRATIVE

After the ANC was banned in 1960 and went into exile, it grew much closer to its key allies, the SACP and the government of the Soviet Union. As early as 1969, it began articulating a new narrative calling for a "revolutionary armed struggle" aimed at "the conquest of power." The 1969 document claimed that the turn to armed struggle was in fact a return to an earlier tradition—that of the "first 250 years" of "unbroken resistance to [white] domination," which featured "regular armed clashes, battles and wars."[13] The older ANC nonracialism was submerged: ANC president Oliver Tambo forthrightly stated in 1971, for example, "Power to the people means, in fact, power to the black people."[14] The ANC renewed its commitment to armed struggle in 1983, when it produced a new strategy document advocating "people's war," arguing that violence was "the only real answer" for the ANC.[15] This document was formally adopted as ANC strategy in 1985.

Continuing throughout the 1980s, the ANC's public statements sounded much like the pronouncements of orthodox Marxist-Leninist rebel groups of that time, including calls for "a revolutionary overthrow of the existing ruling class."[16] Oliver Tambo's rhetoric was martial, as in one 1985 address: "We have planted the seeds of people's war . . . for the forcible overthrow of the racist regime."[17] Tambo's list of the four "pillars" of the ANC's strategy— underground organizing, "mass political action," an "armed offensive," and promoting international pressure—did not include negotiations. Highlighting the ANC's growing ruthlessness, an editorial in the ANC magazine

Sechaba later in 1985 reported that the June "ANC conference, which took the form of a council of war, decided that the distinction between 'hard' and 'soft' [i.e., civilian] targets should disappear."[18] The ANC was openly endorsing terrorism.

On the other hand, the ANC did open its membership to members of all races, and included in its leadership white and Indian Communists such as Joe Slovo and Mac Maharaj. It did not identify the enemy in racial terms as whites; it was primarily the regime that was the target of ANC bile: the "racist monstrosity," the "apartheid regime," and so on. Also targets of ANC animosity were rival black leaders, especially Inkatha and KwaZulu leader Mangosuthu Gatsha Buthelezi. A *Sechaba* editorial called for his assassination in 1985, asserting, "Gatsha Buthelezi . . . has fallen on the side of the people's enemies, on the side of the Pretoria racists, where he belongs. The people will deal with him."[19]

The symbolic predispositions promoted by this narrative were those of a radical authoritarianism: predispositions toward violent struggle, radical change rather than compromise, violent intolerance of competing views— but again, not racial intolerance.

THE APARTHEID NARRATIVE

The Afrikaner narrative begins with the arrival of Jan van Riebeeck and ninety Dutch East India Company settlers at Cape Town in 1652. Emphasizing the theme of Afrikaner commitment to individualism and freedom, the great Afrikaner historian Hermann Giliomee opens his book with a story of a petition by these early Boers for better treatment from the company.[20] A 1987 National Party pamphlet opens with a reference to this and similar events, endorsing the narrative of Afrikaner activism in defense of their "political rights."[21]

The next great event in the Afrikaner narrative is the Great Trek.[22] Piet Retief, one of the early leaders of this movement, articulated the reasons for it as follows. The Boers were angry because their slaves had been emancipated without compensation for the owners, Retief said, and servants now had the legal right to testify in court against their owners. Such policies, he felt, showed "hatred and contempt of the Boer." Blacks could not be legal equals, the Boers argued, because they were the "sons of Ham," destined to be "hewers of wood and drawers of water."[23] In a letter written a few months after this statement, Retief articulated the Boers' political objective in their move: "[We] desire to be considered a free and independent people."[24]

The Great Trek soon led to bloody clashes with the black peoples of the region. Retief's party was massacred by the Zulu King Dingane's warriors when his group appeared, and disarmed, at a parley in 1838. This massacre was avenged in December of the same year, when a large group of over five hundred armed trekkers led by Andries Pretorius (and sporting one bronze cannon) killed some three thousand Zulu warriors at the place thereafter called Blood River. Dingane was killed soon afterward, and his successor Mpande aligned himself with the Boers.[25]

These events took on a central place in Afrikaner mythology. Pretorius's victory was attributed to divine intervention. A historian characterized the Voortrekker movement as a "pilgrimage of martyrdom throughout South Africa." A related theme, as articulated in a 1920s poem, is election by God: the martyrs of the trek were the "first of a new line . . . of an Afrikaner nation, worthy to bear the crown upon the Way of the Cross."[26]

The other "chosen trauma" of the Afrikaner people was the Anglo-Boer War of 1899–1902, a naked British grab for power and for Boer land and wealth.[27] The British conduct of the war was atrocious, responding to the Boers' guerrilla resistance with scorched-earth tactics and a policy of imprisoning Boer civilians in "concentration camps." Before the war was done, over four thousand Boer women and twenty-two thousand Boer children were dead.[28] Afrikaners claimed that this experience reinforced the notion that they had "a national calling and destiny."[29] One prominent text of the time asserted, "We believe that the Afrikaner will . . . arise from the debris and ashes of his defeats . . . and finally become a powerful and victorious people."[30]

South Africa's Calvinist churches took the lead in articulating the racist beliefs of the time. For example, a 1931 church synod declared that "racial leveling" and "bastardization" were "an abomination to every right-minded white and native." In this perspective, the fate of the Tower of Babel demonstrated God's plan to separate the nations of the world. Segregation, one theologian argued, would allow "self-determination . . . to the non-white races on every terrain of life"; as a result, according to another, "the policy of segregation that is promoted by the Afrikaner and his church is in the best interests of both the white and the non-white."[31] The claim of promoting black interests was a thin veil for brutal discrimination, however. For example, future premier J. G. Strijdom denounced mission schools in 1946, asserting that they were "far too eager to . . . [provide] education to *Klein kaffertjies* [little kafirs]."[32]

The key motive for apartheid was survival in the midst of a black majority. Thus one historian at the time, questioning whether Afrikaners had a future, argued that apartheid was necessary to preserve the existence of the Afrikaners because of their minority status. In National Party prime minister D. F. Malan's formulation in 1949, the Voortrekker spirit was threatened by "godless communism," blood mixing, and the disintegration of the white race. In a letter around the same time, Malan asserted that South Africa had to choose "between barbarism and civilization."[33] Apartheid was, as Giliomee argued, a "radical survival plan."[34]

The main architect of apartheid, Hendrik Verwoerd, knitted all these themes together. "The White man," Verwoerd argued, "is of incalculable importance for civilization and for history." Verwoerd emphasized the

Afrikaners' history of overcoming victimhood: "the light of the sun of freedom was extinguished years ago, but not forever. . . . [Now] we are a free, happy and prosperous nation." However, Verwoerd warned, South Africa was under threat, with "attacks surrounding us." The alternative to apartheid was, he suggested, "forced assimilation or absorption of peoples." Rejecting this prospect, he asserted, "True morality . . . [involves] each going his separate road." "We have no ambitions . . . to exploit others," he claimed, ignoring the raft of South African laws and policies that did just that. But racial inclusiveness was not an option: "We will . . . not sacrifice this Republic and its independence and our way of life."[35]

In sum, apartheid was based on racist symbolic predispositions, which encouraged also perceptions of threat to whites' position in every black request or demand for decent treatment.

WHITE LIBERAL NARRATIVES

While liberals in South Africa were in retreat for decades, some did speak out. One was the poet N. P. van Wyk Louw, who on the one hand denounced the idea of majority government as "national suicide" for Afrikaners but on the other insisted that Afrikaners must strive for "survival in justice." He posed the issue this way: "Can a small volk [people] survive for long, if it becomes something hateful, something evil, in the eyes of the best in—or outside—its fold?" He answered, "I would rather go down than survive in injustice."[36] This view would prove important in the end: F. W. de Klerk's brother Willem became a prominent liberal voice, and de Klerk himself ultimately admitted that apartheid was morally wrong and apologized for it.[37]

Others argued that apartheid was unworkable. One early dissenter asserted that he would support apartheid if blacks were given "free government," enough land and capital to make the homelands economically viable, and generous budget subsidies. His point was to make clear that the costs of a genuine policy of "separate but equal development" were far too high for white voters to support; for that reason, Verwoerd consistently opposed all of these measures. A study in 1952 made the point more explicit: if apartheid did not result in the mass migration of blacks back to the homelands—which was never economically possible—then "there was no honorable manner in which we as Christians and democrats will in the long run be able to deny them political and other rights."[38]

Despite all of this, white opponents of apartheid were politically marginalized: from 1961 to 1974, the only member of Parliament (MP) speaking out against apartheid was Progressive Party leader Helen Suzman. Opposing one 1964 measure, Suzman asserted, "This bill . . . strips the African of every basic pretension he has to being a human being, to being a free human being in the country of his birth, and it reduces him to the level of a chattel."[39]

The fiery poet Breyten Breytenbach went further, writing in 1965, "I am ashamed of my people."[40] These critics, however, had no clear alternative policy to propose.

Apartheid supporters, however, were increasingly realizing by the 1980s that the policy was not working. The white population was growing much more slowly than projected, the black population was growing more quickly, and the economy increasingly needed black labor, skilled and unskilled—all just as the early doubters had projected. Thus Piet Cilie, noted for his fiery pro-National Party rhetoric in the 1950s, wrote thirty years later that Afrikaners "had clung too long, against overwhelming evidence, to the dream of a homelands policy."[41]

PREJUDICE IN THE 1980S

The availability of public opinion survey data allows us to assess South Africans' SYPs and other political attitudes. The data come from South Africa's Human Sciences Research Council, which did periodic surveys of South African public opinion throughout the 1980s and 1990s. These data demonstrate that South African whites showed a great deal of racial prejudice in line with their narratives, just as we would expect from Hypothesis 1. For example, as late as July 1992, 73.8 percent of white survey respondents said they opposed mixed marriages, and a plurality opposed racially integrated suburbs. Within the white community, Afrikaners showed more prejudice than did English-speakers. Thus when asked bluntly whether they favored or opposed "racially mixed schools," fully 86 percent of Afrikaners said in 1988 that they opposed it.[42] Similarly, according to the 1992 survey, 27.4 percent of Afrikaners held that race was the most important factor students in a school should have in common (not language or scholastic ability); only 11 percent of English-speaking whites felt the same way.

South Africa's blacks, in contrast, generally rejected racial prejudice. As Patti Waldmeir concluded, after conducting a wide range of interviews in the mid-1990s, "Black South Africans refused to indulge [in] racial hatred."[43] She quoted an ANC supporter who had been abused in prison as follows: "There is no way I can hate whites. To hate whites would be unfair. . . . Our problem is not whites per se. Our problem is the system which made whites the culprits of apartheid."[44] This impression is supported by a late-1990s survey study, which found that only 9 percent of blacks had "strong anti-white sentiment," while the vast majority were not anti-white.[45] Similarly, in 1992, only 13.2 percent of blacks said that they felt close to the Azanian People's Organization (AZAPO), which had a more antiwhite image than the ANC did. On the other side, 21.6 percent of blacks said they felt close to the National Party and nearly 39 percent trusted de Klerk, suggesting that racial concerns were less of a barrier to political loyalty among blacks than among whites.

SYMBOLIC POLITICS OF APARTHEID

Apartheid politics was a classic example of the symbolic politics of protection. As noted earlier in this chapter, Afrikaners' racist narratives inculcated in them strong racial prejudices. That prejudice, in turn (per Hypothesis 2), encouraged whites, especially Afrikaners, to see blacks as a terrible threat, the *swart gewaar*. As Verwoerd articulated it, they felt that their values, identity, and civilization itself were under threat from an alliance of blacks and international Communism. That prejudice and threat perception, in turn, led them to support the discriminatory policies of apartheid (Hypotheses 3 and 4). As late as March 1985, for example, 54 percent of whites continued to support "the policy that prevents Africans from having seats in the current parliament." More specific evidence for Hypothesis 4 comes from a 1987 survey, which found that whites who felt insecure were more likely to defend apartheid repression than those who felt secure. For example, most whites who felt insecure disagreed with the idea that power-sharing with blacks would be a good idea, preferring to keep the apartheid structures that excluded blacks from power; among whites who felt secure, however, 65 percent thought that power-sharing with blacks would be a good thing.[46]

All of this was in keeping with the apartheid narrative that the only alternative to national annihilation was the political exclusion of blacks and the social separation of the races. The assertive rhetoric of leaders like Verwoerd, backed by the organizational muscle of the National Party and allied organizations like the Afrikaner Broederbond, a pro-apartheid secret society, enabled them to win votes and gain control of the government (Hypotheses 5 and 6) and turn these ideas into government policy.

As internal resistance and external criticism of the system grew in the 1980s, South African whites' fears and perceptions of threat at first grew with them, encouraging continued support for apartheid. Whites especially feared that a future black majority government would be a severe threat to their way of life: in surveys from 1985 to 1990, a consistent 86 percent to 93 percent said that a future under an "African majority government" would be "bad." Furthermore, as political violence increased, the proportion of those who said they feared for their own or their family's safety doubled in the late 1980s, increasing from 24 percent in 1986 to 49 percent in April 1990.[47]

P. W. Botha's government used the same assertive frames as its predecessors to maintain support for the protection that apartheid afforded them. State-run radio reiterated the theme of Afrikaner victimization, often recalling "the yoke of British colonialism."[48] Referring to the idea of the *swart gewaar*, Botha asserted in one speech, "The idea of equality did not mean that the white man should sacrifice his right to live in South Africa."[49] Therefore, he stated, his "government was not prepared to [negotiate] on condition that a black majority government should be accepted."[50] Indeed,

Botha claimed, "the battle in South Africa was not between black and white but between Christian civilization and Communism."[51] In an aside to a Cabinet colleague, Law and Order minister Louis LeGrange confirmed the symbolic politics calculation behind this rhetoric: "When you pull the republican flag out of the bucket of blood," he said, "then they vote NP again."[52]

The Symbolic Politics of Accommodation

If apartheid was an example of a politics of protection among South African whites, the politics of accommodation that followed is harder to classify. From the black perspective, of course, the process was a politics of redistribution, but in the face of their demands, most whites *demobilized*, supporting negotiations to end apartheid instead of rallying to its defense. Thus while the stakes for whites were redistributive, the pattern of politics resembled the politics of distribution. This is the puzzle of the end of apartheid: Why did whites support the redistribution of power away from themselves?

What happened is best understood as the exhaustion of the apartheid politics of protection: waving the bloody flag simply did not work anymore. Why? Symbolist theory suggests that group narratives and prejudices may have moderated. Threat perceptions must also have changed, so that accommodating black demands came to seem less threatening to whites than resisting them. Theoretically, this would have led to a decline in support for apartheid policies. In that context, a credible leader could formulate an accommodative framing of the issues that would resonate better than the older, more assertive apartheid frames. As long as the moderates were not then out-organized by the hard-liners, the accommodative politics could then succeed. As I shall show in the following sections, all of these things happened, supporting symbolist expectations.

SHIFTING WHITE ATTITUDES: NARRATIVES, PREJUDICES, AND OTHER SYMBOLIC PREDISPOSITIONS

By the 1980s, the narratives that justified apartheid were starting to come apart.[53] Government leaders denied any belief that nonwhites were racially inferior, and increasingly avoided mentioning the word *apartheid*, focusing instead on their claim that separate development was best for all. But their support was eroding: South Africa's Dutch Reformed Church was expelled from the World Alliance of Reformed Churches in 1982 for its support of apartheid, prompting it to open itself up to nonwhites in 1986 and to condemn apartheid as a sin in 1989.[54] Universities also abandoned the cause, with dissidents even at conservative Stellenbosch University issuing an antiapartheid statement in March 1987. Similarly, by 1986 the Broederbond, long a bastion of apartheid ideology, was arguing against it, asserting that "the exclusion of blacks from the highest level of decision-making"—the keystone of the apartheid system—was "a threat to the survival of whites."[55]

Another prop of the regime, the business community, also abandoned the apartheid narrative as its economic basis crumbled. As early as 1967, one newspaper noted, "Race policies precluded the most economic use of the non-white labor force."[56] For this reason, businesses pushed for loosening restrictions on black migration in the 1970s, and by 1979 big business joined a push to recognize black unions, aiming to create an orderly system of labor relations. As early as 1985, business leaders were sending delegations to meet with the ANC leadership in Zambia.[57] The next year, the Federated Chamber of Industries called for universal suffrage.[58]

As we would expect from Hypothesis 1, these shifting narratives led to a decline in prejudice. For example, according to a 1991 survey, two-thirds of whites—including a majority of Afrikaners—agreed or partially agreed with the proposition "Race or population group should not play any role in the provision of education." These numbers suggest a major shift in Afrikaner opinion. The proportion stating that they opposed "racially mixed schools" had dropped to 52.6 percent in the July 1992 survey, from nearly 74 percent four years earlier.

Closely related to racial prejudice are symbolic predispositions toward political parties. Table 6.1 summarizes the proportions of black and white respondents who told pollsters that they felt either "very close" or "close" to each of the political parties listed (February 1992 survey).

These feelings about the political parties reflect the racial attitudes mentioned earlier in this chapter. Among whites, the 38.4 percent who felt close to the hard-line racist Conservative Party is roughly equal to the overall proportion of whites who rejected the notion of race-blind educational policy at the time, and the 11.8 percent who felt close to the neo-Nazi Afrikaner Weerstandsbeweging (Afrikaner Resistance Movement or AWB) is similar to the proportion of whites whom another study found to be "strongly racist."[59] The roughly two-thirds of whites who felt close to the National Party at this time presumably includes both the NP's longtime

Table 6.1 Favorable symbolic predispositions toward political parties in 1992

Political Party	% Blacks "Close To"	% Whites "Close To"
National Party	21.6	67.3
Inkatha Freedom Party	14.1	25.9
African National Congress	69.0	6.3
Conservative Party	5.6	38.4
Azanian People's Org.	13.2	0
AWB	0.8	11.8

constituents—their old partisan base—and liberals who supported de Klerk's reformist stand.

CHANGING WHITE THREAT PERCEPTIONS

More important than these modest declines in prejudice was a shift in threat perceptions both among elites and in mass opinion, mostly as a result of external events. Because of the power of the South African state, the government could not be dislodged violently, but its leaders understood that they were also unable to impose peace and stability, and all their ideas for unilateral reforms had failed. Members of the cabinet recognized in the late 1980s that in spite of the state of emergency, the country remained largely ungovernable.[60]

At the same time, international pressure was gaining strength, with financial sanctions taking the biggest toll. As the finance minister of the time, Barend du Plessis, recalled in a later interview, the need to repay foreign loans without any new financing drained the country of capital and made it impossible to generate strong economic growth.[61] De Klerk agreed, calling economic stagnation "one of the greatest challenges that we would face" in those years as a result of "capital outflows." At the same time, de Klerk reported, even South Africa's closest allies like British prime minister Margaret Thatcher were pushing him to reform the system.[62]

The threat from the ANC was meanwhile declining. Botha's policy had been based on identifying the ANC as part of a larger international Communist menace. But the 1988 peace agreement for Angola and Namibia led to the withdrawal of Cuban troops and Umkhonto fighters from Angola and demonstrated the feasibility of bargaining with black liberation groups. According to two government leaders of the time, this agreement was an important factor that lowered tensions in South Africa and paved the way for the release of Mandela.[63] After the fall of the Berlin Wall and the collapse of the Communist regimes in Eastern Europe a year later, the notion of the ANC as a Communist threat was no longer plausible.

In this context—internal ungovernability, economic stagnation, external pressure for reform, a weakened ANC, and an evaporating Communist threat—a continuation of the status quo came to appear more threatening than reform would be. When asked in April 1990 to assess the then-current governing structure that included whites, coloreds, and Indians but not blacks, 37 percent of white respondents said they expected a bad future if it continued; only 29 percent expected this system to yield a good future. In other words, only 29 percent supported the apartheid political system. At the same time, fears in the white community were running high. Polled in early 1990, nearly 49 percent of whites said they feared for their family's safety, and 29 percent said they personally felt unsafe.[64] By September 1991, the proportion of whites feeling unsafe had risen to 38.8 percent.

But in the context of a political system that was itself a source of threat, defending it was not a viable option. Whites' future hopes were instead increasingly pinned to the idea of power sharing: when asked in March 1985 about a potential future "under a government consisting of whites, coloureds, Indians and Africans," 47 percent had responded that they thought such a future would be "good," with 32 percent saying it would be "bad." By April 1990, hopes had risen further, with 63 percent considering such a system "good" and only 20 percent rating it as "bad."[65]

PREJUDICE, THREAT, AND POPULAR SUPPORT FOR ACCOMMODATION

The availability of raw public opinion data from South Africa in this period offers an opportunity to perform statistical tests of Hypotheses 2 through 4. According to Hypothesis 2, we should find that more-prejudiced people are more likely to feel threatened than less-prejudiced people. As a measure of people's threat perceptions, we can use answers to the question, "How safe do you feel in South Africa today?" While there is no direct measure of prejudice in the data, we can use attitudes toward racial segregation as a proxy, assuming that those who oppose racial segregation of schools will be less prejudiced than those who support it. The evidence supports the hypothesis. In the September 1991 survey, among whites who opposed segregation, 29 percent said that they felt unsafe or very unsafe, but among those who supported segregation, 49 percent said they felt unsafe or very unsafe. Prejudice does seem to have led to increased perception of threat.

With regard to Hypotheses 3 and 4, we are not interested in support for hostile and discriminatory action, but in the opposite—support for accommodation—which should be associated with lower levels of prejudice and lesser threat perceptions. The best available measure of voters' views on this comes from the question in the same 1991 survey in which people were asked the extent to which they agreed or disagreed with the statement, "The current policies of President de Klerk will bring lasting peace to South Africa." Our expectation would be that lower levels of prejudice, lower threat perceptions, and (inferring from Hypothesis 5) higher levels of credibility for President de Klerk should be associated with greater support for de Klerk's policy of negotiation with the ANC.

Table 6.2 shows the results of the statistical test, which supports all three hypotheses. As expected from Hypothesis 3, less-prejudiced whites were more likely to support de Klerk's policy of negotiations with the ANC than more-prejudiced whites. Two different measures of racial attitudes were important: belief that there was goodwill among races in South Africa (implying the respondent's goodwill toward blacks *and* belief in blacks' goodwill toward whites), and belief that children of different races should be educated together; both strongly predicted support for the policy of negotiation.

Table 6.2 Influences on white support for negotiations (1991)

Model	Unstandardized Coefficient Beta	Std. Error	Standardized Coefficient Beta
Constant	1.063	0.279	
Feel close to National Party	1.227	0.114***	0.407
South Africans share sufficient goodwill for happy future	−0.185	0.034***	−0.192
Your life in new South Africa would be (better or worse)?	0.346	0.067***	0.181
Races should share classrooms	0.489	0.104***	0.166
De Klerk sincere	0.287	0.080***	0.129

Dependent variable: Policies of de Klerk will bring peace. R = 0.742; adj. R square = 0.545; std. error of estimate = 0.99306.
*** Significance: <0.001.

Interestingly, another symbolic predisposition—party identity—was even more important than prejudice. People who felt close to the National Party were much more likely to support de Klerk's policy of negotiation than people who did not. Hypothesis 4 is also supported: respondents who found the idea of a postapartheid future threatening were more likely to oppose the talks, while those who expected a nonracial South Africa to be better tended to support them. Finally, as suggested by Hypothesis 5, de Klerk's credibility was also important: those who believed de Klerk was "sincere" (almost 69 percent of whites in the sample) were more likely to support his negotiation policy than those who did not.

Other evidence also supports the powerful influence of leadership combined with party loyalty among whites. In November 1988, only 30 percent of whites indicated that they supported negotiations with the ANC. Less than two years later, however, after de Klerk announced his and his party's policy of doing just that, popular support for the idea suddenly doubled to 60 percent.[66] De Klerk's immediate associates generally agreed on the importance of the president's role, with one cabinet colleague going so far as to say that voters "blindly" follow their leaders.[67] F. W. de Klerk was not known as a charismatic leader or a powerful orator; his cabinet colleagues generally believed that when a charismatic speech was called for, Foreign Minister R. F. "Pik" Botha was the man for the job. Nevertheless, if we understand leadership the symbolic politics way—whereby positive feelings about a leader (and his party) translate into positive feelings about his policies, then de Klerk was quite good at it.

The simple symbolic politics explanation of support for negotiations summarized in table 6.2 is remarkably powerful, accounting for about 55 percent of the overall variance. If controls for age, sex, education, and poverty are added, none is significant. Even a control for being an Afrikaans-speaker is insignificant, suggesting that my measures of symbolic predispositions explain the difference in views between English-speaking whites and Afrikaners.[68]

De Klerk's own retrospective judgment supports this analysis.[69] When asked how he built support for his policies, his first answer was, "I had the credentials" of a conservative reputation and the respect accorded to the state president—that is, credibility. He also mentioned the immediate symbolic benefits of his opening to the ANC, noting that the public had noticed the positive international reaction. Additionally, he saw a feeling akin to hope—"a sense of relief" among a population that sensed they were leaving the "doomed road" they had been on. He also judged that the decline of the Communist threat was important.

All of this also supports the view that the change in leadership from Botha to de Klerk was itself a critical reason for South Africa's peaceful transition.[70] Botha and his predecessors steadfastly refused to use their leadership authority to promote equal rights for blacks; de Klerk did it. Furthermore, de Klerk's rise came along with a broader generational change in National Party leadership. When de Klerk was elected leader of the National Party, there were initially more votes for his reformist rivals than for him. "My interpretation," de Klerk wrote later, "was that there was an urgent desire among many members of the caucus to move quickly ahead with reform."[71] The shift toward a younger and more reformist leadership continued under de Klerk in the early 1990s, best illustrated by the replacement of hard-line defense minister Magnus Malan with the liberal Roelf Meyer in 1991. These were the people who provided the leadership for South African whites during the transition.

An interesting caveat is that while trust in de Klerk was significant in explaining white support for the negotiation policy, trust in Mandela was not. Theoretically, one would expect that the more South African whites trusted Mandela's intentions, the more likely they would have been to support a policy likely to result in Mandela's rise to power. However, this does not seem to have been true. The 1992 poll found that fewer than 15 percent of whites trusted Mandela. Furthermore, this variable proves insignificant in analyses of white support for political change. This is an important finding: trust in Mandela was *not* an important factor in reassuring whites about their prospects in a black-ruled South Africa, at least not in 1992.

LEADERS' FRAMING OF THE 1992 REFERENDUM

Another reason for the success of the 1992 referendum was the National Party's shrewd advertising campaign using a social threat frame to promote mobilization of voters in support of NP policies (as expected by Hypothesis 5). The key tactic was to frame the issues to suggest that the status quo was more threatening than democratization would be. Since voting against the negotiations process was framed as riskier than voting for it, fear could be made to work in favor of the policy of negotiating with the ANC. The major risk highlighted by NP ads was the economic risk, summarized in a stark two-line ad in an Afrikaans-language newspaper: "Do not vote yourself out of a job. Vote 'Yes' for a solution that will work."[72] De Klerk emphasized the security risks in blunt terms as well, saying at one point, "A 'No' vote would be suicidal. It will scuttle all hopes of so-called white 'survival' because it would isolate whites."[73]

An earlier ad laid out this logic in more detail, stating,

You can vote yourself out of work.

You know that even the smallest "No" vote majority will result in full-scale sanctions and boycotts. Immediately. . . . That means nobody wants the state we seek to make. . . . A "No" vote guarantees labor unrest, large demonstrations, strikes, empty factories, neglected machines . . .

But you also know a "Yes" vote will result in more money pouring into the country. . . . More work for everyone. More money in everyone's pocket.

[V]ote "Yes" for a solution that will work.[74]

The shrewdness of this ad is its manipulation of a wide range of threats. It opens with the threat to individual jobs, and adds a physical threat implied by "labor unrest, . . . unemployment, . . . more crime." It also notes the threats to group status ("nobody wants the state we seek to make"). This ad was so powerfully effective that various versions were printed.

Other symbolic appeals also appeared in the campaign. Some framed the issue as one of basic moral values, as in, "The world is going to judge us according to what we do on 17 March. And if the worst happens . . . future generations will remember. . . . They voted for evil when they could have voted for good."[75] Another ad, seconded by prominent athletes' statements, appealed to another SYP, the national pride that came from South Africa's reinclusion in international sports competitions after de Klerk's reform began.[76] Yet another promoted fear of the neofascist AWB: "This one [swastika symbol] cost 45 million lives and six years of war. How many lives will this one [AWB's similar three-armed symbol] cost?"[77]

To be sure, mixed with the symbolic and emotional appeals were logical arguments and appeals to material interest. Certainly the economic arguments were both of these. Another theme was reassurance on political rights, for example, "We already have an agreement on a Charter of Fundamental Rights that will ensure your right to life, freedom and property."[78] Yet another was to blast the opposition Conservative Party for its alleged inability to propose any alternative path: "They offer you a blank policy."[79] Others mention specific shifts in the security environment and their benefits for individuals, such as "peace in Angola, shorter national service, . . . an end to bombings in fast food joints."[80] Also mentioned were tactical arguments that negotiating now would enable the NP to negotiate from "a position of strength."[81]

The opposition Conservative Party tried to counter by continuing to use the apartheid frames based on prejudice and threat, suggesting that South Africa would become like "the communistic governed countries in darkest Africa [which] count among the most impoverished in the world," and warning about losses of jobs, farms, pensions, and personal security.[82] As noted earlier in this chapter, however, such appeals no longer resonated, as white voters were so pessimistic about the prospects for a continued apartheid system that they felt de Klerk's reform program posed less of a threat to their future.

Black leaders, meanwhile, offered reassurance: "Whites are fellow South Africans and we want them to feel safe," Mandela said.[83] ANC leaders also denied any intentions to seize white-owned farmland or to cut off civil service pensions.[84] On the other hand, black leaders reinforced white fears about the status quo, making clear that a "no" vote would be disastrous for whites. Mandela bluntly stated that if whites voted "no," "then there would be a fight."

The final result in the referendum was a 68.7 percent "yes" vote, a bit more than the 60 percent who had told pollsters they supported negotiations two years earlier.[85] However, the government's internal polls showed a consistent two-thirds level of support for the reform policy, suggesting that the "yes" campaign simply stabilized existing public opinion.[86] If the preceding survey analysis is right, the main reasons for the strong vote of confidence were trust in the National Party, belief in black goodwill, and hope that a more democratic South Africa could be better. After four decades of apartheid, most voters concluded that it had been tried and failed.

WHITE POLITICAL ORGANIZATION

According to Hypothesis 6, a strong organizational network is likely to have been important in de Klerk's success, and evidence suggests it was. As noted earlier in this section, key institutions like the Dutch Reformed Church, the Afrikaner Broederbond, and the universities preceded the National Party's shift by coming out against apartheid in the 1980s. The business community did likewise. The Broederbond's youth wing, called Ruiterwag, also became active in opposing apartheid: one 1970s student activist reported that he was elected to a leading post in the organization *because* of his view that apartheid was not working.[87]

Even more important was de Klerk's ability to maintain control over the institutions of government—especially the security forces—and of the National Party. Party control was eased by the fact that de Klerk himself was the leader of the more conservative wing of the National Party: in the words of one inside observer, he was the "leader of the pack" of those opposing reform in the 1980s.[88] De Klerk's defection left them leaderless for a time. Additionally, National Party leaders realized that they were irretrievably committed to the negotiations: if the talks had failed or they bolted from the party, their political careers would have ended.[89] Thus de Klerk managed to maneuver his more reluctant colleagues into accepting tough compromises. In later interviews, de Klerk's cabinet colleagues widely agreed on the importance of his leadership in keeping the process on track.

The other critical issue of organizational politics was maintaining control of the security forces, especially the military. As de Klerk later noted, this was a problem:

> In my relationship with the security forces, I sometimes felt like a man who had been given two fully grown watchdogs—say, a Rottweiler and a bull terrier. Their previous owner had . . . allowed them to run free and chase cats all over the neighbourhood. I had put a stop to all that. As a result, they did not particularly like me—although they had an ingrained sense of obedience. . . . I could guide them, but I knew that if I pulled [on the leash] too hard, I might choke them—or they might slip their collars and cause pandemonium in the neighbourhood.[90]

There was, in fact, a great deal of illicit security force activity. Two secret military units, the Civilian Cooperation Bureau and the Directorate of Covert Collection were tied, respectively, to assassinations and to promoting the violence in Natal.[91] Yet another military unit, the Fifth Reconnaissance Regiment, was linked to massacres on commuter trains in the early 1990s.[92] The police were at least equally out of control. For example, a secret South African Police hit squad based at the Vlakplaas farm outside Pretoria killed at least seventy people in the 1980s and early 1990s, including some in random attacks on taxi stands.[93] South African police also systematically aided and armed Inkatha fighters in the Natal violence.[94] De Klerk appointed several special commissions to investigate these misdeeds in both police and army, but their probes were constantly blocked, as top-ranking officers destroyed relevant documents and lied to investigators. These security force actions badly undermined de Klerk's strategy of seeking support among black as well as white voters but did not prevent the transition to black majority rule.

The Symbolic Politics of Resistance

The gross injustice of the apartheid system meant that political appeals based on a master frame of "injustice" resonated powerfully with nonwhite communities. When P. W. Botha's policy of reform apartheid opened a window of opportunity for nonwhite political action, the UDF quickly sprang to life behind colored leader Allan Boesak's famous demand to correct injustice: "We want all our rights, we want them here, and we want them now."[95] With the state of emergency that he imposed in 1986, Botha attempted to slam shut that window of opportunity, but the lesson of the episode was that only savage government repression was inhibiting mass nonwhite mobilization.

De Klerk's policy of negotiation with the ANC required that he reopen that window, relegalizing the ANC and allowing it to engage in peaceful mass mobilization. Hypothesis 4 explains what happened: de Klerk's policy shift ended the overwhelming threat that had deterred most blacks from protesting, but apartheid rules remained a threat to black status, rights, and economic prospects. The result was the reemergence of a mass politics of redistribution, demanding full political rights and some economic redistribution in favor of the nonwhite majority. Where blacks differed was in their attitude toward violence: while some, supporters of the Rivonia narrative, preferred to stick to nonviolent mobilization, others responded to the ANC's revolutionary narrative and renewed the violent tactics of the mid-1980s. The challenge of the ANC leadership was how to maneuver between the opportunity provided by de Klerk and the competing preferences of their own followers.

BLACK SYMBOLIC PREDISPOSITIONS IN THE 1990S

As noted earlier in this chapter, most South African blacks in the 1990s rejected racial prejudice, with fewer than 10 percent showing evidence of such SYPs. They did, however, have SYPs toward political parties, with the three most popular being the ANC (to which 69 percent felt close), the National Party (to which 21.6 percent felt close), and Inkatha (to which 14 percent felt close). Only about 13 percent of blacks indicated that they felt close to the more racialist AZAPO. Support for the racialist fringe shrank even further when blacks were asked whether they would advise people close to them to join the Azanian People's Liberation Army (APLA), armed wing of the militant Pan-Africanist Congress: only 1 percent indicated that they would do so. In contrast, 57 percent indicated that they would advise people close to them to join the ANC's armed wing, Umkhonto we Sizwe, and 10 percent indicated similar feelings about Inkatha's armed wing.

Feelings about leaders similarly favored the ANC. In the same 1992 poll, 70 percent of blacks agreed that Nelson Mandela was "sincere when he says that he wants to build a non-racial democratic South Africa." Unsurprisingly, then, Mandela had enormous prestige among South African blacks. Perhaps more surprisingly, de Klerk also had significant credibility among blacks at this time: nearly 39 percent said that he was similarly sincere.

Another important SYP had to do with violence. The 57 percent of blacks who were willing to tell pollsters in 1992 that they would advise someone close to them to join Umkhonto represented a notable vote of confidence in favor of a strategy of armed struggle—that is, violence—which was Umkhonto's raison d'être. The finding is especially striking because by this time the majority of Umkhonto's local "self-defense units" had turned to criminal activity, preying on the very people whose rights they were allegedly "defending."[96] This willingness to overlook the criminal reality of the self-defense units to support the political objective of Umkhonto strongly suggests that many blacks were more symbolically predisposed to support violence than to oppose it.

BLACK HOPES, FEARS, AND THREAT PERCEPTIONS

South African blacks, often living in more dangerous neighborhoods than whites did, were more likely than whites to tell pollsters that they felt unsafe. In March and July 1986, as the township unrest was raging, 63 percent to 64 percent of blacks said they felt unsafe. This fell to 34 percent in July 1988, after the state of emergency had reduced rates of township violence. However, as violence between Inkatha and ANC supporters rose again at the end of the decade, so did feelings of insecurity: 76 percent of black respondents in the July 1989 survey said they felt unsafe.[97]

As blacks began seeing the results of de Klerk's policies, their fears remained strong, but the apartheid context caused these fears to have contradictory effects on their political attitudes. On the one hand, township violence continued to rise, prompting over 61 percent of blacks to agree in the September 1991 survey that "political violence is continuing to threaten the introduction of a genuine democratic order in South Africa." When asked whether they felt safe or unsafe, 65 percent of black respondents replied "Unsafe," and only a minority was optimistic that the problem would be better under a new majority government. Yet there was no significant statistical relationship between these concerns and their hopes for the future: fears did not dampen hopes. And since the violence was a result of the status quo of apartheid, it paradoxically lowered the risk of activism, since clearly the vast majority felt unsafe anyway.

Against this background of fear, blacks were still hopeful in some ways: when asked in 1991 whether "the current policies of Pres. De Klerk will bring lasting peace to South Africa," almost 54 percent of blacks agreed completely or to some extent, with another 31 percent neutral and only 15 percent disagreeing. When asked whether their lives would be better or worse in the future, black survey respondents were more skeptical, with fewer than 39 percent saying life would be better or much better, and 28 percent saying it would be worse. Optimism increased a bit by February 1992, as 49 percent of blacks told pollsters that they imagined people like themselves would be wealthier in a future South Africa. When asked in 1992 and 1993 whether they had more or less hope for a peaceful future than the year before, a steady 52 percent to 54 percent answered that they had "more hope."[98] As far as hopes went, then, blacks were optimistic about peace, but a bit less certain about achieving comity or prosperity.

As ANC elites assessed the threats faced by their movement, they felt a similar mix of hopes and fears. Their symbolic predispositions were generally in favor of militant action, but such tactics did not seem promising. As a result of Botha's offensive against South Africa's neighbors, the ANC lost its base in Zimbabwe in February 1982, and its ability to infiltrate into South Africa through Mozambique after March 1984.[99] In 1988 the circle was closed, as the agreements for peace in Angola and South West Africa (Namibia) called for the evacuation of Umkhonto fighters from Angola. Tambo told his staff that he was under pressure from both Soviet president Mikhail Gorbachev and friendly African states to enter negotiations.[100] By the start of 1990, the Berlin Wall had fallen and the Soviet Union was in crisis, so the ANC was losing its strongest patron. As interim ANC leader Alfred Nzo conceded in January 1990, "We do not have the capacity . . . to intensify the armed struggle in any meaningful way."[101]

The prospects for nonviolent struggle, by contrast, were improving. The UDF had been banned but was quickly replaced by the Mass Democratic Movement, which provided a strong base of popular support for the ANC inside South Africa. Black trade unions had in 1985 coalesced into the Congress of South African Trade Unions (COSATU), which was also openly allied with the ANC. These shifts opened up the opportunity for the key nonviolent elements of the ANC's overall strategy: "mass action" protests inside South Africa plus international sanctions from outside. Negotiations with the regime would fit well with this approach. Continuing with the strategy of "armed struggle," in contrast, increasingly seemed threatening to the ANC's future.

BLACK PUBLIC OPINION

Though the ANC claimed to represent the whole nonwhite community in South Africa, public opinion polls suggest that popular views were more moderate than the ANC's. The best data on this come from a July 1992 survey, which was taken after the ANC's walkout from negotiations with the government. At this time, when all options seemed open, black public opinion was notably moderate, with a majority endorsing strategies more cautious than Nelson Mandela's. Given four options for how the ANC should move forward, the plurality opinion among blacks, 36 percent, was that the parties should just keep on negotiating. Another 15 percent were even more conservative, preferring to leave the current government in power. The second-largest group, 27 percent, advocated Mandela and the mainstream ANC's combined strategy of negotiations and protest rallies (that is, "mass action"). Support for the radical "Leipzig Way" strategy—the ANC strategy of the time aimed at forcing the government to simply hand over power—was 22 percent, a substantial proportion but far from a majority. In sum, the ANC reflected the views only of the more radical half of black opinion. The mainstream popular preference for quiet talks was ignored.

The most powerful influence on black opinion was assessments of Mandela's sincerity, consistent with Hypothesis 5. Blacks who believed Mandela to be sincere tended to support more radical options. Strikingly, then, Mandela had a relatively radical image among both blacks and whites in early 1990s South Africa. Not only did most whites not trust him but the blacks who were listening to him were hearing primarily a radical message. Trust for de Klerk pushed the other way, increasing support for more moderate options. A third symbolic predisposition that mattered was social conservatism: blacks who were more tolerant of homosexuality felt a bit more favorably toward protests and confrontation than were those who disapproved of homosexuals.

The data did not have a good measure of black racial attitudes, but one question might serve as a proxy for SYPs toward whites: the belief that white civil servants should be fired and replaced by blacks, which does imply a certain degree of ethnocentrism. Using this measure yields weak support for Hypothesis 3: those who favored firing white civil servants (73 percent of blacks in the sample) were slightly more likely to favor radical protest strategies than those who did not.

Among the major influences on black opinion, one was pragmatic rather than symbolic: belief that the Leipzig Way could work. Black respondents were split roughly in half between those who thought mass action could topple the government and those who were either unsure or convinced that it would not work. Among those who believed that mass action would work, almost 33 percent favored a revolutionary strategy, as opposed to only 9 percent of the skeptics and 16 percent of the pessimists. Summed up another way, almost three-quarters (74 percent) of the radicals were people convinced mass action would work.[102]

ANC ORGANIZATION

ANC organization inside South Africa was weak before 1990, as government repression prevented it from sinking roots. However, the UDF and its successor, the Mass Democratic Movement, always saw themselves as ANC proxies, so the ANC quickly absorbed them. Since the UDF was an umbrella organization, this meant primarily contacts with its old constituent groups, such as local black civic associations, youth groups, and women's groups; it also inherited the support of the black labor unions under the COSATU umbrella.[103] With this foundation, the ANC grew quickly: by mid-1991, it had half a million members, and six of the fourteen ANC regional organizations had more than fifty thousand members each.[104] As we would expect from Hypothesis 6, the ANC was therefore able to mobilize large numbers of people for mass activities of all kinds. However, its fast growth meant that internal discipline was a problem—one with far-reaching consequences.

ANC FRAMES, RESISTANCE, AND VIOLENCE

After the ANC was unbanned and Mandela released from prison, tensions began growing between defenders of the Rivonia narrative who wanted to focus on negotiations and advocates of the revolutionary narrative who wanted to overthrow the government. On the one hand, the ANC leadership had explicitly opened the door to a negotiated solution in 1987.[105] On the other hand, "armed struggle" remained a major part of ANC strategy until the middle of 1990. Some ANC leaders focused on armed struggle, using physical threat frames to mobilize their supporters for violence. Others focused on nonviolent resistance, using injustice frames to mobilize their supporters for peaceful demonstrations. Both groups, using pieces of the ANC organization, had some success. As noted earlier in this chapter, they were reflecting a split in the ANC's constituency, the majority of which was moderate but which also contained a strong minority of radicals—many of whom formed the hard core of ANC activists. The challenge of the more moderate leaders was not only to mobilize their own backers, but to undermine the efforts of their more radical colleagues so that the violence did not disrupt negotiations.

The difficulty was that while the moderates had Mandela, the radicals also had credible leaders. Hard-liners like the popular Umkhonto chief of staff Chris Hani, and even some ANC intellectuals like Pallo Jordan, long continued to denounce the idea of "cowardly compromises" with a government at war with the ANC.[106] Winnie Mandela, who had famously endorsed necklace killings in the 1980s, was also in this group. Other ANC radicals were focused on the conflict with rival black leaders—especially Inkatha leader Buthelezi, whom the ANC denounced as traitorous. The central ANC figure in this conflict was Harry Gwala, ANC regional leader in the Natal midlands, who pursued what one of his colleagues called a "war to the knife" against Inkatha.[107] It was Gwala who famously stated in May 1992, "Make no mistake, we kill warlords," referring to his Inkatha opponents.[108] Favoring Gwala's position were the facts that it was Inkatha that had initiated the violence in many places, and that the continuing violence between ANC and Inkatha supporters meant threat perceptions were high; Gwala's violent frames therefore resonated with his supporters. Since he had also built a substantial organizational base, he had the ability to pursue his anti-Inkatha war. His colleagues in other parts of the country, notably in Gauteng, did the same.

Mandela's challenge was to articulate a master frame of injustice to mobilize support for his preferred strategy—the combination of street protests and negotiations—while still retaining credibility with the radicals among

ANC leaders and activists. His speech in Soweto two days after his release from prison illustrates how he did this. On the one hand, he affirmed his support for official ANC strategy, stating, "The ANC will pursue the armed struggle against the government as long as the violence of apartheid continues." On the other hand, he began pushing back against black-on-black violence, saying, "We are . . . disturbed that there are certain elements amongst those who claim to support the liberation struggle who use violence against our people. . . . We condemn that. . . . [Progress] is achieved by politically organising our people—not through the use of violence against our people."[109] Mandela also promoted accommodation with whites, saying, "I stated in 1964 that I and the ANC are as opposed to black domination as we are to white domination. . . . We must clearly demonstrate our goodwill to our white compatriots." Two months later, however, he called for the police also to show restraint: "Recently the government has let loose the South African police against our people. . . . President de Klerk, please take notice: If people are becoming angry and intolerant, . . . it must be measured against the activities of your police and your troops."[110]

Speaking to the South African Youth Congress in April 1990, Mandela was already pushing hard for a policy of negotiations while reaching out to radicals, arguing, "Negotiations do not mean the end of the struggle. They are a continuation of the struggle."[111] He also repeated his call for black unity, asserting, "Any form of violence, any form of coercion, any form of harassment is against the policy of the ANC." On the other hand, Mandela had some tough words for traditional black leaders: "It is not the policy of the ANC to condemn the chiefs as such. These are our traditional leaders. . . . [However,] if any chief decides to be a tyrant, to take decisions for his people, he will come to a tragic end in the sense that we will deal with him." This was Mandela's compromise: while calling for peace, he also endorsed the assassination of chiefs who opposed the ANC.

Mandela reiterated his call for restraint to one of his toughest audiences, a rally of the SACP, in July of 1990. He opened with the main point: "Even when we got together with comrade Joe Slovo and others in 1961 to form the People's army, Umkhonto we Sizwe, we understood . . . this did not make the ANC a slave to violence."[112] Rejecting charges that Umkhonto leaders were using violence to undermine negotiations, he defended them but reiterated the Rivonia preference for peaceful change: "Our movement, . . . has itself never abandoned the strategy of non-violent struggle. . . . It cannot now turn against the peaceful resolution of the conflict in our country, precisely at the moment when such a peaceful resolution seems possible. . . . We must move with all possible speed to abolish the apartheid system. . . . We have entered into talks with the government for the realisation of these goals. . . . We insist that the talks must go on."

While Mandela was making this case, de Klerk was supporting it by meeting most of the ANC's preconditions to enter negotiations: in his dramatic speech in February 1990, de Klerk unbanned the ANC and Umkhonto, and he had begun releasing ANC prisoners even earlier. Then, in the middle of 1990, the ANC was embarrassed by the exposure of its Operation Vula, a covert plan to "lay the foundation for a revolutionary armed insurrection."[113] At this point, the ANC finally suspended its armed struggle, reiterating that commitment in the August 1990 "Pretoria Minute" signed with the government and the February 1991 D. F. Malan Accord.[114]

During the next two years, ANC policy continued to oscillate between what it called a "Programme of Mass Action to Destroy Apartheid and Transfer Power to the People"—the revolutionary approach—and a focus on negotiations.[115] An ANC conference in December 1990 decided to continue to recruit and train people for Umkhonto.[116] Even as Mandela and his team pursued preliminary talks with the government, Hani continued to argue that the ANC would have to return to revolutionary warfare.[117] In sum, the ANC's strategy was simultaneously to fight and to talk, with different leaders advocating different mixtures of these tactics.

Mandela's program of pursuing a negotiated transition was not truly approved until a pair of key meetings in July and October 1991. At the ANC's July 1991 national conference, Mandela reiterated his characterization of negotiations as "a theatre of struggle" that promised success,[118] and he received the conference's approval for that program. However, other ANC leaders continued to repeat the revolutionary narrative, arguing for a strategy to gain power in the streets.[119] An October 1991 "Patriotic Front" conference that included both ANC and more radical Pan-Africanist Congress members then ratified the more moderate line, accepting the notion that all-party talks offered the only path forward to the constituent assembly they wanted.[120]

When the negotiations deadlocked in the middle of 1992, however, ANC leaders turned to what Communist Party theoretician Jeremy Cronin called the Leipzig Way: an attempt to topple Pretoria's internal allies, and the government itself, in a series of mass demonstrations and workers' strikes similar to those that had toppled Eastern Europe's Communist governments in 1989.[121] Only about 22 percent of South African blacks supported this effort, but they were enough—in the context of effective leadership and a portion of the ANC organization—to mobilize seventy thousand people for a march led by Ronnie Kasrils and aimed at toppling the homeland government of Ciskei on September 7, 1992. The effort failed, however, as the marchers' radical aims elicited a brutal response: twenty-nine marchers were killed and hundreds injured when Ciskeian security forces opened fire on them. After this tragedy, the ANC finally shifted to a focus on pursuing a negotiated settlement, though it continued to use mass protests and fierce propaganda attacks to strengthen its hand in the negotiations.

Even as the negotiation process moved forward, violence between the ANC and Inkatha was continuing, reaching the proportions of a civil war:

nearly ten thousand people were killed in political violence just in 1990–1992.[122] Mandela signaled moderation in 1990, famously visiting Durban and telling ANC supporters, "Take your guns, your knives and your pangas, and throw them into the sea. . . . End the war now."[123] However, Mandela's ANC colleagues refused to allow him to visit Buthelezi for peace talks in 1990,[124] instead often encouraging the fighting. Even Mandela praised the formation of ANC "self-defense units" and endorsed a "ban" on Inkatha supporters from the Vaal triangle area, implicitly encouraging ANC supporters to enforce this ban violently.[125] The ANC knew that these "self-defense units" were responsible for much of the violence, but Mandela cynically continued to blame the ANC's opponents, while other ANC leaders blamed the government.[126] When ANC moderates finally decided that Gwala had gone too far, they found it was impossible to remove him: his radical position had too much support in the organization.[127] Winnie Mandela was similarly untouchable despite her violent rhetoric because, as ANC official Tokyo Sexwale explained: "Winnie is a symbol."[128]

Mandela finally publicly accepted partial ANC responsibility for the violence in 1993, but by then it was far too late; the death toll would top twenty thousand people, mostly in ANC-Inkatha fighting, before the violence eased.[129] The ANC strategy of blaming the government for the violence, meanwhile, proved extremely effective, playing a pivotal role in undermining the moral authority de Klerk had gained among some South African blacks and in the international community. De Klerk thus gained the image of a man who connived at the killing of blacks while he negotiated with them—while in fact the ANC was much more responsible for the violence than de Klerk was.

A key lesson from this story is that when conditions favor the mobilization of multiple rival movements based on the same constituency, all of them succeed to the extent conditions allow. The obvious social threats posed by apartheid to black status, power, and economic interests meant strong support in the black community for some kind of counteraction (Hypothesis 4). Mandela and the moderates focused on the social threat frame, and that frame resonated with virtually all blacks; the majority who favored mass action were therefore favorably inclined to join in when recruited by local ANC organizers for protest actions (Hypotheses 5 and 6). The pro-negotiation majority was similarly pleased to vote in favor of the negotiation strategy at ANC meetings.

However, radicals like Hani, Kasrils, and Gwala were also credible leaders, and their frames of physical threat resonated with a radical core within the ANC—especially the violent young men in the ANC's self-defense units. Therefore, they also succeeded in mobilizing supporters. Mandela and the moderates had more support, but the only factor that stopped Kasril's revolutionary effort was the military power of the South African state and its allies. Given the radicals' popular support and organizational base, Mandela and the ANC moderates would have needed great organizational strength to rein the radicals in, and they simply lacked that level of organization.

Conclusion

Symbolic politics theory helps us to understand both the politics of apartheid and the negotiation process that ended it. Apartheid itself was a result of the symbolic politics of protection. As we would expect from Hypothesis 1, Afrikaners' self-glorifying and racist narratives contributed to continued racial prejudice among Afrikaners. This prejudice, in turn, led to exaggerated perceptions of the threat from South Africa's black majority, as expected by Hypothesis 2. The political result of these prejudices and threat perceptions was white support for the brutal policies of apartheid (supporting Hypotheses 3 and 4). Apartheid leaders like Verwoerd and P. W. Botha kept their supporters mobilized electorally behind this policy by framing the issues in apocalyptic terms (supporting Hypothesis 5), as in Botha's claims that the ANC menaced white people's "right to live in South Africa." Finally, the organizations of the National Party and allied civil society organizations like the Broederbond (per Hypothesis 6) helped to keep the NP in power.

Apartheid ended because Afrikaners lost faith in it. Prejudice declined somewhat, as whites' increasing acceptance of racial integration showed. More importantly, perceptions of threat shifted, as the collapse of world Communism removed that threat, while South Africa's economic stagnation, internal turmoil, and international isolation finally led even the Broederbond to conclude that maintaining apartheid posed a greater threat to Afrikaners' future than ending it would. In this context, de Klerk and his supporters developed a new set of frames that were responsive to the new SYPs and threat perceptions. Harnessing the deep reservoir of party loyalty to the NP, and also de Klerk's popularity, they addressed concerns about status threat with reference to South Africa's reinclusion in international sporting competitions, pitted against the stark observation quoted earlier in this chapter, "Nobody wants the state we seek to make."[130] They addressed white fears of the economic risk of democratization by pointing to a greater short-term threat: "You can vote yourself out of a job." And they assuaged fears of losing power by feeding hopes of achieving the popular goal of a new power-sharing system.

Finally, superior organization also contributed to de Klerk's defeat of hardline opponents. The big business community, the churches, universities, and the Broederbond had already concluded that apartheid must end; when rallied behind the National Party's organizational resources, they helped de Klerk prevail in the critical 1992 referendum.

The ANC's path to compromise was perhaps more difficult, and much more contentious than is commonly understood, as it entered the 1990s with a strategy of armed struggle and the objective of the violent overthrow of the South African government. The saving grace was that while ANC narratives were fierce, they were political rather than racial, always making clear that the enemy was the apartheid system. This bit of moderation in the narrative was (supporting Hypothesis 1) echoed in the symbolic predispositions of most black people, which in turn meant blacks did not perceive any threat from white people per se, nor did they support vindictive policies toward whites (consistent with Hypotheses 2 and 3). Indeed, black public opinion had remained more loyal to the Rivonia preference for nonviolence than the ANC leadership had. In part because the South African state had overwhelming power available to bring to bear against violent opposition, the black public preferred a negotiated solution to a revolutionary one (as we would expect from Hypothesis 4a).

None of this meant that assertive injustice frames were ineffective; they were, yielding massive protest marches (as we would expect from Hypotheses 4c and 5), as the gross injustice of apartheid was beyond dispute among blacks. While the ANC's organization was much looser and less disciplined than the NP's, it did quickly build enough capacity within the country to mobilize its supporters.

What made the transition period so violent was that hard-line sentiments remained strong among minorities on both sides, so extremist leaders needed little organizational strength to generate disproportional violence. On the government side, the biggest problem was rogue elements within the police and military forces, the so-called third force, who seemed to believe that by fostering violence they could discredit the ANC. They did not realize that they were only discrediting themselves and weakening the hand of the government.

On the ANC side, the biggest problem was the "revolutionary" practice of killing black collaborators with the regime: though "necklacing" declined after the 1980s, gun violence increased massively. Extremist leaders like Harry Gwala combined the anticollaborator rhetoric with physical threat frames to generate the politics of protection ("We kill warlords") that fed the war between the ANC and Inkatha. Inkatha leaders were equally aggressive, so both used their party organizations to build armed militias as well.

In these conditions, neither Mandela nor de Klerk had the ability to prevent violent action by their more extremist constituents. Both mobilized the majority of their communities in favor of accommodation, but both had radical rivals who were able to appeal to those with more extreme SYPs and to mobilize some of them for violent action. Both leaders might have done more. De Klerk might have worked harder to investigate and stop police misconduct, since his metaphorical police Rottweiler had in fact slipped its leash. Mandela certainly could have done more to oppose violence by his own supporters instead of intermittently encouraging it while consistently blaming de Klerk for it. The route Mandela took was tactically shrewd, undermining de Klerk's bargaining leverage and standing with future black voters. However, the black-on-black violence contributed to a legacy of civil disorder on South Africa's streets that continues to haunt it today. South Africa's transition may have been a "miracle," then, but the violence that accompanied it left a permanent stain on the halos of its patron saints, Mandela, and de Klerk—stains from the blood of the more than twenty thousand dead in South Africa's civil war.

The main hero of the negotiation process was President F. W. de Klerk, who courageously passed the point of no return early in his presidency by unbanning the ANC and other opposition groups and who managed to keep his reformist government on the path to a negotiated settlement in the face of fierce opposition by hard-line opponents. Mandela did make efforts to calm white fears before 1994, but his commitment to peace was equivocal at best: his and the ANC's main objective was not peace but "democracy," which for them meant ANC control. They won by defeating their black opponents in combat while blaming de Klerk for the violence. The charges stuck, undercutting de Klerk's negotiating leverage and forcing him to accept an agreement closer to their bottom line than to his.

The Symbolic Politics of Ethnic Peace in Tanzania

As noted in the introduction, mainland Tanzania has long stood as an exceptional case of relative social peace and political stability on a continent brimming with language-group, racial, and religious violence. Tanzania has about 120 different ethnic groups generally speaking mutually unintelligible languages, and its population is divided between Christians and Muslims. Yet there has been very little identity-based violence and no civil war on the mainland. While there has been some ethnic and racial rioting, Tanzania experienced far less of it than did the United States, for example, in the same period. This accomplishment has not gone unnoticed, and a number of studies have delved into the reasons for this pattern of stability.[1]

This chapter answers three questions about Tanzania's accomplishment. First, how did Tanzania's founding leader, Julius Nyerere, manage to mobilize an almost entirely nonviolent movement for national independence in the 1950s—a feat that escaped both Gandhi and Mandela? Second, how did Nyerere manage to order Tanzanian politics to maintain ethnic peace throughout his quarter-century as national leader? Third, how has Tanzania managed to "make peace stay" in the decades since Nyerere stepped down as president in 1985?

The answers are the ones that symbolic politics theory would lead us to expect. Ethnic peace in Tanzania has been maintained because all of the key factors that can promote ethnic conflict—group narratives, symbolic predispositions, threat perceptions, leaders' frames, and organization—instead promote ethnic peace and cooperation. Nyerere's policies boosted inclusive Tanzanian nationalist narratives at the expense of ethnic or "tribal" ones; cultivated symbolic predispositions favoring national unity and opposing prejudice and violence; worked to ameliorate economic inequalities that could grow into perceived economic threats; banned the use of ethnic or religious frames—especially frames of ethnic threat—in politics; and co-opted

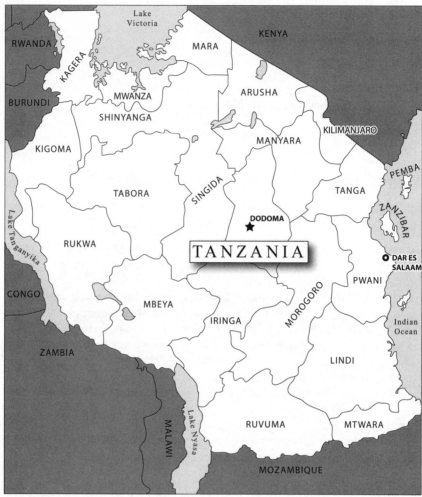

virtually all potentially dissident organizations into his one-party political
system. Even after Nyerere's retirement in 1985, most of these factors remained in place, maintaining an environment in which narratives of ethnic threat do not resonate, so politics remains in the relatively low-conflict
pattern of a politics of distribution.

The chapter is organized as follows. After a brief background section, the
first part details how Nyerere mobilized a movement for national independence that remained nonviolent. The next part examines how Nyerere
avoided ethnic conflict in the decades after independence by cultivating narratives and SYPs and creating an organizational environment promoting
national unity. The final main section explains how Tanzania has maintained

that peace even after the transition to multiparty democracy. After a brief discussion of the partial exception of Zanzibar, the concluding section sums up my findings.

Tanzania's Groups and History

Tanzania's history is as old as humanity. Fossils of early hominids over a million years old have been found there, and contemporary Tanzanians' ancestors began reaching the area over ten thousand years ago.[2] The people of northern Tanzania were making iron in the fifth century BCE.[3] Trade links to the Tanzanian coast from the Middle East and South Asia date back to ancient times, leading to small settlements of Arabs and Shirazi Persians along the coast in late medieval times. Thus when the Portuguese explorer Vasco da Gama landed on Kilwa Island off the Tanzanian coast in 1502, Kilwa had already been the center of a trading empire controlling much of the Tanzanian coast for three centuries.[4] Portugal quickly gained a loose suzerainty over the Tanzanian coastal regions and their Indian Ocean trade, which it held for two centuries. The Portuguese were replaced in the eighteenth century by Omani Arabs, whose sultan found the area so attractive that he transferred his capital to Zanzibar in 1840.

By that time, trade links between Tanzania's coast and hinterland had been growing for centuries. In the eighteenth century, Kilwa was the most important slaving port in East Africa, though trade routes to Zanzibar through northern and central Tanzania were later established as well.[5] This growing trade was accompanied by much violence as African chiefs and kings fought wars over control of trade routes and the sources of trade goods such as ivory and slaves; in some areas, rulers were enslaving their own people for sale to Zanzibari slavers.[6] The northern trade route was the one followed by porters carrying the body of the missionary David Livingstone, who had died shortly after his famous 1871 meeting with Henry Morton Stanley at Ujiji in eastern Tanzania (the occasion of the famous greeting, "Dr. Livingstone, I presume").

British influence over Zanzibar had been growing for decades by this time, leading to the suppression of the slave trade from Zanzibar and Kilwa in the mid-1870s and to Zanzibar's incorporation into the British Empire under a "protectorate" agreement in 1890.[7] German colonial control over the neighboring mainland was established in the same period, as trade treaties were quickly followed by the military conquest of coastal areas and the formal establishment of the German East Africa colony in 1891. When most of the southern part of the colony rose in the Maji Maji Rebellion of 1905–1907, the German commander ended the rebels' guerrilla resistance by starving them out. Estimates of the African casualties of those events range from fifty thousand to three hundred thousand—the latter figure representing one-third of the area's population.[8] British troops conquered the colony during World War I, leading to the establishment of British rule over what was now called Tanganyika under a 1922 League of Nations mandate.

One positive legacy of Germany's system of indirect rule was its use of Swahili—the language of Zanzibaris and coastal traders—as the administrative lingua franca of the region. With a significant number of people throughout Tanganyika already familiar with Swahili, the British maintained that practice, leading to the further spread of the language. Mindful after Maji Maji of the tragic consequences of violent rebellion, Tanganyikans generally avoided violent resistance during the decades of British rule, which ended in 1961. Zanzibar gained independence in December 1963, but a revolution overthrew the sultan—scion of the nineteenth-century Omani sultans—just one month later. To help reestablish order on Zanzibar, Zanzibari revolutionary leader Abeid Karume agreed with Tanganyikan president Nyerere to merge the two countries, leading to the creation later in 1964 of the United Republic of Tanzania.[9]

TANZANIA'S ETHNIC GROUPS

Successive waves of migration brought numerous different groups to what is now Tanzania. Most of Tanzania's more than 120 ethnic groups—including all of the largest such as the Sukuma, Makonde, and Chagga—are Bantu speakers. Other language families represented in Tanzania include the Cushitic, such as the Iraqw and Gorowa peoples, and Nilotics such as the Maasai. Swahili is a Bantu language which, as a result of heavy Muslim cultural influences, came to include a large number of Arabic loan words. The result of Tanzania's ethnic diversity is a plethora of small ethnic groups. Only the Sukuma constitute more than 10 percent of the national population (they constitute about 12.4 percent). All of the other groups are relatively small: the next four largest groups are the Makonde, the Chagga, the Haya, and the Nyamwezi, each estimated at between 3 percent and 4 percent of Tanzania's population.[10]

In addition to linguistic differences, there are a number of other ethnic cleavages in Tanzanian society. The most important is religion: Islam was spread by Arab and other Muslim traders over the course of centuries, while Christian missionaries variously promoted Catholicism and several Protestant sects beginning in the late nineteenth century. The result is a great deal of religious diversity both across ethnic groups and within them, with some groups such as the Meru split between Protestants and Catholics. Racial differences are also important, with a small but significant minority of Asians who, favored by colonial law, established themselves as important in some areas of commerce. Finally, some Tanzanians, especially in Zanzibar, term themselves Shirazis, tracing their descent from ancestors said to have originated in the Persian region of Shiraz.

Tanzania's Peaceful Independence Movement

Tanzania's independence movement was led by the Tanganyikan African National Union (TANU), founded by Nyerere and some associates in 1954 on the basis of a preexisting social organization, the Tanganyikan African Association (TAA). TANU and Nyerere's master frame in the preindependence years was an injustice frame, identifying colonialism as a threat to the status and interests of everyone in Tanganyika.

The status threat frame was particularly notable in Nyerere's rhetoric: "To be ruled is a disgrace," he insisted; "Colonialism is an intolerable humiliation to us."[11] Nyerere built this principle into a political philosophy intelligible to anyone: "Our struggle has been, still is, and always will be a struggle for human rights. As a matter of principle we are opposed . . . to one country ordering the affairs of another country against the wishes of the people of that other country."[12]

The result of political domination was economic exploitation.[13] Exploiting this fact, TANU rhetoric enlarged on the injustice theme, charging that the British and Arabs "sucked our blood," with even Nyerere declaring that there was "no room [in Tanganyika] for land parasites."[14] The answer to these problems, TANU argued, was independence. As historian John Iliffe reports, "Records of TANU speeches, even in remote villages, say little of local issues but much of the large themes of freedom and unity, justice and dignity."[15]

This social threat frame, if successful, should have resulted in mobilization of a relatively nonviolent social movement in a politics of redistribution. This is precisely what happened, for several of the expected reasons. First (recalling Hypothesis 4c), there is evidence that this frame resonated with existing threat perceptions. One Tanzanian veteran of World War I, for example, echoed the TANU frames precisely: "We do not want foreigners to rule here in Tanganyika. . . . The European was poor when he arrived in this country; now he is rich and fat. . . . No man is superior to another here on earth." The economic theme could be potent by itself: local TANU groups were often mobilized primarily on the basis of grievances about agricultural issues. According to Nyerere, "National freedom—*uhuru*—was an uncomplicated principle, and it needed no justification to the audiences of the first few TANU speakers."[16] Significantly, the motivating SYP was not racial prejudice, but the quest for freedom and dignity; since the enemy was colonialism, not white people, there was little impetus for violence against the British.

TANU's message of nonviolent resistance worked because it resonated with Tanganyikan narratives and symbolic predispositions. The most relevant narrative concerned the Maji Maji Rebellion, reinforced by the failure of the 1950s Mau Mau Rebellion in neighboring Kenya, yielding the lesson

213

that violent resistance to European colonialists is foolhardy. The result (consistent with the logic of Hypothesis 1) seems to have been a strong symbolic predisposition against provoking the British. As one village elder explained, "when TANU came we elders resisted strongly . . . lest this Nyerere deceive us" as Maji Maji leaders had.[17] The result of this SYP, in turn (as Hypothesis 4a suggests), was a perception of the British military threat as overwhelming, leading to a reluctance to confront them directly. In this context, the only viable anticolonial strategy was the nonviolent one pursued by TANU. The village elder explained his colleagues' assessment as follows: "When we saw that the Europeans were just watching [Nyerere] and when we were told that it was a war of words, then all of us approved." Nyerere's 1955 appearance at the United Nations and the subsequent arrival of a UN mission in Tanganyika further reassured Tanganyikans that supporting TANU was safe, on the presumption that a movement with such international legitimacy was unlikely to be banned. Tanganyikans now began flocking to join TANU.[18]

To maintain this support and his strategy, Nyerere repeatedly emphasized the importance of nonviolence. In one oft-quoted newspaper article, Nyerere wrote, "The reasons why lunatics have been trying to provoke the people into violence is the fact that they know we are virtually invincible if we remain a law-abiding organization. . . . Fellow Africans, be on your guard. The enemy is losing the cold war because he has no argument against our case. His only chance is to provoke violence so that he may use the gun. Don't give him that chance."[19]

The final element in TANU's mobilizing success (Hypothesis 6) was its ability to build a nationwide organization. Its inclusive message opened the door to such success, but growth was only achieved through a relentless organizing "ground war" sustained over years. Virtually any existing social organization was a potential ally, including the old TAA structures, economic cooperatives, ethnic or tribal unions, and labor unions. TANU leaders and organizers relentlessly toured the country giving speeches, sometimes to audiences numbering a bare handful of people. Among the networks they pressed into service for recruiting purposes were networks of commercial ties. Iliffe reports, "While trading centers and mission stations were initial focal points for leadership [among the Sukuma], the network of contacts spread easily from there into the countryside."[20]

Nyerere's moderate framing was not unopposed. An organization called the African National Congress consistently advocated more confrontational tactics and openly racialist goals. Such ideas did resonate with many Africans, as the harshness of the colonial experience had led to the emergence of racialist symbolic predispositions. As a result, even some local TANU organizers struck racialist themes at times, for example, promising the confiscation of white-owned land and the expulsion of whites and Asians after independence.[21]

A pivotal example of how such arguments were defeated was the TANU debate over participation in the 1958 election. This election was structured by the British to allow black Africans, Tanganyika's 99 percent majority, to elect only one-third of representatives to a new Legislative Council. TANU radicals led by Nyerere's own brother Joseph argued in favor of a boycott of elections for such an unrepresentative body, coupled with a campaign of mass civil resistance. Julius Nyerere, recognizing that such tactics risked an escalation to violence, countered by shrewdly turning the radicals' injustice frame in a moderate direction. His formulation vividly acknowledged his people's resentment of the unfair rules while making a strong pragmatic case for moderation. In his famous speech he argued, "We want that house in which [British governor] Twining is now living. In order to get into it, we must dirty our feet by walking through the mud of an unfair election. What would you rather do? Keep your feet clean and not get the Twining house, or dirty your feet and get the Twining house?"[22] In the event, TANU participated in the election and won such a sweeping victory that the British were forced to accelerate their schedule for Tanganyikan independence and to acquiesce in TANU's growing authority.

The critical importance of this history is the effect it had on Tanzanian symbolic predispositions and national narratives. The narrative of national unity was vindicated, reinforcing nationalism as an important SYP. The narrative of nonviolent action similarly proved itself, leaving in place preexisting SYPs against violent rebellion. Ethnic narratives and ethnic ties, in contrast, received no reinforcement at all, while racial resentments were downplayed. The stage was therefore set for Nyerere to reinforce nationalist sentiments further while continuing to undermine ethnic identities after independence.

Tanzanian Ethnic Politics under Nyerere

When Tanganyika achieved its independence in 1961, the obstacles to successful state-building were significant. As Henry Bienen explained, it was "large, poor, and sparsely settled with a communications system which is underdeveloped even by East African standards," and with a 1961 per capita income estimated as being in the lower third of all African countries.[23] It was also sorely lacking in educated personnel: as late as 1947, there were only twenty-five Tanganyikans studying at the nearest college available to them, Makerere in Uganda, and "there were only 12 fully qualified local doctors in the country" at independence.[24] The obstacles to the successful construction of a coherent national identity out of more than one hundred ethnic groups were thus significant, and the extreme poverty raised the prospect of intense competition for scarce resources that could have led to civil war and a failed state. How was peace maintained?

WEAK ETHNIC NARRATIVES

Even around the time of independence, there is little evidence of widespread, hostile ethnic narratives that could have provided a basis for prejudice among Tanganyikan ethnic groups. Such narratives are typically the creation of previous polities, as among Zulus in South Africa, but such centralized kingdoms were rare in Tanzanian history. On the contrary, the large Sukuma and Chagga groups had little history of any sort of unity and therefore had weak identity narratives: they had first united in tribal federations only in 1946.[25] One of the rare Tanzanian exceptions to this rule, the Shambaa kingdom established in the eighteenth century, had as much of a history of civil war as intertribal conflict, again providing little basis for asserting a strong ethnic identity and ethnic rivalries.[26] Furthermore, those ethnic social organizations that existed in colonial times were mostly nationalist in orientation, working closely with TANU; they did not promote ethnic identities hostile to other Tanganyikan groups.[27]

CONSTRUCTION OF A NATIONAL IDENTITY

While ethnic identities in Tanzania were weak, there were some factors that were favorable to the development of a unifying national identity. One was the availability of Swahili as a unifying national language. Another was a developing nationalist mythology, harking back to the Maji Maji Rebellion of 1905–1907 as an example of what Vamik Volkan would term a "chosen trauma."[28] In the 1920s and 1930s, a number of national associations arose that both embodied and spread the concept of a Tanganyikan identity.[29] After independence, the focus of nationalist ideology was on Nyerere's concept of African socialism or *ujamaa*. The national enemies, in keeping with this socialist ideology, were "exploiters" and "parasites." To the extent that an ethnic identity was attributed to this category, it was most often ethnic Indians: ethnic identity among African groups was thus cemented by emphasis on the cleavage between African blacks and the small Indian minority, who were at times viciously denigrated as blood-suckers and "ticks."[30] This is the one group that was discriminated against: nationalization of property hit Tanzania's Indian community particularly hard, driving half of that community's members to leave Tanzania during the decade 1967–1976.

Nyerere's government made energetic and explicit efforts to cultivate Africans' sense of national identity while undercutting ethnic identity. All primary education was in Swahili, and the school curriculum was intentionally designed to politicize children and promote a national identity.[31] The ruling TANU Party, later retitled Chama cha Mapinduzi (CCM), was also promoted as a symbol of national identity, complete with matching "TANU-green" shirts for members.[32] Younger children were taught to sing pro-TANU and pro-CCM songs, while older students and adults were encouraged to enter local and national arts competitions with original songs extolling the ruling party.[33] Secondary education was in public boarding schools in which all students were assigned to schools outside their home area; as one graduate later recalled, students—that is, all future members of the Tanzanian elite—were thoroughly "de-tribalized" by the time they completed this experience.[34] Nevertheless, Nyerere added another step to further socialize young elites as Tanzanian nationalists, requiring after 1966 that secondary school graduates complete two years of national service.[35]

Efforts to weaken ethnic identity often had a coercive edge, as tribal culture was suppressed by law. For example, women in North Mara were told not to appear in public with bored ears, and Maasai traditional dress was banned.[36] Nyerere also refused to allow tribal identity to be measured in the national census after 1967.[37] No organizations focused on promoting tribal culture were permitted: as one analysis noted, the government refused to allow the operation of any association with "exclusive cultural objectives."[38] References to ethnic identity were also generally banned in public discourse.[39] These weak ethnic identities provided little basis for the growth of ethnic prejudice.

RELATIVE ABSENCE OF ETHNIC THREATS

While it is difficult to provide evidence of an absence, still it seems clear that Tanzanian ethnic groups sensed no threat from each other. There was no recent history of large-scale violence comparable to the 1950s Mau-Mau uprising in neighboring Kenya. While there was a well-established pattern of violent cattle-raiding by some groups (most prominently the Maasai) against their neighbors, it is difficult to find evidence that such activities were seen as threats to the survival of other groups. At worst, it seems that threatened smaller groups assimilated into less-threatening neighbors: Barbaiq pastoralists, for example, settled down and became assimilated with their Iraqw neighbors.[40] Even Maasai cattle-raiding eventually settled down, yielding a relatively high degree of security from physical threat among ethnic groups.

Nyerere maintained this low-threat environment by ensuring that government policy would not come to be seen as threatening to groups' economic interests. Even TANU's forerunner, the TAA, was from the beginning a multiethnic organization. Its officials were often urbanites who had migrated from different parts of the country, and its activities were often aimed at promoting urban-rural cooperation, for example, by providing a service to independently weigh farmers' cotton crop to prevent their being cheated by merchants.[41] TANU itself continued this policy of inclusiveness, including as its founding members representatives from four of the country's five original provinces. Similarly, from the time of the first national elections TANU made sure to have parliamentary candidates from all over the country, including from larger tribes like the Sukuma and Chagga, as well as from smaller tribes like Nyerere's own Zanaki. Overall, at the time of independence, seven of the ten most numerous tribes in Tanzania were also among the eleven best-represented tribes in the national leadership, and members of "other" tribes constituted about 28 percent of that leadership.[42] Tanzania's leadership was, and long remained, about as ethnically representative as feasible.

Economic and development benefits were also widely distributed. The state established a "regional fund . . . to counter-balance regional historical inequality in development [which] was distributed equally to all regions to support development programs."[43] Educational policy was similarly aimed at reducing cross-regional inequality by focusing resources on underserved areas.[44] And of course, the purpose of including officials from all over the country in the executive leadership, and of allowing parliamentary deputies to lobby for their regions, was to ensure that benefits were, as intended, distributed widely.[45]

ORGANIZATIONAL FACTORS

The first constraint on ethnic organization in Tanzania is demography: the fact that Tanzania's population consists of many small ethnic groups means it has always been very difficult to mobilize people on an ethnic basis to project power on a national level.[46] As noted earlier in this chapter, only the Sukuma constitute more than 10 percent of the national population, and they are relatively poor, disunited, and geographical marginal.[47] Nyerere himself noted that this high degree of ethnic diversity favored peace: "The more tribes we have the better," he asserted. "My own tribe is 35,000 people; my brother is the chief. If my brother wanted to be a nuisance, he couldn't be much of a nuisance."[48]

Furthermore, Nyerere quickly acted to eliminate or co-opt what ethnic organizations did exist. He eliminated the official role of tribal chiefs in 1962, replacing them with a new governing structure.[49] He also dissolved all ethnic associations such as the Haya and Chagga unions after independence, instructing their members to join TANU as individuals, while banning all opposition parties and formally establishing Tanzania as a one-party state.[50] Even teachers and the directors of agricultural cooperatives were routinely people from outside the immediate district.[51]

With political organization limited to the government and TANU, Nyerere then organized them to ensure that neither could be used by ethnic leaders to cultivate local bases of political support. Regional and local officials were posted outside their home areas and circulated around the country.[52]

Candidates for Parliament did have to seek local support, but under very tight restrictions: they were forbidden from discussing ethnicity or religion, or even from campaigning in the local language.[53] Preventive detention remained legal and officials seen as threats to public order were imprisoned, sometimes without trial.[54]

The role of MPs was largely to lobby central government bureaucrats to provide material benefits in their districts, but even these activities were strictly limited: in 1968 seven MPs were expelled from Parliament for advocating regional interests too strenuously. And while Nyerere did allow a choice of candidates for parliamentary representatives, all had to be members of TANU, with the central party apparatus having final control over all nominations. That control was exercised tightly: in 1985, one MP was refused renomination after a speech attacking party nepotism.[55] It was thus rendered impossible either for opposition parties to arise on an ethnic basis or for local TANU party organizations to become ethnicized.

To further reduce the chance of political violence, Nyerere acted to ensure both his own control over the security forces and the security forces' control over the population. After a 1964 mutiny, Nyerere dissolved the old colonial army.[56] In building a new army, he began with volunteers from the TANU youth movement, and subsequently required that all military personnel join the ruling party. Military service later became a part of national service, while ideological training for officers became compulsory. Nyerere thus achieved control of the army by politicizing it, in a manner not unlike the method of civilian control of the military in the Soviet Union.[57] Effective civilian control of the military prevented the military itself from becoming a tool of ethnic interests, as it did so often elsewhere in Africa.[58] In this context, with all civil society organizations either dissolved or controlled by the ruling party, with effective party supervision of any dissident or even critical activity by its agents, and with state domination of the economy, there was simply no political space in which dissident or separatist ethnic organizations could have emerged even if there had been any interest in forming them.[59]

NYERERE'S LEADERSHIP

The final factor that favored ethnic peace in Nyerere's time was Nyerere's own charismatic authority. First, as Cranford Pratt explains, Nyerere "had a close and sensitive rapport with ordinary Africans which no other TANU leader could rival. His style of leadership, modest, heavily dependent upon example, humour and simple allegories, fitted the popular mood better than the more flamboyant and more stridently anti-colonial style of some of his colleagues."[60] Additionally, Nyerere's sincerity and personal integrity were beyond dispute. His tactical acumen was widely admired by his colleagues, and TANU's ideology was also his. Finally, even before independence,

Nyerere was the best-known politician in the country; after independence, he was its founding father.

This combination of qualities made the rise of an ethnic challenger to Nyerere nearly impossible. Charisma, as discussed in chapter 1, is a psychological spillover effect in which positive feelings about a leader cause followers to be more positively inclined toward the leader's ideas. Nyerere's stature was such that no rival politician could have credibility, at least on the Tanzanian mainland. If Nyerere was seen as the national ideologist and hero, chief government strategist, and the most gifted political tactician, rivals simply had no basis on which to challenge him. Since any ethnically based leader would also contradict long-standing narratives of national unity, which ultimately became embedded in symbolic predispositions, no such would-be challenger's message could resonate.

In sum, the environment in Nyerere's Tanzania systematically disfavored ethnic activism. There were few organizational resources available that were not controlled by the state, and the state was effective in preventing dissident activities. This organizational structure, combined with the absence of ethnic threats, the relative weakness of ethnic identities, the relative strength of Tanzanian national identity, and Nyerere's charismatic leadership, resulted in the near-absence of ethnic politics in Nyerere's Tanzania.

The political pattern was therefore primarily a politics of distribution—pursuing economic development under the ideology of *ujamaa* and self-reliance. TANU MPs' job was to ensure that their regions received a reasonable share of state resources. The main exception to this pattern was the nationalization program—a policy of redistribution—that was in part aimed at an internal racial minority (Indians) who were portrayed as "exploiters." The other exception was a brief period of a politics of protection during the 1979 war against Idi Amin's Uganda. Here again, the key identity being mobilized was national identity, aimed this time against an external foe.

Tanzania's Contemporary Politics of Distribution

When Nyerere stepped down as president in 1985, he left Tanzania a mixed legacy. His socialist policies had failed to generate economic growth: neighboring Kenya consistently outpaced Tanzania in Nyerere's time, and Tanzania's economy grew more slowly than the sub-Saharan African average during that period.[61] Politically, the legacy of one-party CCM rule has interfered with Tanzania's democratization, obstructing the ability of opposition parties to compete by tilting the political playing field toward a still-dominant CCM. However, Nyerere's retirement set an important precedent, leading to a series of orderly transfers of power with few parallels in Africa. Finally, and most central for this study, Tanzania's ethnic peace has continued for the reasons symbolic politics theory would lead us to expect.

SYMBOLIC PREDISPOSITIONS FAVOR QUIESCENCE

Survey data confirm that levels of ethnic prejudice in Tanzania are low. One Afrobarometer survey found that "Tanzania had the lowest attachment to ethnic affiliation in Africa"; another poll found 83 percent of Tanzanian respondents saying they trusted other tribes.[62] The strength of national identity relative to ethnic identity is striking. According to the 2008 Afrobarometer, for example, 69 percent of Tanzanian respondents said that they "feel only Tanzanian," while an additional 9 percent said that they feel more Tanzanian than their ethnic identity. Only 3 percent identified primarily with their ethnic identity, and only 5 percent identified primarily with their religious group.[63] This is evidence for Hypothesis 1: inclusive and nonhostile narratives in Tanzania promoted nonprejudiced symbolic predispositions among Tanzanians.

Hostility between religions is also strikingly low. According to the 2001 World Values Survey, only 13 percent of Protestants and 16 percent of Catholics indicated that they would object to having a Muslim neighbor, while fewer than 2 percent of Muslims said they would not like a Christian neighbor.[64] Tolerance, not hostility, is the norm: 84 percent of respondents in the same survey indicated that tolerance was an important quality to stress in child-rearing. One result of these attitudes is a strong social norm against even discussing ethnicity. According to one Tanzanian sociologist, "we never ask what kabila [ethnicity] a person is. This is RUDE."[65] In such an environment, appeals to ethnic identity are not likely to get traction.

CCM continues to cultivate these feelings of national unity and to associate itself with that national identity, though some of the means of doing so have changed. For example, the national service program was terminated in 1992 when the number of people required to participate in it grew unmanageably large.[66] However, studies have found that because most current teachers did participate in national service, Tanzanian students have a stronger sense of national identity than do Kenyan students, for example.[67] The existence of a common language also continues to help: as one politician noted, "Kiswahili keeps people from tribalism."[68] Additionally, as Kelly Askew explains, "Singing a national anthem, standing at attention during a state procession, . . . chanting 'CCM Number One' at a political rally, and wearing identical dresses with political portraits emblazoned on the fabric all constitute condensed, symbolically laden, and highly demonstrative strategies for engaging and asserting membership in the nation."[69] As we would expect from Hypothesis 1, these pervasive pro-CCM narratives have resulted in strong pro-CCM SYPs: the 2008 Afrobarometer survey, for example, found that 71 percent of respondents reported feeling closest to CCM among all political parties, and one opposition MP reported in an interview that tribal elders had accused him of violating tradition by opposing CCM.[70]

There is, of course, some variation in national identification, but less variation in ethnic prejudice. Swahili language, carrying with it Tanzanian identity, is well entrenched in most areas: one MP informed me that not only does he never address crowds in his district in the local language; he does not speak that language.[71] In contrast, very few Sukuma speak Swahili, so politicians are forced to address that population in the local language.[72] The same is true in other remote regions, and those who do not speak Swahili often lack a sense of Tanzanian identity.[73] In such areas, informants report that it is impossible to get elected to political office unless the candidate speaks the local language. On the other hand, groups in such remote areas often have few sources of conflict with other ethnic groups, and they show little evidence of ethnic prejudice. As one informant explained it, people in his remote area do not care what other tribes do; they have no opinion or knowledge about them.[74]

Ethnic stereotypes are not completely absent, of course. The most widely mentioned example is the Chaggas, a relatively large and well-educated group whose members are frequently described as showing in-group favoritism in job assignment: Chaggas are alleged to dominate the Treasury and the national rail service, for example. Similar charges are sometimes made against Hayas and Nyakyusas, the latter of whom allegedly dominate in insurance. These negative stereotypes can contribute to conflict: in a fight over control of the Northern Diocese of the Lutheran Church in Meru, for example, the suspicions of ethnic Meru toward the Chagga bishop played a significant role in stoking contention.[75]

Any time such stereotypes are mentioned, however, the caveat is added that discussion of such stereotypes in public is taboo. Additionally, there is very little ethnic resentment or perception of ethnic inequality. For example, when asked about their tribe's influence in politics compared with that of other tribes, 21 percent of Afrobarometer respondents rated their tribes as having *more* influence than others, and 35 percent rated their groups' influence as equal to others', so the majority saw no grounds for any grievance.[76] Similarly, in their ratings of their groups' living standards, 16 percent of respondents rated their group as better off than others, and 36 percent rated their group as equal to others. The majority of Tanzanians do not seem to feel status resentment. By the standards of neighboring countries, these stereotypes and perceptions of inequality are remarkably mild.

ABSENCE OF ETHNIC THREATS

These very low levels of ethnic prejudice have led to a situation in which perceptions of ethnic threat or even nonviolent conflict is virtually absent. As one Tanzanian school principal told a researcher, "This is Tanzania. We do not have that sort of [ethnic conflict] problem here." This researcher found "good" ethnic relations in 97 percent of villages surveyed.[77] Similarly, according to the 2008 Afrobarometer survey, when asked about the most important problems government should address, virtually none mentioned political violence or "political instability/ethnic tensions" as their first concern.[78] This evidence is consistent with Hypothesis 2: in Tanzania, low levels of prejudice are associated with a relative absence of perceived threats.

The most contentious interethnic relationships seem to have been tamed into formalized "joking relations," which involve trading joking invocations of the stereotyped characteristics of participating tribes. But the relationships go beyond jokes: partnership in these joking relationships also includes ritual roles in funerals, circumcisions, and other important ceremonies.[79] Tanzanians frequently quote Nyerere as having said that Tanzanians only ask each other for their tribal affiliation to find out if they can joke with them. Another frequently noted factor is the high rate of intermarriage among members of different ethnic groups, also illustrating positive interethnic relations.

ORGANIZATIONAL FACTORS DISFAVOR ETHNIC MOBILIZATION

Ethnic groups and religious communities in Tanzania remain divided along multiple lines of cleavage, so they cannot provide an organizational base for social mobilization. For example, Meru are divided regionally, between easterners and westerners; split along sectarian lines, between Lutherans and African Methodists; and split into factions even within the Lutheran sect.[80] Arushas, like many other groups, are split subethnically between Ngaramtoni and Ilboru. As for religious communities, there is no overarching Christian organization; all national Christian organizations represent their own sect only. Tanzania's Muslim community is similarly divided, with again many of the fiercest struggles being within a sect, often over control of individual mosques.[81]

An additional obstacle to potential ethnic mobilization is the strength of CCM party institutions that suppress it. The ruling party's organization has a nationwide reach, with structures in many places down to cells of every ten households.[82] It is therefore impossible to engage in efforts at ethnic mobilization without attracting official attention—and since such efforts are legally banned, that means potential legal consequences.[83] There is a highly active National Electoral Commission that enforces regulations, ordering specific campaigns to desist from specific activities, including those with an ethnic tinge.[84] Additionally, police repression of even legal campaign activities is widely reported in every election year, serving as a further deterrent to illegal ethnic mobilization.[85]

Yet another obstacle to ethnic mobilization is the ethnic inclusiveness of the Tanzanian political system. There is, in short, little reason to mobilize on ethnic lines because the ruling CCM includes members from all over the country, as do the opposition parties. Those interested in *political* activism are generally welcome to join either the CCM or the opposition, where in either case they have the opportunity to advocate benefits for their group, as long as the advocacy is cast in regional terms. An oft-cited example of Tanzania's political inclusiveness is that the presidency has, until now, always alternated between Christians and Muslims: the first and third presidents (Nyerere and Benjamin Mkapa) were Christians, while the second and fourth (Ali Hassan Mwini and Jakaya Kikwete) have been Muslim. This can lead to resentment: some Muslims believe that Muslims are underrepresented in government positions, while some Christian politicians feel resentment toward a perceived overrepresentation of underqualified Muslims in the Kikwete cabinet.[86] However, neither religious community can feel wholly excluded, and they can also be fairly confident that if they wait, power will rotate back to their religious group. Thus Hypothesis 6 also helps to explain Tanzania's ethnic peace: any politician who wishes to stir up ethnic conflict is confronted with strong organizations that cut across ethnic lines and an absence of organizations on which to base an ethnic political movement.

THE INEFFECTIVENESS OF ETHNIC FRAMES

In the first two national elections after the transition to a multiparty system, both CCM and opposition parties did make efforts to engage in ethnic identity politics. However, given the low levels of prejudice and feelings of threat, such messages did not resonate with voters (as we would expect from Hypotheses 3 and 4), so the role of ethnic politics has diminished. In 1995, according to one monitoring group, "The ruling party's candidates especially tended to aim at arousing fears of ethnic persecution or favoritism"; they quoted one candidate as having asserted, for example, "A vote for the opposition is a vote for the Chagga people."[87] During the 2000 presidential election campaign, the opposition United Democratic Party tried to mobilize a coalition of the Sukuma with the closely related and relatively large Nyamwezi group. The effort failed, however: UDP came in fourth in both the presidential and parliamentary races with only 4 percent of the nationwide vote, and only 1.4 percent of the seats in Parliament.[88] After such a dismal showing, the effort was not repeated.

THE DISTRIBUTIVE NATURE OF TANZANIAN POLITICS

In these conditions of low prejudice and little threat, the expectation of symbolic politics theory (Hypotheses 4d and 5) is that politics will focus on distribution of benefits. Injustice frames are likely to be tried, but they are likely to be focused primarily on distributive rather than symbolic issues. In this section, I test these expectations by surveying political campaign rhetoric and political attitudes in the 2000, 2005, and 2010 election campaigns.

On the demand side, voters' concerns were, as expected, entirely on distributive issues. In response to one poll done before the 2010 election, for example, 28 percent of participants mentioned education as the most important issue to them, 13 percent mentioned agriculture, 11 percent health care, and 9 percent water.[89] The 2008 Afrobarometer survey also found a primary popular focus on distributive issues, though with somewhat different priorities: infrastructure issues came first, followed by concerns about income, health, and agriculture.[90] Identity and security issues went unmentioned.

While the "supply side" of political rhetoric was somewhat different, the overall pattern was still predominantly distributive.[91] According to a late August 2010 survey of media coverage, the issue to which candidates devoted the most attention was peace (28 percent of their attention). Next most widely discussed was corruption (21 percent), followed by education (12 percent) and health (6 percent). However, as projected by Hypothesis 4, even relatively soft threat frames such as the peace and corruption narratives did not resonate because of people's tolerant SYPs and low perceptions of threat. As a result, the candidates adjusted their focus in the direction of their constituents' concerns: in another survey a month later, education had come to the top of candidates' priorities (with 21 percent of attention), followed by health care (19 percent), peace (18 percent), agriculture (16 percent), and only then corruption (10 percent). Politicians were unable to build support for a politics of protection or of redistribution in that election.

The Issue of Peace. The issue of peace is, of course, a tacit threat frame, but its resonance is relatively limited in Tanzanian elections because of the absence of threat; rather, the debate is over which party can best safeguard peace in Tanzania. In general, CCM has used this frame the most, arguing that it has successfully safeguarded peace and security in Tanzania and that the opposition could not be counted on to do so.

CCM candidates and their proxies offered a number of different arguments on this theme. A typical example was produced by President Mkapa, who during his 2000 reelection campaign warned, "The wrong people may be elected, thereby destroying the peace and security that has existed in the country for a long time."[92] Mkapa's successor Kikwete made a sharper charge in his reelection bid in 2010, accusing opponents "of threatening national security by threatening bloodshed, something which our country has never experienced."[93]

The most inflammatory example of this sort of campaigning reportedly occurred earlier, during a 1994 by-election for a parliamentary seat. According to one account, CCM showed videos of Rwanda and Burundi violence, implying that an opposition victory might lead to such scenes to be played out in Tanzania.[94] In the 2005 election campaign, the regime tried a similar tack: the inspector-general of police reportedly appeared on television holding a machete with the colors of the opposition Civic United Front (CUF), apparently implying that CUF wanted to emulate the machete-wielding violence that had engulfed Rwanda a decade before.[95]

Opposition candidates preferred to focus on other issues, but they did rebut these CCM charges. One argument reportedly offered by CUF presidential candidate Ibrahim Lipumba was to assert that Tanzania's peace was built not by CCM but by Tanzania's citizens: "You are the ones who brought peace," Lipumba asserted.[96] Another response, offered by both Lipumba and Chadema candidate Willibrod Slaa in 2010, was to make well-founded charges that it was the police (at the behest of CCM), not opposition parties, who were responsible for political violence.[97] Another opposition response was simply to publicly call on their supporters to maintain peace and harmony.[98]

All of this is consistent with Hypothesis 4b. The obvious intent of the CCM and security force accusations was to create a terror management effect, raising voters' fears as a way to drive voters in a conservative direction, with CCM, the only ruling party Tanzania has ever known, automatically seen as the safe harbor. However, voters' threat perceptions did not increase, indicating that CCM efforts were not resonating. The opposition responded in just the way that terror management theory would advise: trying to stay away from the issue in order to avoid raising its salience, and working to allay or divert those fears when forced to address them. As a result, most political violence in Tanzania has occurred as the result of disputed elections (which CCM officials have tried to steal), not of ethnic tensions.[99] And of course, the decline in candidates' attention to this issue suggests that it was not resonating with voters.

The Issue of Corruption. If threat frames tend to redound to the benefit of conservatives and incumbents, injustice frames are more useful to challengers. As noted earlier in this chapter, the corruption theme was the main staple of opposition candidates' rhetoric early in the 2010 election campaign. The same appears to have been true in earlier races as well. But in the absence of perceptions of social threat, these appeals for a politics of redistribution have also tended to fail, as we would expect from Hypothesis 4c.

In 2000, for example, opposition presidential candidate Agostino Mrema launched this attack: "The situation in the villages is appalling. There's too much poverty out there, and people are dying for lack of health care. But CCM is buying expensive cars, telling us that the economy has grown. This is nothing but a sin." Furthermore, Mrema charged, CCM officials had been colluding with directors of agricultural cooperatives to "squander farmers' property."[100] When whistleblowers tried to call attention to such abuses, Mrema argued, it was the whistleblowers who were arrested, not the corrupt officials.[101]

In the 2010 campaign, officials of the leading opposition party, Chadema, repeatedly attacked CCM with specific examples of its corruption. Chadema presidential candidate Willibrod Slaa mentioned one case in which four pit latrines were constructed at schools at a cost that would have paid for the construction of one hundred dispensaries. Chadema also launched repeated attacks on CCM, and Kikwete in particular, for a 2005–2006 case of embezzlement from the government's External Debt Payments Account. Slaa tried to connect this issue to voter demands for economic development, asserting, "Once I'm elected to government I'll recover all the government money that has been stashed away in foreign bank accounts and spend some of it on provision of free education and on some other social services."[102]

The fate of these charges illustrates the fact that potentially powerful discourses are not always effective. In spite of the evidence of CCM corruption, and of its connection to high-priority voter issues such as education, agriculture, and health, this line of attack does not seem to have resonated. Only 2 percent of voters reported corruption to have been their top concern in 2010, while the 2008 Afrobarometer found 6 percent emphasizing the corruption issue.[103] Tanzanians seem instead to believe that the corruption problem is under control: 56 percent reported believing that the state was doing fairly well or very well at fighting corruption in government.[104] This illustrates the power of party feelings as a symbolic predisposition: this widespread (and inaccurate) faith in the CCM government's probity should probably be understood as a result of the over 70 percent of Tanzanians who feel closest to CCM among all political parties.

Issues of Economic Development. A great deal of candidate time in Tanzanian elections has focused on the most mundane and straightforward sorts of distributive politics: promising benefits in economic development, education, and health care both nationally and in particular regions. This is consistent with Hypothesis 4d: since threat perceptions are low, it is benefit frames that resonate, resulting in a politics of distribution.

The ruling CCM is energetic in making specific promises of distributive benefits. In 2005, for example, CCM candidate Jakaya Kikwete's election manifesto promised to create one million jobs.[105] In his 2010 reelection campaign, Kikwete followed up with a blizzard of specific pledges, promising to raise workers' wages; to pay the debts of Nyanza Cooperative Union; to buy a ferry ship to connect Mwanza and Bukoba across Lake Victoria; to make Mtwara a major producer of cement, fertilizer, and paper; to provide electricity and water for Lindi and Mtwara; to build a new railroad from Dar es Salaam to the Lake Zone; and to build roads and water facilities in Tabora, inter alia.[106] More general promises included pledges to hire more workers in health centers and dispensaries to improve health services, and to "end water problems across the country."[107] (The promises on health care were reported in an article evocatively titled, "Kikwete Pours Down More Pledges.") CCM candidates for lesser offices offered similar pledges: one promised a tractor for every ward in his district; another pledged to create four thousand jobs in hers.[108]

As the longtime ruling party, CCM also feels obliged to defend its record of promoting economic development and related benefits. During his 2000 reelection campaign, for example, President Mkapa pointed out that his government had built 482 schools and 1,000 km of roads, among other accomplishments.[109] Mkapa's running mate, Dr. Omar Ali Juma, added that the government had achieved the cancellation of Tanzania's foreign debt, the taming of inflation, and increased tax collection.[110] Kikwete, during his 2010 reelection campaign, made similar if more general claims, asserting, "We have delivered in health, education, [and] infrastructure."[111]

When opposition candidates discuss economic development issues, they often try to employ an injustice frame to attack CCM policies. Ibrahim Lipumba of the opposition CUF, for example, frequently attacked "CCM's bad policies which kill" economic growth, especially by taxing small businesses while granting waivers to big business.[112] Attacking CCM policies of privatization, Lipumba asked, "What kind of policies are those which sell all government companies and retrench workers?"[113] Lipumba later tried to extend this injustice frame into a social threat frame, asserting that the CCM policy of grabbing small-holders' farms to give to investors might foment civil strife.[114] The overall tenor of Lipumba's campaigns was thus a populist attack on an allegedly elitist set of CCM economic policies. This was reinforced by the usual pledges to upgrade infrastructure, including roads and electric power; to make education more available by cutting school fees; to eliminate the poll tax; and so on.[115]

Another opposition approach, taken by Chadema's Dr. Slaa in his 2010 campaign, was to counter Kikwete's blizzard of promises with a blizzard of his own. In September 2010, for example, Slaa pledged tax cuts and subsidies on building materials; free education up to Form 6; free university for all students passing A-level exams; dispensaries providing free health care in all villages; and the revival of an agricultural price stabilization fund.[116] At the regional level, Chadema MPs reported in interviews that pledges to address infrastructure issues such as water, roads, and electricity were especially important in their campaigns.[117] Thus simple distributive politics is pervasive in Tanzania at both the national and the regional levels.

An interesting illustration of this tendency is the response of one CCM candidate for Parliament to journalists' charges that candidates were ignoring foreign policy issues. The candidate replied, "I have no option but to address local issues such as health, water supply, education, animal husbandry and infrastructure which most directly affect the electorate."[118]

SYMBOLIC POLITICS OF IMAGE MANIPULATION

The ruling CCM, as the most widely known and respected political party, has the most room for engaging in the symbolic politics of image manipulation, and it does so relentlessly. One of the most prominent examples of this tendency was a 2000 campaign speech by President Mkapa, which was reported under the headline, "Opposition Parties Are Like an Uncircumcised Person"—that is, children who have not yet undergone the rites of passage to adulthood.[119] Mkapa also relentlessly attacked opposition candidates as unreliable and unable to honor commitments.[120] His successor Kikwete used the same line of attack—for example, denouncing his opponent Slaa's promise of free primary education as a "false and impossible promise."[121]

In 2010, Slaa also found himself repeatedly forced to counter widespread inaccurate rumors that were widely assumed to have been spread by CCM. One week, for example, Slaa was forced to deny rumors that he was anti-Islam; the following week, he was denouncing a rumor spread in churches that he had endorsed Tanzanian membership in the Organization of the Islamic Conference (OIC).[122] Similarly, Slaa (a former Catholic bishop) was charged alternately with having been expelled from his church and with having been ordered by the church to run for office.[123] Yet another line of attack traced back to CCM was to call attention to Slaa's alleged involvement in an extramarital affair.[124]

At the same time that it was attacking its opponents' images, CCM continued its efforts to polish its own image and those of its candidates. A particularly striking example of the latter is the willingness of religious leaders to endorse certain CCM candidates. One CCM MP admitted to me that church leaders in his district had openly endorsed him.[125] Even more striking was the endorsement of Kikwete by one bishop, a personal friend of his, as "the choice of God."[126] In the case of Kikwete, experts widely assess that personality played an important role: especially in his first campaign in 2005, Kikwete seems to have attracted a substantial amount of attention, and a substantial number of votes, based on his attractive personality. Finally, references to CCM as the party of the still-revered Nyerere are also common. Thus in one speech to tribal elders, Kikwete "cited the late Thabit Kombo and Mwalimu Julius Nyerere as some of the elders who made it possible for him to become a successful politician."[127]

In attempting to respond in kind, opposition parties are hobbled by the strong pro-CCM SYPs (including the 71 percent level of support cited earlier in this chapter) that CCM accumulated in its more than fifty years of rule. One way they have responded has been to associate themselves with CCM symbols such as Nyerere: most opposition leaders are, in any case, former members of CCM. For example, opposition presidential candidate Freeman Mbowe told a newspaper reporter in 2005, "My late parents . . . were very close to the late Mwalimu Julius Nyerere. . . . Anybody who reads Nyerere's works realizes that he was an exemplary leader. . . . That's why Nyerere is still my role model."[128]

The alternative route taken by opposition leaders is to try to undermine the CCM's reputation. One graphic example is the response of opposition presidential candidate Augustine Mrema in 2000 to the question of whether he would consider returning to CCM: "I can't return to CCM. I'm not a dog to eat my own vomit. CCM has not changed. It stinks of sins and oppression."[129] Another example is from Ibrahim Lipumba of CUF the same year: "Wherever I went, people said they were tired of CCM. There is no development, so people have no faith in it anymore."[130] This latter is a common theme frequently repeated by opposition politicians, but as noted earlier in this chapter, they have not yet gained traction with these attacks: the attacks do not resonate because CCM retains respect and support from most Tanzanians.

ORGANIZATIONAL POWER: BUYING VOTES AND GOOD OPINIONS

One reason for CCM's continued popularity is its immense advantage in material resources and organization over its rivals, as we would expect from Hypothesis 6. When Tanzania was officially a one-party state, CCM accumulated a wide variety of lucrative assets, the most commonly cited being its ownership of sports venues. CCM also owns most "independent" radio stations and newspapers, giving it a powerful ability to spin the news. Radio is especially important, the primary source of information for most voters.[131] It is thus significant that according to one survey, 48 percent of radio coverage of the 2010 campaign focused on CCM, as opposed to 27 percent for Chadema, 16 percent for CUF, and 9 percent for other parties. Furthermore, a survey of newspaper coverage found that though CCM received more attention overall, Chadema received slightly more total *negative* coverage than CCM did, and there was a least one report of a newspaper being threatened by the government for coverage that was too favorable to the opposition.[132] In short, CCM retains the ability to use the media to continue to reinforce SYPs in favor of itself and its leaders while cultivating negative SYPs toward its opponents.

Additionally, CCM reportedly uses its revenues directly to buy votes. Opposition leaders widely report that CCM cadres give out free T-shirts and caps in rural areas during election campaigns, gifts that are well received in these deeply impoverished areas. Other gifts distributed by CCM at election time include sugar and other consumer items. CCM's revenue streams and control over patronage also enable it to maintain a nationwide organizational structure down to the level of ten-household cells, an organizational advantage its opponents cannot begin to match. Opposition politicians are also not immune to the allure of this wealth: one CUF official was reported as having defected to CCM in 2010 "because of hunger."[133]

EXCEPTIONS TO THE PEACEABLE RULE

While tensions and even ethnic identification among ethnic groups in Tanzania are extremely low, identity conflict is not entirely absent from mainland Tanzania. The potentially most dangerous cleavage is religion. In the 1980s, for example, a number of "crusades" by fundamentalist Christians prompted public Muslim counterpreaching in an open contest for religious converts.[134] As noted earlier in this chapter, there is also enough tension between Muslims and Christians for CCM operatives to attempt to exploit it in election campaigns. Furthermore, there are some symbolic religious issues that have stirred the waters of Tanzanian politics.

The two most commonly mentioned are two demands of Muslim activists: Tanzanian or Zanzibari membership in the OIC and the establishment of officially recognized and government-funded religious courts known as "Kadhi's courts" that would enforce shari'a. The first issue arose in 1992, when Zanzibar, exceeding its constitutional authority in foreign affairs, joined the OIC. The Union government soon forced it to withdraw, but Islamist activists kept the issue alive. Kadhi's courts had existed in Tanganyika throughout colonial times but were abolished in 1962. CCM revived the issue during the 2005 election campaign, promising a resolution of the issue, but opponents blocked the change, arguing that such courts would unconstitutionally undermine Tanzania's status as a secular state.[135]

There have also been a few episodes of violence between religious communities. In April 1993, for example, a mob incited by a fringe Muslim organization attacked butcher shops selling pork in Dar es Salaam; the sponsoring organization was quickly banned. Later in 1993–1994, Reverend Christopher Mtikila, an independent church leader, "openly incited hostility against Muslims and non-Africans living in Tanzania and led violent attacks on Indian and Arab shopowners, including some African Muslims wearing [Muslim garb]."[136] Specifically, Mtikila called Asians "enemies of the nation" and labeled Indians and Arabs as "thieves," calling for their expulsion.[137] In February 1998, riots broke out in the area of the Mwembechai Mosque outside Dar es Salaam in response to the arrest of members of the Islamist group Khidmat Daawat Islamiya; a total of forty people were injured in two days of rioting, and two were killed by police bullets. Some analysts termed these incidents part of a "struggle of Muslims against the state."[138]

Such violent episodes remain rare on the mainland, however, and they may well have been side effects of the transition to multiparty politics that had just gotten underway. According to a survey performed in 2000, 78 percent of Tanzanians assessed relations between Christians and Muslims as positive.[139] Still, religious tensions continue to exist, and some politicians and experts fear that there may well be more Christian-Muslim conflict in the future.

The other axis of identity conflict in Tanzania, as illustrated by Mtikila's rhetoric cited earlier in this section, is the racial one, primarily between black Africans on the one side and Arabs and Indians on the other. Given the small size of the targeted populations, these tensions do not carry the threat of future civil war, but because they resonate with existing SYPs, they have had a greater impact on Tanzanian politics than religious prejudices have. Before the 1960s wave of nationalizations which disproportionately harmed them, Asians had been relatively affluent, the beneficiaries of colonial-era discriminatory policies. The economic liberalization policies of the 1980s benefited these groups, provoking verbal attacks by African businessmen. At the same time, the introduction of the multiparty system led to open references to race in Tanzanian politics for the first time in decades.[140] These tensions continued to the point that in the late 1990s, the government felt pressured to act on a discriminatory "indigenization" bill, with "corruption" and "exploitation" being used as racial code words denoting Asians.[141]

There are occasional reports that ethnic rivalries have also played a role in regional politics. At least one informant told me that in multiethnic districts, candidates for Parliament do sometimes appeal to members of their tribe for support on the basis that a candidate from another tribe would be likely to favor his own tribe at the expense of theirs. A more extreme example, playing on anti-Chagga sentiment, came from Moshi, where a CCM official reportedly charged that Chadema planned to expel all non-Chaggas from the district.[142] As of this writing, however, these maneuvers seem to be relatively rare events.

THE ZANZIBAR EXCEPTION?

In contrast to Tanzania's mainland, the autonomous island region of Zanzibar has a reputation for political and racial violence. For this reason, Zanzibar is sometimes cited as an exception to the rule of relatively peaceful Tanzanian ethnic politics. It therefore merits a brief look.

Zanzibar's violent reputation is based mostly on the bloody events of its revolution in January 1964, one month after it gained independence from Britain. During the revolution, radicals among the black majority on Zanzibar's main island overthrew the Arab sultan and began attacking the privileged ethnic Arab minority.[143] Hundreds of Arabs were killed—mostly poor Arabs, not the elite—leading many more Arabs and Asians to flee.[144] Feelings were different on the smaller island of Pemba, however, where 43 percent of Zanzibar's population lived. Pemba's economy was dominated by a large number of small landowners among whom the difference between Arabs and blacks was unimportant.[145] As a result, the anti-Arab Afro-Shirazi Party (ASP), whose youth wing led the revolution and which gained power after it, never had substantial support on Pemba.[146]

After the revolution, ASP leader Abeid Karume quickly engineered the merger with mainland Tanganyika. Concerned with establishing order and maintaining his own power, Karume agreed to form the new union of Tanzania in exchange for significant autonomy for Zanzibar's leadership—that is, himself.[147] Unlike TANU on the mainland, however, Karume's ASP "rejected multiracialism," building a regime openly hostile to Arabs and responsive only to the ASP's prerevolutionary base. Pemba was exploited: heavily dependent on its clove production, its growers received only 10 percent of the export price in the late 1960s.[148] Thus when TANU and ASP merged to form CCM in the 1970s, the new ruling party inherited the divisive legacy of the ASP in Zanzibar.

As a result, as soon as the multiparty system was introduced in Tanzania, Pembans were at the forefront of the emerging opposition, quickly emerging as one of the main bases for the opposition Civic United Front (CUF). Zanzibar has divided almost evenly between CCM and CUF ever since: in the first contested presidential election in Zanzibar in 1995, the CCM candidate claimed a victory with 50.2 percent of the vote—a claim CUF disputed.[149]

CCM's response in the 2000 election was aggressive: it derided CUF leaders as "Arabs" who wanted to return to the prerevolutionary system, denigrated Pembans as "bumpkins and fools," and deployed army troops to try to intimidate voters.[150] Since these campaign tactics were ineffective, CCM resorted to "widespread, internationally condemned election fraud in Zanzibar," canceling the vote tally in Pemba and claiming an improbable two-thirds of the vote for its candidate for Zanzibari president.[151] CUF organized nationwide protests the following January, which came off peacefully on the mainland, but on Zanzibar, security forces repeatedly opened fire on unarmed demonstrators, killing at least thirty-five and injuring over six hundred according to a Human Rights Watch tally. This was the worst case of violence on Zanzibar since its union with the mainland, but while it was surrounded by racial rhetoric, its nature was primarily political: the violence was aimed by the regime and ruling party against CUF supporters.

Some religious tensions have also arisen to color local politics. A Salafi movement called Ansar Sunnah has arisen in Zanzibar, aided by the establishment of two Islamic universities supported by Kuwaiti and Saudi funding.[152] CCM spokesmen attempted to tie this group to CUF in the early 2000s, implying that CUF included "fundamentalist elements."[153] The extremist fringe of this Salafi movement did briefly veer into terrorism: one of the activists implicated in the 1998 bombing of the U.S. Embassy in Dar es Salaam was from Pemba, and Zanzibar town was rocked by several nonlethal bomb attacks on bars in early 2002.[154]

Zanzibar's partisan political violence has meanwhile diminished. While the 2005 election campaign resulted in renewed political violence between CCM and CUF supporters, this time the police showed more restraint, leading to a death toll an order of magnitude lower than in 2000: CUF claimed five of its supporters had been killed, with aid workers confirming only one of those deaths.[155] To head off further political violence, CUF and CCM agreed ahead of the 2010 balloting on a procedure for forming a Government of National Unity in Zanzibar. This agreement was effective: while CCM again won the Zanzibar presidency by a slim and suspicious margin (50.1 percent to 49.1 percent), violence during the campaign was minimal. A key monitoring group gave the election a "qualified free and fair" rating, and the power-sharing government was formed as promised.[156]

In sum, while Zanzibar experienced severe racial violence before its union with the mainland, the union has generally helped to improve stability on Zanzibar. While Zanzibar has experienced political violence, the worst of it has been partisan rather than ethnic, the legacy of Pemban exclusion from the benefits of CCM rule. Even Zanzibar has experienced very little ethnic violence since the merger.

Conclusion

Tanzania is a relatively peaceful example of the politics of distribution, and it has remained so for the reasons that symbolic politics theory would predict. The usual narrative of how Tanzania avoided ethnic conflict in the Nyerere years and afterward is notably consistent with the hypotheses of symbolic politics. Consistent with Hypothesis 1, Nyerere's relentless efforts to promote a national identity—by disempowering tribal leaders, promoting nationalism through universal primary education, and maintaining cross-regional secondary boarding schools and national service—resulted in strong nationalist symbolic predispositions. Parallel and massive CCM efforts to promote its party image have been similarly effective at generating pro-CCM SYPs. Ethnic prejudice seems to have been low from the start, and Nyerere's repression of ethnic organization and any efforts to appeal to ethnicity worked to prevent the emergence of ethnic identities that might lead to prejudice. As expected by Hypotheses 2 and 3, these favorable SYPs have resulted in quite low perceptions of ethnic threat, and no support for hostile policies directed against other African ethnic groups.

Another cause of Tanzania's ethnic peace is the one projected by Hypothesis 6: an organizational environment that continues to favor and allow party political mobilization while disfavoring ethnic mobilization. In this environment (Hypothesis 4), threat and injustice frames do not resonate with the Tanzanian public. Instead, the appeals that resonate the most reflect distributive frames—simple promises to deliver economic goods. The one sort of symbolic politics that is prominent is the politics of image manipulation— parties' efforts to boost their own images and those of their candidates, while denigrating the image of opponents.

Hypothesis 5, regarding the role of leaders' frames, was most important during the Nyerere era, when nationalist narratives and SYPs were not as strong as they would be later. In these early decades, it was Nyerere's relentless focus on a unifying nationalist narrative frame instead of a divisive ethnic or religious one, plus his careful structuring of the organizational environment, that prevented ethnic politics from taking off. Once Nyerere was done, the enduring factors of moderating narratives, SYPs, and organizations reduced the role of leaders' frames from a cause to a result of the system: when leaders try to use threat or injustice frames, those frames simply do not resonate, so ethnic mobilization cannot result.

Ultimately, the decisive factors in Tanzanian elections in the multiparty era have probably been the enormous CCM advantage in financing and organizational strength, coupled with the deep-rooted SYPs in favor of the party. With cells in virtually every village, control over much of the media, and generous flows of money from stadium ownership and other economic assets, CCM has the ability to overpower opposition efforts to get their messages across while maintaining its own image. These advantages, plus the traditional advantages of incumbency and the occasional resort to repressive tactics and vote fraud, have kept CCM in power ever since the transition to a multiparty system in the early 1990s.

In applying symbolic politics theory to explain these patterns, I do not claim to have generated a startlingly new account of the politics of that country. All of the key elements of the symbolist explanation have been proposed before: the importance of Nyerere's leadership is consensus opinion, and the importance of Tanzania's strong national identity, weak ethnic identities, tolerant atmosphere, and organizational environment have all been widely recognized in the literature. The advantage of symbolist theory is that it provides a more systemic explanation than alternative ones, demonstrating why certain factors play a positive role in Tanzania even though they do not elsewhere. For example, some accounts emphasize that Tanzanian ethnic groups are divided by cross-cutting cleavages of clan, age-set, and sometimes religion.[157] Others emphasize the large number of different ethnic groups in Tanzania as a factor impeding ethnic mobilization. As some scholars have pointed out, however, cross-cutting cleavages are universal in all ethnic groups, and some countries with huge numbers of groups, such as Uganda, Congo, Sudan, and Russia, have still suffered ethnic civil wars.[158]

So why do these factors help in Tanzania but not elsewhere? The short answer is symbolic predispositions and the organizational environment. Ethnic fractionalization and cross-cutting cleavages prevent ethnic mobilization in Tanzania because Tanzania does not have organizations that can mobilize people on ethnic or religious grounds across those divides, nor are there ethnic prejudices that chauvinist elites can manipulate. Largely for these reasons, perceptions of ethnic threat are also low. The organizational environment and

SYPs, however, are a legacy of Nyerere's leadership, not something inherent to Tanzanian society. Similar conditions can be cultivated elsewhere.

Symbolist theory can also tell us how this stability might be threatened in the future. Mobilization along either religious (Muslim vs. Christian) or racial (African vs. Indian) lines is possible, as a few outbursts in the mid-1990s demonstrated. The Indian minority is so small that the worst plausible outcome is a series of riots, but the religious divide could get much uglier. The following elements would be required. First, extremist political-religious narratives would have to emerge, probably including Islamist ideas spreading from the Middle East, and must cause the spread of symbolic predispositions of religious intolerance. Next, charismatic leaders would have to emerge capable of manipulating religious symbols in a way that resonates with the Tanzanian population, further fostering an atmosphere of ethnoreligious fear. Finally, these extremist leaders would have to capture or build mobilizing organizations.

The worst-case scenario might come if a future CCM presidential candidate were credibly accused of winning by fraud against an opposition candidate of the other religion. If violence between political parties, which does sometimes occur in Tanzania, were to begin over a contest for Tanzanian president across the religious divide, it might encourage mobilization along religious lines. In that case, what begins as political violence might well turn into genuine religious or communal violence, setting a precedent for additional such violence in the future. Tanzania has always avoided such a scenario before, and such a scenario is not likely now, but as stockbrokers often warn their clients, past performance is no guarantee of future results.

Conclusion

Symbolic Politics—Ethnicity and Beyond

The main argument of this book is that when we think about people's be-havior, our first question should not be about the person's "rational" inter-ests, but about his or her biases. The foundation of political behavior is in people's symbolic predispositions, which guide them in defining what their interests are and shape their emotional responses to events. To mix Jonathan Haidt's metaphor mentioned in chapter 1, we need to focus on the elephant in a person's head—on the power of the intuitive decision-making system—in driving what people do. This insight suggests the basic principle of sym-bolic politics: because people make decisions based primarily on their sym-bolic predispositions, the way leaders gain support is by using symbols to manipulate those SYPs.

This primary role of intuitive decision making applies not only to ordi-nary citizens but also to elites of all kinds. Consider the case of term-limited national leaders. Most scholars assume that politicians of all kinds want first to maximize their own power. From this point of view, most leaders should echo Ferdinand Marcos's (perhaps apocryphal) remark: "Only fools leave the Malacanang [presidential palace]." Marcos himself went to extraordinary lengths not to do so, preempting the election in which he should have been replaced by declaring martial law, thereby turning himself into a dictator and extending his stay in power for an additional fourteen years. The point, how-ever, is that Marcos's behavior *was* unusual: the vast majority of elected na-tional leaders do leave office peacefully when their terms are up. The reason for this behavior lies not in their interests or in government institutions, but in their SYPs and those of their subordinates. Most national elites in such systems are concerned enough for the interest of their nations to value the laws, institutions, and stability of their country over their own desire for power.

As shown in this book, SYPs are even more central to explaining ethnic politics. Nationalism or ethnic loyalty is nothing but a cluster of SYPs—the inclination to favor one's own group over competing groups, the tendency to become more loyal to the group when it is under threat, and so on. Yet many political scientists, irrationally wedded to the fallacy that political behavior is rational, persistently ignore this basic fact. For example, in a carefully researched book, Daniel Posner notes how Zambians consistently want to put their own coethnic in the presidency. His argument is that they believe that a coethnic as president will favor his own ethnic group in economic policy.[1] Yet Posner finds that at least one Zambian president did not favor his home region, which may well have received less development funding than other regions.[2] In other words, Posner's image of Zambians is that they are rational in their political behavior except for the fact that their fundamental premise is false. The more logical assumption is that Zambians are symbolically predisposed to have a coethnic as national leader for reasons of group pride and status, and *feel* that they benefit from it even if the benefit is intangible.

Thinking about symbolic predispositions allows us to see this pattern—in Zambia or in the cases discussed in this book—in a completely different light. First, as social identity theory tells us, people tend to be biased in favor of members of their own group, Zambians as much as anyone else. Second, as prejudice theory tells us, people tend to evaluate out-group members on the basis of stereotypes and sometimes prejudice. Third, as constructivist theories of nationalism (and Hypothesis 1) would predict, the stronger group identity narratives are, the stronger the biases toward the in-group and against the out-group are likely to be.

Because symbolic predispositions tend to be enduring, focusing on SYPs that are widely believed by the mass population helps us understand stability and continuity in politics: Why did the Sudanese fall into the same trap of religious intolerance and civil war in 1983 that they had fallen into two decades before? Why did Filipino Christians so consistently fear and discriminate against Muslims? Why did Rwandan Hutus so persistently discriminate against Tutsis, and what made them morally capable of committing genocide against them? Long-standing prejudices are an essential part of the answer. This is the logic of Hypothesis 3: the more prejudiced people are, the more likely they are to support such policies.

Short-term changes in politics have to be explained against the background of these widespread SYPs, but on the basis of other factors. The most important of these is threat perceptions. For example, while racial prejudice put genocide on the agenda in Rwanda, it was the immensity of the threats they faced that motivated the genocidaire leaders and their followers to act: the military threat from the RPF, the context of the bloodshed in next-door Burundi, the political threat to the power of the ruling elite. Hypotheses 2 and 4 help us understand this. First (Hypothesis 2), it was prejudice that made plausible the idea that ordinary Hutus' unarmed Tutsi neighbors were so threatening that they had to be slaughtered. Prejudice tends to increase threat perceptions. Then (Hypothesis 4), once the obvious threat from the RPF and the ambiguous "threat" from ordinary Tutsis combined into a perception of extreme physical threat, ordinary Hutus increasingly supported the idea of the genocide.

Another factor is the leader's SYPs: one way to think about the timing of the Rwandan genocide, for example, is that it began with the death of the relatively cautious President Habyarimana and his replacement by the fanatically anti-Tutsi genocidaires led by Colonel Bagosora. Similarly, South Africa's transition came when the thuggish President Botha was replaced by the more tolerant de Klerk. Leaders then try to mobilize support for their preferred policies by framing issues in terms of values, such as Ferdinand Marcos's anti-Communism or Jaafar al-Numayri's Islamism. These appeals work, however, only if the leader is credible in using that frame: Marcos was seen as a credible anti-Communist (and anti-Muslim) strongman, and so he benefited from a "rally-around-the-flag" effect; Numayri, however, was not seen as a credible Islamist, so he was replaced by the sectarian leader Sadiq al-Mahdi, who was. This is the logic of Hypothesis 5: support for any policy remains latent in politics until credible leaders propose it and offer a resonant frame to justify its adoption.

While some constructivists see the value in paying attention to SYPs and threat perceptions in explaining which frames and narratives resonate, others argue that it is inappropriate. A combination of such psychological and social factors, scold the prominent constructivists Ronald Krebs and Patrick Jackson, "relies on incompatible microfoundations."[3] Constructivists of this variety see norms or values as essentially social, existing only in narratives or discourse (or, in some versions, in social relationships); psychologists see them as individual, residing in people's heads. They argue that you cannot assume both at the same time.

The argument of this book, however, is that not only is it possible to look at values and SYPs from both points of view; it is necessary. The two notions rely on each other. Where do individual-level symbolic predispositions come from? From discourse, mostly—from socializing by parents transmitting values and stereotypes, by schools and media purveying narratives of national identity, and so on. This, again, is Hypothesis 1. On the other hand, why do some narratives resonate with an audience while others do not? Because of SYPs, mostly: Gandhi's Hindu- and Buddhist-based discourse of nonviolence was inspiring to Hindus and Buddhists, but resonated much less with Muslims. Hypothesis 3 is just a specific version of this core logic of symbolic politics theory: the more policies and frames resonate with their SYPs, the more likely people are to agree with them.

Applying these insights together requires that we pay attention to the fact that different questions are being addressed here. Narratives, prejudices, and other SYPs help to explain why people might be inclined to support aggressive or hostile ethnic policies and why leaders may be inclined to adopt them. Perceptions of threat also help explain this, additionally explaining why policy preferences may shift: while SYPs tend to be stable, threats may grow or shrink, motivating different policy responses. Organization and leadership, on the other hand, explain how and when preferences are translated into action.

This is why the symbolic politics theory presented in this book is a multi-step theory, as depicted in figure 1.1 (see chapter 1). The core theoretical logic is depicted by the heavy black lines in the figure. Narratives influence SYPs in the first step; SYPs and the other group's behavior influence threat perceptions in the second step; SYPs, threats, and frames together influence political support for mobilization (or any other policy) in the third step; and then hostile framing by leaders, public support, and organization are all necessary for mobilization to occur in the fourth step. Going from mobilization to war is yet another step, requiring hostile mobilization on both sides, as the feedback from one's own mobilization to the other group's behavior creates a security dilemma spiral that causes escalation to war. This is the implication of the arrow leading back from mobilization to the other group's behavior—"our" mobilization might prompt "them" to mobilize in response.

Constructivists see these relationships as mutually constitutive rather than causal, and this is an important insight. Narratives and SYPs, for example, coevolve. I incorporate this insight by adding the other thin black lines and arrows in figure 1.1, which I understand as feedback effects. Thus narratives are influenced by SYPs (as narratives that do not resonate with SYPs lose prominence) and also by leaders' frames. SYPs, in turn, may be influenced not only by narratives but by leaders' frames (some of which may be seen as "candidate narratives," while others reinforce or appeal to existing narratives). Others' behavior and threat perceptions also influence SYPs— for example, threatening behavior reinforces hostile SYPs. Finally, there are some "forward" effects that logically follow from the theory but which I lacked the space and data to test. Organization, for example, is not independent of the other factors, as both leaders' framing and public support for mobilization influence organizational strength.

Moving from step 3 to step 4—from SYPs, threats, and policy preferences on the one hand to frames and organization on the other—involves a shift in the level of analysis, from thoughts and feelings that we measure at the individual level (e.g., through survey data) to social action. The causal mechanisms involved are different. Thus the "air war" of narratives and discourse influences people's SYPs, perceptions, and preferences, but its effectiveness for mobilizing political action is limited. Psychology and sociology agree that it is personal, often face-to-face contact that is most effective here, so analysis must shift from the "air war" of words and frames to the "ground war" realm of organizations and networks. To explain social movements, in other words, constructivism and individual psychology are not enough; they must turn to mobilization theory. This is the logic of Hypothesis 6: a leader's ability to mobilize followers mostly depends on the strength of the organizational network supporting that leader.

Symbolic politics theory also offers a useful understanding of charisma, with two factors emerging as particularly important in enabling charismatic leadership. The first is positive SYPs toward the leader, enabling an "affect transfer" effect whereby positive feelings about the leader spill over into positive feelings about the proposed policy. The second factor is the leader's credibility in using a particular frame. Thus the foul-mouthed, longtime secularist and whiskey-swilling Numayri was not a credible Islamist, and as a dry technocrat he evoked limited personal devotion. In contrast, Mandela's record of violent activism and long imprisonment gave him unimpeachable credibility with even ANC radicals, while his personal magnetism proved invaluable in reassuring South African whites after his inauguration as president. Ergo, Mandela was an effective charismatic leader; Numayri was not.

Summing up, symbolic politics theory asserts that we can understand when and why ethnic politics becomes violent and when it remains nonviolent, by focusing on the four factors of symbolic predispositions, threat, leadership, and organization. If feelings of threat are low, politics follows a distributive pattern that is normal in well-functioning democracies. People mobilize for the more contentious politics of redistribution if they feel a social threat to their status, identity, or interests and if they have the organizational tools and leadership to do so. The violent politics of protection occurs when a physical threat is met by the leadership and organizational resources to mobilize against it. People are more likely to perceive a threat, whether social or physical, the more strongly their SYPs incline them that way—that is, the more prejudiced they are. Finally, if people are powerfully and effectively threatened by security forces, then they are demobilized in a politics of submission.

The hypotheses generated by the theory are intentionally stated in probabilistic terms instead of the terms of "necessary and sufficient" causes. For the first few hypotheses, this is the only possible formulation. Hostile group narratives are likely to promote prejudice, but they are neither necessary (prejudice may be learned from the family rather than from group narratives) nor sufficient to produce prejudice (narratives may be new or unpopular). Similarly, while prejudice makes the perception of threat more likely, it is also neither necessary (an open attack generates threat perceptions without prior prejudice) nor sufficient (a disliked but quiescent out-group may not be seen as threatening). Finally, support for hostile action against an out-group need not come from either prejudice or threat perception—greed may be sufficient, for example. The logic of symbolic politics theory is that given what we understand about the relevant psychology, those factors are likely to be critically important in most cases of ethnic conflict, but there may be exceptions. In practice, cases of violent mobilization that are not based on prejudice or fear are not likely to be ethnic. If greed is the motivation, for example, the result will be something like the conflicts over Africa's "blood diamonds," in which ethnic identity plays little role.

With regard to the roles of leadership and organization, the causal connections are different. It is certainly possible to say, as I do, that some degree of organization is necessary for sustained political action or mobilization. However, it is also accurate, and more useful, to state the effect in terms of relative probability: the better the group's organization, the greater the likely degree of mobilization. As we find in the cases, there are often multiple groups mobilizing for different purposes, so thinking about organization in more-or-less rather than yes-or-no terms is more useful for explaining relative degrees of success. The same logic applies to the role of leadership: some degree of leadership can be said to be a necessary condition for political mobilization, but again there is variation. Sporadic violence (e.g., rioting) may occur with high-ranking leaders playing little if any role, and to some extent, better organization can substitute for effective leadership and vice versa. Again, therefore, speaking of relative probabilities makes more sense: more assertive frames and more credible leadership increase the likely scale of ethnic mobilization.

Evidence for the Theory

The evidence summarized in the six case studies in this book generally supports the theory I have outlined. I review the evidence point by point here.

NARRATIVES AND SYMBOLIC PREDISPOSITIONS

Of the six cases studied in this book, five suffered some form of ethnic war. In all five of those cases, at least one side had group narratives justifying hostility to the other, and as a result showed evidence of prejudice toward that group, as we would expect from Hypothesis 1. Tanzania was the sole exception on all these counts: there, inclusive narratives promoted low levels of prejudice. In several but not all of the violent cases, warrior self-images on one or both sides were also important. The typical pattern was that prejudice on the side of the dominant group justified repression against the subordinate group, eventually motivating the subordinate group to rebel. Prejudice seems to be more typically a disorder of the rulers than of the ruled.

In the Philippine case, the national narrative identifies the Philippine nation with the Christians of the north and depicts the Muslim southerners as primitive and violent people who should be modernized by converting them to Christianity. The result of this narrative is the violent "moro image"—and a strong accompanying prejudice. This prejudice showed up repeatedly in surveys, with one finding, "The Muslim image is exclusively negative for all nine traits [measured]."[4] On the Muslim side, the key narrative is one of an imagined family linked by their Muslim identity and history of opposition to the authorities in Manila, whether Spanish or Filipino. Muslim narratives also define those ethnic groups, such as the Tausug and the Maguindanao, as warrior peoples. The resulting SYPs, therefore, favor violence and resistance to the government. As anthropologist Ruth Moore noted, the Tausug believe "being Muslim is synonymous with being in militant opposition to the Philippine government."[5] These attitudes explain much about their willingness to resort to force.

Sudan had the opposite religious demography: northern Muslims controlled the government, while Christians and animists were the oppressed southerners. Yet Sudan showed a similar pattern of narratives and SYPs. The northern narrative defined the national identity as an Arab and Muslim one and depicted southerners as primitive and violent infidels, a slave people who should be taught Islam. The result was open prejudice that made it common for northerners to refer to southerners as "slaves." Non-Muslim groups like the Dinka, in contrast, associated northerners with violent repression, recalling the Mahdiya as a time when "the world was spoiled." The resulting SYP among Sudanese southerners was deep distrust for the government. Southern Sudanese groups like the Dinka and Nuer also had a warrior self-image that reinforced SYPs toward violent resistance to threat.

In Rwanda, by 1994 the hostile narratives and prejudices exceeded even Sudan's viciously racist standards. The national narrative of the ruling Hutus identified the minority Tutsis as invaders from afar who had no legitimate rights in Rwanda and as arrogant and cruel former rulers who constantly plotted against Hutus. As a result, stereotypes of Tutsis as aggressive, conniving, and untrustworthy abounded and were later magnified to genocidal intensity by extremist media outlets like *Kangura* (with its "Hutu Ten Commandments") and the "hate radio" station RTLMC.

Though I did not intend to focus on Hindu-Muslim violence in the India case, I found it impossible to ignore. Anti-Muslim narratives such as the story of the Marathi ruler Shivaji and his opposition to the Mogul emperor Aurangzeb were widespread in some regions, resulting in strong SYPs against Muslims. Prejudice was so pervasive that even Gandhi endorsed stereotypes such as "The Mussulman as a rule is a bully, and the Hindu as a rule is a coward." Gandhi's philosophy of nonviolence was based on Hindu values and symbols, so it failed as a way to bridge the Hindu-Muslim divide.

The South African case is the one case studied in this book in which ethnic war was resolved by negotiation before a worst-case scenario unfolded. One reason for this outcome was that white narratives mellowed, as Afrikaners stopped claiming that blacks were inferior or that apartheid was fair. Prejudice also declined, with whites increasingly acceptant of racial integration in schools and workplaces. Among blacks, the key factors allowing negotiated peace were the ANC narrative defining apartheid, rather than whites, as the enemy and a striking absence of antiwhite prejudice among the vast majority of blacks.

Like the ANC, the Tanzanian ruling party diligently promoted a narrative of national identity that was broadly inclusive, and it too was successful in minimizing ethnic prejudice. National identity was tied to the widely disseminated Swahili language, to the national policy of socialist development (in the 1960s and 1970s), and to the ruling party and the image of Nyerere himself. Identification with ethnic groups was relatively weak. As a result, prejudice among black ethnic groups was minimal, and even religious tensions are relatively low. Genuine prejudice was confined to feelings about ethnic Indian merchants and to Zanzibar, which lacked the mainland's inclusive history.

In sum, while these factors are hard to measure comparatively, the nastiness of identity narratives and the intensity of prejudice in each case seem roughly to predict the scale of the violence that occurred. Sudan and Rwanda, both with vicious racist narratives and racial prejudice, experienced violence on a genocidal scale. Filipino Christians' narratives of national identity were nearly as nasty, as was their prejudice against Muslims, resulting in violence that similarly killed hundreds of thousands of people. In South Africa and India, the moderate narratives of the ANC, the Indian National Congress, and key leaders like de Klerk, Mandela, and Gandhi kept the scale of violence lower than it could otherwise have been. Tanzania has managed, up to this writing, to keep ethnic violence essentially off the national agenda.

THREAT PERCEPTIONS

Hostile narratives and prejudice help distinguish *where* violence is likely to happen; changes in feelings of threat help to determine the timing. All influence the scale of violence that results. More specifically, according to Hypothesis 2, higher levels of prejudice increase the likelihood that the prejudiced people will perceive threats. Hypotheses 3 and 4 then assert that prejudice and threat perceptions tend to increase support for the kinds of hostile policies that lead to ethnic violence. The cases bear out these expectations, with one particular pattern common. Specifically, it was the dominant group that was typically the prejudiced side; these prejudices led to perceptions of physical or social threat from the subordinate group that were used to justify hostile policies such as Sudan's imposition of shari'a on non-Muslims. Such policies, in turn, eventually became so threatening to the subordinate group that the group rebelled.

Thus in each of the first three cases examined, the outbreak of war can be directly traced to increased feelings of threat on the side of the rebels. In the Philippines, Marcos's imposition of martial law, his attempt to disarm the

244

population, and massacres by the Ilaga and security troops were together felt to be imminent threats to Muslims. In Sudan, Numayri's dissolution of the south's autonomous government and imposition of shari'a were threatening to southerners, while the effort to transfer southern troops to the north was an immediate threat to those troops. For Rwandan Tutsis, the threatened loss of their refuge in Uganda was a last straw impelling the RPF invasion, while that invasion and the violence in Burundi stoked Rwandan Hutus' fears and helped motivate the genocide. In all of these cases, physical threats led to a politics of protection and intense violence.

Peaceful outcomes, on the other hand, tend to be the result of the decline or absence of physical threats. In South Africa, the decline in the threat of Communism was critical in giving white leaders the confidence to engage with the ANC, as was the defeat of the mid-1980s township uprisings. The ANC's relations with the regime therefore turned into a politics of redistribution, with the ANC using primarily nonviolent actions against the government, and the government responding to its claims of injustice. In Tanzania, the inclusive national identity meant that no group felt particularly threatened, and the strong state apparatus prevented any violent mobilization. This enabled a politics of distribution: Nyerere and his successors made a point of spreading both symbolic and tangible benefits widely across regions and groups. And in India, while Gandhi's Salt March did not stir widespread Muslim participation, it also posed no threat to Muslims and therefore did not spark communal violence. Gandhi's was a politics of redistribution, but it was not aimed against Muslims; it targeted the British and could benefit Muslims.

A common thread here is political exclusion: all five cases of ethnic or nationalist mobilization involved a rebellious group that was excluded politically. Since routine politics promised no benefits, people had to resort to extraordinary efforts at political mobilization. Tanzania, the sole example of calm, was the only one that did not exclude important constituents from government benefits.

Repression, on the other hand, had mixed effects. Hypothesis 4a asserts that mobilization is unlikely in the face of an overwhelming threat from the state, and this tends to be the case, as in South Africa in the 1960s. However, states sometimes fail to make the threat overwhelming enough. Attempts to increase repression were what sparked the rebellions in Sudan and the Philippines. Similarly in India, British savagery at Amritsar did not prevent renewed nonviolent activism or the Moplah revolt in the following years. On the other hand, it was decreased repression—the political openings of the mid-1980s apartheid reforms and de Klerk's unbanning of the ANC in 1990—that permitted black mobilization in South Africa. We cannot, therefore, look to repression to explain patterns of ethnic mobilization. Effective repression may just shift the base of mobilization outside the country, as in the case of RPF mobilization in Uganda.

NATIONALIST MOBILIZATION: ORGANIZATION, SYMBOLS, AND LEADERSHIP

Narratives, prejudices, and threats explain people's motives for ethnic conflict. However, to turn motivation into social action requires leadership and organization. This is our expectation from Hypotheses 5 and 6, and again the evidence supports them. What made possible the mass Indian protest campaigns of 1920 and 1930, for example, was Gandhi's conversion of the Indian National Congress from an elite debating society into a mass political party with branches widely spread across India. Similarly, South African black activism of the 1980s required the creation of the UDF, a legal, nationwide structure coordinating the antiapartheid activities of a wide range of nonwhite organizations, headed by a network of leaders such as Allan Boesak.

Social networks and organizations were also essential for the violent rebellions. The Mindanao conflict could escalate because the leaders of Muslim private armies such as the Blackshirts came together under the auspices of established leaders like Matalam and Lucman and drew in up-and-coming young elites such as Nur Misuari; the MNLF evolved from those social networks. In southern Sudan, the key network was of southern military officers such as John Garang who plotted the initial uprising and sought early support from Ethiopia and from their future Anyanya II rivals and who quickly set up the SPLA. In Rwanda, the core network was of former officers in Yoweri Museveni's Ugandan rebel force, led by Fred Rwigyema and Paul Kagame, who were being squeezed out of the Ugandan army after Museveni's victory; they networked with the Rwandan Tutsi diaspora to create the RPF.

External aid was important in providing the resources for all of the violent uprisings. The Philippine rebels had assistance from Malaysia and Libya. Southern Sudanese rebels had bases in Ethiopia and assistance from several countries. The RPF had their supply base in Uganda and financial help from the Rwandan Tutsi diaspora. The ANC had material aid from the Soviet Union. India never launched a serious twentieth-century rebellion against British rule, in large part because it never had that kind of foreign backing. Had the British tried to stay in India after the Communist victory in neighboring China, that situation would probably have changed.

THE SYMBOLIC POLITICS OF MOBILIZATION

The processes hypothesized in symbolic politics theory were the way all of these elements came together to produce ethnic war or peace. The roots of the wars are in the symbolic politics carried out by the leaders of the dominant groups, whose power was based on mobilizing their followers against an ethnic enemy. Numayri's decisions to revoke southern autonomy and impose shari'a nationwide are clear examples. These moves were of course applause-seeking stunts aimed at securing Numayri's power, but the reason they were popular was their symbolic value in appealing to the SYPs of Sudanese Arabs. The war was government led—Numaryi started the war by having his troops attack balky southern troops—but the sense of threat on the southern side was what motivated so many southerners to pick up arms to resist. The popularity of the war on the northern side was proved after Numayri's ouster, when his civilian successors proved too afraid of an Islamist backlash to stop it until two decades had passed.

The patterns in Rwanda and the Philippines were similar. In Rwanda, Habyarimana denigrated Tutsis using code phrases such as "feudal mentality" to help justify his Hutu-dominated regime. After the RPF invasion, regime and *akazu* propaganda became openly racist and increasingly genocidal, as with the "Hutu Ten Commandments." In South Africa, apartheid involved mobilizing the white minority, based on Afrikaner narratives, against the "black threat" and the "Communists." The Philippines also had a long history of discrimination against Muslims, so Marcos's effort to consolidate power inadvertently provoked a Muslim uprising even though it was initially aimed against the Communists. In their repressiveness, all of these regimes richly deserved to be rebelled against.

Such symbolic politics and the underlying prejudices and narratives are important for understanding the excesses that resulted. While senseless violence by individuals or small groups may be explained by the thuggish inclinations of the perpetrators,[6] senseless violence by institutions can be explained only by prejudice-fueled ideology. Thus in the Philippines, events like the massacre in Magsaysay carried out by Philippine security forces are explicable only by strong prejudices—a mentality that all Muslims were equally the enemy. The most extreme example of such a mentality, of course, is Rwanda, where prejudice and fear created a mad cognitive universe where extremist elites believed that their power could be safeguarded only by genocide, even though the genocide actually proved to be their downfall.

Apartheid, too, makes sense only as the Kafkaesque product of racist symbolic politics. Afrikaners were so committed to the narrative of the need for white rule that they blinded themselves not only to the injustice of apartheid but also to its infeasibility. The "homelands" could never have become viable. This brutal absurdity in turn justified others, such as security forces spreading mayhem in black townships in the belief that order would result. Racism, of course, was what justified the cavalier disregard for human life when the victims were black.

Symbolic politics was also the process by which the subordinate groups organized their resistance efforts. Gandhi's nonviolent campaigns are the clearest example here, as Gandhi turned himself into the symbol of a righteous, downtrodden India finally standing up for its rights, thereby inspiring millions to follow him. Allan Boesak's similar appeal in 1980s South

Africa—"We want all our rights. We want them here. And we want them now"—is another classic example of an injustice frame being used to inspire mobilization for a politics of redistribution.

In the cases of open war, the rebels matched the regimes' use of threat frames to motivate politics of protection. In the Philippines, for example, the most effective mobilizing appeal for the rebels was a straightforward argument for physically protecting either the local community or the Muslim population as a whole. Similarly in Sudan, the return of northern troops—in the context of a previous civil war ending only eleven years earlier—was all that was necessary to make a similar threat frame strongly resonant.

IMPLICATIONS FOR CONFLICT MANAGEMENT
AND CONFLICT RESOLUTION

As we have seen throughout this book, it is very easy to turn ethnic identity into a divisive force and difficult to prevent that outcome. This does not mean that ethnicity is "inherently" conflictual, but it is often so. Social identity theory tells us that people tend to discriminate in favor of their in-group and that increased attention to the group distinction increases the discriminatory effect. Prejudice theory tells us that negative stereotypes and negative feelings about members of other groups can distort judgment so subtly yet powerfully that people do not realize they are being biased. And terror management theory tells us that even subtle feelings of physical threat can enhance all of those effects. All of these effects have been demonstrated in psychology experiments and in the cases in this book.

In a book entitled *Reducing Intergroup Bias*, Samuel Gaertner and John Dovidio propose a solution to these problems, which they term the "common ingroup identity model."[7] Their central argument is that ethnic tensions are best overcome by promoting an overarching identity that unites the different subgroups. This "recategorization" works in multiple ways. It reduces the effect of stereotypes, because thinking of another person as one among a larger "us" instead of a narrower "them" triggers different connections in associative memory—bypassing, for example, negative stereotypes. Affective reactions will also be more positive, because people systematically give in-group members more sympathy than out-group members. The result, Gaertner and Dovidio show, is to make people more likely to cooperate and help others.[8]

The findings of this book support Gaertner and Dovidio's theory: appealing to separate group identities increases the likelihood of conflict, but building a common identity reduces it. In the Indian case, even Gandhi's message of nonviolence had the ironic effect of strengthening the appeal of Hindu extremists because it was a message pitched primarily to Hindu ears. Even his calls for Hindu-Muslim "heart-unity" reinforced the divide by emphasizing the distinction between the two groups. According to this theory, Gandhi's great failure was in not focusing on entrenching a common Indian identity for members of all religions—though he would have faced long odds against success had he tried to do so.

The Tanzanian case, in contrast, is the epitome of promoting a common identity. Nyerere did everything he could to keep a common Tanzanian identity at the forefront of political discourse, and to keep narrower identities out. Promoting Swahili as a common language, circulating students and officials around the country, distributing economic benefits widely—all of these efforts were aimed at keeping people's attention focused on Tanzanian unity rather than disunifying factors such as ethnicity and religion. The policy was carried out coercively and to that extent it may not be a model that should be widely copied. But it did work.

Similarly, what made South Africa's negotiated transition possible was the existence of a common South African identity that united blacks and whites. Most whites realized that the right-wing dreams of an Afrikaner homeland were just that—pipe dreams—just as very few blacks ever accepted the notion that the apartheid "homelands" were really their homelands. As a result, de Klerk and his followers never had any difficulty in accepting the idea that they were negotiating over a constitution for a united South Africa; the contest was over the provisions of that constitution, not the borders of the state. The ANC was genuinely multiracial, and if it was dominated by blacks, that fact is unsurprising in a country whose demography was almost 80 percent black. The ANC's inclusive rhetoric was also a critical element in making agreement possible.

All of this, in turn, supports the ethnic conflict management approach known as "centripetalism." In this approach, "the explicit aim is to engineer a centripetal spin to the political system—to pull the parties towards moderate, compromising policies and to discover and reinforce the centre."[9] The centerpiece of such systems is to create incentives for politicians to attract votes across ethnic lines, ideally by ensuring that few politicians can succeed without doing so. To make this work, "centripetal" political systems are designed to promote multiethnic political parties or alliances and government institutions that create forums for interethnic swapping of political support. One centripetal device that has been used successfully in two giant multiethnic countries, Indonesia and Nigeria, is to require that presidential candidates get a certain minimum quota of votes from across the nation, rather than being based solely in any one part of the country—or one ethnic group.[10] Tanzania's system is centripetal in that all of the political parties are multiethnic.

The other prominent model that has been suggested to manage ethnic conflict is a specific system of power sharing called "consociationalism."[11] Instead of trying to create multiethnic parties, consociational systems are built to get leaders of ethnic parties to cooperate with each other in government. Some of the key elements of a consociational system are a grand coalition that includes all major groups, a "mutual veto" over major government decisions for each of those groups, proportional representation in Parliament, and the distribution of government benefits and jobs to the different groups also according to their proportions of the population. Some degree of group autonomy is also included. At the heart of consociationalism, then, is ethnic separation: separately represented groups that cooperate in a grand coalition. The diversity of ethnic identities is not downplayed, but placed at the center of attention.

Among the cases in this study, variations on consociationalism were tried in British India, South Africa, and Rwanda and did not do well. In India, the main consociational bargain was the 1915 "Lucknow Pact," a deal between the Indian National Congress and the Muslim League that promised Muslims would be overrepresented in any future national Parliament; Muslims would be kept on separate voter rolls and be able to elect one-third of all representatives, though they constituted only about one-fourth of the population. The idea was power sharing and a guarantee for minority interests, but the deviation from the rule of proportionality was the idea's undoing, because it sparked a Hindu backlash. The Hindu Mahasabha was formed as a Hindu pressure group within the Congress, and it concentrated its fire on this disproportionality, which the Muslim League just as stubbornly tried to protect. This was the issue over which Hindu-Muslim political unity collapsed in the late 1920s and that provoked the "parting of the ways" between the Muslim League and the Congress, and also between Gandhi and his longtime Muslim allies.

In South Africa, Botha's reform apartheid with its racially divided tricameral Parliament was conceived as a kind of consociationalism. The father of consociational theory, Arendt Lijphart, was invited to advise National Party officials. Yet for this very reason, ANC negotiators constantly rejected any explicit power-sharing arrangement as merely another attempt to reform apartheid instead of replacing it. The idea of consociationalism had been discredited. The lasting regret of "conservatives" in de Klerk's final cabinet was their failure to get key elements of consociationalism in the permanent constitution—especially a mutual veto over government decisions that would have given them some leverage in ANC-led governments. The ANC dismissed this idea out of hand as incompatible with democracy as they conceived it.

Consociationalism could not have failed more egregiously than in Rwanda. The Arusha accords between Habyarimana's government and the RPF were for a consociational-style, power-sharing "grand coalition" including the Hutu opposition parties as well as the ruling party and the Tutsi-led RPF. As with the Lucknow Pact, the Arusha deal deviated from proportionality by guaranteeing the RPF half of all officer posts in the new Rwandan army, as well as 40 percent of all enlisted soldier positions. This continuation of

Tutsi military power, seen in the context of what another Tutsi military had done in Burundi, was the source of much of the Hutu opposition to the Arusha arrangement. For the *akazu*, of course, broad power sharing meant the loss of most of their own power, so it was unacceptable. The ironic result was that the mere attempt to institute consociationalism motivated and triggered the Rwanda genocide.

Despite this pattern, we cannot conclude that consociationalism is a bad idea. To take one positive example, the 1998 Good Friday accord that settled the conflict in Northern Ireland is a consociational arrangement, and for all its imperfections, it is unlikely that anything much different would have worked in that case. Something similar is true even for Rwanda. No matter how catastrophically the Arusha process failed, that is not evidence that any other approach would have succeeded. Because of the uneven demographic balance and deeply felt prejudices in Rwanda, a centripetal approach would not have been feasible. And because there were terribly evil people in Rwanda who were powerful in the outgoing system, the only way there could have been a decent outcome would have been through a powerful international peace enforcement mission to secure the implementation of the Arusha accords, or some deal like it.

The distinction to make, perhaps, is between conflict management and conflict resolution. In cases of conflict management, when ethnic tensions exist but ethnic war has not occurred—in short, when feelings of threat are low enough that a politics of protection does not arise—then the centripetal approach is feasible. Because it is compatible with Gaertner and Dovidio's, this approach to conflict management can work to take ethnic conflict out of politics. Its political message is that ethnic identity is not that important, cross-ethnic coalitions are routine, and there is plenty of room to build a common group identity to bring people together.

One criticism that is made of the common in-group identity model is that it failed in the Soviet Union and Yugoslavia, despite the enormous efforts both of those states put into creating common Soviet and Yugoslav identities and despite their savage repression of ethnic nationalism. But we can now see where they made their mistake: their attempts to build a common identity were undercut by their government organization, which embodied a sort of coercive consociationalism. Yugoslavia was a federal system composed of autonomous Republics of Serbia, Croatia, Slovenia, and so on. This organization kept the ethnic identities of Serbs, Croats, and Slovenes not only alive, but at the center of Yugoslavia's political structure. The republic governments inevitably turned into incubators of nationalist sentiments for Serbs, Croats, and Slovenes no matter how many times Tito tried to repress them.

In sum, if we compare Tanzania and Yugoslavia, the lesson is that while coercive centripetalism can help make common identity building work, coercive consociationalism blocks common identity building. If Yugoslavia had been divided into, say, fourteen federal units instead of eight ethnically defined ones, Tito's efforts to promote "brotherhood and unity" and a common Yugoslav identity might have made more progress. Ethnic identity would have been less central to politics, and it would have been easier to promote a common Yugoslav historical narrative in schools while playing down discordant ethnic themes. Also, as Henry Hale has pointed out, a Croatia and a Serbia divided into several pieces would have found it more difficult to seek independence.[12] Add together a stronger national narrative, weaker ethnic narratives justifying hostility, and weaker organizations that could promote nationalism, and the result would have been weaker ethnonationalist separatism. Yugoslavia might well have succeeded.

The same logic applies to the former Soviet Union. If Stalin had declared the nationality problem "solved" and dissolved the Soviet Republics of Russia, Ukraine, and the rest into their constituent one hundred or so regions, the Soviet Union probably would not have broken up in 1991. The Soviet republics were all multilingual anyway, so language policy could have been decentralized to very local levels, while there would have been no republic governments to preserve or develop mutually hostile national narratives. And when reforms began, the big groups at the core of the union— Russians, Ukrainians, Kazakhs, and Belarusians—would have had no republic governments to coordinate their independence drives. While some of the smaller and more nationalistic groups like the Estonians and Lithuanians would probably have sought independence anyway, the core of the Soviet Union might well have survived.

But this is all conflict management. Tanzania's mildly coercive centripetalism worked because mutual hostility and threats were low to begin with. The Soviet Union and Yugoslavia promoted their common identities using brutal totalitarian controls. When the problem is resolution of ethnic civil wars and totalitarian repression is not an option, power sharing of the consociational type is often the only plausible solution. Even for conflict management, the consociational efforts discussed in this book failed in part because of their deviation from the formula. The Lucknow Pact in India was not viable because it promised Muslims not proportional representation, but disproportional power. Consociationalism in South Africa was discredited because it came to be associated with apartheid, which embodied not power sharing, but the exclusion of the majority. In Rwanda, the problem was not the consociational terms of the Arusha accords, but the power of the extremists.

In sum, centripetalism is the preferable solution for ethnic conflict management when it is feasible—when feelings of threat are low—because it allows the growth of a common group identity that can genuinely take ethnic conflict off the political agenda. However, when threat feelings are high, conflicting ethnic identities have to be acknowledged, not ignored, so consociational approaches are most appropriate.

Beyond Ethnicity: A Symbolic Theory of Politics

As I mentioned in the introduction, symbolic politics theory is not only applicable to explaining ethnic politics; it is a paradigm for understanding all
kinds of politics, serving as an alternative to approaches that assume rational decision making. Its basic paradigmatic assumption is that human decision making is based primarily on intuitive reactions stemming from symbolic predispositions—values, ideology, prejudices, party identity, and other
biases—more than on rational calculations related to material interests. It
has the potential to work as an overarching theory of politics because it explains behaviors and outcomes where rationalist approaches do not do well,
while also offering a logic for why rationalist analyses sometimes do work
and the conditions under which competing rationalist approaches work.

As an example of an area in which it does not work well to assume that
people rationally seek to maximize their material interests, I suggest the areas of public opinion and voting behavior. Symbolist theory was originally
built by David Sears and others to explain just such behavior in the U.S. context. The second category—defining the conditions under which rationalist
analysis works—is illustrated by the case of rational institutional analysis,
which works well when the bureaucrats' SYPs match the ostensible values
of the organization. Symbolist theory is superior, however, for explaining
corruption, which is what happens when bureaucrats' SYPs diverge from
organizational values. The third use for symbolist theory is to explain what
to do when competing theories propose different rationalist logics, as in the
case of the debate between realist and liberal international relations theory.
The competing logics derive from the different SYPs that realist and liberal
theorists assume underlie state behavior; we can determine the conditions
under which each approach is applicable by examining which SYPs are most
important in which kinds of cases.

I outline in the following sections each of these uses for symbolic politics
theory.

PUBLIC OPINION, VOTING, AND ELECTIONS

The theorizing in chapter 1 is based largely on the findings of political
psychologists like David Sears and Drew Westen who study U.S. public
opinion and voting behavior. What the cases in this book show is that their
general approach, supplemented by the logic of terror management theory, works for explaining public opinion and voting in several African and
Asian countries as well. Detailed public opinion data were available only for
South Africa, but those data showed that the views of both white and black
voters could be explained quite well just by focusing on symbolic predispositions like prejudice, party identity, and trust in leaders, plus overall

measures of the atmosphere of fear and hope. Proxy measures of economic interest, such as income level, were in contrast not significant in explaining people's views.[13]

Furthermore, the overall picture for all six cases showed a consistent pattern of both government and opposition leaders seeking popular support by engaging in symbolic politics. Once we start looking for symbolic politics, it becomes clear that public opinion and election campaigns on at least three continents make no sense without considering the roles of symbolic predispositions, hopes, fears, and symbolic appeals. And this applies not only to ethnic politics but, as the Tanzanian and U.S. cases show, also to "routine" politics that is not mostly about ethnicity.

The most sophisticated effort to date to build something like a symbolic politics theory of voting behavior is Milton Lodge and Charles Taber's *The Rationalizing Voter*. Lodge and Taber start with the neural elephant, writing about "the ubiquity of unconscious thinking," and they carefully describe and model the mental processes that are involved.[14] Their central focus is on "hot cognition," the recognition that "all thinking is suffused with feeling"—most importantly symbolic predispositions.[15] "Spreading activation" is the process that calls up other thoughts that are linked to the original one in associative memory. As this broader thinking starts to happen, it is strongly influenced by "affect transfer" as feelings toward the initial object spill over to the associated ones—for example, liking for Obama increases liking for Democrats, or vice versa.

What is impressive about Lodge and Taber's effort is that they find evidence for each of these mental processes in a series of carefully designed experiments. One set of experiments analyzed respondents' attitudes about illegal immigration, for example.[16] They found evidence for the importance of symbolic predispositions: prior attitudes directly influenced subjects' policy judgments through the "affect transfer" process and related kinds of emotional thinking. They found an even stronger effect from efforts to influence subjects' mood, which powerfully influenced people's political evaluations. The moral of this story is to show how much emotions swamp logic in political reasoning, and it underlines the importance of mood-setting political symbolism. Candidates smile, wave flags, kiss babies, and play upbeat music at campaign rallies and in advertisements to improve voters' moods, hoping the positive mood will spill over onto themselves, their parties, and their ideas.

After all of this, Lodge and Taber put together a sophisticated model of political decision making that is built to predict the attitudes of voters of different ideological persuasions, which works remarkably well.[17] Their model represents a huge improvement over the old political science conceit that campaigns have only "minimal effects." Other work has returned similar findings.[18] On the one hand, symbolic politics theory—and the research of Sears, Donald Kinder, and Westen—explains why campaigns make little difference for most people: most people have such strong symbolic predispositions toward one side or the other that their votes are not up for grabs. On the other hand, a new literature also details how campaigns do matter, making a clear distinction between the role of the "air war" and of the "ground war."

In the "air war" what matters most, as we would expect, is how the frames that are used resonate with voters' symbolic predispositions. Lynn Vavreck has shown, for example, that the candidate favored by the economy emphasizes an economic message, while the opposing candidate runs an "insurgent" campaign that tries to change the subject to almost anything else— foreign policy, candidates' personal qualities, and so on.[19] Another study adds that the daily give-and-take between candidates in the media is critically important in shaping who wins this air war by shaping SYPs toward the candidates.[20] Concerning the ground war, networks should of course matter in getting voters to the polls. One study found, for example, that the Obama campaign's advantage in its number of field offices seems to have been important enough to change the outcome in three swing states in 2008: Florida, North Carolina, and Indiana.[21]

A huge advantage to the symbolic politics way of thinking about politics, as these examples illustrate, is that it makes what candidates and journalists actually do in campaigns more intelligible theoretically: their words are not mere noise that academics may safely ignore. The obsessive focus on candidates' image is not superficial puffery; it is part of the critically important battle to influence voters' symbolic predispositions about the candidates. The daily media back-and-forths are battles in the campaign to win the "air war" over whether the election will turn on economic or noneconomic issues— which in turn decides whether swing voters will be influenced by symbolic predispositions that favor one candidate or the other. The campaigns' mobilization of armies of volunteers and paid staffers add the network element that is so critical to mobilizing voters. And the endless money hunt, of course, is about providing the main resource that powers both the air war and the ground war.

INSTITUTIONAL BEHAVIOR

Symbolic politics theory assumes that people are not rational decision makers, but impulsive ones whose decisions are biased by emotion and SYPs and then rationalized after the fact. Yet rationalist analysis, especially principal-agent theory, seems to have an excellent track record in explaining how political institutions work.[22] The approach is intuitively reasonable: an employer, or principal, hires a worker, or agent, but faces the problem of ensuring that the worker will work as directed instead of "shirking." How does the principal motivate a rational agent to work instead of shirk? Most studies of U.S. political institutions focus on monitoring, arguing that workers work if they are monitored well and that the trick is to find a way to monitor them not only well but also efficiently, without too much effort. Some scholars add that the monitoring needs to be supplemented by some system of punishment—if the agent is shirking but goes unpunished even if detected, why should he work?[23] Scholars have shown that these considerations explain a lot about who works and who shirks in U.S. institutions.

Where this model runs into trouble, however, is in explaining corruption. In many parts of the world, even if bureaucrats work, they take bribes, and if they shirk, they steal as well. Monitoring is not the issue; the bosses know that the bureaucrats take bribes, but they permit it and typically demand a cut for themselves. Suggest to a Russian that improved monitoring and punishment will improve bureaucratic behavior, and the response will be, "Oh, no! If they know they will soon be detected and punished, they will steal even more while they can!"

The contribution of symbolic politics theory is to provide a way of determining when "rationalist" models of institutional behavior are appropriate and when they are not. Essentially, rationalist models work when the actors' symbolic predispositions and opportunity structure accord with the theorist's assumptions about what is "rational." They often do not.

Let us return to comparing the typical Russian and U.S. bureaucrats. The U.S. bureaucrat, first of all, probably has a symbolic predisposition against corruption. Furthermore, other U.S. citizens also have such a SYP—they do not like paying bribes, or being stolen from; they have a free press that has an incentive to expose corruption; and as voters they may make the bureaucrat's boss—the principal—pay with his job if he permits corruption. This is the environment the rationalist theorist assumes: the principal has strong incentives not to permit corruption, the agent is inclined to be honest (but possibly lazy or disobedient), and the client is more likely to report a demand for a bribe than to comply with it. If the agent is interested in finding creative ways to make money, she will go into the private sector.

None of this is true for the Russian bureaucrat. First, few in Russia really think stealing from the state is wrong; such theft is so widespread that one prominent book on Russian privatization was called *Stealing the State*.[24] For this reason, everyone expects to pay bribes, recognizing that they would themselves probably demand bribes should they be in a position to do so. Entrepreneurship, on the other hand, is a less attractive alternative because, unlike in the United States, it is *legally* hazardous: even an honest businessman will be forced to pay bribes, and powerful people may at any time use the legal system to confiscate his business. Finally, the corruption of the legal system means that there is no connection between dishonesty and punishment—the relatively honest may be punished, while the most dishonest may not. Justice is "telephone justice": the judge makes her decision on the basis of telephoned orders from bosses higher up. Finally, Russian voters have few opportunities to punish the corrupt in Russia's one-party system, and Russian journalists can be intimidated into silence about specific allegations of corruption.

The way to start thinking about institutional behavior, therefore, is to ask the same question that symbolic politics theory asks about mass behavior: What are people's symbolic predispositions? In a well-run and noncorrupt bureaucracy, the bureaucrats' symbolic predispositions accord with the purposes of the institution: police want to fight crime, soldiers want to protect the country, and labor and environmental regulators want to protect workers and the environment. Significantly, these SYPs may not fully accord with popular ones. In the United States, for example, police and military values are more authoritarian than the average among civilians, while regulators may be less favorable to free enterprise. The question therefore becomes, how do institutions end up with workers whose SYPs accord with the purposes of the organization in some cases but not in others?

Social psychology provides answers. The first and most well-known is *socialization*: new recruits are taught to accept the values of the institution. Much of this socialization happens tacitly, not explicitly, as new workers emulate the views and behaviors of their colleagues and bosses. In other cases it is explicitly drilled in: obedience to orders is the first value military recruits are taught, for example. A second process is *role assignment*, which influences people to adopt the values and behaviors of the role they are given. If my job is to prevent forest fires, I may become unusually authoritarian toward people lighting unsafe campfires. Third is *commitment*: the *less* reason people have for taking some action or attitude, the more likely they are to maintain it. All three of these factors reinforce each other, as commitment and role assignment are part of the socialization process.

On the other hand, selection effects also influence bureaucrats' SYPs: those who join the organization may already be inclined to accept or reject the organization's values. If they already accept the organization's basic values, socialization will be easy and quick. On the other hand, if regulators' initial SYPs mirror those of the industry they are regulating, the result will be "regulatory capture" and regulations that do little to restrain the industry.

Symbolic politics theory would hypothesize, therefore, that noncorrupt and effective institutions are ones in which workers' SYPs correspond with their duties and that this will be true when the institution has effective procedures for recruitment and socialization. While opportunity structures—such as monitoring and punishment processes—are important, the main expectation will be that corruption and shirking are the result of incongruent values.

The symbolic approach also allows us to explain what the institutional interest is—or, more precisely, what the bureaucrats think the institution's interest is. Asking that question allows us to get more interesting answers out of an earlier wave of theory, 1970s-era bureaucratic politics theory. For example, trying to understand how the U.S. Navy shaped its force structure—that is, what sorts of ships it emphasized building and maintaining—Edward Rhodes asked whether it mattered if the Navy's top admiral rose through the ranks as a submarine officer, an aircraft pilot, or a surface ship officer.[25] Rhodes found that the admirals' specialty did not matter; the key fact was that all of the admirals shared an "image of naval warfare" that was "strongly influenced by the teachings of Alfred Thayer Mahan."[26] Briefly, Mahan argued that command of the sea depended on the number of capital ships a navy could maintain—battleships in his day, aircraft carriers during World War II and ever since. Thus Rhodes found that all post–World War II navy commanders made maintaining the navy's fleet of aircraft carriers their top priority. In other words, what Rhodes found was a navy-wide symbolic predisposition (which is inculcated throughout the Navy's system of schools) in favor of Mahan's ideas about command of the sea and maintaining capital ships.

As Rhodes notes, Mahan's influence on U.S. Navy thinking is widely known and of long standing. Franklin D. Roosevelt's Navy secretary, Henry Stimson, complained about this phenomenon, referring to "the peculiar psychology of the Navy Department, which frequently seemed to retire from the realm of logic into a dim religious world in which Neptune was God, Mahan his prophet, and the United States Navy the only true church."[27] It would be hard to find a clearer statement of the influence of symbolic predispositions on institutional behavior.

Furthermore, there is a long history of studies of institutions making similar points. Herbert Kaufman's classic *The Forest Ranger*, for example, chronicles the U.S. Forest Service's evolution from a symbolic predisposition to put out all forest fires to a more sophisticated method of forest management.[28] Morton Halperin noted that the "organizational essence" of the U.S. Air Force "is the development of a capability for combat flying," especially strategic bombing and interdiction of supply lines.[29] This view, based on a line of theory originating with Giulio Douhet and Billy Mitchell, has caused the Air Force to resist procuring aircraft designed for close air support of ground troops on the battlefield, forcing the Army to build helicopters for that purpose.[30] Finally, in *The Ideology of the Offensive*, Jack Snyder demonstrates that an extreme bias in favor of offensive action impelled the French army to adopt an aggressive and immensely unwise war plan in 1914 that nearly led to complete disaster.[31]

Government institutions are not the only kinds of organizations that can be understood in this way. The best example of organizations that are well structured to produce rational-looking political behavior is lobbying organizations, especially business lobbies. The rationalist assumption is that business groups have a clear material interest in promoting the prosperity of their businesses, and so lobby the government for favorable regulations, subsidies, low taxes, and other benefits. The principals—the business leaders—

can easily monitor the results achieved by the agents (the lobbyists), giving the lobbyists every incentive to provide evidence of their efforts (especially if results fall short of hopes). Thus monitoring is easy. And given that clear system of monitoring, the lobbyists themselves are either self-selected or socialized to accept the ideological views of their clients. In sum, the system cultivates symbolic predispositions in favor of the businesses' bottom lines. The result is the vast array of business lobbying groups in early twenty-first-century Washington, D.C., that do exactly what a rationalist would expect.

This story seems so inescapably logical that it obscures the fact that it was not always true. But it was not; narrow business interests did not have dominant power before the 1970s. As journalist Nicholas Confessore has pointed out,

> For many years, most business leaders adopted a conciliatory approach to the new [post–New Deal] system and accepted its basic premises. But during the 1970s, . . . businesses began funding a new wave of aggressively ideological think tanks and advocacy groups to challenge the intellectual underpinnings of Democratic governance. . . . Between the early 1970s and mid-1980s, the number of trade associations doubled; between 1981 and 1985 [alone], the number of registered lobbyists in Washington quadrupled, vastly augmenting business power.[32]

In sum, for several decades in the middle of the twentieth century, business leaders did not try rationally to maximize their bottom lines by lobbying to dismantle the New Deal system of economic redistribution. Instead, they took a "conciliatory approach" because the New Deal system was compatible with their symbolic predispositions—they "accepted its basic premises." While it is not clear why, the reasons are not difficult to guess. Industrial leaders got used to close collaboration with the government during World War II, and continued regulation after the war did not impede rapid economic growth. Banks included the lessons of the 1929 crash into the symbolic predispositions they cultivated—SYPs favoring caution and financial stability. And everyone remembered the shared pain of the Depression, leading businessmen to accept workers as important stakeholders in their businesses.

Only an ideological shift can explain what happened next. It is not simply a matter of market conditions. Germany, for example, faced the same global marketplace that the United States did, yet it kept most of its labor-friendly regulations and its welfare state while remaining a powerhouse exporter of manufactured goods. In the United States, however, right-wing ideologues articulated a new set of values that better resonated with business leaders' interests—essentially, that greed is good, and the market is always best except when government intervention directly aids one's own bottom line. Especially as Depression-era and World War II–era business leaders left the scene, new generations of business leaders cultivated new, more narrowly self-interested SYPs. To a 1970s-era corporate manager raised during the Depression, shutting a profitable factory and outsourcing its functions was unthinkable; for 1990s-era managers of the baby boom generation, it was routine, and a justification for a massive bonus for the manager if higher profits were projected to follow. That is the normative context in which lobbying grew into a $3 billion per year business in Washington, D.C., in the early 2010s.[33]

INTERNATIONAL RELATIONS

As in other areas of political science, international relations theory generally starts by assuming rational behavior—by states rather than individuals—with theorists differing in their assumptions about what it is rational for states to do. For Hans Morgenthau, Thucydides's notion of human nature is accurate: "Of the gods we believe, and of men we know, that it is a necessary law of their nature that they rule wherever they can"; Morgenthau therefore understands "international politics as a struggle for power."[34] Kenneth Waltz argues, in contrast, that states seek security, not untrammeled power, and that in the quest for security, they form balances of power.[35] Rational behavior for Waltz, therefore, is to maintain a state's security by maintaining a balance of power. John Mearsheimer adjusts Waltz's logic to reach Morgenthau's conclusion: if states seek security, he argues, they can best achieve it by making themselves hegemonic in their region of the world.[36] These are all versions of "realism," assuming that international politics is inherently dangerous and conflictual.

The opposing camp of rationalists, the liberals, argues that rational international behavior is often cooperative rather than competitive, primarily because of interdependence. States can often gain wealth and improve their security cooperatively, and as rational actors, they often do so. They sign and abide by treaties that promote trade, with widespread benefits; they engage in arms control, dispatch peacekeeping missions, provide humanitarian aid, and collaborate to reduce pollution, in each case doing more to restrain the competition for power than to pursue it. One result, as John Mueller has noted, is "the obsolescence of major war": great powers fought each other with horrific regularity for millennia, but none have done so since 1953.[37] To liberals, then, rationality means more cooperation than competition for power.

The first point these opposing arguments prove is the futility of assuming "rational" behavior, as there is no way of reaching objective agreement on what behavior that assumption leads us to expect. The source of the debate is likely that theorists are expressing symbolic predispositions of their own. One set of relevant SYPs is a cluster of attitudes called "social dominance orientation" (SDO)—an inclination to see intergroup relations as competitive and hierarchical and to believe that tough-mindedness is necessary in such a world.[38] This is the realist view: most realists seem to be people inclined toward SDO. Another set of SYPs that leads to support for militant action is right-wing authoritarianism (RWA): RWAs tend to be highly reactive to threat and to favor hawkish policies, while those who are less reactive tend to prefer liberal policies.[39] A third factor is willingness to trust. As Brian Rathbun notes, psychologists have shown that some people are simply more inclined to trust potential partners than are others.[40] Liberals, therefore, would be those inclined to trust others, and therefore to advocate cooperation; realists and unilateralists are skeptics about cooperation, and so assume relations are typically or necessarily conflictual.

Recognizing these effects—and recognizing that politicians as well as political scientists vary in their inclinations toward SDO, RWA, and trust for others—we reach the apparently tautological conclusion that realist theory should work when leaders are competitive, reactive to threat, and distrustful, and liberal theory should work when leaders are more egalitarian, less reactive to threat, and more trusting. But how do we know when each applies?

A third school of thought in international relations theory, the constructivist approach articulated by Alexander Wendt, suggests a way forward. Wendt's classic formulation is that the international system "is what states make of it."[41] Essentially, Wendt argues, if states act aggressively, then they will create a realist world; if they act cooperatively, then they will create a liberal world. They create these worlds through their patterns of behavior: for example, repeated cooperation creates a "social identity" as a cooperator, making it easy for others to cooperate.

Still, if the question is "When is international politics likely to be cooperative rather than conflictual?" each of the three approaches offers a different answer. Realists simply deny that it ever is, repeating their nostrums about the omnipresence of international violence and the irrelevance of international institutions.[42] The trouble is that they are wrong, as international war decreased dramatically in frequency after World War II, while cooperation has led to a vast increase in international economic links and broader effectiveness of international law in many areas.[43] Liberals led by Bruce Russett argue that these trends are all connected, providing evidence that the world is more peaceful because more countries are governed by democratic institutions and because they participate more in international trade and international organizations.[44] The trouble with that argument is that there is also evidence against it: massive economic interdependence in 1914 did not prevent World War I, and a potent (on paper) League of Nations utterly failed to prevent World War II. And while it is true that democracies rarely if ever fight each other, they do have a propensity to fight nondemocracies.

Constructivists try to settle this dispute by referring to international norms and identities, which emerge from international communication or discourse. One example is the "taboo" on the use of nuclear weapons.[45] Another

261

is the democratic peace, which may be the result of a combination of liberal values and democratic institutions.[46] This kind of sophisticated combination of liberalism and constructivism offers some of the best explanations available of specific puzzles like the democratic peace, but it does not offer a general answer to the question of when international politics looks more "realist" or more "liberal." It does not, for example, explain why even nondemocracies do not fight foreign wars very often since World War II. What explains when dictators follow international norms and when they do not?

Symbolic politics theory would suggest starting from a different strand of liberal theory, the domestic politics liberal approach that argues that international behavior is the result of domestic politics, not any single logic imposed by the international system.[47] A key influence on domestic politics is the terror management effect: it matters whether the state's leaders and people perceive a physical threat. The threat may be an obvious one, like a military buildup; but if there is an ambiguous threat from another state that is already seen as an enemy (that is, if one side is predisposed to see the other as hostile), the result will be the same. In either case, if state leaders feel threatened, the terror management effect will cause them to react aggressively. The effect works at the level of public opinion as well. For example, as discussed in the introduction, because U.S. citizens were feeling generally threatened after the 9/11 terrorist attacks, they were more inclined to support hostile action toward another outside target seen as hostile—Iraq—even though Iraq had nothing to do with 9/11. The terror management effect, in other words, is the psychological process that causes the security dilemma. It also explains why the security dilemma is a general one that tends to expand beyond any specific bilateral relationship.

But this same logic also explains why the security dilemma is a variable, not a constant as realists assume. Leaders of states with mutually hostile national narratives (such as Pakistan and India) will be symbolically predisposed to feel threatened by ambiguous behavior from each other, while leaders of states with mutually friendly narratives and SYPs are unlikely to threaten or to feel threatened. This logic would explain why most international conflict comes in the context of enduring rivalries.[48] For example, citizens of the United States and the Soviet Union saw each other as enemies in part because each nation subscribed to an ideology that defined the other as hostile: U.S. citizens hated and feared Communism, and Soviet citizens hated and feared capitalist "imperialism."

The international atmosphere is also important: since the terror management effect is a general one, states or groups feeling threatened from one source are more likely to be reactive against another. On the other hand, if the international environment is peaceful, states are less likely to react aggressively to potential threats. This logic also explains why international crises increase the danger of war: the terror management effect pushes both leaders' and citizens' preferences toward aggressive action *on both sides*, creating an intense security dilemma where there was not one before.

These ideas point toward a symbolic politics explanation of the democratic peace. Democracies can be hostile toward nondemocracies because the latter are inherently symbolic threats: they threaten democratic values by challenging them. At the same time, as the "common in-group identity model" would suggest, democracies would tend to see a fellow democracy as part of a common in-group: not only not inherently threatening, but one of "us," deserving of the psychological benefit of the doubt that common in-group membership affords. After four decades of the Cold War alliance among western democracies, this common in-group identity was well-enough established that it outlived the context of rivalry with Communism that had created it.

A symbolist argument would also expand on Owen's point about liberal values and combine it with constructivist logic to explain the contemporary power of the international norm against aggression. Discourses create norms, but the norms are accepted only to the extent that they resonate with existing symbolic predispositions. Democracies, of course, work only if their populations accept liberal values such as the rule of law and nonviolent conflict management—that is, if their people are symbolically predisposed to accept a norm of nonaggression. Thus people in democracies embrace the international norm of nonaggression because it resonates with SYPs that democracies cultivate for domestic interactions.

In sum, the same set of arguments that explains ethnic war and peace can also explain international war and peace. Symbolic predispositions, whether they promote a warrior ethos or a value for nonaggression, provide the starting point. Discourses promoting peaceful norms—or violence—may be influential, but only if they resonate with those SYPs. However, especially in the context of enduring rivalries, SYPs may incline some states to perceive threats, which can trigger the terror management effect and create security dilemmas: India versus Pakistan, for example, or Israel versus the Arabs. Another factor is the symbolic predispositions of leaders. Authoritarian, dominance-seeking, and distrustful leaders, such as George W. Bush or Saddam Hussein, will see more need for aggressive policy than more peacefully disposed leaders will. In sum, the symbolist argument sees international war and peace as flowing from the interaction of national narratives, popular symbolic predispositions, threat perceptions, and the leaders and organizations of international actors.

Another advantage to building international relations theory this way is that it solves the problem of who the actors are. Realism is stuck to the notion that states are the only important actors in international politics, unable to account for the obvious importance of international organizations, multinational corporations (MNCs), terrorist groups, and nonprofit nongovernmental organizations (NGOs), among others. The 1970s wave of liberal theorizing tried to challenge the state-actor assumption, but never came up with a suitable alternative.[49] Liberals have theorized the importance of international organizations, but only by starting with states.

Symbolic politics theory, however, starts from the question of when ethnic or nationalist groups mobilize. In other words, it provides a practical way of starting from the assumption proposed by Gilpin that groups, not states, are the main actors in world politics.[50] What kinds of groups? Obviously, nation-states will be very potent because they combine the symbolic power of nationalism with the institutional power of the state. States that are not nation-states, lacking the power resource provided by nationalism, should be weaker than nation-states, though they may still function as institutions. But nonstate nations—that is, politicized ethnic groups—are important actors too, as this book has shown, because they can become belligerents in ethnic wars, turning non-nation-states into battlegrounds instead of independent actors.[51]

Nonnational and nonethnic groups can engage in symbolic politics as well. Organized-crime groups and greed-motivated warlords (such as those who exploit "blood diamonds") use a very simple sort of symbolic politics. The relevant SYPs are greed and brutality (that is, these organizations tend to attract greedy thugs and to socialize their recruits into those values), and their terrorizing creates a politics of submission for those under their control. At the other end of the spectrum, NGOs that promote human rights are pure players in symbolic politics, using their organizational networks to appeal to and reinforce the humanitarian SYPs of their audiences and using the resulting resources of money and political support to pursue their causes. MNCs are in the middle of this spectrum, relying primarily on greed like the warlords but using legal and nonviolent methods like the NGOs. From this point of view, the pornography and prostitution industries form a unique category because they work on the basis of an unusual mix of SYPs: greed on the part of the organizers, lust on the part of the customers, and often fear to motivate the work force. This powerful mix of motivations helps to explain why these industries are so difficult to suppress.

Another area where symbolic politics can inform international relations theorizing is conflict management and conflict resolution. Since the vast majority of armed conflicts in the early twenty-first century are internal conflicts—civil wars, including ethnic wars—the conclusions of this book are directly relevant. Achieving any sort of peace requires reducing the parties' perceptions of threat so they do not feel impelled to fight, or else allowing one side to win and impose a politics of repression on the other. Peacekeeping troops and other international interventions can be critical here. But, as William Long and Peter Brecke showed for one sample of cases, achieving lasting internal stability requires reconciliation, including changing group narratives in ways that promote positive symbolic predispositions toward past rivals. Achieving that, in turn, requires public truth-telling and acknowledgment of each side's unjust behavior, and also partial justice that reconciles the need for accountability and for forgiveness and pragmatic accommodation.[52]

In international politics, this sort of deep reconciliation is not necessary for peace, but it is necessary for the sort of security community that exists in the West, where war is essentially unthinkable. The pioneering case here is western Europe, and especially Franco-German relations: it took a concerted effort by French and West German historians and civil society to construct narratives of national identity—and history textbooks—that promoted positive rather than negative symbolic predispositions in each country toward the other.[53] Charles Kupchan surveyed a number of such cases, finding that a necessary condition for this kind of reconciliation is compatible domestic institutions and values.[54] Kupchan's finding makes sense in symbolic politics terms: states with incompatible domestic institutions and values will find each other a symbolic threat and therefore be predisposed to rivalry.

This logic also explains exceptions to the rule of democratic peace, such as the Northeast Asian "history problem." South Korea and Japan, in particular, are fellow democracies and fellow U.S. allies, but they continue to cultivate mutually incompatible national narratives, especially about World War II. The result is strong, mutually hostile symbolic predispositions, so diplomatic crises between them have been common, and a security alliance has been impossible.[55]

Symbolic politics theory, in sum, is built to fuse the main insights of constructivism (with its emphasis on discourse or narrative) and realism (with its emphasis on threat). At the same time, by recognizing the importance of values, institutions, and leadership, it also includes the key insights of liberalism. The unique contributions of the symbolist approach include explaining when and how international norms work (by creating or resonating with symbolic predispositions); what explains the usual contemporary pattern of international peace (SYPs, norms, low threat, institutions); and why peace sometimes breaks down (threat perceptions magnified by hostile SYPs). The symbolist approach also allows the problem of who the main international actors are to be decided empirically, instead of by assumption, by examining the symbolic and institutional resources available to different groups.

FINAL WORDS

Beyond its usefulness in explaining ethnic conflict and ethnic cooperation, symbolic politics theory has two great virtues. The first is that it is transdisciplinary: instead of starting from just one source, such as the economic logic of rational choice theory, or the social-theory foundation of constructivism, it explicitly works to bring together the insights of all of the social sciences. In this way, it provides the best available vehicle for turning political science into what Aristotle suggested it should be, the "master science."

End

Though symbolic politics theory starts first with insights from psychology, it uses those insights to indicate when the findings of other social sciences are important. Public opinion, of course, is primarily the realm of political psychology. But symbolic predispositions are also cultural, so symbolic politics theory also includes key insights from anthropology, exemplified in this book by the attention to narratives of national identity. These two approaches go together well enough that one cousin to symbolic politics theory is called the psychocultural approach.[56]

The insights of other social sciences are also included. Symbolist logic explains why economic-style rationalist analysis works well for studying U.S. institutions, including government bureaucracies and private businesses. It also explains the limits of the rationalist approach, applying primarily to institutions that socialize their employees effectively and operate in a stable legal environment, as in most advanced industrialized democracies. On the other hand, sociology's emphasis on social ties and networks is critical for explaining political mobilization and collective political behavior: personal and face-to-face ties are critical in turning feelings and opinions into action. Finally, within international relations theory, symbolic politics helps explain how threats and hostile symbolic predispositions motivate states, like ethnic groups, to shift from cooperative to conflictual relations.

The second virtue of symbolic politics theory is that it allows the return of common sense and normative clarity to political science. Rationalist theorists like to look for rare examples of counterintuitive behavior. Symbolic politics, in contrast, shows us how to apply common sense to common behavior. It tells us that people's prejudices, values, biases, and fears matter, for leaders and the mass public alike. That, in turn, tells us that it matters enormously if leaders are bad people—if they are ruthless, bigoted, aggressive, or dominance seeking, symbolic politics gives them the tools to gain support for their plans. In other words, this approach reminds us that political conflict is rooted in part in common human weaknesses—fear, pride, greed, hate. It also tells us why politicians engage in so much absurd-seeming theater and why journalists pay so much attention to it: those theatrical gestures influence us, whether we like to admit it or not.

At the same time, symbolic politics tells us that psychology is not everything. Political outcomes depend heavily on political institutions, but the institutions work as expected only when symbolic predispositions and institutional rules are aligned. Political outcomes also depend on material facts and resources that enable institutions to act. Institutions succeed only when they have money, whether to buy television advertising or guns for the troops. And institutions succeed only in a favorable legal environment. The point is that symbolic politics theory allows us to put all of these pieces together in a coherent framework, so analysts of politics can talk *to* each other, instead of past each other like blind men trying to describe an elephant.

Notes

Introduction

1. I am indebted to Mark Bowden for suggesting this opening statement.

2. Wars and armed conflicts are enumerated in Lotte Themner and Peter Wallensteen, "Armed Conflicts, 1946–2012," *Journal of Peace Research* 50, no. 4 (July 2013): 509–21. Assessment of their ethnic character is mine.

3. See, e.g., Paul Collier and Anke Hoeffler, "Greed and Grievance in Civil War," *Oxford Economic Papers* 56 (2004): 563–95.

4. Key works that make this argument include Donald Horowitz, *Ethnic Groups in Conflict* (Berkeley: University of California Press, 1985), and Andreas Wimmer, *Ethnic Boundary Making: Institutions, Power, Networks* (New York: Oxford University Press, 2013).

5. Quoted in Horowitz, *Ethnic Groups in Conflict*, 53.

6. The notion of an "imagined family" is, of course, a variation on Benedict Anderson, *Imagined Communities: Reflections on the Origin and Spread of Nationalism* (Norfolk, UK: Thetford Press, 1983). Donald Horowitz (*Ethnic Groups in Conflict*, 57) has made a similar point, noting that ethnicity has "a kinship with kinship."

7. See Anthony D. Smith, *The Ethnic Origins of Nations* (New York: Blackwell, 1986).

8. Rogers Brubaker, *Ethnicity without Groups* (Cambridge, MA: Harvard University Press, 2004).

9. Stathis N. Kalyvas, *The Logic of Violence in Civil War* (Cambridge: Cambridge University Press, 2006).

10. John Mueller, "The Banality of 'Ethnic War,'" *International Security* 25, no. 1 (Summer 2000): 42–70.

11. Fearon and Laitin, "Ethnicity, Insurgency, and Civil War," *American Political Science Review* 97, no. 1 (February 2003): 75–90; Collier and Hoeffler, "Greed and Grievance in Civil War."

12. Paul Collier, Anke Hoeffler, and Dominic Rohner, "Beyond Greed and Grievance: Feasibility and Civil War," *Oxford Economic Papers* 61, no. 1 (January 2009): 23.

13. Monica Duffy Toft, *The Geography of Ethnic Violence: Identity, Interests, and the Indivisibility of Territory* (Princeton, NJ: Princeton University Press, 2003); Erin K. Jenne, *Ethnic Bargaining: The Paradox of Minority Empowerment* (Ithaca: Cornell University Press, 2007).

14. Collier, Hoeffler, and Rohner, "Beyond Greed and Grievance," 1–27.

15. Lars-Erik Cederman, Nils B. Weidmann, and Kristian Skrede Gleditsch, "Horizontal Inequalities and Ethnonationalist Civil War: A Global Comparison," *American Political Science Review* 105, no. 3 (August 2011): 478–95.

16. More precisely, the finding was that a "feasibility" model of civil war tested in a logistic regression had a pseudo-R-square of 0.28, in Collier, Hoeffler, and Rohner, "Beyond Greed and Grievance," 9.

17. The seminal work in this school of thought is David A. Lake and Donald Rothchild, eds., *The International Spread of Ethnic Conflict: Fear, Diffusion and Escalation* (Princeton, NJ: Princeton University Press, 1998).

18. Stuart J. Kaufman, "Symbolic Politics or Rational Choice? Testing Theories of Extreme Ethnic Violence," *International Security* 30, no. 4 (Spring 2006): 45–86.

19. Henry Hale has proposed a sophisticated version of rational choice theory that draws on some findings in psychology, but his approach is still limited in its ability to explain why leaders like Numayri choose such exploitative policies. See Henry E. Hale, *The Foundations of Ethnic Politics: Separatism of States and Nations in Eurasia and the World* (Cambridge: Cambridge University Press, 2008).

20. See, for example, Doug McAdam, John D. McCarthy, and Mayer N. Zald, eds., *Comparative Perspectives on Social Movements* (Cambridge: Cambridge University Press, 1996); Doug McAdam, Sidney Tarrow, and Charles Tilly, *Dynamics of Contention* (Cambridge: Cambridge University Press, 2001); and Charles Tilly, *Identities, Boundaries and Social Ties* (Boulder, CO: Paradigm, 2005).

21. Tilly, *Identities, Boundaries and Social Ties*.

22. Ibid., 6.

23. See, e.g., Eric Chaisson and Steve McMillan, *Astronomy: A Beginner's Guide to the Universe*, 5th ed. (Upper Saddle River, NJ: Pearson Prentice Hall, 2007), 243–59, 330–31.

24. I first heard a version of this satiric comparison from Edward Rhodes, personal communication.

25. I use the concept of "paradigm" here in the sense proposed in Thomas S. Kuhn, *The Structure of Scientific Revolutions* (Chicago: University of Chicago Press, 1970).

26. David O. Sears, Leonie Huddie, and Lynita G. Schaffer, "A Schematic Variant of Symbolic Politics Theory, as Applied to Racial and Gender Equality," in *Political Cognition: The 19th Annual Carnegie Symposium on Cognition*, ed. Richard R. Lau and David O. Sears (Hillsdale, NJ: Lawrence Erlbaum Associates, 1986), 159–202.

27. Bruce D. Bartholow and Cheryl L. Dickter, "Social Cognitive Neuroscience of Person Perception: A Selective Review Focused on the Event-Related Brain Potential," in *Social Neuroscience: Integrating Biological and Psychological Explanations of Social Behavior*, ed. Eddie Harmon-Jones and Piotr Winkielman (New York: Guilford Press, 2007), 376–400.

28. David O. Sears and Jack Citrin, *Tax Revolt: Something for Nothing in California* (Cambridge, MA: Harvard University Press, 1982).

29. For example, Alec MacGillis, "The Unelectable Whiteness of Scott Walker," *New Republic*, June 30, 2014, 16–27.

30. Roza N. Musina, "Contemporary Ethnosocial and Ethnopolitical Processes in Tatarstan," in *Ethnic Conflict in the Post-Soviet World: Case Studies and Analysis*, ed. Leokadia Drobizheva et al. (Armonk, NY: M.E. Sharpe, 1996), 202.

31. A good review of these findings is Blake M. Riek, Eric W. Mania, and Samuel L. Gaertner, "Intergroup Threat and Outgroup Attitudes: A Meta-Analytic Review," *Personality and Social Psychology Review* 10, no. 4 (2006): 336–53.

32. See, for example, Jeff Greenberg, Tom Pyszczynski, Sheldon Solomon, Abram Rosenblatt, Mitchell Veeder, Shari Kirkland, and Deborah Lyon, "Evidence for Terror Management Theory II: The Effects of Mortality Salience on Reactions to Those Who Threaten or Bolster the Cultural Worldview," *Journal of Personality and Social Psychology* 58, no. 2 (1990): 308–18.

33. William A. Gamson, *Talking Politics* (New York: Cambridge University Press, 1992).

34. Theodore J. Lowi, "American Business, Public Policy, Case Studies and Political Theory," *World Politics* 16 (July 1964): 677–715; William Zimmerman, "Issue Area and Foreign-Policy Process: A Research Note in Search of a General Theory," *American Political Science Review* 67, no. 4 (1973): 1204–12.

35. On this point see William J. Long and Peter Brecke, *War and Reconciliation: Reason and Emotion in Conflict Resolution* (Cambridge, MA: MIT Press, 2003).

36. I expand on these points in Stuart J. Kaufman, "Escaping the Symbolic Politics Trap: Reconciliation Initiatives and Conflict Resolution in Ethnic Wars," *Journal of Peace Research* 43, no. 2 (March 2006): 201–18.

37. George W. Bush, "Text of Bush's Address," delivered September 11, 2001, http://articles.cnn.com/2001-09-11/us/bush.speech.text_1_attacks-deadly-terrorist-acts-despicable-acts?_s=PM:US.

38. I discuss the nature of ethnic security dilemmas in Stuart J. Kaufman, *Modern Hatreds: The Symbolic Politics of Ethnic War* (Ithaca: Cornell University Press, 2001.

39. Martin Luther King Jr., "I've Been to the Mountaintop," delivered April 3, 1968, http://www.americanrhetoric.com/speeches/mlkivebeentothemountaintop.htm.

40. Dan Miller, "Queens Is Out in Force Joining Mayor Bloomberg in Columbus Day Parade," *Queens Gazette*, October 14, 2009, http://m.qgazette.com/news/2009-10-14/Features/Queens_is_Out_In_Force_Joining_Mayor_Bloomberg_in_.html.

41. Garth Johnston, "Bloomberg Gets St. Patrick's Day Jeers (and Some Cheers)," *Gothamist*, March 18, 2011, http://gothamist.com/2011/03/18/jeers_some_cheers_greet_bloomberg_o.php#photo-1.

1. Symbolic Predispositions and Ethnic Politics

1. Crawford Young, "The Dialectics of Cultural Pluralism: Concept and Reality," in *The Rising Tide of Cultural Pluralism: The Nation-State at Bay?*, ed. Crawford Young (Madison: University of Wisconsin Press, 1993): 3–35.

2. Examples of the synthesis include, e.g., Ted Robert Gurr, *Minorities at Risk* (Washington, DC: U.S. Institute of Peace, 1993); and Anthony D. Smith, *Nationalism and Modernism* (London: Routledge, 1998).

3. Clifford Geertz, "The Integrative Revolution: Primordial Sentiments and Civil Politics in the New States," in *Old Societies and New States: The Quest for Modernity in Asia and Africa*, ed. Clifford Geertz (New York: Free Press, 1963), 109, emphasis added.

4. James D. Fearon and David D. Laitin, "Violence and the Social Construction of Ethnic Identity," *International Organization* 54, no. 4 (Autumn 2000): 874.

5. Donald Rothchild, "Collective Demands for Improved Distribution," in *State versus Ethnic Claims: African Policy Dilemmas*, ed. Donald Rothchild and Victor Olorunsola (Boulder, CO: Westview, 1983), 173.

6. Anthony D. Smith, *The Ethnic Origins of Nations* (New York: Blackwell, 1986), 15–16 and passim.

7. Lewis Coser, *The Functions of Social Conflict* (Glencoe, IL: Free Press, 1956), 7.

8. Jonathan St. B. T. Evans and Keith Frankish, "The Duality of Mind: An Historical Perspective," in *In Two Minds: Dual Processes and Beyond*, ed. Jonathan St. B. T. Evans and Keith Frankish (New York: Oxford University Press, 2009), 15.

9. Jonathan Haidt, *The Righteous Mind: Why Good People Are Divided by Politics and Religion* (New York: Pantheon, 2012), 46; cf. Jonathan Haidt, *The Happiness Hypothesis: Finding Modern Truth in Ancient Wisdom* (New York: Basic Books, 2006).

10. Malcolm Gladwell, *Blink: The Power of Thinking without Thinking* (New York: Little, Brown, 2005), 8–9.

11. George E. Marcus, W. Russell Neuman, and Michael MacKuen, *Affective Intelligence and Political Judgment* (Chicago: University of Chicago Press, 2000), 36–68.

12. Tiffany A. Ito, Eve Willadsen-Jensen, and Joshua Correll, "Social Neuroscience and Social Perception: New Perspectives on Categorization, Prejudice and Stereotyping," in *Social Neuroscience: Integrating Biological and Psychological Explanations of Social Behavior*, ed. Eddie Harmon-Jones and Piotr Winkielman (New York: Guilford Press, 2007), 401–21.

13. Rose McDermott, "The Feeling of Rationality: The Meaning of Neuroscientific Advances for Political Science," *Perspectives on Politics* 2, no. 4 (2004): 691–706, 700.

14. Jonathan Mercer, "Emotional Beliefs," *International Organization* 64 (Winter 2010): 1–31.

15. Gladwell, *Blink*.

16. Ibid.; Eliot R. Smith and Elizabeth C. Collins, "Dual-Process Models: A Social Psychological Perspective," in Evans and Frankish, *In Two Minds*, 203.

17. Haidt, *Righteous Mind*.

18. Drew Westen, *The Political Brain: The Role of Emotion in Deciding the Fate of the Nation* (New York: PublicAffairs, 2007), 3.

19. Ibid., 62.

20. George Lakoff, *The Political Mind: Why You Can't Understand 21st-Century Politics with an 18th-Century Brain* (New York: Viking, 2008), 83–84, 128.

21. David O. Sears, "The Role of Affect in Symbolic Politics," in *Citizens and Politics: Perspectives from Political Psychology*, ed. James H. Kuklinski (New York: Cambridge University Press, 2001), 16.

22. Westen, *Political Brain*.

23. Gian Vittorio Caprara, Shalom Schwartz, Cristina Capanna, Michele Vechione, and Claudio Barbaranelli, "Personality and Politics: Values, Traits and Political Choice," *Political Psychology* 27, no. 1 (February 2006): 1–28.

24. Marina F. Barnea and Shalom H. Schwartz, "Values and Voting," *Political Psychology* 19, no. 1 (March 1998): 17–40; Haidt, *Righteous Mind*.

25. Smith and Collins, "Dual-Process Models," 198–99.

26. Jonathan L. Freedman, David O. Sears, and J. Merrill Carlsmith, *Social Psychology* (Englewood Cliffs, NJ: Prentice-Hall, 1978), 162–63.

27. Ibid., 158–86.

28. Haidt, *Righteous Mind*, 58–59.

29. Milton Lodge and Charles S. Taber, *The Rationalizing Voter* (New York: Cambridge University Press, 2013), 58.

30. Louis Wirth, "The Unfinished Business of American Democracy," *Annals of the American Academy of Political and Social Science* 44 (March 1946): 1–9.

31. Joshua Correll, Bernadette Park, Bernd Wittenbrink, and Charles M. Judd, "The Police Officer's Dilemma: Using Ethnicity to Disambiguate Potentially Threatening Individuals," *Journal of Personality and Social Psychology* 8, no. 6 (2002): 1314–29.

32. Haidt, *Righteous Mind*, 53–54.

33. Freedman, Sears, and Carlsmith, *Social Psychology*, 137.

34. Irving L. Janis and Leon Mann, *Decision Making: A Psychological Analysis of Conflict, Choice and Commitment* (New York: Free Press, 1977), 120–25.

35. Linda M. Isbell and Victor C. Ottati, "The Emotional Voter: Effects of Episodic Affective Reactions on Candidate Evaluation," in *The Social Psychology of Politics*, ed. Victor C. Ottati et al. (New York: Kluwer Academic, 2002), 55–74.

36. Ted Brader, "Striking a Responsive Chord: How Political Ads Motivate and Persuade Voters by Appealing to Emotions," *American Journal of Political Science* 49, no. 2 (2005): 388–405.

37. McDermott, "Feeling of Rationality," 694–95.

38. Marcus, Neuman, and MacKuen, *Affective Intelligence and Political Judgment*, 1.

39. David O. Sears, Richard R. Lau, Tom R. Tyler, and Harris M. Allen Jr., "Self-Interest vs. Symbolic Politics in Policy Attitudes and Presidential Voting," *American Political Science Review* 74, no. 3 (September 1980): 679; cf. David O. Sears, Leonie Huddie, and Lynita G. Schaffer, "A Schematic Variant of Symbolic Politics Theory, as Applied to Racial and Gender Equality," in *Political Cognition, the 19th Annual Carnegie Symposium on Cognition*, ed. Richard R. Lau and David O. Sears (Hillsdale, NJ: Erlbaum, 1986), 159–202.

40. George E. Marcus, "The Structure of Emotional Response: 1984 Presidential Candidates," *American Political Science Review* 82, no. 3 (September 1988): 752.

41. Larry M. Bartels, "Beyond the Running Tally: Partisan Bias in Political Perceptions," *Political Behavior* 24, no. 2 (June 2002): 134.

42. Westen, *Political Brain*, 107–8.

43. Ibid., 109–11.

44. David P. Redlawsk, "Hot Cognition or Cool Consideration? Testing the Effects of Motivated Reasoning on Political Decision Making," *Journal of Politics* 64, no. 4 (November 2002): 1021–44.

45. Westen, *Political Brain*, 35.

46. Quoted in Haidt, *Righteous Mind*, 204.

47. Summarized in Rupert Brown, *Prejudice and Its Social Psychology*, 2nd ed. (Malden, MA: Wiley-Blackwell, 2010), 40–43.

48. Ibid., 40; Henry Hale, *Foundations of Ethnic Politics: Separatism of States and Nations in Eurasia and the World* (Cambridge: Cambridge University Press, 2008) 19.

49. Hale, *Foundations of Ethnic Politics*, erroneously attributes this view to me.

50. Henri Tajfel, "Social Psychology of Intergroup Relations," *Annual Review of Psychology* 33 (1982): 1–39.

51. Marilynn B. Brewer and Donald T. Campbell, *Ethnocentrism and Intergroup Attitudes: East African Evidence* (New York: John Wiley and Sons, 1976).

52. Marilynn B. Brewer, "The Psychology of Prejudice: Ingroup Love or Outgroup Hate?" *Journal of Social Issues* 55, no. 3 (1999): 429–44.

53. Vamik Volkan, *Bloodlines: From Ethnic Pride to Ethnic Terrorism* (New York: Farrar, Straus and Giroux, 1997).

54. Anthony D. Smith, *Ethno-Symbolism and Nationalism: A Cultural Approach* (London: Routledge, 2009).

55. Smith, *Ethnic Origins of Nations*.

56. Ernest Gellner, *Nations and Nationalism* (Ithaca: Cornell University Press, 1983).

57. Mercer, "Emotional Beliefs."

58. David Cuillier, Blythe Duell, and Jeff Joireman, "The Mortality Muzzle: The Effect of Death Thoughts on Attitudes toward National Security and a Watchdog Press," *Journalism* 11, no. 2 (2010): 185–202.

59. John Duckitt, "Prejudice and Intergroup Hostility," in *Oxford Handbook of Political Psychology*, ed. David O. Sears, Leonie Huddy and Robert Jervis (Oxford: Oxford University Press, 2003), 571–73. See also Thierry Devos, Lisa A. Silber, Diane M. Mackie, and Eliot R. Smith, "Experiencing Intergroup Emotions," in *From Prejudice to Intergroup Emotions: Differentiated Reactions to Social Groups*, ed. Diane M. Mackie and Eliot R. Smith (New York: Psychology Press, 2002), 111–34; Susan T. Fiske, Amy J. C. Cuddy, and Peter Glick, "Emotions Up and Down: Intergroup Emotions Result from Perceived Status and Competition," in Mackie and Smith, *From Prejudice to Intergroup Emotions*, 247–64.

60. Marilynn B. Brewer and Michele G. Alexander, "Intergroup Emotions and Images," in Mackie and Smith, *From Prejudice to Intergroup Emotions*, 214.

61. Fiske, Cuddy, and Glick, "Emotions Up and Down."

62. Brown, *Prejudice and Its Social Psychology*, 163.

63. Diana Dumitru and Carter Johnson, "Constructing Interethnic Conflict and Cooperation: Why Some People Harmed Jews and Others Helped Them During the Holocaust in Romania," *World Politics* 63, no. 1 (2011): 1–42.

64. Duckitt, "Prejudice and Intergroup Hostility," 564–65.

65. Donald R. Kinder, "Opinion and Action in the Realm of Politics," in *The Handbook of Social Psychology*, 4th ed., ed. Daniel T. Gilbert, Susan T. Fiske, and Gardner Lindzey (Boston: McGraw-Hill, 1998), 808, 831.

66. John F. Dovidio, Adam R. Pearson, Samuel L. Gaertner, and Gordon Hodson, "On the Nature of Contemporary Prejudice: From Subtle Bias to Severe Consequences," in *Explaining the Breakdown of Ethnic Relations: Why Neighbors Kill*, ed. Victoria M. Esses and Richard A. Vernon (Malden, MA: Blackwell, 2008), 49.

67. Brown, *Prejudice and Its Social Psychology*, 161. See also Brewer, "Psychology of Prejudice."

68. Duckitt, "Prejudice and Intergroup Hostility," 582–86.

69. Blake M. Riek, Eric W. Mania, and Samuel L. Gaertner, "Intergroup Threat and Outgroup Attitudes: A Meta-Analytic Review," *Personality and Social Psychology Review* 10, no. 4 (2006): 336–53, 339.

70. Brewer, "Psychology of Prejudice"; Muzafer Sherif, *Group Conflict and Cooperation: Their Social Psychology* (London: Routledge, 1966); Lawrence Bobo, "Whites' Opposition to Busing: Symbolic Racism or Realistic Group Conflict?" *Journal of Personality and Social Psychology* 45, no. 6 (1983): 1196–1210.

71. Sears, Huddie, and Schaffer, "Schematic Variant of Symbolic Politics Theory," 159–202.

72. Donald Horowitz, *Ethnic Groups in Conflict* (Berkeley: University of California Press, 1985); Duckitt, "Prejudice and Intergroup Hostility," 586.

73. Riek, Mania, and Gaertner, "Intergroup Threat and Outgroup Attitudes"; Walter G. Stephan and C. Lausanne Renfro, "The Role of Threat in Intergroup Relations," in Mackie and Smith, *From Prejudice to Intergroup Emotions*, 191–208.

74. Duckitt, "Prejudice and Intergroup Hostility," 586; Dovidio et al., "On the Nature of Contemporary Prejudice," 52–53.

75. Stephan and Renfro, "Role of Threat in Intergroup Relations."

76. Jeff Greenberg, Tom Pyszczynski, Sheldon Solomon, Abram Rosenblatt, Mitchell Veeder, Shari Kirkland, and Deborah Lyon, "Evidence for Terror Management Theory II: The Effects of Mortality Salience on Reactions to Those Who Threaten or Bolster the Cultural Worldview," *Journal of Personality and Social Psychology* 58, no. 2 (1990): 308–18; Cuillier, Duell, and Joireman, "Mortality Muzzle"; Tom Pyszczynski, Jeff Greenberg, and Sheldon Solomon, "Why Do We Need What We Need? A Terror Management Perspective on the Roots of Human Social Motivation," *Psychological Inquiry* 8, no. 1 (1997): 1–20.

77. Florette Cohen, Daniel M. Ogilvie, Sheldon Solomon, Jeff Greenberg, and Tom Pyszczynski, "American Roulette: The Effect of Reminders of Death on Support for George W. Bush in the 2004 Presidential Election," *Analyses of Social Issues and Public Policy* 5, no. 1 (2005): 177–87.

78. Ibid.

79. Devos et al., "Experiencing Intergroup Emotions."

80. Leonie Huddy, Stanley Feldman, Charles Taber, and Gallya Lahav, "Threat, Anxiety, and Support of Antiterrorism Policies," *American Journal of Political Science* 49, no. 3 (2005): 593–608.

81. Murray Edelman, *Politics as Symbolic Action: Mass Arousal and Quiescence* (New York: Academic Press, 1971); Edelman, *Political Language: Words That Succeed and Policies That Fail* (New York: Academic Press, 1977); cf. Edelman, *The Symbolic Uses of Politics* (Urbana: University of Illinois Press, 1964).

82. Edelman, *Politics as Symbolic Action.*

83. Edward Aspinall, "Democratization and Ethnic Politics in Indonesia: Nine Theses," *Journal of East Asian Studies* 11 (2011): 289–90, 103–5.

84. Bert Klandermans, "The Demand and Supply of Participation: Social-Psychological Correlates of Participation in Social Movements," in *The Blackwell Companion to Social Movements*, ed. David A. Snow, Sarah A. Soule, and Hansbeter Kriesi (Malden, MA: Blackwell, 2004), 343–52; Omar Shahabudin McDoom, "The Psychology of Threat in Intergroup Conflict: Emotions, Rationality, and Opportunity in the Rwandan Genocide," *International Security* 37, no. 2 (Fall 2012): 119–55.

85. Michael Brown, "International Dimensions of Internal Conflict," in *International Dimensions of Internal Conflict*, ed. Michael Brown (Cambridge, MA: MIT Press, 1996), 580.

86. V. P. Gagnon Jr., *The Myth of Ethnic War: Serbia and Croatia in the 1990s* (Ithaca: Cornell University Press, 2004).

87. William A. Gamson and Andre Modigliani, "The Changing Culture of Affirmative Action," in *Research in Political Sociology*, vol. 3, ed. R. G. Braungart and M. M. Braungart (Greenwich, CT: JAI press, 1987), 143.

88. Robert D. Benford and David A. Snow, "Framing Processes and Social Movements: An Overview and Assessment," *Annual Review of Sociology* 26 (2000): 611–39.

89. Ibid., 619–22.

90. William A. Gamson, *Talking Politics* (Cambridge: Cambridge University Press, 1992).

91. Stephen Ellingson, "Understanding the Dialectic of Discourse and Collective Action: Public Debate and Rioting in Antebellum Cincinnati," *American Journal of Sociology* 101, no. 1 (1995): 100–44.

92. Gamson, *Talking Politics.*

93. Klandermans, "Demand and Supply of Participation"; McDoom, "Psychology of Threat in Intergroup Conflict."

94. Stuart J. Kaufman, *Modern Hatreds: The Symbolic Politics of Ethnic War* (Ithaca: Cornell University Press, 2001).

95. Mario Diani, "Networks and Participation," in *The Blackwell Companion to Social Movements*, ed. David A. Snow, Sarah A. Soule, and Hanspeter Kriesi (Malden, MA: Blackwell, 2004), 339–59. See also Doug McAdam, John D. McCarthy, and Mayer N. Zald, eds., *Comparative Perspectives on Social Movements* (Cambridge: Cambridge University Press, 1996).

96. Westen, *Political Brain*; Lakoff, *Political Mind*.

97. Ervin Staub and Daniel Bar-Tal, "Genocide, Mass Killing and Intractable Conflict: Roots, Evolution, Prevention and Reconciliation," in *Oxford Handbook of Political Psychology*, ed. David O. Sears, Leonie Huddy, and Robert Jervis (Oxford: Oxford University Press, 2003), 710–51; Dovidio et al., "On the Nature of Contemporary Prejudice," 56.

98. Staub and Bar-Tal, "Genocide, Mass Killing and Intractable Conflict," 720.

99. Daniel Jonah Goldhagen, *Hitler's Willing Executioners*, suggests the concept of eliminationist ideology.

100. Benjamin A. Valentino, *Final Solutions: Mass Killing and Genocide in the Twentieth Century* (Ithaca: Cornell University Press, 2004); Staub and Bar-Tal, "Genocide, Mass Killing and Intractable Conflict."

101. Lodge and Taber, *Rationalizing Voter*, 56–57.

102. Freedman, Sears, and Carlsmith, *Social Psychology*, 388, 313.

103. Karl D. Jackson, *Traditional Authority, Islam, and Rebellion: A Study of Indonesian Political Behavior* (Berkeley: University of California Press, 1980), 240–76.

104. Charles Tilly, *Identities, Boundaries and Social Ties* (Boulder, CO: Paradigm, 2005).

105. For example, see Michael Massing, "The Volunteer Army: Who Fights and Why?" *New York Review of Books*, April 3, 2008, accessed at http://www.nybooks.com/articles/archives/2008/apr/03/the-volunteer-army-who-fights-and-why/?page=1, September 11, 2011.

106. Gurr, *Minorities at Risk*; Monica Duffy Toft, *The Geography of Ethnic Violence* (Princeton, NJ: Princeton University Press, 2003).

107. James D. Fearon and David D. Laitin, "Ethnicity, Insurgency, and Civil War," *American Political Science Review* 97, no. 1 (2003): 75–90; Nicholas Sambanis, "Do Ethnic and Nonethnic Civil Wars Have the Same Causes?: A Theoretical and Empirical Inquiry (Part 1)," *Journal of Conflict Resolution* 45, no. 3 (2001): 259–82; Havard Hegre and Nicholas Sambanis, "Sensitivity Analysis of Empirical Results on Civil War Onset," *Journal of Conflict Resolution* 50, no. 4 (2006): 508–35.

108. Fearon and Laitin, "Ethnicity, Insurgency, and Civil War"; Gurr, *Minorities at Risk*; Hegre and Sambanis, "Sensitivity Analysis."

109. Marta Reynal-Querol, "Ethnicity, Political Systems, and Civil Wars," *Journal of Conflict Resolution* 46, no. 1 (2002): 29–54; Patrick M. Regan and Daniel Norton, "Greed, Grievance, and Mobilization in Civil Wars," *Journal of Conflict Resolution* 49, no. 3 (2005): 319–36; Zeynep Taydas, Jason Enia, and Patrick James, "Why Do Civil Wars Occur? Another Look at the Theoretical Dichotomy of Opportunity versus Grievance," (n.d.), unpublished manuscript.

110. Gurr, *Minorities at Risk*.

111. Louk Hagedoorn and Maykel Verkuyten, "Prejudice and Self-Categorization: The Variable Role of Authoritarianism and In-Group Stereotypes," *Personality and Social Psychology Bulletin* 24, no. 1 (January 1998): 99–110.

112. Robert Jervis, "Cooperation under the Security Dilemma," *World Politics* 30, no. 2 (January 1978): 167–214; Barry R. Posen, "The Security Dilemma and Ethnic Conflict," *Survival* 35, no. 1 (1993): 27–47; Chaim Kaufmann, "Possible and Impossible Solutions to Ethnic Wars," *International Security* 20, no. 4 (1996): 136–75; Jack Snyder and Robert Jervis, "Civil War and the Security Dilemma," in *Civil Wars, Insecurity, and Intervention*, ed. Barbara F. Walter and Jack Snyder (New York: Columbia University Press, 1999), 15–37.

113. Stuart J. Kaufman, "Symbolic Politics or Rational Choice? Testing Theories of Extreme Ethnic Violence," *International Security* 30, no. 4 (2006): 45–86.

114. Inspired by William Zimmerman, "Issue Area and Foreign-Policy Process: A Research Note in Search of a General Theory," *American Political Science Review* 67, no. 4 (1973): 1204–12;

cf. Theodore J. Lowi, "American Business, Public Policy, Case Studies and Political Theory," *World Politics* 16 (July 1964): 677–715.

115. Lowi, "American Business, Public Policy"; Zimmerman, "Issue Area and Foreign-Policy Process."

116. For example, Peter J. Katzenstein, ed., *The Culture of National Security: Norms and Identity in World Politics* (New York: Columbia University Press, 1996); Ted Hopf, *Social Construction of International Politics: Identities and Foreign Policies, Moscow, 1955 and 1999* (Ithaca: Cornell University Press, 2002); Thomas U. Berger, *Cultures of Anti-Militarism: National Security in Germany and Japan* (Baltimore: Johns Hopkins University Press, 1998); Ron E. Hassner, *War on Sacred Grounds* (Ithaca: Cornell University Press, 2009). Kaufman, *Modern Hatreds*, demonstrates a similar approach. David L. Rousseau, *Identifying Threats and Threatening Identities: The Social Construction of Realism and Liberalism* (Stanford, CA: Stanford University Press, 2006), explicitly works to bring insights from psychology to international relations constructivism.

117. For example, Patrick Thaddeus Jackson and Ronald R. Krebs, "Twisting Tongues and Twisting Arms: The Power of Political Rhetoric," *European Journal of International Relations* 13, no. 1 (2007): 35–66.

118. Marc Howard Ross, *Cultural Contestation in Ethnic Conflict* (Cambridge: Cambridge University Press, 2007).

119. Alexander George and Andrew Bennett, *Case Studies and Theory Development in the Social Sciences* (Cambridge, MA: MIT Press, 2005).

120. George and Bennett, *Case Studies and Theory Development.*

121. Adam Przeworski and Henry Teune, *The Logic of Comparative Social Inquiry* (New York: Wiley, 1970), first suggested this label.

2. The Muslim Rebellion in the Philippines

1. Aijaz Ahmad, "Class and Colony in Mindanao," in Eric Gutierrez et al., *Rebels, Warlords and Ulama: A Reader on Muslim Separatism and the War in Southern Philippines* (Quezon City: Institute for Popular Democracy, 2000), 26.

2. Ibid., 13.

3. R. J. May, "The Philippines," in *The Politics of Muslim Reassertion*, ed. Mohammed Ayoob (London: Croon Helm), 211.

4. This and the following paragraphs are based on Cesar Adib Majul, *Muslims in the Philippines* (Quezon City: University of Philippines Press, 1999 ed.).

5. Ibid., 155–81.

6. For the history of this period, see Peter Gordon Gowing, *Mandate in Moroland: The American Government of Muslim Filipinos 1899–1920* (Quezon City: New Day Publishers, 1983).

7. Patricio N. Abinales, *Making Mindanao: Cotabato and Davao in the Formation of the Philippine Nation-State* (Quezon City: Ateneo de Manila University Press, 2000).

8. W. K. Che Man, *Muslim Separatism: The Moros of Southern Philippines and the Malays of Southern Thailand* (Singapore: Oxford University Press, 1990), 24.

9. Ruth Laura Perry Moore, "Women and Warriors: Defending Islam in the Southern Philippines" (PhD diss., University of California–San Diego, 1981), 77.

10. Peter G. Gowing, "Muslim Filipinos between Integration and Secession," *South East Asia Journal of Theology* 14, no. 2 (1972): 67–68.

11. Abinales, *Making Mindanao*, 98.

12. Population increase figure from ibid. Provincial data calculated from B. R. Rodil, *The Minoritization of the Indigenous Communities of Mindanao and the Sulu Archipelago* (Davao: Alternate Forum for Research in Mindanao, 2004), 122.

13. Abinales, *Making Mindanao*, 2–14.

14. James B. Goodno, *Philippines: Land of Broken Promises* (London: Zed Books, 1991), 55; George, *Revolt in Mindanao*, 137–42.

15. Sterling Seagrave, *The Marcos Dynasty* (New York: Harper and Row, 1988), 211.

16. Goodno, *Philippines*, 59.

17. Seagrave, *Marcos Dynasty*, 217–18.

18. Goodno, *Philippines*, 61.

19. Eufronio M. Alip, *Philippine History: Political, Social, Economic* (based on the Course of Study of the Bureau of Public Schools) (Manila: Alip and Brion, 1951), 166, 288, 331ff.

20. Peter G. Gowing, "Christians and Moros: The Confrontation of Christianity and Islam in the Philippines," *South East Asia Journal of Theology* 10, no. 2–3 (1969): 84–85.

21. Robert D. McAmis, "Muslim Filipinos: 1970–72," in *The Muslim Filipinos: Their History, Society, and Contemporary Problems*, ed. Peter G. Gowing and Robert D. McAmis (Manila: Solidaridad, 1974), 53.

22. Thomas M. McKenna, *Muslim Rulers and Rebels: Everyday Politics and Armed Separatism in the Southern Philippines* (Berkeley: University of California Press, 1998), 164.

23. Quoted in McAmis, "Muslim Filipinos: 1970–72," 44.

24. Alip, *Philippine History*, 155–68, 173.

25. Majul, *Muslims in the Philippines*, 262–77.

26. For an example of a Christian call for Muslim conversion, see Moore, "Women and Warriors," 83.

27. Quoted in McAmis, "Muslim Filipinos," 43.

28. Moore, "Women and Warriors," 38. This view is sometimes endorsed by Christian Filipino accounts. See, e.g., Alip, *Philippine History*, 33.

29. Thomas M. Kiefer, quoted in Gowing, "Christians and Moros," 97.

30. McKenna, *Muslim Rulers and Rebels*, 191.

31. Majul, *Muslims in the Philippines*, 6.

32. Francisco L. Gonzalez, "Sultans of a Violent Land," in Gutierrez et al., *Rebels, Warlords and Ulama*, 97.

33. G. Carter Bentley, quoted in Eric Gutierrez, "In the Battlefields of the Warlord," in Gutierrez et al., *Rebels, Warlords and Ulama*, 79.

34. Majul, *Muslims in the Philippines*, 97.

35. Gowing, "Christians and Moros," 81–82.

36. Ibid., 95; cf. McKenna, *Muslim Rulers and Rebels*, 143–44; and May, "The Philippines," 218.

37. Moore, "Women and Warriors," 92.

38. Gutierrez, "In the Battlefields of the Warlord," 67.

39. Personal interview A, June 2006.

40. Peter G. Gowing and Robert D. McAmis, *The Muslim Filipinos: Their History, Society, and Contemporary Problems* (Manila: Solidaridad, 1974), 117–19.

41. Ibid., 105.

42. Gowing, "Christians and Moros," 85.

43. McKenna, *Muslim Rulers and Rebels*, 36.

44. Luis Q. Lacar and Chester L. Hunt, "Attitudes of Filipino Christian College Students toward Filipino Muslims and Their Implications for National Integration," *Solidarity* 7, no. 7 (July 1972): 8.

45. Filipinas Foundation, *Philippine Majority-Minority Relations and Ethnic Attitudes* (Makati, Rizal: Filipinas Foundation, 1975), 122, 137, 158, 196.

46. Congress of the Philippines, House of Representatives, 1955, quoted in A. C. Glang, *Muslim Secession or Integration?* (Quezon City: A. C. Glang, 1969), 35.

47. Moore, "Women and Warriors," 124.

48. T. J. S. George, *Revolt in Mindanao: The Rise of Islam in Philippine Politics* (Kuala Lumpur: Oxford University Press, 1980), 150.

49. Moore, "Women and Warriors," 17, 92–93, 101–2.

50. Thomas M. Kiefer, *The Tausug: Violence and Law in a Philippine Moslem Society* (New York: Holt, Rinehart and Winston, 1972), 53–55.

51. George, *Revolt in Mindanao*, 137–38.

52. Personal interview, June 2006.

53. Gowing, "Christians and Moros," 80.

54. Moore, "Women and Warriors," 14, 28, 85.

55. Gowing, "Christians and Moros," 80.

56. McKenna, *Muslim Rulers and Rebels*; Moore, "Women and Warriors," 83.

57. McAmis, "Muslim Filipinos," 45; cf. Soliman M. Santos Jr., *The Moro Islamic Challenge: Constitutional Rethinking for the Mindanao Peace Process* (Quezon City: University of Philippines Press, 2001), 208.

58. Gowing, "Christians and Moros," 98.

59. Elisio Mercado, "Culture, Economics, and Revolt in Mindanao: The Origin of the MNLF and the Politics of Moro Separatism," in *Armed Separatism in Southeast Asia*, ed. Lim Joo Jock (Singapore: Institute of Southeast Asian Studies, 1984), 158.

60. George, *Revolt in Mindanao*, 145.

61. Hilario M. Gomez Jr., *The Moro Rebellion and the Search for Peace: A Study on Christian-Muslim Relations in the Philippines* (Zamboanga City: Silsilah Publishers, 2000), 140, 160.

62. Ibid., 157, 161.

63. Salah Jubair, *Bangsa Moro: A Nation under Endless Tyranny*, 3rd ed. (Kuala Lumpur: IQ Marin, 1999), 139.

64. Author interview J, June 2006.

65. For a detailed account of this episode, see Marites Danguilan Vitung and Glenda M. Gloria, *Under the Crescent Moon: Rebellion in Mindanao* (Quezon City: Ateneo Centre for Social Policy and Public Affairs, 2000), 2–23.

66. McKenna, *Muslim Rulers and Rebels*, 141.

67. Ibid., 145–47.

68. Quoted in Mercado, "Culture, Economics, and Revolt," 156.

69. McAmis, "Muslim Filipinos"; McKenna, *Muslim Rulers and Rebels*.

70. George, *Revolt in Mindanao*, makes the point about Matalam's credibility.

71. Ibid., 152.

72. Author interview S, June 2006.

73. Author interview C, June 2006.

74. McAmis, "Muslim Filipinos," 45–46.

75. The name "Ilaga-Blackshirt War" is suggested in Gomez, *Moro Rebellion*, 126.

76. McKenna, *Muslim Rulers and Rebels*, 150–51; Mercado, "Culture, Economics, and Revolt," 157–58.

77. McKenna, *Muslim Rulers and Rebels*, 150–51; Mercado, "Culture, Economics, and Revolt," 157–58; George, *Revolt in Mindanao*, 143–50.

78. Moore, "Women and Warriors," 12.

79. McKenna, *Muslim Rulers and Rebels*, 151–53. One of my informants claimed direct personal knowledge of this connection, but I have not yet been able to verify the claim.

80. Jubair, *Bangsamoro*, 137–40; cf. George, *Revolt in Mindanao*, 151.

81. Jubair, *Bangsamoro*, 138–39.

82. Mercado, "Culture, Economics, and Revolt," 158.

83. Ibid.; May, "The Philippines," 219; Cesar Adib Majul, *The Contemporary Muslim Movement in the Philippines* (Berkeley, CA: Mizan Press, 1985); McAmis, "Muslim Filipinos."

84. Author interview J, June 2006.

85. George, *Revolt in Mindanao*, 164.

86. Gomez, *Moro Rebellion*, 126, 134–40; George, *Revolt in Mindanao*, 171–77.

87. George, *Revolt in Mindanao*, 175; on Almendras, see Abinales, *Making Mindanao*.

88. Majul, *Contemporary Muslim Movement*, 113.

89. Author interview F, June 2006.

90. Gomez, *Moro Rebellion*, 156–58.

91. Ibid., 147.

92. McKenna, *Muslim Rulers and Rebels*, 146–47, makes this point.

93. Author interview D, June 2006.

94. McKenna, *Muslim Rulers and Rebels*, 148; Samuel K. Tan, *Internationalization of the Bangsamoro Struggle* (Quezon City: University of the Philippines Center for Integrative and Development Studies, 1995), 78; author interview E, June 2006.

95. Jubair, *Bangsa Moro*, 151–52.

96. Eliseo J. Mercado Jr., "The Moro People's Struggle for Self-Determination," in *Mindanao: Land of Unfulfilled Promise*, ed. Mark Turner, R. J. May, and Lulu Respall Turner (Quezon City: New Day Publishers, 1992), 161.

97. Author interviews A and S, June 2006.

98. See, e.g., Che Man, *Muslim Separatism*, 139.

99. Author interview J, June 2006.

100. Author interview D, June 2006.

101. Author interviews D, F, and G, June 2006.

102. Author interview M, June 2006.

103. Che Man, *Muslim Separatism*, 97.

104. Author interview C, June 2006.

105. Tan, *Internationalization of the Bangsamoro Struggle*, 55–72.

106. Author interview A, June 2006.

107. George, *Revolt in Mindanao*, 181–82.

108. David A. Rosenberg, ed., *Marcos and Martial Law in the Philippines* (Ithaca: Cornell University Press, 1979), 225–41.

109. Guillermo L. Loja, "Martial Law: Philippine Experience in Relation to Peace and Order, 1972–73" (MA thesis, National Defense College of the Philippines, Ft. Bonifacio, Rizal, 1972–1973), 64, 72.

110. Author interviews I, K, June 2006.

111. Ferdinand Marcos, "The Continuing Revolution," speech of November 30, 1973, in *A Dialogue with My People: Selected Speeches of Ferdinand E. Marcos, September 1972–September 1973*, ed. F. S. Tatad (Manila: Department of Public Information, 1973), 39–45.

112. Fortunato U. Abat, *The Day We Nearly Lost Mindanao: The CEMCOM Story*, New Updated Edition (FCA Incorporated); author interview with General Abat.

113. Mercado, "Culture, Economics, and Revolt," 161.

114. McKenna, *Muslim Rulers and Rebels*, 183.

115. Ibid., 24.

116. Author interview J, June 2006.

117. Che Man, *Muslim Separatism*, 84.

118. Tan, *Internationalization of the Bangsamoro Struggle*, 55–72.

119. Author interview H, June 2006.

120. Author interview C, June 2006.

121. For an account of the subsequent fighting from the perspective of the Philippine army commander in the region, see Abat, *Day We Nearly Lost Mindanao*.

122. Mercado, "Culture, Economics, and Revolt," 161–63.

123. Reprinted in Majul, *Contemporary Muslim Movement*, 117–19.

124. "Cultural Genocide in the Philippines," speech delivered by Nur Misuari, October 1997, in Alliance for Philippine National Democracy (UGNAYAN), *The Moro People's Struggle: Documents from the Moro National Liberation Front (MNLF)* (Detroit, MI: Cellar Book Shop, 1980); cf. McKenna, *Muslim Rulers and Rebels*, 164.

125. Tan, *Internationalization of the Bangsamoro Struggle*, 55–72.

3. The North-South War in Sudan

1. Elijah Malok, *The Southern Sudan: Struggle for Liberty* (Nairobi: Ujuzi Books, 2009), 124–28; John Garang, *John Garang Speaks*, ed. Mansour Khalid (London: KPI, 1987), 22.

2. Robert O. Collins, *A History of Modern Sudan* (Cambridge: Cambridge University Press, 2008), 19, 139–40.

3. On the terms of the Addis accords, see Collins, *History of Modern Sudan*, 137–40; 146–47. For warnings by southerners, see, e.g., interview with Joseph Oduho, in "Sudanese Rebel Radio Interviews with SPLM Leaders," BBC Summary of World Broadcasts, November 8, 1984, transcript from Radio SPLA in English 1300 gmt, November 3, 1984.

4. Randolph Martin, "Sudan's Perfect War," *Foreign Affairs* 81, no. 2 (March–April 2002): 111.

5. B. Yongo-Bure, "The Underdevelopment of the Southern Sudan since Independence," in *Civil War in the Sudan*, ed. M. W. Daly and Ahmad Alawad Sikainga (London: British Academic Press, 1993), 51, 67–68, 70, 75–76; Indexmundi.com.

6. Douglas H. Johnson, *Root Causes of Sudan's Civil Wars* (Oxford: James Currey, 2003), 45–46.

7. G. Norman Anderson, *Sudan in Crisis: The Failure of Democracy* (Gainesville: University Press of Florida, 1999), 38.

8. Collins, *History of Modern Sudan*, 4–8; Amir H. Idris, *Sudan's Civil War—Slavery, Race and Formational Identities* (Lewiston, NY: Edwin Mellen, 2001), 5–6.

9. A useful discussion is Ann Mosely Lesch, *The Sudan–Contested National Identities* (Bloomington: Indiana University Press, 1998); cf. Sharon Elaine Hutchinson, *Nuer Dilemmas: Coping with Money, War, and the State* (Berkeley: University of California Press, 1996).

10. Scopas S. Poggo, *The First Sudanese Civil War: Africans, Arabs, and Israelis in the Southern Sudan, 1955–1972* (New York: Palgrave Macmillan, 2009), 11–12.

11. Poggo, *First Sudanese Civil War*, 13–14, 119.

12. http://countrystudies.us/sudan/, retrieved March 2013.

13. Poggo, *First Sudanese Civil War*, 17; http://countrystudies.us/sudan/, retrieved March 2013.

14. Alex de Waal, "Who Are the Darfurians?" *African Affairs* 104, no. 415 (April 2005): 182–90; Johnson, *Root Causes of Sudan's Civil Wars*, xviii.

15. Collins, *History of Modern Sudan*, 6.

16. Francis M. Deng, *War of Visions: Conflict of Identities in the Sudan* (Washington, DC: Brookings Institution, 1995), 42, 69; Idris, *Sudan's Civil War*, 38.

17. Gabriel Warburg, *Islam, Sectarianism and Politics in Sudan since the Mahdiyya* (Madison: University of Wisconsin Press, 2003), 6.

18. Warburg, *Islam, Sectarianism and Politics in Sudan*, 38, 94–95.

19. Collins, *History of Modern Sudan*, 21–30.

20. Warburg, *Islam, Sectarianism and Politics in Sudan*, 111.

21. Collins, *History of Modern Sudan*, 35.

22. Ibid.; Deng, *War of Visions*, 92, 128–31; Poggo, *First Sudanese Civil War*, 34–36.

23. Poggo, *First Sudanese Civil War*, 34–39.

24. Ibid., 56, 131; Deng, *War of Visions*, 144.

25. Johnson, *Root Causes of Sudan's Civil Wars*, 35.

26. Poggo, *First Sudanese Civil War*, 172–73.

27. J. Millard Burr and Robert O. Collins, *Africa's Thirty Years' War: Libya, Chad, and the Sudan 1963–93* (Boulder, CO: Westview, 1999), 72.

28. Poggo, *First Sudanese Civil War*, 123, 158–60; Malok, *Southern Sudan*, 84; Donald Rothchild, *Managing Ethnic Conflict in Africa: Pressures and Incentives for Cooperation* (Washington, DC: Brookings, 1997); Bona Malwal, *The Sudan: A Second Challenge to Nationhood* (New York: Thornton Books, 1985), 11.

29. Deng, *War of Visions*, 5 and passim; Collins, *History of Modern Sudan*, 4–5; Ahmad Alawad Sikainga, "Northern Sudanese Political Parties and the Civil War," in Daly and Sikainga, *Civil War in the Sudan*, 78–96.

30. Makris is quoted in Idris, *Sudan's Civil War*, 43.

31. Deng, *War of Visions*, 4–5.

32. Idris, *Sudan's Civil War*.

33. Poggo, *First Sudanese Civil War*, 92.

34. Warburg, *Islam, Sectarianism and Politics*, 167.

35. Poggo, *First Sudanese Civil War*, 102.

36. Deng, *War of Visions*, 223.

37. Ibid., 226.

38. M. W. Daly, "Broken Bridge and Empty Basket: The Political and Economic Background of the Sudanese Civil War," in Daly and Sikainga, *Civil War in the Sudan*, 4.

39. Idris, *Sudan's Civil War*, 15–17, 113.

40. Quoted Poggo, *First Sudanese Civil War*, 36. Italics and translation as in the original.

41. Quoted Idris, *Sudan's Civil War*, 100.

42. Poggo, *First Sudanese Civil War*, 101.

43. Quoted in Sikainga, "Northern Sudanese Political Parties," 82.

44. Deng, *War of Visions*.

45. Quoted in Sikainga, "Northern Sudanese Political Parties," 83.

46. Warburg, *Islam, Sectarianism, and Politics in Sudan*, 145–48.

47. Deng, *War of Visions*, 70–75.

48. Ibid., 70.

49. Ibid., 70, 73.

50. Idris, *Sudan's Civil War*, 24; cf. Warburg, *Islam, Sectarianism and Politics*, 140; Catherine Jendia, *The Sudanese Civil Conflict 1969–85* (New York: Peter Lang, 2002), 27, 39.

51. Deng, *War of Visions*, 224.

52. Quoted in ibid., 261.

53. Poggo, *First Sudanese Civil War*, 70.

54. Malok, *Southern Sudan*, 123–24.

55. Poggo, *First Sudanese Civil War*, 93–101.

56. Ibid., 45–53, 75–76, 83–88; Deng, *War of Visions*, 137–43.

57. Hutchinson, *Nuer Dilemmas*, 9, 133.

58. Deng, *War of Visions*, 145–46.

59. Poggo, *First Sudanese Civil War*, 119–21, 135, 139–43; Malok, *Southern Sudan*.

60. Quoted in Deng, *War of Visions*, 195.

61. Deng, *War of Visions*, 226–27.

62. Collins, *History of Modern Sudan*, 153.

63. Abdelwahab El-Affendi, *Turabi's Revolution: Islam and Power in Sudan* (London: Grey Seal, 1991), 104–7, 121–22.

64. Ibid., 122.

65. Deng, *War of Visions*, 170.

66. "The Address of H. E. Jaafer Mohamed Nimeiri, President of the Sudanese Socialist Union at the Opening Session of the Central Committee Meetings" (Khartoum: Sudanese Socialist Union, Central Committee, 1981), 7.

67. "Numayri's 22nd February Address to People's Assembly: Unity in the South," BBC Summary of World Broadcasts, February 25, 1982, Thursday SOURCE: Sudan News Agency 1450 gmt, February 22, 1982, Excerpts from dispatch datelined Khartoum, February 22, Section: Part 4 The Middle East and Africa; A. The Middle East; ME/6963/A/1.

68. Affendi, *Turabi's Revolution*, 121.

69. Lesch, *Sudan*, 49–55.

70. Affendi, *Turabi's Revolution*, 191, 124; cf. Lesch, *Sudan*.

71. Foreign Broadcast Information Service Daily Report: Middle East and Africa (hereinafter abbreviated FBIS), October 13, 1983, Q3; and FBIS, October 17, 1983, Q2.

72. "Numayri's Address to New Sudanese Cabinet," BBC Summary of World Broadcasts May 8, 1984, SOURCE: Sudan News Agency 1415 gmt, May 6, 1984, text of dispatch datelined Khartoum, May 6, Section: Part 4 The Middle East, Africa and Latin America; A. The Middle East; ME/7637/A/1.

73. T. Abdou Maliqalim Simone, *In Whose Image? Political Islam and Urban Practices in Sudan* (Chicago: University of Chicago Press, 1994), 26.

74. Collins, *History of Modern Sudan*, 146–47.

75. Warburg, *Islam, Sectarianism and Politics in Sudan*, 154.

76. Collins, *History of Modern Sudan*.

77. Sikainga, "Northern Sudanese Political Parties," 80.

78. Malwal, *Sudan*, 32.

79. Collins, *History of Modern Sudan*, 145; Warburg, *Islam, Sectarianism and Politics in Sudan*, 155.

80. Affendi, *Turabi's Revolution*, 113–20.

81. Collins, *History of Modern Sudan*, 146.

82. Affendi, *Turabi's Revolution*, 121; Abdel Salam Sidahmed, *Politics and Islam in Contemporary Sudan* (Richmond, UK: Curzon Press, 1997), 120–34.

83. Collins, *History of Modern Sudan*, 127–31; Affendi, *Turabi's Revolution*, 120.

84. Collins, *History of Modern Sudan*, 141.

85. Malwal, *Sudan*; Malok, *Southern Sudan*, 96, 107.

86. Jendia, *Sudanese Civil Conflict*, 102; Malok, *Southern Sudan*, 96; Collins, *History of Modern Sudan*, 133.

87. Collins, *History of Modern Sudan*, 134–36; Malwal, *Sudan*, 31; Malok, *Southern Sudan*, 97.

88. Deng, *War of Visions*, 178, 124, 184.

89. Affendi, *Turabi's Revolution*, 121–23, 126–27.

90. Ibid., 191, 124; cf. Lesch, *Sudan*.

91. Lesch, *Sudan*.

92. Malok, *Southern Sudan*, 157.

93. Affendi, *Turabi's Revolution*, 124.

94. FBIS April 15, 1985, Q8; FBIS April 19, 1985, Q8.

95. Abdelwahab El-Affendi, " 'Discovering the South': Sudanese Dilemmas for Islam in Africa," *African Affairs*, no. 356, July 1990, 384.

96. FBIS April 17, 1985, Q7; and, e.g., FBIS May 16, 1985, Q3.

97. FBIS April 18, 1985, Q5; FBIS May 2, 1985, Q6–7.

98. Lesch, *Sudan*, 42–43, 66–72.

99. FBIS May 9, 1985, Q4.

100. FBIS April 19, 1985, Q8; FBIS May 2, 1985, Q7.

101. FBIS May 13, 1985, Q8–Q9.

102. John Garang, *The Call for Democracy in Sudan* (London: Kegan Paul International, 1992), 143.

103. Collins, *History of Modern Sudan*, 165–66.

104. Ibid., 166–68.

105. Lesch, *Sudan*, 82; Johnson, *Root Causes*, 84.

106. Kamal Osman Salih, "The Sudan, 1985–89: The Fading Democracy," *Journal of Modern African Studies* 28, no. 2 (June 1990): 218.

107. Collins, *History of Modern Sudan*, 170.

108. Douglas A. Johnson and Gerard Prunier, "The Foundation and Expansion of the Sudan People's Liberation Army," in Daly and Sikainga, *Civil War in the Sudan*, 121–22.

109. Malok, *Southern Sudan*, 143; Collins, *History of Modern Sudan*, 140.

110. Randall Fegley, *Beyond Khartoum: A History of Subnational Government in Sudan* (Trenton, NJ: Red Sea Press, 2011), 55; Collins, *History of Modern Sudan*, 6.

111. Collins, *History of Modern Sudan*, 139.

112. Johnson and Prunier, "Sudan People's Liberation Army," in Daly and Sikainga, *Civil War in the Sudan*, 126.

113. Malok, *Southern Sudan*, 144–55.

114. Johnson and Prunier, "Sudan People's Liberation Army," 127–35.

115. Garang, *Call for Democracy in Sudan*, 26–30.

116. Ibid., 20, 23.

117. Interview with Joseph Oduho, in "Sudanese Rebel Radio Interviews with SPLM Leaders," BBC Summary of World Broadcasts, November 8, 1984, transcript from Radio SPLA in English 1300 gmt, November 3, 1984.

118. Garang, *Call for Democracy in Sudan*, 124.

119. Ibid., 25–26, 36.

120. Ibid., 134. For a similar statement by Oduho, see BBC Summary of World Broadcasts, November 8, 1984.

121. Interview with Kerubino Kuanyin Bol, in "Sudanese Rebel Radio Interviews with SPLM Leaders," BBC Summary of World Broadcasts, November 8, 1984, transcript from Radio SPLA in English 1300 gmt, November 2, 1984, Section: Part 4 The Middle East, Africa and Latin America; A. The Middle East; ME/7795/A/1.

122. Garang, *Call for Democracy in Sudan*, 130–32.

123. See, e.g., FBIS April 11, 1985, Q2; cf. Carolyn Fluehr-Lobban, "Islamization in Sudan: A Critical Assessment," in *Sudan: State and Society in Crisis*, ed. John O. Voll (Bloomington: Indiana University Press, 1991), 71.

124. Steven K. Hindy, "New Islamic Laws Alarm Non-Moslems in Sudan," Associated Press, Khartoum, December 19, 1983, Monday, AM cycle.

125. Interview with Oduho, BBC Summary of World Broadcasts, November 8, 1984.

126. Garang, *Call for Democracy in Sudan*, 27.

127. Interview with Kerubino Kuanyin Bol, BBC Summary of World Broadcasts, November 8, 1984.

128. Peter Adwok Nyaba, *The Politics of Liberation in South Sudan: An Insider's View* (Kampala, Uganda: Fountain Publishers, 1997), 32.

129. Garang, *John Garang Speaks*, 24–27. It is notable that the Koka Dam Declaration (in ibid., 145), incorporates most of Garang's language and themes.

130. Jack Snyder and Robert Jervis, "Civil War and the Security Dilemma," in *Civil Wars, Insecurity, and Intervention*, ed. Barbara Walter and Jack Snyder (New York: Columbia University Press, 1999), 16, 21.

131. See, e.g., Garang, *John Garang Speaks*, 27.

132. Lesch, *Sudan*, 49.

133. Quoted in Deng, *War of Visions*, 154.

4. Ethnic War and Genocide in Rwanda

1. Three excellent sources are Gerard Prunier, *The Rwanda Crisis: History of a Genocide* (New York: Columbia University Press, 1995); Johan Pottier, *Re-Imagining Rwanda: Conflict, Survival and Disinformation in the Late Twentieth Century* (Cambridge: Cambridge University Press, 2002); and Mahmood Mamdani, *When Victims Become Killers: Colonialism, Nativism, and the Genocide in Rwanda* (Princeton, NJ: Princeton University Press, 2001).

2. James D. Fearon and David D. Laitin, "Ethnicity, Insurgency, and Civil War," *American Political Science Review* 97, no. 1 (2003): 75–90.

3. Rui J. P. de Figueiredo and Barry Weingast, "The Rationality of Fear: Political Opportunism and Ethnic Conflict," in *Civil Wars, Insecurity, and Intervention*, ed. Barbara F. Walter and Jack Snyder (New York: Columbia University Press, 1999), 261–302; Benjamin A. Valentino, *Final Solutions: Mass Killing and Genocide in the 20th Century* (Ithaca: Cornell University Press, 2004).

4. Lee Ann Fuji, *Killing Neighbors: Webs of Violence in Rwanda* (Ithaca: Cornell University Press, 2009), 101.

5. Aimable Twagilimana, *The Debris of Ham: Ethnicity, Regionalism, and the 1994 Rwandan Genocide* (Lanham, MD: University Press of America, 2003), 53.

6. Rene Lemarchand, *Rwanda and Burundi* (New York: Praeger, 1970) 19–20.

7. Pottier, *Re-Imagining Rwanda*, 13.

8. Lemarchand, *Rwanda and Burundi*, 25–26.

9. Ibid., 22–27, 37, 42, 62.

10. Pottier, *Re-Imagining Rwanda*, 13.

11. Prunier, *Rwanda Crisis*, 33.

12. This and the following paragraphs are based on Lemarchand, *Rwanda and Burundi*, 79, 84, 106–8, 114, 158–98, 216, 223–24.

13. Peter Uvin, "Prejudice, Crisis, and Genocide in Rwanda," *African Studies Review* 40, no. 2 (September 1997): 96.

14. Stephen Weissman, quoted in Rene Lemarchand, *Dynamics of Violence in Central Africa* (Philadelphia: University of Pennsylvania Press, 2009), 71.

15. Twagilimana, *Debris of Ham*, 80–81.

16. Pottier, *Re-Imagining Rwanda*, 23.

17. Phillip Verwimp, "Peasant Ideology and Genocide in Rwanda Under Habyarimana," in *Genocide in Cambodia and Rwanda: New Perspectives*, ed. Susan E. Cook (Transaction Publishers, 2006), 18; Paul J. Magnarella, "The Hutu-Tutsi Conflict in Rwanda," in *Perspectives on Contemporary Ethnic Conflict: Primal Violence or the Politics of Conviction?*, ed. Santosh C. Saha (Lanham, MD: Lexington Books, 2006), 118.

18. Jan Vansina, *Antecedents to Modern Rwanda: The Nyiginya Kingdom* (Madison: University of Wisconsin Press, 2004), 37.

19. Lemarchand, *Rwanda and Burundi*, 33, 43; Lemarchand, *Dynamics of Violence*, 53.

20. Quoted in Twagilimana, *Debris of Ham*, 65.

21. Ibid., 37–38.

22. Mamdani, *When Victims Become Killers*, 90.

23. Lemarchand, *Rwanda and Burundi*, 32–33.

24. Prunier, *Rwanda Crisis*, 47.

25. Twagilimana, *Debris of Ham*, xxiv, 48.

26. Quoted in Prunier, *Rwanda Crisis*, 11.

27. Twagilimana, *Debris of Ham*, 53.

28. Prunier, *Rwanda Crisis*, 38.

29. Pottier, *Re-Imagining Rwanda*, 110.

30. Prunier, *Rwanda Crisis*, 80, 45.

31. Quoted in Lemarchand, *Rwanda and Burundi*, 223–34, 285.

32. Prunier, *Rwanda Crisis*, 56–62; Lemarchand, *Rwanda and Burundi*.

33. Quoted in Marcel Kabanda, "Kangura: The Triumph of Propaganda Refined," in *The Media and the Rwanda Genocide*, ed. Allan Thompson (Ottawa: International Development Research Centre, 2007), 70.

34. Ibid.

35. Verwimp, "Peasant Ideology," 16–20.

36. Joan Kakwenzire and Dixon Kamukama, "The Development and Consolidation of Extremist Forces in Rwanda 1990–94," in *The Path of a Genocide: The Rwanda Crisis from Uganda to Zaire*, ed. Howard Adelman and Astri Suhrke (New Brunswick, NJ: Transaction Publishers, 1999), 72.

37. Aaron Phillip Karnell, "The Role of Radio in the Genocide of Rwanda" (PhD diss., University of Kentucky, 2003), 175–76.

38. Quoted in Mamdani, *When Victims Become Killers*, 199.

39. Omar McDoom, "The Micro-Politics of Mass Violence: Authority, Security and Opportunity in Rwanda's Genocide" (PhD diss., London School of Economics, 2008), 68.

40. Twagilimana, *Debris of Ham*, 101.

41. This and the following quotations are from Jean Hatzfeld, *Machete Season: The Killers in Rwanda Speak* (New York: Farrar, Straus and Giroux, 2005), 216–18.

42. McDoom, "Micro-Politics of Mass Violence," 176.

43. Hatzfeld, *Machete Season*, 216–18.

44. Stanley Milgram, *Obedience to Authority: An Experimental View* (New York: Harper and Row, 1974).

45. Prunier, *Rwanda Crisis*, 70–73; Mamdani, *When Victims Become Killers*, 173, 182.

46. Uvin, "Prejudice, Crisis and Genocide," 98.

47. Lemarchand, *Rwanda and Burundi*, 256.

48. Omar McDoom, "Why Men Kill: The Microfoundations of Ethnic Radicalization and Extremism: Insights from Rwanda" (paper presented at International Studies Association Convention, March 2007); cf. Scott Straus, *The Order of Genocide* (Ithaca: Cornell University Press, 2006).

49. Mamdani, *When Victims Become Killers*.

50. Prunier, *Rwanda Crisis*, 116–17.

51. Colin M. Waugh, *Paul Kagame and Rwanda: Power, Genocide and the Rwandan Patriotic Front* (Jefferson, NC: Mcfarland and Company, 2004), 52.

52. On the absence of looting, see Mamdani, *When Victims Become Killers*, 187. On Kagame's charisma, see Bruce D. Jones, *Peacemaking in Rwanda: The Dynamics of Failure* (Boulder, CO: Lynne Rienner, 2001), 30.

53. Lemarchand, *Dynamics of Violence*, 81.

54. The narrative in this paragraph is from Prunier, *Rwanda Crisis*, 93–113; and Mamdani, *When Victims Become Killers*, 183–87.

55. Prunier, *Rwanda Crisis*, 85–87.

56. Twagilimana, *Debris of Ham*, 91.

57. The next two paragraphs are based on the accounts in Uvin, "Prejudice, Crisis and Genocide," 106–8; and Prunier, *Rwanda Crisis*, 84–97.

58. Twagilimana, *Debris of Ham*, 165.

59. Andrew Wallis, *Silent Accomplice: The Untold Story of France's Role in the Rwandan Genocide* (London: I. B. Tauris, 2006).

60. Prunier, *Rwanda Crisis*, 136; Twagilimana, *Debris of Ham*, 93.

61. Twagilimana, *Debris of Ham*, 102–3.

62. The previous paragraphs are based Prunier, *Rwanda Crisis*, 129–50, 168–88.

63. Allison Des Forges for Human Rights Watch, *Leave None to Tell the Story: Genocide in Rwanda* (New York: Human Rights Watch, 1999), 109–10.

64. Prunier, *Rwanda Crisis*, 174–80, 186–92, 200.

65. Twagilimana, *Debris of Ham*, 140.

66. Prunier, *Rwanda Crisis*, 203–4, 211–12.

67. Twagilimana, *Debris of Ham*, 99–100.

68. Des Forges, *Leave None to Tell*, 77.

69. Karnell, "Role of Radio," 188–89.

70. Twagilimana, *Debris of Ham*, 96.

71. Ibid., 105–6.

72. Frank Chalk, "Hate Radio in Rwanda," in *The Path of Genocide: The Rwanda Crisis from Uganda to Zaire*, ed. Howard Adelman and Astri Suhrke (New Brunswick, NJ: Transaction Publishers, 1999), 95.

73. Prunier, *Rwanda Crisis*, 189.

74. Twagilimana, *Debris of Ham*, 96.

75. RTLMC transcript 162.45, June 14, 1994, as published in Jean-Pierre Chretien, *Les Medias du Genocide* (Paris: Karthala, 1995), trans. Nathalie Ricci-Whaley.

76. Prunier, *Rwanda Crisis*, 200–201.

77. McDoom, "Micro-Politics of Mass Violence," 111–12, 117.

78. Chalk, "Hate Radio in Rwanda," 95–99; cf. Karnell, "Role of Radio."

79. Prunier, *Rwanda Crisis*, 200–201.

80. Quoted in African Rights, *Rwanda: Death, Despair and Defiance* (London: African Rights, 1994), 572.

81. Straus, *Order of Genocide*, 159, emphasis added.

82. McDoom, "Micro-Politics of Mass Violence," 117.

83. Quoted in Mamdani, *When Victims Become Killers*, 191; cf. Jones, *Peacemaking in Rwanda*, 40.

84. The quotations in this section are from Hatzfeld, *Machete Season*, 58–59, 132, 219–20.

85. Straus, *Order of Genocide*, 9 and passim.

86. Prunier, *Rwanda Crisis*, 200.

87. Des Forges, *Leave None to Tell*, 97–100, 127.

88. Prunier, *Rwanda Crisis*, 185; Des Forges, *Leave None to Tell*, 113.

89. Des Forges, *Leave None to Tell*, 87.

90. Prunier, *Rwanda Crisis*, 74.

91. Republic of Rwanda, "Committee of Experts Investigation of the April 7, 1994 Crash of President Habyarimana's Dassault Falcon—50 Aircraft, Media Guide," January 2010, 3 and passim. Bagosora's title is reported in Twagilimana, *Debris of Ham*, 123.

92. Des Forges, *Leave None to Tell the Story*, 8, 223; Jones, *Peacemaking in Rwanda*, 39.

93. Prunier, *Rwanda Crisis,* 268.

94. Ibid.,113; Jones, *Peacemaking in Rwanda*, 30–33; cf. Mamdani, *When Victims Become Killers*, 206–7.

95. Mamdani, *When Victims Become Killers*, 215.

96. Arguments for this thesis include Josias Semujanga, *Origins of the Rwandan Genocide* (Amherst, NY: Humanity Books, 2003); Twagilimana, *Debris of Ham*; and Uvin, "Prejudice, Crisis, and Genocide."

97. Prunier, *Rwanda Crisis*, 142.

98. On "blowback," see Jack Snyder, *Myths of Empire: Domestic Politics and International Ambition* (Ithaca: Cornell University Press, 1990). On akazu views of their own propaganda, see Mamdani, *When Victims Become Killers*, 207.

99. Des Forges, *Leave None to Tell*, 8, 225.

100. Ibid., 83–84; Prunier, *Rwanda Crisis*, 137–38.

101. David A. Lake and Donald Rothchild, "Spreading Fear: The Genesis of Transnational Ethnic Conflict," in *The International Spread of Ethnic Conflict*, ed. Lake and Rothchild (Princeton, NJ: Princeton University Press, 1998), 19.

102. McDoom, "Micro-Politics of Mass Violence," 158, 160.

103. Ibid., 158.

104. Ibid.; cf. Fuji, *Killing Neighbors*.

105. Straus, *Order of Genocide*, 61.

106. Prunier, *Rwanda Crisis*, 247.

107. Bruce D. Jones, "Military Intervention in Rwanda's 'Two Wars': Partisanship and Indifference," in *Civil Wars, Insecurity, and Intervention*, ed. Barbara Walter and Jack Snyder (New York: Columbia University Press, 1999), 116–17.

108. Benjamin A. Valentino, *Final Solutions: Mass Killing and Genocide in the 20th Century* (Ithaca: Cornell University Press, 2004), 186.

109. De Figueiredo and Weingast, "Rationality of Fear," 282. I refute their argument more specifically in Kaufman, "Symbolic Politics or Rational Choice?"

5. Gandhi's Nonviolence, Communal Conflict, and the Salt March

1. David Arnold, *Gandhi: Profiles in Power* (Harlow, UK: Longman, 2001).

2. Gitika Commuri, *Indian Identity Narratives and the Politics of Security* (New Delhi: Sage, 2010); Jawaharlal Nehru, *The Discovery of India* (New York: Day, 1946).

3. Sumit Sarkar, *Modern India: 1885–1947* (New York: St. Martin's Press, 1989), 151.

4. Ibid., 53–54, 156.

5. Ibid., 148–53.

6. See Kerry Brown, *The Essential Teachings of Hinduism* (London: Rider, 1988).

7. Milton B. Singer, *Krishna: Myths, Rites, and Attitudes* (Chicago: University of Chicago Press, 1971); Lionel D. Barnett, *Hindu Gods and Heroes* (New York: Hesperides Press, 2006).

8. Eknath Easwaran, *The Bhagavad Gita: A Classic of Hindu Spirituality* (Berkeley, CA: Nilgiri Press, 2007).

9. George Feuerstein and Ken Wilbur, *The Yoga Tradition: Its History, Literature, Philosophy and Practice* (New Delhi: Motilal Banarsidass, 2002).

10. K. R. Sundararajan and Bithika Mukerj, *Hindu Spirituality: Post Classical and Modern* (New York: Crossroad, 2003).

11. Arnold, *Gandhi*, 63.

12. Tomara I. Sears, *Worldly Gurus and Spiritual Kings: Architecture and Asceticism in Medieval India* (New Haven, CT: Yale University Press, 2014), 35–35.

13. Chakravarti Rajagopalachari, *Mahabharata* (Mumbai: Bharatiya Vidya Bhavan, 1976).

14. Albert Schweitzer, *The Teaching of Reverence for Life* (New York: Henry Holt, 1965).

15. Malavika Vartak, "Shivaji Maharaj: Growth of a Symbol," *Economic and Political Weekly* 34 (1999): 1126–34.

16. William Roy Smith, *Nationalism and Reform in India* (New Haven, CT: Yale University Press, 1983), 49–50.

17. Clare Anderson, *The Indian Uprising of 1857–8: Prisons, Prisoners and Rebellion* (London: Anthem Press, 2007); K. C. Yadav, *Mohammad Ali Khan: An Autobiographical Discourse* (Delhi: Hope India Publications, 2008).

18. Rajat Kanta Ray, *The Felt Community: Commonalty and Mentality before the Emergence of Indian Nationalism* (Oxford: Oxford University Press, 2003), 467.

19. C. J. Ferguson-Davie, "Communal Trouble in India," *Times* (London), April 15, 1929.

20. S. Balaram, "Product Symbolism of Gandhi and Its Connection with Indian Mythology," *Design Issues* 5 (1989): 68–85; Peter Gottschalk, *Beyond Hindu and Muslim: Multiple Identity in Narratives from Village India* (New York: Oxford University Press, 2000).

21. Arnold, *Gandhi*, 87, 97–99.

22. *Times* (London), March 28, 1921; see also Victor A. G. R. Lytton, "Hindu-Moslem Unity," *Annals of the American Academy of Political and Social Science* 145, pt. 2 (1929): 175–80, 176–77.

23. David Hardiman, "Purifying the Nation: The Arya Samaj in Gujarat 1895–1930," *Indian Economic and Social History Review*, 44, no. 1 (2007): 48.

24. *The Collected Works of Mahatma Gandhi* (Electronic Book) (New Delhi, Publications Division Government of India, 1999, 98 vols.), vol. 28, p. 49. Hereinafter cited as Gandhi, *Collected Works*.

25. *Times* (India), March 31, 1924.

26. *Times* (India), February 14, 1929.

27. Hardiman, "Purifying the Nation," 43, 47.

28. Peter van der Veer, *Religious Nationalism: Hindus and Muslims in India* (Berkeley: University of California Press, 1994), 10.

29. Mushirul Hasan, "Pan-Islamism versus Indian Nationalism? A Reappraisal," *Economic and Political Weekly* 21, no. 24 (June 14, 1986): 1074–79, p. 1076.

30. Quoted in Commuri, *Indian Identity Narratives*, 64.

31. Ray, *Felt Community*, 528.

32. Angus Stewart Woodburne, "The Present Religious Situation in India," *Journal of Religion* 3, no. 4 (1923): 387–97, 390.

33. Lytton, "Hindu-Moslem Unity," 176.

34. *Times* (India), March 31, 1924.

35. W. Crooke, "The Veneration of the Cow in India," *Folklore* 23, no. 3 (September 1912): 278.

36. *Times* (India), January 1, 1929.

37. *Times* (India), June 1, 1923.

38. *Times* (India), January 30, 1924.

39. *Times* (India), December 31, 1929.

40. *Times* (India), January 1, 1929.

41. Sheila McDonough, *Gandhi's Response to Islam* (New Delhi: D. K. Printworld, 1994), 37. In contemporary Indian politics, elites often appeal to many of the symbolic predispositions and fears cited here to stoke communal violence between Hindus and Muslims. See Paul. R. Brass, *Theft of an Idol: Text and Context in the Representation of Collective Violence* (Princeton: Princeton University Press, 1997); Paul. R. Brass, *The Production of Hindu-Muslim Violence in Contemporary India* (Seattle: University of Washington Press, 2003); and Ashutosh Varshney, *Ethnic Conflict and Civic Life: Hindus and Muslims in India* (New Haven, CT: Yale University Press, 2003).

42. Kathryn Tidrick, *Gandhi: A Political and Spiritual Life* (New York: IB Tauris, 2006), 97–103.

43. Gopal Das Khosla, *Tales of Love and War from the Mahabharat: Stories from the Mahabharat* (New York: Oxford University Press, 1994); Thomas Weber, *Gandhi as Disciple and Mentor* (Cambridge: Cambridge University Press, 2004).

44. R. K. Prabhu and U. R. Rao, *The Mind of Mahatma Gandhi* (Ahmedabad: Navajivan, Pub. House, 1967).

45. Mohandas K. Gandhi, *The Bhagavad Gita According to Gandhi* (Berkeley, CA: North Atlantic Books, 2009).

46. Erik H. Erikson, *Gandhi's Truth: On the Origins of Militant Nonviolence* (New York: W. W. Norton, 1993).

47. Balaram, "Product Symbolism of Gandhi," 72–73.

48. Tidrick, *Gandhi*, 97.

49. Balaram, "Product Symbolism of Gandhi," 72–73.

50. Tidrick, *Gandhi*, 103.

51. Balaram, "Product Symbolism of Gandhi"; Gottschalk, *Beyond Hindu and Muslim*.

52. Karl H. Potter, "Explorations in Gandhi's Theory of Nonviolence," in *The Meanings of Gandhi*, ed. Paul F. Power (Honolulu: University Press of Hawaii, 1971), 91–117; Amrut Nakhre, "Meanings of Nonviolence: A Study of Satyagrahi Attitudes," *Journal of Peace Research* 13, no. 3 (1976): 185–96.

53. Nakhre, "Meanings of Nonviolence," 191.

54. Mohandas K. Gandhi, *The Economics of Khadi* (Ahmedabad: Navajiva Press, 1941); Ainslie T. Embree, "The Function of Gandhi in Indian Nationalism" in *The Meanings of Gandhi*, ed. Paul F. Power (Honolulu: University Press of Hawaii, 1971), 59–76; Susan S. Bean, "Gandhi and Khadi: The Fabric of Indian Independence," in *Cloth and Human Experience*, ed. Annette B. Weiner and Jane Schneider (Washington, DC: Smithsonian, 1989), 355–76; Buddhadeva Bhattacharyya, *Evolution of the Political Philosophy of Gandhi* (Calcutta: Calcutta Book House, 1969).

55. Louis Fischer, *The Life of Mahatma Gandhi* (New York: Harper and Row, 1962), 69.

56. Embree, "Function of Gandhi."

57. Balaram, "Product Symbolism of Gandhi," 83.

58. J. T. F. Jordens, *Gandhi's Religion: A Homespun Shawl* (London: Macmillan, 1998).

59. Romesh Dutt, *The Economic History of India under Early British Rule* (New York: Routledge, 2001).

60. Shiri Ram Bakshi, *Gandhi and Civil Disobedience Movement* (New Delhi: South Asia Books, 1986).

61. Arnold, *Gandhi*, 83–88; Yogesh Chadha, *Rediscovering Gandhi* (London: Century Books, 1997), 218–25.

62. Sarkar, *Modern India*, 183.

63. Tidrick, *Gandhi*, 121.

64. Arnold, *Gandhi*, 89.

65. Tidrick, *Gandhi*, 124.

66. Sarkar, *Modern India*, 187–88.

67. Ibid., 191–93; Arnold, *Gandhi*, 111.

68. *The Collected Works of Mahatma Gandhi* (Electronic Book), New Delhi, Publications Division Government of India, 1999, 98 vols.; Mohandas K . Gandhi, *Collected Works* (New Delhi: Publications Division, 1971), 184–85.

69. Arnold, *Gandhi*.

70. Tidrick, *Gandhi*, 144–45, 161–62.

71. Arnold, *Gandhi*, 121.

72. Ibid., 120–21.

73. Jaswant Singh, *Jinnah: India—Partition—Independence* (Oxford: Oxford University Press, 2010), 95.

74. Roland E. Miller, "Indian Muslim Critiques of Gandhi," in *Indian Critiques of Gandhi*, ed. Harold Coward (Albany: State University of New York Press, 2003), 211.

75. Akbar S. Ahmed, *Jinnah, Pakistan, and Islamic Identity: The Search for Saladin* (London: Routledge, 1997), 100.

76. Ibid., 100–102.

77. Ibid., 66.

78. Fred Dallmayr, "Gandhi and Islam: A Heart-and-Mind Unity?" in *History of Science, Philosophy, and Culture in Indian Civilization*, vol. 10, pt. 7: *Political Ideas in Modern India: Thematic Expressions*, ed. Vrajendra Raj Mehta and Thomas Pantham (New Delhi: Sage, 1994), 211.

79. Ahmed, *Jinnah, Pakistan, and Islamic Identity*, 104.

80. Cited in ibid., 103–4.

81. Arnold, *Gandhi*, 124.

82. Roland E. Miller, "Indian Muslim Critiques of Gandhi," in *Indian Critiques of Gandhi*, ed. Harold Coward (Albany: State University of New York Press, 2003), 203–4.

83. Dallmayr, "Gandhi and Islam," 212.

84. Tidrick, *Gandhi*, 176–80.

85. Ibid., 179.

86. McDonough, *Gandhi's Response to Islam*, 43; Roland E. Miller, *The Mapila Muslims of Kerala* (Madras: Orient Longman, 1992), 130.

87. Miller, "Indian Muslim Critiques of Gandhi," 210.

88. *Times* (India), August 23, 1923.

89. T. C. A. Raghavan, "Origins and Development of Hindu Mahasabha Ideology: The Call of V D Savarkar and Bhai Parmanand," *Economic and Weekly Review* 18, no. 5 (1983): 595–600.

90. Gordon, Richard, "The Hindu Mahasabha and the Indian National Congress, 1915–26," *Modern Asian Studies* 9, no. 2 (1975): 145–203, 169.

91. Singh, *Jinnah*, 103.

92. S. R. Bakshi, *Gandhi and Civil Disobedience Movement* (New Delhi: South Asia Books, 1986), 98.

93. Singh, *Jinnah*, 112–42; Sandhya Chaudhuri, *Gandhi and the Partition of India* (New Delhi: Sterling Publishers, 1984) 17–20.

94. Tidrick, *Gandhi*, 211, 219.

95. Mushirul Hasan, "Communal and Revivalist Trends in Congress," *Social Scientist* 8, no. 7 (1980): 52–66, 60.

96. Quoted in Tidrick, *Gandhi*, 221.

97. Gandhi, *Collected Works*, vol. 43, pp. 181, 297, 525. .

98. Tidrick, *Gandhi*, 219–20.

99. Arnold, *Gandhi*, 129, 139–40.

100. Tidrick, *Gandhi*, 216–17.

101. Ibid., 222–24.

102. Gandhi, *Collected Works*, vol. 43, pp. 84, 182.

103. Ibid., 60, 79, 141, 182–83, 162.

104. Ibid., 213, 218.

105. Sarkar, *Modern India*, 289.

106. Ibid., 222, 293, 304.

107. Ibid., 297–99.

108. Rao B. Shiva, *India's Freedom Movement: Some Notable Figures* (New Delhi: Orient Longman, 1972), 248.

109. Martin Green, *Gandhi: Voice of a New Age Revolution* (New York: Continuum, 1993), 314.

110. Sarkar, *Modern India*, 288.

111. Ibid., 291, 298, 300.

112. Ibid., 284.

113. Mohandas K. Gandhi, *Collected Works*, vol. 18 (New Delhi: Publications Division, 1971), 351.

114. Arnold, *Gandhi*, 144.

115. Green, *Gandhi*, 293; Tidrick, *Gandhi*, 205–6.

116. Dennis Dalton, *Mahatma Gandhi: Nonviolent Power in Action* (New York: Columbia University Press, 2001), 105.

117. Chadha, *Rediscovering Gandhi*, 291–92.

118. Dalton, *Mahatma Gandhi*, 108–11.

119. Arnold, *Gandhi*, 147.

120. Dalton, *Mahatma Gandhi*, 101.

121. Tidrick, *Gandhi*, 230.

122. Rajhoman Gandhi, *Gandhi: The Man, His People, and the Empire* (Berkeley: University of California Press, 2008), 313–15.

123. Webb Miller and Roy W. Howard, *I Found No Peace: The Journal of a Foreign Correspondent* (New York: Simon and Schuster, 1936), 192.

124. Gandhi, *Gandhi*, 315.

125. Ibid., 193.

126. Gandhi, *Collected Works*, vol. 18, 142.

127. Miller and Howard, *I Found No Peace*; Tidrick, *Gandhi*, 233.

128. Ray, *Felt Community*, 466.

129. Ibid., 528.
130. Tidrick, *Gandhi*, 106–7
131. Gandhi, *Collected Works*, vol. 43, 399–400.

6. The End of Apartheid in South Africa

1. Patti Waldmeir, *Anatomy of a Miracle: The End of Apartheid and the Birth of the New South Africa* (New York: W. W. Norton, 1997).
2. I detail the argument for calling this a civil war in Stuart J. Kaufman, "The Violent Death of Apartheid: South Africa's Civil War, 1985–1996" (paper presented at Political Studies Association conference, London, England, April 20, 2011).
3. Calculated from midyear estimates by Statistics South Africa, news release P0302, retrieved from http://www.nda.agric.za/docs/abstract04/Population.pdf, August 8, 2014.
4. Hermann Giliomee, *The Afrikaners: Biography of a People* (Charlottesville: University of Virginia Press, 2009); Roger B. Beck, *The History of South Africa* (Westport, CT: Greenwood Press, 2000).
5. P. Eric Louw, *The Rise, Fall and Legacy of Apartheid* (Westport, CT: Praeger, 2004), 44–50.
6. South African Defence Force Nodal Point (SADF 1994), "Submission IRO the Former SADF: South African Defence Force Involvement in the Internal Security Situation in the Republic of South Africa" (document submitted to TRC, accessed at University of Witwatersrand, Historical Documents Collection, Kairos Documents Accession #AG2918, file no. 4.3.1.2).
7. Kaufman, "Violent Death of Apartheid."
8. F. W. de Klerk, *The Last Trek: A New Beginning* (London: Pan Macmillan, 1999).
9. J. Tengo Jabavu, "The South African Races Congress: Inaugural Address by J Tengo Jabavu, President, South African Races Congress" (1912), retrieved at http://www.anc.org.za/show.php?id=4346, July 22, 2012.
10. Nelson R. Mandela, "Nelson Mandela's Statement from the Dock at the Opening of the Defence Case in the Rivonia Trial" (1964), retrieved at http://www.anc.org.za/show.php?id=3430, July 22, 2012.
11. Ibid.
12. "Music, Laughter and Tears on Tutu's Triumphal Sunday," *Sydney Morning Herald*, September 9, 1986, 6.
13. Ben Turok, ed., *Readings in the ANC Tradition*, vol. 1: *Policy and Praxis* (Auckland Park, South Africa: Jacana, 2011), 99, 102.
14. Oliver R. Tambo, *Preparing for Power: Oliver Tambo Speaks*, compiled by Adelaide Tambo (London: Heinemann 1987), 94.
15. Howard Barrell, "Conscripts to Their Age: African National Congress Operational Strategy, 1976–1986," (PhD diss., St. Antony's College, Oxford, 1993), 314.
16. Joe Slovo, " 'Reforms' and Revolution in South Africa," *Sechaba* (February 1985): 3–11.
17. Oliver R. Tambo, "Render South Africa Ungovernable, President O.R. Tambo's Message Delivered in Lusaka on January 8, 1985," *Sechaba* (March 1985): 12.
18. "We Are Revolutionaries, Internationalists and Africans," unsigned editorial, *Sechaba* (August 1985): 1–2.
19. "Apartheid—A Wounded Beast," unsigned editorial, *Sechaba* (October 1985): 1.
20. Giliomee, *Afrikaners*, 1.
21. Stoffel van der Merwe, "And What about the Black People?" (Cape Town: Federal Information Service of the National Party, 1987).
22. Giliomee, *Afrikaners*, 162.
23. T. Dunbar Moodie, *The Rise of Afrikanerdom: Power, Apartheid and the Afrikaner Civil Religion* (Berkeley: University of California Press, 1975), 3, 29.

24. Giliomee, *Afrikaners*, 157.

25. Ibid., 163–165.

26. Quoted in Moodie, *Rise of Afrikanerdom*, 5–6, 14.

27. On the concept of chosen trauma, see Vamik Volkan, *Bloodlines: From Ethnic Pride to Ethnic Terrorism* (New York: Basic Books, 1998); on the Afrikaner narrative of the Boer War, see Giliomee, *Afrikaners*, 233, 245–48.

28. Ibid., 256–57.

29. Ibid., 385.

30. Quoted in Moodie, *Rise of Afrikanerdom*, 13–14.

31. Ibid., 459–62.

32. Ibid., 507.

33. Ibid., 470, 488, 499.

34. Giliomee, *Afrikaners*, 447.

35. Hendrik F. Verwoerd, "Speech on the Occasion of the First Quinquennial Celebration of the Republic of South Africa, at Monument Hill, Pretoria," repr. in *Verwoerd Speaks: Speeches 1948–1966*, ed. A. N. Pelzer (Johannesburg: APB Publishers, 1966), 720–29.

36. Giliomee, *Afrikaners*, 472–74.

37. De Klerk, *Last Trek*, 378.

38. Ibid., 483–84.

39. Helen Suzman, "On the Bantu Laws Amendment Bill of 1964," retrieved at http://www.cortland.edu/cgis/suzman/quotes.html, July 2012.

40. Quoted in Giliomee, *Afrikaners*, 556.

41. Quoted in Giliomee, *Afrikaners*, 597.

42. Kate Manzo and Pat McGowan, "Afrikaner Fears and the Politics of Despair: Understanding Change in South Africa," *International Studies Quarterly* 36, no. 1 (1992): 1–24, 7.

43. Waldmeir, *Anatomy of a Miracle*, xi.

44. Ibid., 61.

45. Timothy B. Smith and Christopher R. Stones, "Perception of Social Change and Cross-Cultural Differences among South African Adolescents," in *Socio-Political and Psychological Perspectives on South Africa*, ed. Christopher R. Stones (New York: Nova Science Publishers, 2001), 167.

46. Chris de Kock, "Movements in South African Mass Opinion and Party Support to 1993," in *Launching Democracy in South Africa: The First Open Election, April 1994*, ed. R. Richard William Johnson and Lawrence Schlemmer (New Haven, CT: Yale University Press, 1996), 42–44.

47. De Kock, "Movements in South African Mass Opinion," 37, 45.

48. BBC, "S African Prime Minister's Speech on Flexibility in Politics" (Johannesburg radio in English for abroad, 30 July 1979, 11:12 gmt, transcribed in BBC Summary of World Broadcasts, August 1, 1979, ME/6182/B/7).

49. BBC, "Zambia and Southern Africa: In Brief; P.W. Botha's interview for 'Time on Whites' Fears" (Johannesburg radio home service in English, November 26, 1979, 6:00 gmt, transcribed in BBC Summary of World Broadcasts, November 28, 1979, ME/6283/B/5).

50. BBC, "P.W. Botha's Warning to Neighbouring States and Rejection of Black Rule" (Johannesburg in English for abroad, June 23, 1980, 3:00 gmt, transcribed in BBC Summary of World Broadcasts, June 24, 1980, ME/6453/B/1).

51. BBC, "Southern Africa: In Brief; P.W. Botha's Rustenburg meeting speech" (Johannesburg home service in English, March 18, 1981, 5:00 gmt, transcribed in BBC Summary of World Broadcasts, March 19, 1981, ME/6677/B/8).

52. Interviews. Personal interviews conducted with South African elites, September–October 2010. Participants' confidentiality maintained whenever possible.

53. Waldmeir, *Anatomy of a Miracle*, 132.

54. Giliomee, *Afrikaners*, 620.

55. Ibid., 621. Emphasis in original.

56. Quoted in Giliomee, *Afrikaners*, 598.

57. Waldmeir, *Anatomy of a Miracle*, 25–27, 73.

58. David Welsh, *The Rise and Fall of Apartheid* (Charlottesville: University of Virginia Press, 2009), 262.

59. Smith and Stones, "Perception of Social Change," 157–72.

60. Interview no. 12.

61. Personal interview, October 2010.

62. De Klerk, *Last Trek*, 141, 154.

63. Interviews no. 11, 14.

64. De Kock, "Movements in South African Mass Opinion," 37, 47.

65. Ibid., 46–48.

66. Ibid., 40.

67. Interview no. 5.

68. Further analysis of these data is reported in Julio F. Carrión and Stuart J. Kaufman, "Public Opinion and the End of Apartheid" (paper presented at International Studies Association convention, Toronto, Canada, March 2014).

69. F. W. de Klerk, personal interview, October 2010.

70. A prominent argument for the importance of Botha's removal is in Allister Sparks, *Tomorrow Is Another Country* (New York: Hill and Wang, 1995).

71. De Klerk, *Last Trek*, 134.

72. Advertisement, *Volksblad*, March 9, 1992, 11. Quotations translated by Andre Dumon.

73. Quoted in Annette Strauss, "The 1992 Referendum in South Africa," *Journal of Modern African Studies* 31, no. 2 (1993): 339–60, 341.

74. Advertisement, *Volksblad*, March 6, 1992, 5; cf. *Die Burger*, March 12, 1992, 8.

75. Advertisement, *Volksblad*, March 1, 1992, 13.

76. Advertisement, *Volksblad*, March 5, 1992, 7; Strauss, "1992 Referendum in South Africa," 343–45.

77. Advertisement, *Volksblad*, March 13, 1992, 15.

78. Advertisement, *Volksblad*, March 9, 1992, 9.

79. Advertisement, *Volksblad*, March 11, 1992, 7.

80. Advertisement, *Volksblad*, March 4, 1992, 9.

81. Strauss, "1992 Referendum in South Africa," 346.

82. Ibid., 340.

83. Quoted in Thomas A. Moriarty, *Finding the Words: A Rhetorical History of South Africa's Transition from Apartheid to Democracy* (Westport, CT: Praeger, 2003), 58.

84. Strauss, "1992 Referendum in South Africa," 342–46.

85. Welsh, *Rise and Fall of Apartheid*, 441.

86. Interview no. 14.

87. Interview no. 10.

88. Interview no. 1.

89. Interview no. 17.

90. De Klerk, *Last Trek*, 264.

91. Welsh, *Rise and Fall of Apartheid*, 468.

92. Pierre Steyn, "Executive Summary on: Steyn Report," compiled by Research Department, Truth and Reconciliation Commission (n.d.); *Truth and Reconciliation Commission of South Africa Report*, vol. 2 (Cape Town: The Commission, 1999), 612.

93. Jeremy Gordin, "Foreword," in Eugene de Kock, *A Long Night's Damage: Working for the Apartheid State* (Saxonwold, South Africa: Contra Press, 1998), 19; Stephen Ellis, "The Historical Significance of South Africa's Third Force," *Journal of Southern African Studies* 24, no. 2 (1998): 261–99, 285.

94. Thula Bopela and Daluxolo Luthuli, *Umkhonto we Sizwe: Fighting for a Divided People* (Alberton, South Africa: Galago, 2005).

95. Tom Lodge and Bill Nasson, *All, Here, and Now: Black Politics in South Africa in the 1980s* (South Africa Update Series, London: Hurst 1991).

96. Johannes M. Rantete, *The African National Congress and the Negotiated Settlement in South Africa* (Pretoria: J. L. van Schaik, 1998), 36.

97. De Kock, "Movements in South African Mass Opinion," 55.

98. Ibid.

99. Barrell, "Conscripts to Their Age," 276; Thula Simpson, "The Role of the African National Congress in Popular Protest during the Township Uprisings, 1984–89," in *Popular Politics and Resistance Movements in South Africa*, ed. William Beinart and Marcelle C. Dawson (Johannesburg: Witwatersrand University Press, 2010), 76–92.

100. Interview no. 3.

101. Quoted in Rantete, *African National Congress*, 151.

102. Additional analysis of the Human Sciences Research Council data on all of the preceding issues can be found in Julio F. Carrion and Stuart J. Kaufman, "Public Opinion and the End of Apartheid" (paper prepared for presentation at International Studies Association Convention, Toronto, Canada, March 2014).

103. On the UDF and its constituent parts, see Lodge and Nasson, *All, Here, and Now*, 34 and passim.

104. Rantete, *African National Congress*, 15–16.

105. Quoted in Rantete, *African National Congress*, 145.

106. Rantete, *African National Congress*, 202.

107. Mac Maharaj, personal interview, October 2010.

108. Quoted in Anthea Jeffery, *People's War: New Light on the Struggle for South Africa* (Johannesburg: South African Institute of Race Relations, 2009), 315.

109. Nelson R. Mandela, "Nelson Mandela's Address to Rally in Soweto," February 13, 1990, Nelson Mandela Centre of Memory, NMS017, retrieved at http://db.nelsonmandela.org/speeches/pub_view.asp?pg=item&ItemID=NMS017&txtstr= Dates: 1990–1990.

110. Nelson R. Mandela, "Nelson Mandela's Address to the Youth," April 13, 1990, Nelson Mandela Centre of Memory, NMS026, retrieved at http://db.nelsonmandela.org/speeches/pub_view.asp?pg=item&ItemID=NMS026&txtstr= Dates: 1990–1990.

111. Ibid.

112. Nelson R. Mandela, "Speech of the Deputy President of the African National Congress, Nelson Mandela, at the Rally to Relaunch the South African Communist Party," July 29, 1990, Nelson Mandela Centre of Memory, NMS049, retrieved at http://db.nelsonmandela.org/speeches/pub_view.asp?pg=item&ItemID=NMS049&txtstr= Dates: 1990–1990.

113. Rantete, *African National Congress*, 186.

114. Welsh, *Rise and Fall of Apartheid*, 393–96.

115. Johannes Rantete, *Room for Compromise: The African National Congress and Transitional Mechanisms* (Cape Town: Human Sciences Research Council, Centre for Policy Studies, CPS Transition Series, 1992), 3.

116. Janet Smith and Beauregard Tromp, *Hani: A Life Too Short* (Cape Town: Jonathan Ball, 2009), 220.

117. Ibid., 224.

118. Martin Meredith, *Nelson Mandela: A Biography* (New York: St. Martin's, 1998), 447.

119. Rantete, *African National Congress*, 202.

120. Steven Friedman, ed., *The Long Journey: South Africa's Quest for a Negotiated Settlement* (Braamfontein: Ravan, 1993), 17.

121. Jeffery, *People's War*, 324; Welsh, *Rise and Fall of Apartheid*, 448.

122. Pierre Du Toit, *South Africa's Brittle Peace: The Problem of Post-Settlement Violence* (Houndmills, Hampshire: Palgrave, 2001), 35.

123. Quoted in Jeffery, *People's War*, 240.

124. Welsh, *Rise and Fall of Apartheid*, 394.

125. Ibid., 249; Jeffery, *People's War*, 249.

126. Rantete, *African National Congress*, 190; Jeffery, *People's War*; Welsh, *Rise and Fall of Apartheid*, 449.

127. Rantete, *African National Congress*, 211.

128. Ibid., 176.

129. Quoted in Meredith, *Nelson Mandela*, 495.

130. Advertisement, *Volksblad*, March 6, 1992, 5.

7. The Symbolic Politics of Ethnic Peace in Tanzania

1. See, e.g., Edward Miguel, "Tribe or Nation? Nation Building and Public Goods in Kenya vs. Tanzania," *World Politics* 56, no. 3 (April 2004): 327–62; and Aili Mari Tripp, "The Political Mediation of Ethnic and Religious Diversity in Tanzania," in *The Accommodation of Cultural Diversity: Case Studies*, ed. Crawford Young (New York: St. Martin's, 1999), 38–68.

2. Rodger Yeager, *Tanzania: An African Experiment*, 2nd ed., rev. (Boulder, CO: Westview Press, 1989), 6.

3. Peter Schmidt and Donald H. Avery, "Complex Iron Smelting and Prehistoric Culture in Tanzania," *Science* 201, no. 4361 (September 22, 1978): 1085–89.

4. William Redman Duggan and John R. Civille, *Tanzania and Nyerere: A Study of Ujamaa and Nationhood* (Maryknoll, NY: Orbis Books, 1976), 17; Yeager, *Tanzania*, 8.

5. John Iliffe, *A Modern History of Tanganyika* (Cambridge: Cambridge University Press, 1979), 40–41.

6. Steven Feierman, *The Shambaa Kingdom: A History* (Madison: University of Wisconsin Press, 1974), 185–86 and passim.

7. Iliffe, *Modern History of Tanganyika*, 49; Yeager, *Tanzania*, 9.

8. Iliffe, *Modern History of Tanganyika*, 88–98, 200; Duggan and Civille, *Tanzania and Nyerere*, 21.

9. Yeager, *Tanzania*, 25–28.

10. Bruce Heilman, "Identity and Politics in Tanzania," *African Review* 34, no. 1–2 (2007): 6.

11. Iliffe, *Modern History of Tanganyika*, 537; Julius K. Nyerere, *Freedom and Unity: Uhuru na Umoja, A Selection from Writings and Speeches, 1952–65* (Dar es Salaam: Oxford University Press), 59.

12. Nyerere, *Freedom and Unity*, 76.

13. On economic exploitation, see Ronald Aminzade, *Race, Nation, and Citizenship in Post-Colonial Africa: The Case of Tanzania* (Cambridge: Cambridge University Press, 2013), 31–41.

14. James R. Brennan, "Blood Enemies: Exploitation and Urban Citizenship in the Nationalist Political Thought of Tanzania, 1958–75," *Journal of African History* 47, no. 3 (2006): 393–94.

15. Iliffe, *Modern History of Tanganyika*, 535–36.

16. Ibid., 519, 527, 536.

17. The elder's specific reference was to Hongo, the name of the spirit which the Maji Maji leader Bokero claimed as his inspiration. Quoted in ibid., 520.

18. Iliffe, *Modern History of Tanganyika*, 517.

19. Nyerere, *Freedom and Unity*, 59–60.

20. Iliffe, *Modern History of Tanganyika*, 523.

21. Aminzade, *Race, Nation, and Citizenship*, 67.

22. Quoted in ibid., p. 71.

23. Henry Bienen, *Tanzania: Party Transformation and Economic Development* (Princeton, NJ: Princeton University Press, 1967), 264.

24. A. G. Ishumi and T. L. Maliyamkono, "Education for Self-Reliance," in *Mwalimu: The Influence of Nyerere*, ed. Colin Legum and Geoffrey Mmari (London: Britain-Tanzania Society, 1995), 47; Bienen, *Tanzania*, 266; and Colin Legum, "The Nyerere Years," in *Tanzania After Nyerere*, ed. Michael Hodd (London: Pinter, 1988), 4.

25. Bienen, *Tanzania*, 33–34.

26. Feierman, *Shambaa Kingdom*.

27. C. K. Omari, "Ethnicity, Politics and Development in Tanzania," *African Study Monographs* 7 (March 1987): 70.

28. Bienen, *Tanzania*, 37; Vamik D. Volkan, *Bloodlines: From Ethnic Pride to Ethnic Terrorism* (New York: Farrar, Straus and Giroux, 1997).

29. A. J. Temu, "The Rise and Triumph of Nationalism," in *A History of Tanzania*, ed. I. N. Kimambo and A. J. Temu (Nairobi: East African Publishing House, 1969), 191.

30. Brennan, "Blood Enemies," 393–97.

31. David Court, "The Education System as a Response to Inequality," in *Politics and Public Policy in Kenya and Tanzania*, ed. Joel D. Barkan (New York: Praeger, 1984), 274–75; Miguel, "Tribe or Nation?," 335.

32. Duggan and Civille, *Tanzania and Nyerere*, 57.

33. Heilman, "Identity and Politics in Tanzania," 14; Kelly Askew, *Performing the Nation: Swahili Music and Cultural Politics in Tanzania* (Chicago: University of Chicago Press, 2002), 290–92.

34. Heilman, "Identity and Politics in Tanzania"; Askew, *Performing the Nation*, 47; Author interview, January 2012.

35. F. S. Swai, "The Politicisation of the Tanzania Defence Force," in *Rethinking the Arusha Declaration*, ed. Jeanette Hartmann (Copenhagen: Centre for Development Research, 1991), 96.

36. Michael Jennings and Claire Mercer, "Rehabilitating Nationalisms: Conviviality and National Consciousness in Postcolonial Tanzania," *Politique Africaine* 121 (March 2011): 12–13.

37. Heilman, "Identity and Politics in Tanzania," 14.

38. Jennings and Mercer, "Rehabilitating Nationalisms," 15.

39. Tripp, "Political Mediation," 43–45.

40. Author interview, January 2012.

41. G. Andrew Maguire, *Toward "Uhuru" in Tanzania: The Politics of Participation* (Cambridge: Cambridge University Press, 1969), 65–67.

42. Omari, "Ethnicity, Politics and Development."

43. Ibid., 76.

44. Court, "Education System," 269, 275.

45. Tripp, "Political Mediation," 44.

46. Goran Hyden, *Political Development in Rural Tanzania* (Nairobi: East African Publishing House, 1969), 39.

47. Heilman, "Identity and Politics in Tanzania," 6.

48. Quoted in Bienen, *Tanzania*, 42.

49. Omari, "Ethnicity, Politics and Development," 68.

50. Askew, *Performing the Nation*, 64; Tripp, "Political Mediation," 43; Omari, "Ethnicity, Politics and Development," 69.

51. Askew, *Performing the Nation*, 47; Heilman, "Identity and Politics in Tanzania," 14.

52. See, e.g., Julius E. Nyang'oro, *JK: A Political Biography of Jakaya Mrisho Kikwete, President of the United Republic of Tanzania* (Trenton, NJ: Africa World Press, 2011).

53. Tripp, "Political Mediation," 43–45; Heilman, "Identity and Politics in Tanzania," 10.

54. Duggan and Civille, *Tanzania and Nyerere*, 63; Jeanette Hartman, "President Nyerere and the State," in *Tanzania after Nyerere*, ed. Michael Hodd (London: Pinter, 1988), 165.

55. Tripp, "Political Mediation," 46; Robert Pinkney, *Democracy and Dictatorship in Ghana and Tanzania* (Houndmills, Hampshire, UK: Macmillan, 1997), 99.

56. Bienen, *Tanzania*, 366.

57. Swai, "Tanzania Defence Force." On the Soviet case, see Roman Kolkowicz, *The Soviet Military and the Communist Party* (Princeton, NJ: Princeton University Press, 1967).

58. On military involvement in ethnic politics, see Donald Horowitz, *Ethnic Groups in Conflict* (Berkeley: University of California Press, 1985).

59. Max Mmuya and Amon Chaligha, *Towards Multiparty Politics in Tanzania* (Dar es Salaam: Dar es Salaam University Press, 1992), 5.

60. Cranford Pratt, *The Critical Phase in Tanzania, 1945–1968: Nyerere and the Emergence of a Socialist Strategy* (Cambridge: Cambridge University Press, 1976), 80.

61. World Bank, *Tanzania at the Turn of the Century: Background Papers and Statistics* (Washington, DC: World Bank, 2002), 4–7.

62. Miguel, "Tribe or Nation?," 337, 351.

63. Jennings and Mercer, "Rehabilitating Nationalisms," 7.

64. World Values Survey data base, http://wvsevsdb.com/wvs/WVSAnalizeQuestion.jsp, accessed February 11, 2014.

65. Aili Mari Tripp and Crawford Young, "The Accommodation of Cultural Diversity in Tanzania," in *Ethnopolitical Warfare: Causes, Consequences, and Possible Solutions*, ed. Daniel Chirot and Martin E. P. Seligman (Washington, DC: American Psychological Association, 2001), 259.

66. Author interview, January 2012.

67. Miguel, "Tribe or Nation?," 336.

68. Author Interview, January 2012.

69. Askew, *Performing the Nation*, 290–91.

70. *Afrobarometer Summary of Results: Round 4 Afrobarometer Survey in Tanzania*, compiled by Policy Research and Development (REPOA) and Michigan State University (2008), Afrobarometer.org, 56; Author interview, January 2012.

71. Author interview, January 2012.

72. Author interview, January 2012.

73. Author interview, January 2012.

74. Author interview, January 2012.

75. Tim Kelsall, *Contentious Politics, Local Governance and the Self: A Tanzanian Case Study* (Uppsala, Sweden: Nordiska Afrikainstitutet, 2004), Research Report no. 129, 21.

76. *Afrobarometer Summary of Results* (2008), 53–54.

77. Miguel, "Tribe or Nation?," 359.

78. *Afrobarometer Summary of Results* (2008), 31.

79. Tripp, "Political Mediation," 61.

80. Kelsall, *Contentious Politics*, 51.

81. Heilman, "Identity and Politics in Tanzania," 9–10.

82. Author interview, January 2012.

83. Tripp, "Political Mediation," 43, 45.

84. See, e.g., *Guardian* (Dar es Salaam), September 7, 2010, 1.

85. See, e.g., "Tanzania Police Kill Two in Arusha at Chadema Protest," BBC News Africa, March 20, 2012, accessed at http://www.bbc.co.uk/news/world-africa-12126861; "We'll Ensure Peace and Security—Mkapa," *Nipashe* (Dar es Salaam), August 20, 2000. This and all subsequently cited articles in Swahili-language newspapers trans. by Kelvin Mathayo, 2012.

86. Author interview, January 2012.

87. International Foundation for Election Systems (IFES), *Republic in Transition: 1995 Elections in Tanzania and Zanzibar, IFES Observation Report 1995* (Washington, DC: IFES, December 1995), 41.

88. Heilman, "Identity and Politics in Tanzania," 6. For vote totals, see Electoral Institute for Sustainable Democracy in Africa (EISA), "Tanzania: 2000 Parliamentary Election Results," at http://www.eisa.org.za/WEP/tan2000resultsp.htm; and EISA, "Tanzania: 2000 Presidential Election Results," at http://www.eisa.org.za/WEP/tan2000results.htm, accessed August 4, 2013.

89. *Guardian*, October 9, 2010, 1–2.

90. *Afrobarometer Summary of Results* (2008).

91. Tanzanian Election Monitoring Committee (TEMCO), *The 2010 Tanzania General Elections: Report of the Tanzania Election Monitoring Committee* (Dar es Salaam: Tanzania Election Monitoring Committee, 2011), 114.

92. Keneth Simbaya, "It Is Not Sensible Trying to Vote For the Opposition—Mkapa," *Nipashe*, September 5, 2000.

93. *Guardian*, October 13, 2010, 2.

94. Author interview, January 2012.

95. Author interview, January 2012.

96. Author interview, January 2012.

97. *The Citizen* (Dar es Salaam), October 2, 2010, 1, and *The Citizen*, October 6, 2010, p. 18. For evidence supporting Slaa's charges, see *Guardian,* September 9, 2010, 4.

98. See, e.g., Slaa, quoted in *The Citizen*, October 6, 2010, 18.

99. See, e.g., BBC, "Tanzania Police Kill Two in Arusha at Chadema Protest," BBC News Africa, 2011, accessed at http://www.bbc.co.uk/news/world-africa-12126861, March 20, 2012.

100. Simon Mhina, "A Ban against Mrema Is Thrown Out," *Nipashe*, August 21, 2000.

101. Agnether Kasenene, "Mrema Says He Will Not Retaliate if He Becomes President," *Nipashe*, August 30, 2000.

102. Frederick Katulanda and Kizitto Noya, "Kikwete Pledges Bright Future for Small-Scale Businesspeople," *Mwananchi* (Dar es Salaam), October 27, 2010.

103. *Guardian*, October 9, 2010, 1–2; *Afrobarometer Summary of Results* (2008), 35.

104. *Afrobarometer Summary of Results* (2008), 35.

105. Midraji Ibrahim, "Kikwete To Create 1,000,000 Jobs," *Mwananchi*, August 20, 2005.

106. *Guardian*, September 1, 2010, 1; TEMCO, *The 2010 Tanzania General Elections*, 115; *Guardian*, October 15, 2010, 1; *The Citizen*, October 6, 2010, 18.

107. Suleiman Abeid, "Kikwete Pours Down More Pledges," *Majira* (Dar es Salaam), October 1, 2010; *Guardian*, October 2, 2010, 2.

108. *Guardian*, October 7, 2010, 5; *Guardian*, October 11, 2010, 4.

109. "We'll Ensure Peace and Security—Mkapa," *Nipashe*, August 20, 2000; Jumbe Ismailly, "Opposition Parties Are Like an Uncircumcised Person—Mkapa," *Nipashe*, September 19, 2000.

110. "We'll Ensure Peace and Security—Mkapa," *Nipashe*, August 20, 2000.

111. Katulanda and Noya, "Kikwete Pledges Bright Future," *Mwananchi*, October 27, 2010; *Guardian*, October 13, 2010, 2.

112. Agnether Kasenene, "Lipumba Blames CCM's Policies for Dismal Economy," *Nipashe*, August 29, 2000.

113. Nico Mwaibale, "Those Who See CCM as Their Property Are Mad, Claims Lipumba," *Nipashe*, September 7, 2000.

114. *The Citizen*, October 6, 2010, 18.

115. George Ramadhani, "Lipumba Says He Will Abolish Poll Tax if He Wins the Election," *Nipashe*, September 29, 2000; Mwaibale, "Those Who See CCM as Their Property," *Nipashe*, September 7, 2000; *The Citizen*, October 6, 2010, 18.

116. *Guardian*, September 2, 2010, p. 2; *Guardian*, September 9, 2010, 2; *Guardian*, September 3, 2010, p. 5; *Guardian*, September 4, 2010, 1, 2.

117. Author interviews, January 2012.

118. *Guardian*, October 5, 2010, 2.

119. Ismailly, "Opposition Parties Are Like an Uncircumcised Person," *Nipashe*, September 19, 2000.

120. Nelson Goima, "Mkapa Insinuates the Candidate Who Failed to Fulfill His Promise," *Nipashe*, September 12, 2000.

121. *Guardian*, September 15, 2010, 1.

122. *The Citizen*, October 13, 2010, 18, and October 20, 2010, 18.

123. *Guardian*, September 3, 2010, 5.

124. TEMCO, *The 2010 Tanzania General Elections*, 127.

125. Author interview, January 2012.

126. *The Citizen*, October 3, 2010, 2.

127. "Kikwete Mends Fences with the Elderly," *Mwananchi*, July 26, 2005.

128. "Mbowe: It Is Ignominious That Our Programs Are Prepared in Washington," *Mwananchi*, November 27, 2005.

129. Susama Susama, "After Being Asked to Return to CCM: Mrema Says He Is Not a Dog to Eat His Own Vomit," *Nipashe*, July 27, 2000.

130. "Lipumba: Now I Have High Hopes of Winning the Election," *Nipashe*, July 6, 2000.

131. *Afrobarometer Summary of Results* (2008).

132. TEMCO, *The 2010 Tanzania General Elections*, 144–55.

133. *Guardian*, October 4, 2010, 4.

134. Bruce E. Heilman and Paul J. Kaiser, "Religion, Identity and Politics in Tanzania," *Third World Quarterly* 23, no. 4 (August 2002): 691.

135. Simeon Mesaki, "Religion and the State in Tanzania/La religion et l'etat en Tanzanie," *Cross-Cultural Communication* 7, no. 2 (June 30, 2011): 249.

136. Tripp, "Political Mediation," 58.

137. Erik Larson and Ron Aminzade, "Nation-Building and Post-colonial Nation-States: The Cases of Tanzania and Fiji," *International Social Science Journal* 59, no. 192 (June 2008): 160.

138. Mesaki, "Religion and the State."

139. Heilman and Kaiser, "Religion, Identity and Politics," 692.

140. Tripp, "Political Mediation," 51.

141. Larson and Aminzade, "Nation-Building and Post-colonial Nation-States," 174.

142. TEMCO, *2010 Tanzania General Elections*, 110.

143. Don Petterson, *Revolution in Zanzibar: An American's Cold War Tale* (Boulder, CO: Westview, 2002), 11.

144. Aili Mari Tripp and Crawford Young, "The Accommodation of Cultural Diversity in Tanzania," in *Ethnopolitical Warfare: Causes, Consequences, and Possible Solutions*, ed. Daniel Chirot and Martin E. P. Seligman (Washington, DC: American Psychological Association, 2001), 267; cf. Barbara G. Brents and Deo Mshigeni, "Terrorism in Context," *American Sociologist* 35, no. 2 (2004): 66.

145. Abdul Sheriff, "Race and Class in the Politics of Zanzibar," *Africa Spectrum* 36, no. 3 (2001): 301–18.

146. Issa G. Shivji, *Pan-Africanism or Pragmatism? Lessons of Tanganyika-Zanzibar Union* (Dar es Salaam: Mkuki na Nyota Publishers, 2008), 45.

147. Shivji, *Pan-Africanism or Pragmatism*, 54.

148. Ibid., 25, 119.

149. IFES, *Republic in Transition.*

150. Greg Cameron, "Zanzibar's Turbulent Transition," *Review of African Political Economy* 29, no. 92 (June 2002): 315–16, 326.

151. Human Rights Watch, " 'The Bullets Were Raining': The January 2001 Attack on Peaceful Demonstrators in Zanzibar," *Human Rights Watch* 14, no. 3 (A) (2002): 3.

152. Simon Turner, " 'These Young Men Show No Respect for Local Customs'—Globalization and Islamic Revival in Zanzibar," *Journal of Religion in Africa* 39 (2009): 237–61.

153. Cameron, "Zanzibar's Turbulent Transition," 327.

154. *New York Times*, March 6, 2002, A4.

155. *New York Times*, November 2, 2005, A8.

156. TEMCO, *Report on the 2010 Zanzibar General Elections* (Dar es Salaam: Tanzania Election Monitoring Committee, 2011): 73, 103, 116.

157. For example, Tripp, "Political Mediation."

158. The former point was suggested by Marc Howard Ross. On the latter, see Elliot Green, "The Political Economy of Nation Formation in Modern Tanzania: Explaining Stability in the Face of Diversity," *Commonwealth and Comparative Politics* 49, no. 2 (2011): 234.

Conclusion

1. Daniel N. Posner, *Institutions and Ethnic Politics in Africa* (New York: Cambridge University Press, 2005).

2. Ibid., 97.

3. Ronald Krebs and Patrick Thaddeus Jackson (2007), "Twisting Tongues and Twisting Arms: The Power of Political Rhetoric," *European Journal of International Relations* 13, no. 1 (2007): 35–66, 40.

4. Filipinas Foundation, *Philippine Majority-Minority Relations and Ethnic Attitudes* (Makati, Rizal: Filipinas Foundation, 1975), 122, 137, 158, 196.

5. Moore, "Women and Warriors," 124.

6. John Mueller, "The Banality of 'Ethnic War,'" *International Security* 25, no. 1 (Summer 2000): 42–70.

7. Samuel L. Gaertner and John F. Dovidio, *Reducing Intergroup Bias: The Common Ingroup Identity Model* (Philadelphia: Taylor and Francis, 2000). This work builds on the pioneering findings of Muzafer Sherif and his colleagues in Sherif et al., *Intergroup Conflict and Cooperation: The Robbers Cave Experiment* (Norman, OK: University Book Exchange, 1961).

8. Gaertner and Dovidio, *Reducing Intergroup Bias*, 47 and passim.

9. Timothy D. Sisk, quoted in Benjamin Reilly, "Centripetalism," in *Routledge Handbook of Ethnic Conflict*, ed. Karl Cordell and Stefan Wolff (London: Routledge, 2011), 289.

10. Ibid., 290–92.

11. The seminal contributions to this school of thought are those of Arend Lijphart. See, e.g., Lijphart, *Democracy in Plural Societies: A Comparative Exploration* (New Haven, CT: Yale University Press, 1977).

12. Henry E. Hale, "Divided We Stand: Institutional Sources of Ethnofederal State Survival and Collapse," *World Politics* 56, no. 2 (2004): 165–93.

13. For detailed analysis, see Julio F. Carrion and Stuart J. Kaufman, "Public Opinion and the End of Apartheid" (paper presented at International Studies Association convention, Toronto, March 2014).

14. Milton Lodge and Charles S. Taber, *The Rationalizing Voter* (New York: Cambridge University Press, 2013), 2.

15. Ibid., 19.

16. Ibid., 142–46.

17. Ibid., 170–205.

18. Kathleen A. Frankovic, "The 1984 Election: The Irrelevance of the Campaign," *PS: Politics and Political Science* 18, no 1. (1985): 39–47; Steven E. Finkel, "Reexamining the 'Minimal Effects' Model in Recent Presidential Campaigns," *Journal of Politics* 55, no. 1 (1993): 1–21.

19. Lynn Vavreck, *The Message Matters: The Economy and Presidential Campaigns* (Princeton, NJ: Princeton University Press, 2009).

20. Janet M. Box-Steffensmeier, David Damofal, and Christian A. Farrell, "The Aggregate Dynamics of Campaigns," *Journal of Politics* 71, no. 1 (2009): 309–23.

21. Seth Masket, "Did Obama's Ground Game Matter? The Influence of Local Field Offices During the 2008 Presidential Election," *Public Opinion Quarterly* 73, no. 5 (2009): 1023–39.

22. Peter D. Feaver, *Armed Servants: Agency, Oversight, and Civil-Military Relations* (Cambridge, MA: Harvard University Press, 2003), 55–68.

23. Ibid., 56.

24. Steven Lee Solnick, *Stealing the State: Control and Collapse in Soviet Institutions* (Cambridge, MA: Harvard University Press, 1998).

25. Edward Rhodes, "Do Bureaucratic Politics Matter? Some Disconfirming Findings from the Case of the U.S. Navy," *World Politics* 47, no. 1 (1994): 1–41.

26. Ibid., 34.

27. Steve Vogel, *The Pentagon: A History* (New York: Random House, 2008), 280.

28. Herbert Kaufman, *The Forest Ranger: A Study in Administrative Behavior* (Baltimore: Published for Resources for the Future by Johns Hopkins University Press, 1960).

29. Morton H. Halperin, "Why Bureaucrats Play Games," *Foreign Policy* 1, no. 2 (Spring 1971): 79.

30. David MacIsaac "Voices from the Central Blue: The Air Power Theorists," in *Makers of Modern Strategy: From Machiavelli to the Nuclear Age*, ed. Peter Paret (Princeton, NJ: Princeton University Press, 1986), 624–47.

31. Jack Snyder, *The Ideology of the Offensive: Military Decision Making and the Disasters of 1914* (Ithaca: Cornell University Press, 1984).

32. Nicholas Confessore, "Welcome to the Machine: How the GOP Disciplined K Street and Made Bush Supreme," *Washington Monthly*, July–August 2003, 33.

33. Opensecrets.org, "Lobbying Expenditures Slump in 2011," Open Secrets Blog, January 12, 2012, http://www.opensecrets.org/news/2012/01/lobbying-expenditures-slump-in-2011.html, retrieved July 10, 2013.

34. Hans J. Morgenthau, *Politics among Nations: The Struggle for Power and Peace*, 5th ed., rev. (New York: Knopf, 1978), xxi, 4, 38.

35. Kenneth L. Waltz, *Theory of International Politics* (Reading, MA: Addison-Wesley, 1979).

36. John J. Mearsheimer, *The Tragedy of Great Power Politics* (New York: W. W. Norton, 2001).

37. John Mueller, *Retreat from Doomsday: The Obsolescence of Major War* (New York: Basic Books, 1989).

38. J. Sidanius and F. Pratto, *Social Dominance: An Intergroup Theory of Social Hierarchy and Oppression* (Cambridge: Cambridge University Press, 1999).

39. Bob Altemeyer, "The Other Authoritarian Personality," *Advances in Experimental Social Psychology* 61: 47–91, repr. in *Political Psychology: Key Readings*, ed. John T. Jost and Jim Sidanius (New York: Psychology Press, 2004), 85–107; Douglas R. Oxley et al., "Political Attitudes Vary with Physiological Traits," *Science* 321, no. 5896 (September 19, 2008): 1667–70.

40. Brian C. Rathbun, *Trust in International Cooperation: International Security Institutions, Domestic Politics and American Multilateralism* (Cambridge: Cambridge University Press, 2011).

41. Alexander Wendt, *Social Theory of International Politics* (Cambridge: Cambridge University Press 1999).

42. Kenneth N. Waltz, "Structural Realism after the Cold War," *International Security* 25, no. 1 (Summer 2000): 5–41; John J. Mearsheimer, "The False Promise of International Institutions," *International Security* 19, no. 3 (Winter 1994–1995): 5–49.

43. Joseph S. Nye Jr., *The Future of Power* (New York: PublicAffairs, 2011), 29–33; Helen V. Milner and Andrew Moravcsik, eds., *Power, Interdependence, and Nonstate Actors in World Affairs* (Princeton, NJ: Princeton University Press, 2009); Bruce Russett and John Oneal, *Triangulating Peace: Democracy, Interdependence, and International Organizations* (New York: W. W. Norton, 2001); Michael N. Barnett and Raymond Duvall, *Power in Global Governance* (Cambridge: Cambridge University Press, 2005).

44. Bruce Russett, *Grasping the Democratic Peace: Principles for a Post-Cold War World* (Princeton, NJ: Princeton University Press, 1993); John R. Oneal and Bruce Russett, "The Kantian Peace: The Pacific Benefits of Democracy, Interdependence, and International Organizations, 1885–1992," *World Politics* 52, no. 1 (October 1999): 1–37.

45. Nina Tannenwald, "The Nuclear Taboo: The United States and the Normative Basis of Nuclear Non-Use," *International Organization* 53, no. 3 (Summer 1999): 433–68.

46. John M. Owen, "How Liberalism Produces Democratic Peace," *International Security* 19, no. 2 (Fall 1994): 87–125.

47. Andrew Moravschik, "Taking Preferences Seriously: A Liberal Theory of International Politics," *International Organization* 51 (Autumn 1997): 513–33.

48. Paul K. Huth, "Enduring Rivalries and Territorial Disputes, 1950–1990," *Conflict Management and Peace Science* 15, no. 1 (Spring 1996): 7–41.

49. Robert O. Keohane and Joseph Nye, *Power and Interdependence* (Boston: Little, Brown, 1977).

50. Robert Gilpin, *War and Change in World Politics* (Cambridge: Cambridge University Press, 1981).

51. A sophisticated discussion of the "state-nation balance" in international politics is Benjamin Miller, *States, Nations, and the Great Powers: The Sources of Regional War and Peace* (Cambridge: Cambridge University Press, 2007).

52. William J. Long and Peter Brecke, *War and Reconciliation: Reason and Emotion in Conflict Resolution* (Cambridge, MA: MIT Press, 2003).

53. Alice Ackermann, "Reconciliation as a Peace-Building Process in Postwar Europe: The Franco-German Case," *Peace and Change* 19, no. 3 (July 1994): 242.

54. Charles A. Kupchan, *How Enemies Become Friends: The Sources of Stable Peace* (Princeton, NJ: Princeton University Press, 2010).

55. Ji Young Kim, "Symbolic Politics, the History Problem, and the Japan–South Korea Security Relationship during the Post–Cold War Period" (PhD diss., University of Delaware, 2011).

56. Marc Howard Ross, *Cultural Contestation in Ethnic Conflict* (New York: Cambridge University Press, 2007).

Index